Pan-Asianism

ASIA/PACIFIC/PERSPECTIVES

Series Editor: Mark Selden

Pan-Asianism

A Documentary History

Volume 1: 1850–1920

Edited by
Sven Saaler and
Christopher W. A. Szpilman

ROWMAN & LITTLEFIELD PUBLISHERS, INC.
Lanham • Boulder • New York • Toronto • Plymouth, UK

Published by Rowman & Littlefield Publishers, Inc.
A wholly owned subsidiary of The Rowman & Littlefield Publishing Group, Inc.
4501 Forbes Boulevard, Suite 200, Lanham, Maryland 20706
http://www.rowmanlittlefield.com

Estover Road, Plymouth PL6 7PY, United Kingdom

British Library Cataloguing in Publication Information Available

Library of Congress Cataloging-in-Publication Data
Pan-Asianism : a documentary history / edited by Sven Saaler and Christopher W.A. Szpilman.
    p. cm. — (Asia/Pacific/perspectives)
    Includes bibliographical references and index.
    ISBN 978-1-4422-0596-3 (v. 1 : cloth : alk. paper) — ISBN 978-1-4422-0598-7 (v. 1 : electronic) — ISBN 978-1-4422-0599-4 (v. 2 : cloth : alk. paper) — ISBN 978-1-4422-0601-4 (v. 2 : electronic)
    1. East Asia—History—19th century—Sources. 2. East Asia—History—20th century—Sources. 3. Regionalism—East Asia—Sources. 4. East Asians—Ethnic identity—Sources. 5. Nationalism—East Asia—History—Sources. 6. National characteristics, East Asian—Sources. I. Saaler, Sven, 1968– II. Szpilman, Christopher W. A., 1951–
    DS504.5.P36 2011
    950.4—dc22
                                                                    2010049256

∞™ The paper used in this publication meets the minimum requirements of American National Standard for Information Sciences—Permanence of Paper for Printed Library Materials, ANSI/NISO Z39.48-1992.

Printed in the United States of America

Contents

Preface and Acknowledgments

Pan-Asianism has been an ideology that has shaped the history of Asia over the past century and a half. It has been used both to express transnational aspirations to Asian regionalism and integration and to legitimize aggression and empire building. Whereas the former application makes Pan-Asianism highly relevant today in connection with various initiatives for regional integration, the latter has discredited Pan-Asianism to such an extent that for many years historians treated it as a taboo. The result is that there is no comprehensive book of materials on Pan-Asianism in English or, for that matter, in any Western language. This sad state of affairs has in effect hampered the study of modern Asian and Japanese history in which Pan-Asianism has played a decisive role. This book is intended to remedy this glaring gap. It is hoped that it will promote research into modern Asian history and throw some light on those many aspects of international relations in Asia that have remained underresearched because of shortage of easily accessible sources.

This project is the fruit of several years' collaboration by three dozen scholars on four continents. Several contributors to this project cooperated also on a collection of articles titled *Pan-Asianism in Modern Japanese History*, which was published in 2007. The preface to that volume stressed the need for further research on Pan-Asianism that would not be limited only to Japan but cover also the rest of Asia. For, although pan-Asian ideology was most frequently articulated in Japan, it had numerous and important advocates also in other Asian countries. For a number of practical reasons, however, it was necessary to limit the focus of the 2007 volume only to Japan. In recent years, however, Pan-Asianism as an academic field has shown rapid growth with a number of important publications on Pan-Asianism appearing in English, Japanese, and Chinese (see the introduction for further details). But the difficulty of obtaining access to primary sources is the root cause of the various problems that plague the field and the main obstacle on research that transcends both national boundaries and the limitations of historical periodization. The difficulty is also compounded by linguistic problems since only few, if any, scholars are competent in all the diverse languages of Asia that are required to engage in a comparative study of Pan-Asianism. To remedy these difficulties, the editors decided it would be a good idea to publish a collection of important primary sources in English. But when we started putting together documents along these lines, we ended up with more "seminal documents" than could fit in a single volume. As we kept working on it over a period of three years, our collection expanded into two hefty volumes of more than 100,000 words each. Yet, in spite of the size of this work, it was unfortunately impossible to include some very important documents. Some of the texts included in the work in their original languages can be accessed online on the following home page (see http://asianism.japanesehistory.de). The home page, which also includes additional sources of relevance as well as photographic material, will be expanded in the future as new sources come to our attention. Needless to say, the editors would have been unable to complete such a huge enterprise on their own. In this connection, we owe a great debt of gratitude to a number of institutions and individuals without whose cooperation, assistance, and support this publication would not have seen the light of day.

The editors, speaking also on behalf of the contributors to this volume, would like to express their gratitude, first of all, to the Toshiba International Foundation for providing funds vital for the completion of this project. We are also enormously grateful to Mark Selden for his advice and assistance and for agreeing to contribute at a very late stage of the project. We also thank the authors of the primary sources or their families for allowing us to reprint the texts included in this collection. Every effort has been made to trace copyright holders, but in the event of any omissions, the editors would be glad to hear from the copyright holders.

We would also like to thank all the contributors for their patience and cooperation in responding to our questions and suggestions, Paul Sorrell and Elena Neufeld for editorial assistance, and Nicholas Warren and Izabela Grocholski for their thoughtful comments. At Rowman & Littlefield, we are enormously grateful to Susan McEachern and Carrie Broadwell-Tkach for their support and help in bringing the production of this volume to fruition. We would also like to thank Rowman & Littlefield for their willingness to publish this collection, which, because of its size, must be a major commitment in terms of publishing policy. Finally, a word of appreciation for Skype and Dropbox, the providers of twenty-first-century communication technology. If they had not existed, the editors, who live 1000 miles apart, would have found it very difficult to overcome the vast distances between themselves and the contributors who live all over the globe.

Note on Transliteration
and Translation

Transliteration was understandably a major challenge in a collection that includes primary sources from close to a dozen Asian countries and regions. We are in great debt to a number of contributors for the advice on how to transliterate personal names and place-names in English.

We have rendered East Asian names in the original order, surname first (however, the order in the English-language sources has been left unchanged), and have Romanized East Asian languages according to the Hepburn system for Japanese, the Revised Romanization of Korean from 2000 for Korean, and Pinyin for Chinese. When Japanese place names are established in English, macrons are omitted (e.g., Tokyo, not Tōkyō; Osaka, not Ōsaka; Ryukyu, not Ryūkyū; and so on). They were also not added when missing in the English-language original. In cases where the Wade-Giles Romanization for Chinese terms is commonly used in the West, it has been added in brackets on the first appearance of the term in each chapter. Cross references in brackets refer to volume and chapter number, i.e., II:10 refers to vol. 2, chapter 10 of this work. In the case of personal and place-names in Chinese and Korean that are long familiar in the West, such as Chiang Kai-shek or Sun Yat-sen, we have adhered to the common usage. In such cases, the Pinyin Romanization is given in brackets on the first mention.

Most texts included have been translated into English expressly for this collection. In such cases, the name of the translator (contributor) appears at the heading of the source. Some texts, however, were originally written and published in English. Such texts are reproduced faithfully with only obvious typographical errors being corrected. Any additions by the editors or contributors are placed in square brackets.

In order to ensure coherence and the uniformity of this work, the editors felt it necessary to make some editorial changes to the commentaries and translation. Generally, we gave priority to the readability over literalness and close philological adherence to the original. The editors assume the responsibility for any errors that may have resulted from this editorial policy.

Introduction

The Emergence of Pan-Asianism as an Ideal of Asian Identity and Solidarity, 1850–2008

Sven Saaler and Christopher W. A. Szpilman

Asia is one. The Himalayas divide, only to accentuate, two mighty civilizations, the Chinese with its communism of Confucius, and the Indian with its individualism of the Vedas. But not even the snowy barriers can interrupt for one moment that broad expanse of love for the Ultimate and Universal, which is the common thought-inheritance of every Asiatic race, enabling them to produce all the great religions of the world. . . . (Okakura 1920: 1)

Asia is not one. This is the reality, which the grave experience of the Sino-Japanese War [from 1937] has taught us. (Ozaki Hotsumi 1939, quoted in Yonetani 2006: 166)

The economic and political power of Asia, the world's largest continent, is increasing rapidly. According to the latest projections, the gross domestic products of China and India, the world's most populous nations, will each surpass that of the United States in the not-too-distant future. China's economy, like Japan's, is already larger than that of any single European country. With this new economic might comes diplomatic influence. On the world scene Asian countries pull more weight now than ever before. The twenty-first century, many pundits agree, will be an Asian century. This undisputed Asian success story, together with its accompanying tensions and discontents, has attracted much media and scholarly attention. Yet for all this talk of Asia, there is no consensus on what Asia actually stands for as a whole. Is the vast Asian landmass a single entity? As the previous quotations show, there has never been—and perhaps never will be—universal agreement on this question.

Attempts to define Asia are almost as old as the term itself. The word "Asia" originated in ancient Greece in the fifth century BC. It originally denoted the lands of the Persian Empire extending east of the Bosphorus Straits but subsequently developed into a general term used by Europeans to describe all the lands lying to the east of Europe. (The point where Europe ended and Asia began was, however, never clearly defined.) Often, this usage connoted a threat, real or perceived, by Asia to Europe—a region smaller in area, much less populous, poorer, and far less significant than Asia in terms of global history (see Arrighi, Hamashita, and Selden 2003: introduction).

The term "Asia" arrived in East Asia relatively late, being introduced by Jesuit missionaries in the sixteenth century. The term is found, written in Chinese characters (亞細亞), on Chinese maps of the world made around 1600 under the supervision of Matteo Ricci (1552–1610),[1] one of the founders of the Jesuit mission in China. However, it took two more centuries before the name gained wide currency in the region. For it was only with the resumption of European colonialist expansion in the nineteenth century that "Asia" ceased to be a technical term used by East Asian cartographers and, in reaction to the threat of Western colonialism, came to represent a specific geopolitical space bound together by such commonalities as a shared history, close cultural links, a long record of diplomatic relations, trade exchanges, and the notion of a "common destiny." Although the definitions of Asia were diverse and often contradictory, the real or perceived Western threat caused an increasing number of intellectuals, politicians, and activists throughout Asia to argue for a strengthening of "Asian" solidarity in relation to "the West."

These arguments about the definition and nature of Asia in reaction to the impending Western threat marked the beginnings of Pan-Asianism[2] as an ideology and a movement. Vague sentiments about strengthening Asian solidarity were gradually developed into concrete policy proposals for a united defense of Asia against the encroachments of Western imperialism. In many cases, such calls for Asian solidarity, integration, and unity were accompanied by endeavors to create an Asian identity by postulating commonalities and identifying traditions of interaction and interrelationship. Some thinkers took for granted the existence of an Asian identity. Others argued that such an identity must be deliberately forged as a necessary condition for realizing the ultimate objective of unifying Asia. Although individual writers in different places and at different times advocated a wide variety of strategies and views on the nature of Asian unity, we can nonetheless observe a certain degree of uniformity in the development of pan-Asian rhetoric from the nineteenth century down to the present—a pattern discussed further at the end of the introduction.

In this way, then, a pan-Asian worldview or "style of thought"[3] became established and diffused throughout the region. It can be identified in the writings of intellectuals, political statements, popular slogans, and even in songs and poems in a number of Asian states and nations. A representative selection of such texts, all of which are of great significance in the history of Pan-Asianism and Asian regionalism, is included in this collection. They were written or collected in various parts of Asia, from Japan, through Korea, China, Indonesia, and India to the Ottoman Empire, over the past 150 years. These texts, most of which have been translated into English from a number of Asian languages, are brought to the Western reader for the first time in an easily accessible form. Each source is accompanied by a commentary that provides essential information, such as a biographical sketch of the author and the historical context of the document under consideration.

A number of collections of pan-Asian texts have been published in Japanese.[4] The most important of these is Takeuchi Yoshimi's (1910–1977) volume *Asianism* (Takeuchi 1963a), which, in addition to providing a selection of sources, examines the significance of Pan-Asianism and attempts to place it in its historical context. Much less useful is the recently published three-volume anthology, *Ajiashugishatachi no Koe* (Pan-Asianist Voices; Tōyama et al. 2008; Miyazaki et al. 2008; Kita Ikki et al. 2008), which merely reproduces snippets of texts seemingly at random without any critical contextualization. Pan-Asianism, however, receives scant attention in widely available English-language source collections on Asia such as the volumes in the Introduction to Asian Civilizations series—*Sources of Japanese Tradition* (Tsunoda et al. 1958), *Sources of Chinese Tradition* (de Bary et al. 1960), *Sources of Korean Tradition* (Lee et al. 2000), and *Sources of Indian Tradition* (de Bary 1964).

The end of the Cold War in 1989 produced a surge of interest in issues of regionalism and transnational identity in contemporary East Asia (Katzenstein and Shiraishi 1997; Morishima 2000; Kang 2001; Wada 2003; Rozman 2004; Shindō and Hirakawa 2006; Hamanaka 2009). This new interest in contemporary regionalism was followed only a decade later by the recognition of the long-term historical developments underlying the geopolitical formation of the East Asian region and the idea of Asian solidarity (i.e., the ideology of Pan-Asianism) as important research subjects. Few works on Pan-Asianism were published before 2000 in any language (notable exceptions are Jansen 1954, Takeuchi 1963a, Hay 1970, Matsuzawa 1979, Hatsuse 1980, Hatano 1996, and the seven-volume series *Asian Perspectives* [Mizoguchi 1993–1994]). But since the beginning of the twenty-first century there has been an upsurge of interest in the historical development of Pan-Asianism, reflected in a stream of book-length publications on various aspects of Pan-Asianism (in English they include Saaler and Koschmann 2007, Hotta 2007, Aydin 2007b, Hamashita 2008, Tankha 2009, and Zachmann 2009; in Japanese, Yamamuro 2001, Miyadai 2004, Nakajima 2005, Inoue 2006,

Yonetani 2006, Matsuura 2007b, Li Cai-hua and Suzuki 2007, and Matsuura 2010; and, in Chinese, Wang 2004). In addition, a number of important articles have been published on the subject over the years.[5] Notwithstanding these publications, however, our knowledge of Pan-Asianism and its role in modern Asia remains fragmented, unsystematic, and unbalanced.[6]

This collection aims to remedy the situation by providing readers, first of all, with the seminal documents of Pan-Asianism and thus a comprehensive overview of the development of the ideals of Asian solidarity and regionalism in the hope of stimulating further research and providing the foundations for a synthesis of earlier work. The major difficulty with researching Pan-Asianism is a linguistic one, for it would be very difficult, if not impossible, for any one scholar to master all the languages necessary for a comprehensive study of the subject. So, while the community of scholars interested in issues of Asian regionalism continues to grow, linguistic difficulties and the barriers of specialization have prevented them from studying Pan-Asianism as an ideology that transcends linguistic boundaries and national narratives and examining the processes of regional integration in East Asia from the perspective of the *longue dureé*. We hope that this collection, with its comprehensive approach, will help scholars to look beyond the scope of their narrow specializations and open new possibilities for transnational cooperation in research on Asian regionalism.

The sources collected are arranged in chronological order, with some exceptions allowed for the presentation of a coherent sequence of texts. The book allows the reader to trace the development of Pan-Asianism and Asian regionalism from the mid-nineteenth century down to the present day and provides an insider's view of intra-Asian debates. The material discussed in each chapter falls roughly into three often overlapping and never mutually exclusive categories: 1) attempts to define Asia and assess the region's contribution to world civilization; 2) calls for Asian solidarity, integration, and unity; and 3) debates about Asia's role in world politics and, above all, about Asia's relations with Europe.

THE ORIGINS OF PAN-ASIANISM: MACRONATIONALISM AND TRANSNATIONALISM

The term "Asia" came into common use in East Asia only in the mid-nineteenth century in response to the increasing diplomatic, military, and economic presence of the Western powers, and their territorial expansion in East Asia. The Opium War of 1839–1842 was a watershed in the history of Asian–European encounters. The British victory led to the recognition, throughout East Asia, of Europe as a common threat, and it was at that time that intellectuals and politicians throughout the region began to consider the questions of "Asia" and Asian solidarity. With a view to giving the concept of solidarity some substance, they began exploring Asian cultural commonalities and the common historical heritage of the continent. It is of course true that, as Hamashita Takeshi (2008) and other scholars have pointed out, East Asian countries had a long history of interaction before the nineteenth century. This took the form of an interstate system, centered on China. It was this Sinocentric system (sometimes also known as the tributary system) to which the Western powers had to accommodate themselves when they first came into contact with East Asian states (see Fairbank et al. 1989: 195–96 and passim). But it was the acute sense of crisis brought about by the Chinese defeat in the Opium War that finally forced Asian writers and thinkers actively to pursue the agenda of a united Asia, an Asia with a common goal—the struggle against Western imperialism.

Ideas of Asian solidarity came in a large variety of forms, as did the geographical definitions underlying claims for regional solidarity (Arano 2007). Some forms of the concept were based on assumptions of racial unity, following, curiously enough, racial notions that had originated in the West (Hannaford 1996; Dikötter 1997). Others tended to emphasize commonalities in culture and language (more accurately written language). This was especially the case in East Asia, often referred to in the West as the "Orient" (Japanese: *Tōyō*; Korean: *Tong'yang*; Chinese: *Dongyang*), a region which for thousands of years had been under the powerful influence of Chinese civilization. (The term "East Asia" was used from the late nineteenth century on [Japanese: *Tōa*; Korean: *Dong-a*; Chinese: *Dong-ya*].) In this context, some thinkers saw the new quest for solidarity as a strengthening of the existing networks of economic and cultural exchange. Others were inspired by pan-movements emerging almost simultaneously in Europe and America. The various approaches to Pan-Asianism, however, all shared a common emphasis on transnationalism and Asian unity.

As some contributions in this collection show, Pan-Asianism was at times used to legitimize Japan's territorial aggrandizement and colonial expansion (see the next section for a discussion of this issue). One of the few detailed studies of pan-movements in general, Snyder's (1984) *Macro-Nationalisms*, characterizes pan-movements as "Nationalism Writ Large" or "extended nationalisms." However, as the present volume shows, advocacy of Pan-Asianism also reflected reservations about the concepts of nation and nationalism, which were also imported in their modern forms to Asia from the West in the nineteenth century. The popularity of a transnational Pan-Asianism and the transnational political activities of revolutionaries (see I:3, I:5, I:10, I:11, and so on) show that the nation was not, as is often believed, an absolute and unquestioned value in Asia. (The rise of pan-movements in other parts of the world, too, has been seen as an expression of skepticism over the absolute character of the "nation;" cf. Duara 1998.) To be sure, in a number of Asian countries protonationalism had already developed before the arrival of the European powers in the region (Mitani 1997; Hamashita 2008). Within the Sinocentric international order, the elites of tributary states in East Asia had developed their own sense of nationhood. However, in the nineteenth century new forms of nationalism developed in East Asia. In the same way as Pan-Asianism, they represented a reaction to Western colonialism and over time developed into national independence movements. Yet again, these nationalist aspirations and the independence movements they spawned were characterized by strong *trans*national links, alliances that were apparent in the activities of Asian revolutionaries described in this volume: Indians, Vietnamese, Indonesians, Filipinos, and activists from other Asian countries who went into exile in Japan, where they exchanged ideas, promoted pan-Asian solidarity, developed networks, and worked together to achieve national independence. Benedict Anderson has brilliantly traced the process by which the elites of colonized nations developed a sense of national identity and a desire for independence from their colonial masters during periods of residence in the metropole (Anderson 1983). It could be argued that a similar process was at work in the case of the revolutionary members of the Asian elites. When they found themselves in Japan, whether as students or exiles, they interacted with other Asians and in this way developed a common Asian consciousness.

In Japan they came also into contact with Japanese Pan-Asianists, many of whom supported independence movements throughout Asia (see I:11 for an example). The Japanese triumph in the war with Russia in 1904–1905 was an important turning point (Aydin 2007a), an event that accelerated the spread of pan-Asian ideas throughout the continent. Many Asians now believed that Japan would soon assume leadership in the struggle against the tyranny of the Western imperialist powers. Even in distant Egypt, a delighted Arab announced the news of the Russian defeat to the Chinese revolutionary leader Sun Yat-sen (Zhongshan; Japanese: Son Bun, 1866–1925), who was traveling by boat through the Suez Canal. "The joy of this Arab, as a member of the great Asiatic race," Sun recalled many years later, "seemed to know no bounds" (Jansen 1954: 117). However, as we describe here, disillusionment with Japan soon set in when it embarked on a program of carving out its own colonial empire at the expense of other Asian nations and justified these expansionist policies with pan-Asian rhetoric.

Pan-Asian cooperation was institutionalized in the form of numerous pan-Asian associations founded all over Asia and was also reflected in pan-Asian conferences that took place in Japan, China, and Afghanistan in the 1920s and 1930s (see II:8). These developments showed the diversity and interconnectedness of anti-Western movements throughout Asia. A few examples will suffice to illustrate this phenomenon. In 1907, socialists and anarchists from China, Japan, and India joined forces to found the Asiatic Humanitarian Brotherhood in Tokyo (I:16). In 1909 Japanese and Muslim pan-Asianists in Japan established the Ajia Gikai (Asian Congress; cf. Worringer 2006, which also includes a translation of the association's foundation manifesto) with the goal of promoting the cause of Asian solidarity and liberation. It was almost certainly this Ajia Gikai that a British intelligence report referred to when it mentioned "an Oriental Association in Tokyo attended by Japanese, Filipinos, Siamese, Indians, Koreans, and Chinese, where Count Okuma [Shigenobu, 1838–1922] once delivered an anti-American lecture" (Eliot to Curzon, 30 April 1921, 77B Foreign Office Documents pertaining to Japan, FO 371/6678, Public Record Office, Kew, Richmond). In 1921, the Pan-Turanian Association was founded in Tokyo to rally Japanese support for the unification of the Turks of Central Asia and their liberation from Russian rule. The association cooperated closely with the Greater Asia Association (Dai Ajia Kyōkai) and other Japanese pan-Asian organizations (cf. Dai Ajia Kyōkai/Dai Tsuran Kyōkai 1922).

The transnational character of Pan-Asianism was also apparent in its publishing activities. Indian pan-Asianists published material in Japan (Bose 1922; Das 1917a, 1944; see also I:24), China (Das 1917b), the United States (Das 1936), and Germany (e.g., Raja Mahendra Pratap in the *Zeitschrift für Geopolitik* [Journal of Geopolitics]; also Sarkar 1922); Japanese pan-Asianists published in China (Kodera Kenkichi; see I:26), India (Okakura Tenshin; see I:7 and I:8), and the United States (Kawakami 1919, 1921; Rōyama 1941). Koreans, too, such as the court noble An Kyongsu (1853–1900), published their works in Japan (An 1900). Journals with a clear pan-Asian message—the source of many of the documents in this collection—were published in Japan, China, and Southeast Asia (discussed here).

Although such writings might be dismissed as mere "propaganda" (on prewar Japanese propaganda activities, see O'Connor 2004–2005; Kushner 2006), there is no doubt that a significant number of Westerners were sympathetic to the ideals of Asian solidarity and Pan-Asianism. At the center of pan-Asian activities in Japan at the end of World War I stood the now obscure French mystic, Paul Richard (1874–1967; see I:29), whose works were published in Japan, India, and the United States and certainly widely read, at least in Japan. In the 1920s and 1930s, the famous editor of the *Zeitschrift für Geopolitik*, Karl Haushofer (1869–1946), paid tribute to the pan-Asian movement in his publications (e.g., Haushofer 1931), seeing it as proof of his theory that international relations would come to be dominated by regional blocs. Haushofer (1931: 14f) introduced to his readers the writings and activities of pan-Asianists such as Sun Yat-sen (see II:5), Rabindranath Tagore (1861–1941), and Benoy Kumar Sarkar (1887–1949; see I:21). The writings of these Asian activists and revolutionaries, Haushofer was convinced, reflected a trend toward a future world order that would be dominated by large, regional blocs, replacing the existing order characterized by the sovereign nation-state. Another proponent of pan-ideas, Richard Nikolaus Count von Coudenhove-Kalergi (1894–1972), the founder of the pan-European movement and the publisher of the journal *Pan-Europa*, also praised the pan-Asian movement; a Japanese translation of an enthusiastic article by him appeared in the journal *Dai Ajiashugi* (Greater Asianism; see II:13) (Coudenhove-Kalergi 1931, 1932).

As a final striking example of the appeal of Pan-Asianism to Westerners, in 1934 an anonymous Greek wrote a letter addressed "to the Eastern Asiatic people of the Mongolian race and colour," which he sent to the Japanese consulate at Surabaya in the Dutch East Indies (present-day Indonesia).[7] The letter called on Asians to

> cultivate the Pan-Mongolian consciousness, in feeling, in thought and above all in action; harmonize, cultivate and facilitate in every possible way the Inter-Mongolian race intercourse and understanding by adopting an official and compulsory taught and used Inter-Mongolian language composed of Words of Chinese, Japanese and Siamese languages; Eliminate from your mind and from your dictionaries the word FOREIGNER, and cultivate the Inter-Mongolian fellowship and community of interest; Harmonize your national, political, social, economic and religious life. . . . [F]orm and organize THE INTER-MONGOLIAN AND INTER-CONTINENTAL HARMONIZED AWAKENING, in every city, town, village and hamlet.

This bizarre letter was apparently inspired by the Japanese Foreign Ministry's so-called Amau Statement, which declared "special responsibilities for Japan in East Asia" and which was often interpreted as a declaration by Japan of an "Asian Monroe Doctrine,"[8] that is, a call for noninterference by Western powers in China (cf., e.g., Wang 1934). As far as one can tell, this eccentric appeal to an inter-Asian consciousness elicited no reaction either in Japan or elsewhere in Asia. Nevertheless, Pan-Asianism was stimulated, both positively and negatively, by Western influences. For example, the Japanese politician Kodera Kenkichi (1877–1949; see I:26), who had studied international relations in Europe and the United States for almost a decade, justified his advocacy of Pan-Asianism by constantly referring to the positive role of pan-movements in the West. In contrast to Kodera, Prince Konoe Fumimaro (1891–1945; see I:32) chose to stress the negative aspects of the West by rejecting the universalist pretensions of the League of Nations (founded 1919) when he proclaimed the need for Asian solidarity under Japanese leadership. Both Kanokogi Kazunobu (1884–1949; II:14) and Hirano Yoshitarō (1897–1980; see II:30) were strongly influenced by German ideas, as were the 1930s proponents of a regional bloc in East Asia such as the political scientist Professor Rōyama Masamichi (1895–1980; see II:18) and Kada Tetsuji (1895–1964; Kada 1939: 577ff).

While the West was important as a reference point, Pan-Asianism as an ideology also posed a significant challenge to the traditional Sinocentric order discussed previously—an order not limited to China proper but also appropriated by the nomadic conquerors of China and by states on the periphery such as Korea and Japan. In this context, the seemingly "more modern" ideology of Pan-Asianism served as an integrating force, helping to fulfill the requirement for the "de-centering of China" (Schmid 2002).

Arguably, in many cases the Sinocentric hierarchical view of the world influenced the thinking of some Japanese pan-Asianists who appropriated it faithfully with one significant change. For them it was Japan, not China, that was to be the new "Middle Kingdom" and the leader of Asia (Miwa 1973: 389–90). Although, as we show here, early forms of Pan-Asianism often envisioned cooperation on equal terms, insistence on Japanese leadership (*meishu*) in Asia increased in proportion to the growth and expansion of Japan's power in East Asia (on this "Meishuron" version of Pan-Asianism, see Hotta 2007: 44–49).

For advocates of this "Meishuron" Asianism, Japan's leadership was justified on moral grounds as well as by the realities of international relations. Japan qualified as the leader of Asia because it was morally superior to China, which was in political turmoil, and had always been as a result of its frequent dynastic changes. In contrast, Japan, many believed, was qualified to lead Asia because of its divine imperial dynasty that was "unbroken through ages immemorial." Japan, in this view, was a "chosen" country, the "Land of the Gods"—qualities that uniquely fitted it for a special "mission" to liberate Asia from Western oppression, become the leader of the region, and, as its more imaginative supporters asserted, unite the whole world under the benevolent rule of the Japanese emperor, following the ancient slogan *hakkō ichiu*, or "The Eight Corners of the World [United] under One Roof." Rather than drawing on the foundational myths, other pan-Asian writers justified Japan's leadership of Asia on the grounds of Japan's successful modernization program, an effort they contrasted with the failure of the rest of Asia in this regard. From this perspective, Japan's technological advances served as evidence of Japanese superiority. But whatever the grounds for such claims, the fact remains that many Japanese pan-Asianists, in various ways, consciously or unconsciously, provided justification for Japan's colonial rule and territorial expansion in Asia.

PAN-ASIANISM AND EMPIRE

One of the reasons why, for a long time after 1945, Pan-Asianism was largely ignored by researchers—not to mention politicians and diplomats—was its fateful connection to Japanese imperialism and the role it played as an ideology that legitimized Japan's empire-building project in the first half of the twentieth century. While some commentators insist that Japan never officially pursued a pan-Asian foreign policy (Aoki Kazuo, quoted in Yamamuro 2001: 573; see also I:12) before or even during the Asia-Pacific War (1931–1945), it is undeniable that the Japanese government frequently utilized pan-Asian rhetoric in the 1930s and 1940s in order to bolster claims to Japanese leadership in East Asia and legitimize its colonial rule over parts of Asia.

In *The Origins of Totalitarianism*, Hannah Arendt suggested a close link between nineteenth-century Pan-Germanism and Pan-Slavism and twentieth-century totalitarianism and expansionism. "Nazism and Bolshevism," she contended, "owe more to Pan-Germanism and Pan-Slavism (respectively) than to any other ideology or political movement. This is most evident in foreign policies, where the strategies of Nazi Germany and Soviet Russia have followed so closely the well-known programs of conquest outlined by the pan-movements before and during the First World War . . ." (Arendt 1985: 222). Although it would be an exaggeration to claim that Pan-Asianism formed an important component of any totalitarian developments in modern Asia, one cannot overlook the connection between Pan-Asianism and Japanese ultranationalism (which will be discussed in more detail here) and also the contribution of this ideology to the legitimization of Japanese colonial rule and Japanese empire building in Asia in the first half of the twentieth century (Oguma 1998: 225–30; 272; 321–44; 644–54).[9]

As early as 1910, pan-Asian rhetoric was used by the Japanese government to legitimize the annexation of Korea. The Annexation Treaty referred specifically to commonalities between Japanese and Koreans, such as racial origins, a common history and culture, and a shared destiny. This remained the orthodox way of justifying and legitimizing Japanese rule in Korea throughout the colonial period and was reiterated time and again in both public and private statements[10] (see I:4; Oguma 1995; I:5; Oguma 1998: 163–66). The same pan-Asian rhetoric was continuously reaffirmed and also applied to other colonial territories. For example, in 1939, in the semi-official journal *Contemporary Japan*, a writer insisted that contrary to the general assumption held abroad, and even entertained by some Japanese, Chosen [Korea], Taiwan, and even Manchukuo are not Japanese colonies according to the Western way of thinking. . . . "To make the world one household" is an expression used by the Japanese to indicate their moral principle of co-existence and co-prosperity. . . . Although their languages and customs are now different, Japan and Korea were especially close to each other until about thirteen centuries ago, there having been a large intermixture of both blood and culture before that time. . . . Japan's annexation of the peninsula might be taken as a reversion of the two countries to their ancient status of being one homogeneous whole. (Matsuzawa 1939: 455, 462f)

The assertion of racial and cultural commonalities presented here went hand in hand with the legitimization of Japanese superiority on the grounds that Japan was a country chosen by the gods (see the previous discussion). As early as the late 1910s, a number of writers, such as Kanokogi Kazunobu (II:14), Kita Ikki (I:27), and Ōkawa Shūmei (II:4), spoke of a divine Japanese "mission" to liberate Asia. This high-sounding objective was often difficult to distinguish from the substitution of one form of colonial oppression (by Europeans) for another (by fellow Asian Japanese). And a belief in Japan's divine mission was by no means limited to radical reformists. Even mainstream writers who eschewed ideologically driven rhetoric and sought to explain international relations in terms of Realpolitik, such as Tokutomi Iichirō (better known as Sohō, 1863–1957; see I:28), urged Japan to establish an "Asian Monroe Doctrine." In doing so, Tokutomi may have been applying an idea of Western provenance to international relations in East Asia, but he still believed, just like Kita and Kanokogi, that Japan had a special "mission" to accomplish in East Asia (Tokutomi 1917).

In the 1930s, claims that Japan's empire was an embodiment of pan-Asian ideals were voiced more frequently and much more openly than before. This was due to the impact of "regional bloc thinking" that was highly influential at the time. For example, the previously mentioned Rōyama Masamichi insisted in 1934 that "the Pan-Asiatic movement" was a "decisive influence responsible for the establishment of the Empire." Though he lamented that this movement lacked "any coherent programme under any prominent leader," he nevertheless regarded it as full of promise for the future. As evidence, he noted with satisfaction that "many small groups of so-called Pan-Asianists loosely affiliated through study organizations . . . have sprung up like mushrooms during the past two years in both Japan and Manchuria" (Rōyama 1934: 29f). Rōyama's notion of an "East Asian bloc," as introduced in II:18, gained wide prominence in Japan in the late 1930s, amplified by a fusion with the geopolitical ideas of Karl Haushofer and Carl Schmidt (1888–1985) and with earlier concepts of an "Asian Monroe Doctrine" (see

I:28 and Miwa 1990: 146–49). The notion of an "East Asian bloc" was also popular with Marxists and socialists, as can be seen in the writings of Taka-hashi Kamekichi (1894–1977; cf. Hoston 1984) and of some members of the Shōwa Kenkyūkai, the brain trust founded by Prince Konoe Fumimaro, prime minister in 1937–1939 and 1940–1941 (see II:20).

The intimate connection of Pan-Asianism with Japan's empire-building ambitions leads us to another central problem of Pan-Asianism—the inherent ambiguity of the concepts involved.[11] It is clear that, from the outset, pan-Asian thought was riddled with ambiguity and contradictions that made this ideology capable of being used to legitimize both the anticolonial struggle against the West and the domination of one Asian nation by another. This ambiguity is also inherent in the terminology used to describe the ideology, a question to which we shall turn next.

PROBLEMS OF TERMINOLOGY

As stated at the start of this introduction, Pan-Asianism poses a problem as a topic of scholarly inquiry even at the level of terminology. The object of inquiry is hard to define and is almost as elusive as a continuously shifting target. There is no scholarly consensus on the definition of "Asia," on pan-movements, or on ideologies with a transnational focus that have evolved over time. Likewise, the question of how Pan-Asianism is related to other pan-movements is far from settled.

As we have seen, the emergence of Pan-Asianism was inseparable from the rise of Japan as a major power and Japan's struggle with China for leadership in Asia. But Pan-Asianism also reflected attempts by East Asian elites to forge Asian unity by bringing Japan and China together. Thus, early manifestations of the movement were characterized by the close cooperation of ideologues, activists, and politicians from Japan, China, and Korea. But the need for cooperation and, thus, compromise resulted in pan-Asian ideas being characterized by a marked lack of specific content. The diffusion of the term over time is a case in point. Although this collection treats the subject from the mid-nineteenth century on, the term "Pan-Asianism" (or Asianism, Greater Asianism) was not in use in China, Korea, and Japan before the 1890s and occurs only infrequently prior to the 1910s.

Around the turn of the century, Western writers who were clamoring about the threat of the Yellow Peril (on the Yellow Peril, see Thompson 1978) oc-casionally used the terms "Pan-Asianism" or "pan-Asiatic league" in warn-ing of the dangers a united Asia would pose for Western supremacy (for an early example, see Brandt 1903).[12] The Japanese government was quick to lay any Western suspicions on this score to rest, particularly after the start of the war with Russia, a Western power, in 1904 (cf. Matsumura 1987). It took this popular Western agitation so seriously that on many occasions it officially disclaimed any interest in promoting closer relations with its (weak) Asian neighbors (see, e.g., "No 'Yellow Peril.' Minister Kurino Denies That Japan Wants to Organize the Asiatics," *New York Times*, 18 February 1904). Japanese diplomats were dispatched to Europe and the United States expressly to dispel any Western suspicions as to Japan's pan-Asian ambitions. For example, in the United States, Harvard-educated Baron Kaneko Kentarō (1853–1942) dismissed rumors voiced in the "yellow" press that Japan was aiming to form an Asian federation, as did diplomat Suematsu Kenchō (1855–1920) in Europe (see I:12; for Suematsu's remarks, see *New York Times*, 21 February 1904 for Kaneko). As late as 1919, Takekoshi Yosaburō (1865–1950) ridiculed the idea of a Japanese-led Asian alliance against the West in a publication funded by the Japanese government:

Among our own people, there are some who do not rightly interpret the history of their own country, and who do not take their national strength into proper consideration and who, being prompted by certain fanatical ideas, advocate the alliance of the yellow races against the white, an alliance of which Japan should be the leader, and with that object in view, they favour the partition of China. Those who argue in this strain have evidently lost their mental balance. (Takegoshi [*sic*] 1919: 83)

Just as the government went to great lengths to deny any association with Pan-Asianism, the opposition placed a strong emphasis on Pan-Asianism, calling for the unification of the "yellow race," that is, the Asian peoples. As early as 1874, Ueki Emori (1857–1892), a prominent member of the opposition freedom and People's Rights Movement (*jiyū minken undō*), had attacked what he considered the pro-Western policy of the government and, insisting that the West was Japan's enemy, called for the formation of an Asian League (*Ajia rengō*) (cf. Kuroki 2002: 19). Ueki held a version of Pan-Asianism that assumed equality among Asian nations. He even advocated independence for the Ryukyu archipelago (present-day Okinawa Prefecture), a previously independent kingdom that was annexed by Japan in the 1870s (Kuroki 2002: 24).[13] An anonymous writer in the journal *Ajia* (Asia) (see I:1) and the antigovernment activist and politician Tarui Tōkichi (1850–1922; see I:5) again made similar proposals in the 1880s. It was not until 1903 that the first acknowledgment of the potential of Pan-Asianism as a significant factor in international relations was made, when the art critic Okakura Tenshin (1862–1913), famous for coining the phrase "Asia is one," stated in his book *The Awakening of the East* that a "Pan-Asiatic Alliance" would "in itself constitute an immense force" (I:7). However, the impact of this statement may have been somewhat reduced in Japan by the fact that Okakura had written his book in English for an Indian and not a Japanese audience.

While the term "Pan-Asianism" entered the mainstream political vocabulary only in the 1910s, in the nineteenth century advocates of Asian unity could draw on a number of terms and slogans when propagating their ideals. In the 1880s, the term *Kōa*, or "Raising (or Developing) Asia," was the most widely used slogan, implying the need for Asia to modernize in order to catch up with the technologically advanced West. The term was not without its problems, however. For example, an organization called the Kōakai (Raising Asia Society) was founded in Tokyo in 1880 (see I:2 and Kuroki 2007). Its membership was predominantly Japanese—they had chosen the group's name—but it included some Koreans and Chinese who objected to the name on the grounds that it implied—in contrast to successful, modern Japan—that Asia was backward, oppressed, and downtrodden and could be saved only by "raising" it through Japanese leadership and advice. Following such criticism, the Kōakai was renamed Ajia Kyōkai (Asia Association) in 1883. But it was not only Japanese pan-Asianists who believed in Japanese superiority; many Asians also acknowledged their political and economic backwardness in relation to Japan. Many Chinese recognized the failure of modernization, at least implicitly, in their nation, accounting for the formation of political associations with names such as the Raise China Society (Xingzhonghui), founded by Sun Yat-sen in 1894, and the China Revival Society (Huaxinghui), founded in Hunan in 1904.

Another early term used to describe pan-Asian solidarity was the classical Chinese phrase *hosha shinshi* (Chinese: *fuche chunchi*; Korean: *poch'a sonch'i*), which means "mutual dependence" or, literally, "a relationship as close as that between the lips and the teeth or between the chassis and the wheels of a cart." This image implied a high degree of interdependence (Hashikawa 1980), but, in contrast to the potentially hierarchical Kōa, it presumed equal relations among Asian nations. Its origin also indicates the influence of Chinese classical scholarship on early Pan-Asianism. This phrase was used by early pan-Asianists particularly in the 1870s and 1880s, but it can be found in many of the texts presented in this collection well into the twentieth century.

A third influential slogan used to express pan-Asian sentiment and activism that was very popular at the turn of the century was "Same Culture, Same Race" (Japanese: *dōbun dōshu*; Chinese: *tongwen tongzhong*; Korean: *tongmun tongjong*), which likewise did not imply hierarchical relations between Asian nations or make claim to the superiority of any one country. In Japan, the term was used particularly often by Prince Konoe Atsumaro (1863–1904), who, uncharacteristically for an early pan-Asianist, was a member of Japan's ruling elite (I:6), and by the Tōa Dōbunkai (East Asian Common Culture Society; see I:9). The term also appears frequently in Japanese journals of the day and seems to have received some acceptance in other Asian countries. Closely related to the rise of racial thinking in Japan and East Asia, this slogan also has to be seen as an expression of the growing fear in Japan of a future "clash of races," that is, a war fought along racial lines in which Japan would have no choice but to side with the Asian, or "colored," peoples against the white powers of the West (cf. Saaler 2008a). Parallel with the development of this kind of racial thinking in Asia, the idea of the "White Peril" also gained ground (see Nagai 1913; Duus 1971; I:14). It was an inversion of the "Yellow Peril" hysteria that affected Europe at the time. The proponents of the "White Peril," including some Europeans (e.g., Gulick 1905), believed that the threat to civilization came not from the "yellow" peoples of Asia but from the predatory European powers (cf. Mori 1904; Kodera 1916).

It was only in the 1910s that the term "Pan-Asianism" made its debut in intellectual discourse. Japanese political scientist Ōyama Ikuo (1880–1955) used the term for the first time to describe Chinese political associations which were promoting "Greater Asianism" (*Da Yazhouzhuyi*) "in secretly published pamphlets" with the intention of spreading anti-Western sentiment in China.[14] Ōyama himself rejected Asianism because he saw the emergence of this ideology as a sign of increasing nationalistic and xenophobic tendencies in Japan (Ōyama 1916). While Ōyama criticized Asianism from his position as a liberal intellectual,[15] the Japanese government remained wary of pan-Asian proposals because it feared that such tendencies might undermine Japan's good relations with the Western powers. Between its signing in 1902 and 1921–1922, when it was superseded by the Washington treaty system, the Anglo-Japanese Alliance was always at the heart of Japan's foreign policy. The alliance, however, would be in jeopardy if it transpired that Japan was supporting an independence movement in India as part of a pan-Asian foreign policy. On several occasions, Britain showed suspicion over Indian–Japanese relations, particularly during World War I when members of the Indian independence movement were cooperating with Germany (see II:9). For example, the visit of the celebrated poet and first Asian Nobel laureate, Rabindranath Tagore, to Japan in 1916 caused "considerable uneasiness in London" over "a Japanese–Indian understanding that could eventually take a political and anti-British form" (Hay 1970: 80–81). The British intelligence service kept close tabs on Indian independence activists in Japan (and China) and their Japanese sympathizers.[16]

If only to avoid alienating its British ally and other Western powers, both the Japanese government and the press tended to be highly critical of pan-Asian schemes. The hostile tone adopted by Japanese newspapers during a short public debate on Pan-Asianism in 1913 well illustrates this point. In a debate with the British journalist and diplomat Sir Valentine Chirol (1852–1929), the celebrated American naval strategist Admiral Alfred Thayer Mahan (1840–1914) defended the 1913 California "Alien Land Bill" (cf. Daniels 1977), which would prevent Asian immigrants from owning land or property in the state on the grounds that America would not be able to "digest and assimilate the strong national and racial characteristics which distinguish the Japanese." Mahan seemed moreover to believe that in excluding the Japanese, Californians were acting in the interests not only of the United States but also of "the whole community of European civilization" (*The Times*, 23 June 1913). In the debate Chirol, who had retired from his position at *The Times* two years before and joined the Foreign Office, criticized the Land Bill. However, it appears that he was a voice in the wilderness. Even the editors of the *Times* seemed to support Mahan when they criticized Japan for what they regarded as contradictions in its foreign policy:

> On the one hand, she [Japan] demands recognition because her people are not as other Asiatics. On the other hand, . . . her publicists are now asserting that "to Japan is assigned the leadership in the claim of the 'coloured' races against the 'non-coloured.'" These two sets are mutually destructive. Japan cannot have it both ways. . . . She must make up her mind whether she wishes to present herself as aloof from other Asiatic races, or as the avowed champion of Pan-Asiatic ideals. (*The Times*, 23 June 1913)

Such criticisms clearly struck a sensitive chord in Japan. Throughout June and July 1913, these various statements were discussed at great length by Japan's leading newspapers, including the *Osaka Asahi Shinbun*, the *Osaka Mainichi Shinbun*, and the *Tokyo Nichinichi Shinbun*.[17] The *Asahi* unequivocally declared that it considered "Pan-Asianism an illusion (*kūsō*)," while the *Nichinichi* ridiculed the notion that Japan would "lead the Asian peoples to fight against the Euro-American white powers" as "useless and reckless." It was in these articles dismissing the accusations made by Mahan and the *Times* that the terms Han-Ajiashugi ("Pan-Asianism," *Mainichi* and *Nichinichi*) and Zen-Ajiashugi ("All-Asianism," *Asahi*) made their first appearance in the Japanese language. They were coined specifically to express the English term "Pan-Asianism," which previously had had no exact Japanese equivalent. At this stage, as indicated by the critical, derisory tone of the newspaper articles cited, these neologisms were used in a derogatory sense.

Yet, little by little, the negative connotations of the term "Asianism" were lost in the aftermath of World War I. The bloodbath in Europe made Japan the dominant power in East Asia and brought about an upsurge in Japan's self-confidence. At the same time, it stimulated international attempts to establish a new world order after the war, an order that would guarantee peace—if not permanent peace,[18] then at least peace for the foreseeable future. Within these developments, Japan's newly found self-confidence resulted in an outpouring of pan-Asian writings during the last two years of the war (see I:26). These writings should be seen as a Japanese contribution to the debate on how a new international order could guarantee peace. But Japanese writers were not alone in arguing for the necessity of regional integration. There were also notably some Chinese commentators who, while critical of Japanese Pan-Asianism, nonetheless advocated regional integration on the grounds that only a regional, pan-Asian order would result in the achievement of a permanent peace (see, e.g., I:22). When the idea of a League of Nations surfaced during World War I,[19] pan-Asian writers in Japan reacted by proposing an East Asian League (*Tōa renmei*) that would guarantee peace on a regional basis (e.g., Sugita 1916).[20]

By the war's end, pan-Asianist visions of regional integration had thus come to be accepted, at least by public opinion and some politicians, as a realistic scenario for future international relations in East Asia. Certainly, in contrast to the vague professions of pan-Asian unity that had been the norm up until the beginning of the twentieth century, the ideology of Pan-Asianism had by 1918 become concrete and well defined. It had gained recognition in public discourse and was no longer confined to the political fringes. Terms such as Pan-Asianism (*Han Ajiashugi*), Greater Asianism (*Dai Ajiashugi*), All-Asianism (*Zen Ajiashugi*), and the "Asian Monroe Doctrine" (*Ajia Monrōshugi*), largely absent from public discourse until then, now began to appear frequently in newspapers and journals. This proliferation of neologisms reflected a growth of diverse and sophisticated approaches to the issue of Asian solidarity in all its ramifications. The wide range of these responses can be gleaned from the flood of articles (e.g., Ōyama 1916; Sawayanagi 1917; Uchida 1917; Kita 1917a; Horiuchi 1918; Ukita 1918; Sawayanagi 1919b; Bose 1922) and books (Kodera 1916; Sawayanagi 1919a; Mitsukawa 1921; Ōkawa 1922; Tanaka 1924; Murobuse 1926) on Pan-Asianism that appeared during and after the war. While these works indicated the spread and acceptance of the term "Pan-Asianism" in Japanese discourse, perhaps more important they also defined Asianism in concrete terms and demanded that Japan act in accordance with pan-Asian principles in international relations.

The new popularity of Pan-Asianism in Japanese intellectual discourse and politics received a boost when news of a new immigration law that would bar Japanese from immigration to the United States (part of the 1924 Immigration or Johnson-Reed Act) reached Japan. Protests against the act were held through the length and breadth of Japan, events that in many cases turned into demonstrations of pan-Asian solidarity (see I:26 and Stalker 2006). In this climate of anti-American agitation, a number of new associations sprang up whose names—such as the Federation of East Asian Races (Ajia Minzoku Gikai, founded in 1923) or the Oriental Co-Existence Society (Tōyō Kyōzonkai)—proclaimed their pan-Asian orientation. The invigoration of popular interest in Pan-Asianism as a result of America's exclusionist policies was also attested to by a slew of articles on the subject in the Japanese press. For example, the influential journal *Nihon oyobi Nihonjin* (Japan and the Japanese) brought out a special issue on "Greater Asianism" (Dai Ajiashugi) in October 1924, and the Asian Newspaper Company published a call for the "Foundation of a Greater East Asian Federation" (Miyai 1925).

Not all pan-Asian slogans and catchphrases—like some of the new associations—survived for long. Many enjoyed a brief popularity and then quickly disappeared from public discourse. Some terms, however, resurfaced in later years, often in different contexts. The notion of an "East Asian League," for example, exemplified the entrenchment of the term "East Asia" in Japanese public discourse around the turn of the century. However, after the wave of anti-American protests subsided in 1924, "East Asia" receded from public discourse, only to return to the mainstream discussion in the late 1930s, in somewhat modified form, as the "East Asian Cooperative Community" (*tōa kyōdōtai* or *tōyō kyōdōtai*; see II:18 and II:20). The formation of a "Greater Asian League" (*Dai Ajia rengō*) was also proposed in the founding manifesto of the Dai Ajia Kyōkai (Greater Asia Association) in 1933. This manifesto, drafted a year after Japan had left the League of Nations, insisted that such a league was necessary given the global trend toward the formation of regional blocs (II:13).

"All-Asianism" (*Zen Ajiashugi*), another term for "Asianism" or "Pan-Asianism," was launched by Ōkawa Shūmei in the wake of the 1913 Chirol–Mahan debate in articles he contributed to *Tairiku* (The Continent) (Ōkawa 1916: 32). However, the term did not "catch on" and vanished from public discourse in the early 1920s. In any event, all these terms were used largely interchangeably. Even Ōkawa on occasion used *Han Ajiashugi* in the same context (Ōkawa 1916) as *Zen Ajiashugi*, and he appears to have made no distinction between the two.

The term "Kōa" perhaps enjoyed the most remarkable career of any pan-Asian term. Kōa first appeared in the 1880s (see I:2 and I:4), when it was used as the main slogan to express pan-Asian solidarity. However, as we have seen, it was quickly discarded because it implied Japanese leadership of the pan-Asian movement. But the term was not forgotten completely, as it reappeared in the 1930s at a time when Japan was adopting a form of Pan-Asianism in its foreign policy. By then, Japan had begun to abandon its policy of cooperation with the Anglo-American powers and was openly pursuing a strategy of destroying the political status quo in East Asia. The unity of Asia and, at the same time, the establishment of Japanese hegemony in East Asia had become Japan's ultimate objective. Although no government decrees contained the terms "Asianism" or "Pan-Asianism" even in the 1930s, the Japanese government demonstrated its commitment to the pan-Asian cause in 1938 by creating the Kōa-in, the Agency for the Development of Asia (sometimes also known in English as the East Asia Development Board). The Kōa-in was a cabinet-level agency with the primary task of coordinating political, economic, and cultural activities in regard to China. While it engaged in research on Chinese affairs and published its findings in the *Kōa-in Chōsa Geppō* (Kōa-in Monthly Research Bulletin), some scholars argue that it was also involved in the recruitment and management of forced labor and even in the opium trade in China. Such were the powers of this agency that only formal diplomatic relations with China remained within the jurisdiction of the Ministry of Foreign Affairs. The Kōa-in was integrated into the Ministry of Greater East Asia (Daitōa-shō) in 1942, which from that time on directed Japan's political and diplomatic relations with the members of the newly declared Greater East Asian Co-Prosperity Sphere (see II:24 and II:27).

This official endorsement of what is probably the oldest pan-Asian term caused a veritable boom in the use of Kōa. Newspapers used the term frequently; journals incorporating it in their title—such as *Kōa Kyōiku* (Education to Raise Asia) or simply *Kōa*—were founded, while politicians, diplomats, and intellectuals discussed the new Kōa policy (e.g., Ōtani 1939). These figures included a foreign minister (Matsuoka 1941b), and a prime minister who proclaimed the "Raising of Asia" a "holy task" (Tōjō 1943). Under the circumstances it is no surprise to learn that, in Japanese schools, children were taught from a "Colonial Kōa Textbook" (Hanzawa 1940). Newly founded political organizations and a number of political conferences held in the late 1930s and early 1940s also were characterized as contributing to the policy of "Raising Asia." In 1941, the Dai Nihon Kōa Dōmei (Greater Japanese League for Raising Asia) was founded.[21] Its members and advisers included venerable pan-Asianists such as Tōyama Mitsuru (1855–1944) and Kuzuu Yoshihisa (1874–1958), party politicians well known for their pan-Asian sympathies such as Nagai Ryūtarō (1881–1944; see I:14), as well as a large number of senior military figures, such as Araki Sadao (1877–1966), Yanagawa Heisuke (1879–1945), Koiso Kuniaki (1880–1950), Ōi Shigemoto (1863–1951), Hayashi Senjūrō (1876–1943), Honjō Shigeru (1876–1945), Matsui Iwane (1878–1948), and Abe Nobuyuki (1875–1943). This impressive lineup, which included two former (Hayashi and Abe) and one future prime minister (Koiso), reflected a growing interest in the potential of Pan-Asianism in military circles.

In the atmosphere of social mobilization that thickened as the war escalated, the League became a central organization, incorporating fifty-three associations and institutions of pan-Asian character under its umbrella. These included the Tōa Dōbunkai (I:9), the Dōjinkai (Comrades' Society), the Tōa Renmei Kyōkai (East Asian League Association; II:19 and II:22), the Tōa Kensetsu Kyōkai (Association for Constructing East Asia), the Tōa Kyōkai (East Asia Association), and the Tōyō Kyōkai (Oriental Association), in addition to think tanks engaged in research on East Asia, such as the Dōmei Tōa Kenkyūkai (Alliance East Asia Research Association), the Tōa Chōsakai (East Asia Investigation Association), the Tōa Kenkyūjo (East Asia Research Institute), and the Tōa Chitsujo Kenkyūkai (East Asian Order Research Association).

These wartime efforts to "raise Asia" had also an international dimension. A year before the founding of the League, a "Raising Asia Welfare Congress" (Kōa kōsei taikai) was held in Osaka in October 1940 that was attended by representatives of eleven countries, including Japan's Asian and also its two European allies, Germany and Italy (Tano 2009). Even today, the name of a Japanese insurance company, Nippon Kōa Sonpo, which was originally founded in 1944, reminds us of the former popularity of this pan-Asian term.

Another term pan-Asianists began to use in the late 1920s (see II:5 and II:12) was "Kingly Way" (Chinese: *wangdao*; Japanese: *ōdō*). In the 1930s it was used with increasing frequency as a way of emphasizing the region's legacy of Confucian values and the significance of Confucianism as a potential basis for the unification of Asians.[22] The "Kingly Way" implied benevolent rule and was used as a fundamental concept to help legitimize Japan's construction of the new state of Manchukuo after 1932 (cf. Duara 2003). Japanese "guidance" of this new, ostensibly independent state—in reality it was a puppet state—was seen in paternalistic, Confucian terms as the kindly direction and advice offered to a younger brother (Manchuria) by his elder brother (Japan) (see II:16). In fact, as is well known, under Japan's "benevolent" guidance Manchukuo became a cornerstone of the Japanese Empire. It was ruthlessly exploited to provide material for the Japanese war effort (see, e.g., Yamamuro 1993, who describes Manchukuo as a "concentration camp state"), and this economic exploitation, carried out under the cloak of paternalistic benevolence, contributed significantly to the discrediting of pan-Asian ideology—the subject to which we turn next.

PAN-ASIANISM AND THE ASIANS

As we have argued here, Pan-Asianism was particularly important in the framework of intellectual debate and policy formulation in Japan, but other

Asians also made an important contribution to the discussion—comment that was sometimes supportive, sometimes critical. While in China the term apparently made its debut in the 1910s, in Korea similar terms were used to express similar sets of ideas a decade or so earlier. At the turn of the century, the term "Easternism" (*Tong'yangjuyi*) was first found in Korean writings on the subject to describe the idea of close cooperation between Korea, China, and Japan (I:15). Although Koreans were on the whole suspicious of Pan-Asianism as a concept that served to cloak Japanese attempts to establish their leadership of East Asia, anxiety over a future "race war" with the West was just as widespread in Korea as in Japan. In fact, one of the first concrete pan-Asian policy proposals was penned by a Korean, An Chung-gŭn (Ahn Choong Kun, 1879–1910), a member of the anti-Japanese movement in Korea (I:20). In 1910, while imprisoned on death row for assassinating Prince Itō Hirobumi (1841–1909), Japan's minister-resident in Korea, he wrote a visionary essay in which he talked of a united Asia facing the reality of a coming war between the yellow and white races. In order to prepare for this conflict, An advocated a transnational military force and even a single currency for an East Asian political union. Although not very realistic in the climate of the time, An's vision testified to the increasing importance of Pan-Asianism in international relations in East Asia.

As official and public support for Pan-Asianism as a tool for establishing Japanese hegemony in East Asia grew stronger in Japan, the likelihood of the acceptance of pan-Asian ideals waned in other Asian countries. This tendency to distrust the ideology of Pan-Asianism was particularly pronounced in East Asia, where the Japanese threat was at its most palpable. In Korea, for example, Pan-Asianism became marginalized. Korea was a special case because of its geographical proximity to Japan. As Kim (2007) shows (see also I:15 and I:18), most Korean intellectuals and political activists had been fairly skeptical about the idea of Asian solidarity even in the nineteenth century, even if some pro-Japanese modernizers, such as Kim Ok-kyun (1851–1894), had promoted Pan-Asianism as a useful tool for cooperation with Japan against the threat posed by imperial Russia. In spite of Korean suspicions over Japanese ambitions for the Korean peninsula, many Korean intellectuals, strongly influenced by social Darwinism during the final years of the nineteenth century (cf. Shin 2005), were convinced that for historical reasons the Koreans—"a backward and thus inferior race"—had no choice but to form an alliance with China and Japan as a result of Korea's proximity to its two neighbors. Others, who feared the much-trumpeted Western peril much more than any alleged racial inferiority, reached the same conclusions (e.g., the series of articles on the prospects of a Sino-Japanese-Korean Alliance by reformer An Kyongsu published in a Japanese journal in 1900; see An 1900).

After Korea became a Japanese protectorate in 1905 and a Japanese colony in 1910, Korean writers naturally became highly suspicious of their powerful neighbor and advocated resistance and "self-strengthening" as a way of regaining their independence. Under Japanese rule, the appeal of Pan-Asianism to Koreans was greatly limited. But it was not extinguished completely. Some Korean pan-Asianists continued to advocate a more or less equal "union of the Korean and Japanese cultures within the context of a broader Asian alliance," or within "a pan-Asian community," until the end of Japanese colonial rule in 1945 (Caprio 2009: 173, 184–86, 200; cf. also Shin 2006: chap. 1). Some Koreans who continued to adhere to the ideal of pan-Asian solidarity even interpreted the outbreak of war with the United States in 1941 (or the "Greater East Asian War," as it was officially called in the Japanese Empire) as the beginning of "a real war of races—the Yellow against the White" (quoted in Caprio 2009: 184). For these Koreans it was clear that Korea, as an Asian nation, had to side (temporarily at least) with Japan in this war of the races, even though Koreans were unhappy with Japanese colonial rule.

Some Chinese intellectuals and activists also continued to adhere to Pan-Asianism in the first decades of the twentieth century, as is evident from the quotation by Sun Yat-sen discussed here. However, open criticism of Japanese Pan-Asianism as a tool of Japanese expansionism was voiced as early as 1907, when the scholar and revolutionary Zhang Taiyan (1868–1936; see I:16) described Japan as the "public enemy" (*kōteki*) of Asia (Yamamuro 2005). Zhang gave vent to his conviction that Japan was an imperialist predator rather than a victim of imperialist oppression to which calls for Asian solidarity could properly be directed (see I:11 for a similar criticism from within Japan). Zhang also questioned the validity of pan-Asian ideals in general. Rejecting the simplistic scheme of "oppressed yellow Asians" and "white oppressors," he stressed what he called the "double enslavement of the Chinese"—bondage by Western imperialism and by "foreign," that is, Manchu, rule. His argument led him to emphasize the urgent need to establish Chinese nationalism as a counterforce to Manchu rule (Kondō 1979: 17). However, these advanced views did not prevent him from forming the Asiatic Humanitarian Brotherhood to promote cooperation with other Asian peoples.

Another revolutionary leader of modern China, Li Dazhao (1888–1927), also rejected Pan-Asianism as advocated by its Japanese exponents. In 1919, he harshly criticized Japanese pan-Asian writings as an expression of Japanese expansionism. However, while rejecting Japanese forms of Asianism, Li nevertheless conceded that some kind of regional cooperation was necessary to counter the threat of Western imperialism and called for the formulation of a "New Asianism" that presumably would be untainted by Japanese distortions (I:22). The tense atmosphere of pan-Asian conferences organized by Japanese and Chinese groups in Nagasaki in 1926 and Shanghai in 1927, however, clearly demonstrated that Chinese hostility to Japanese versions of Pan-Asianism had undermined any realistic expectation of close Sino–Japanese cooperation in an atmosphere of true solidarity (II:8). Some Chinese, such as Sun Yat-sen (until his death in 1925) and his confidant Wang Ching-wei (1883–1944; see I:25, II:5, and II:23), remained hopeful that Pan-Asianism might yet play a constructive role in Asia's fight against Anglo-Saxon imperialism, and a group of Chinese Pan-Asianists published a journal, *Asiatic Asia*, in Shanghai from 1941. However, in the end Japanese efforts to legitimize its various forms of aggression, including the war against China (1937–1945), as a pan-Asian "holy war" (see II:15) completely discredited the idea of Asian solidarity in China for many years to come.

In India, by contrast, Pan-Asianism left few negative legacies, probably because, unlike Korea and China, that country had never come under Japanese rule. In India, attempts to secure Japanese support for the national independence movement had a long tradition and resulted in close connections with Japan (cf. Nakajima 2005, 2009; Hotta 2006; Matsuura 2007a). A number of Indian revolutionaries found asylum there, and some even used Japan as a base for their pan-Asian activities. Among them was Taraknath Das (1884–1958; see I:31), who frequently published in Japan under the pseudonym "An Asian." In works published in Japan and China, Das called on "Asian Youth" to resist the West: "Every Asian youth . . . who possesses even a tiny bit of the feeling of self-respect should strive to achieve the goal of assertion of Asia to the fullest sense of its meaning" (Das 1917a, 1917b). Clearly Japan's invasion of China did nothing to dampen Das's hopes for Japan as the liberator of Asia, for as late as 1941 he insisted that Japan was "the only Eastern Power which can challenge the mighty forces of the West. . . . People of the East . . . have set their eyes on [Japan] as their possible saviour."[23] Rash Behari Bose (1886–1945), who was naturalized as a Japanese subject in 1923, also used his Japanese contacts to campaign on behalf of Pan-Asianism and Indian independence. As his speech reproduced in I:24 shows, he was an influential advocate of a Japan-centered Pan-Asianism and remained so until his death in 1944. His compatriot Subhas Chandra Bose (no relation, 1897–1945), who met Hitler in his attempt to marshal support for Indian independence (cf. Hauner 1981), also entertained great hopes for Japan as Asia's savior. He held meetings with Japanese leaders to encourage their support for his nationalist cause and participated in the Assembly of the Greater East Asiatic Nations in 1943 (see II:27).

The celebrated writer and cultural nationalist Rabindranath Tagore also deserves mention in this context. Tagore, who is not given a separate chapter in this collection, was a longtime friend of Okakura Tenshin (I:7 and I:8; on the relationship between the two, see also Bharucha 2006) and visited

Japan several times in the 1910s and 1920s. During his first visit, Tagore condemned Japanese nationalism as an imitation of Western practices (cf. Hay 1970: 69f). However, in 1924, when demonstrations against the United States Asian Exclusion Act erupted in Japan, Tagore spoke out on a number of occasions in favor of pan-Asian unity to audiences of several thousand. Announced at these rallies as "The Pride of the Orient," Tagore called on his fellow Asians to "awake, arise, agitate, agitate and agitate against this monstrous and inhuman insult which America has heaped upon us" (cited in Stalker 2006: 166). He hoped that the discriminatory U.S. immigration law would "unite the Asiatic races who will awake from their long sleep and . . . prove invulnerable against the attacks of the White Races" and motivate them to erect an "Empire of Asia . . . [that would] spring roaring into the arena of the world's politics" (Stalker 2006: 166f).

South East Asians became suspicious of Japanese Pan-Asianism only in the late 1930s—much later than the Koreans and Chinese. The main reason for this was, unlike in Korea and China, the Japanese were not perceived as a threat to a region dominated by the Western powers. Consequently, Japanese-directed Pan-Asianism enjoyed great appeal throughout Southeast Asia. In the Philippines, Japanese pan-Asianists had already supported the independence movement under Emilio Aguinaldo (1869–1964) as early as 1898 (Jansen 1954: 68–74). In 1915, a Pan-Oriental Society was formed in Manila. The society was headed by General Jose Alejandrino (1870–1951), who had gained his rank in the struggle against the United States and, after surrendering in 1901, went on to enjoy a career as a senator. British intelligence reported that "he speaks and writes Japanese and speaks with the authority of the Japanese Foreign Office." To the British, the anti-Western position of the Pan-Oriental Society was clear. At its meetings "speeches are made favoring an 'Oriental Monroeism' headed by Japan." But it would be wrong to dismiss the society as nothing more than a front for Japanese propaganda. Alejandrino took a wider interest in Asian affairs and wrote newspaper articles in which he mentioned the Indian Independence Party and even discussed the possibility of a free India. And there was some evidence of contacts with other Asian proindependence movements. According to the British intelligence report, "an intercepted letter, written by a Filipino student returned from Tokyo, shows that there might be a danger of a connection between these Filipino students and disaffected Indians in Japan" (Eliot to Curzon 30 April 1921, 77B Foreign Office Documents Pertaining to Japan, FO 371/6678, Public Record Office, Kew, Richmond).

In Malaya, too, some looked to Japan as a liberating force. For example, the nationalist journalist Ibrahim bin Haji Yaacob (1911–1979) founded, with Japanese support, the pro-Japanese and pan-Malay (if not pan-Asian)

Kesatuan Melayu Muda (League of Malay Youth). Its members cooperated with the Japanese forces during the invasion of the Malay Peninsula against the British and continued to do so throughout the Japanese occupation (Bayly and Harper 2007: 17–18).

The Japanese occupation of Southeast Asia in the wake of Pearl Harbor and the economic exploitation of the region that followed called into question the sincerity of pan-Asian rhetoric. However, even under the Japanese occupation, Pan-Asianism remained an important factor in Japan's relations with Southeast Asia. The Japanese certainly milked pan-Asian sentiment to help mobilize the region's resources for the war effort. At the same time some Southeast Asians, such as the contributors to the *Greater Asia* newspaper in Indonesia (II:26) and to the eponymous newspaper in Burma (cf. Sareen 2004), embraced the anti-Western component of pan-Asian rhetoric.

However, relations between Japan and the leaders of independence movements in Southeast Asia remain a controversial subject in Asian historiography. The position of those Southeast Asians who supported the Japanese war effort was much more ambivalent than is generally believed. The Indonesian independence activist Mohammed Hatta (1902–1980) is a case in point. Hatta is known for his collaboration with the Japanese occupation authorities during the war, but even at that time he was no Japanese puppet. And even before the war, in the 1930s, he was capable of a sober critique of the problems inherent in the Japanese version of Pan-Asianism. This is made clear by an article that he published in 1934, shortly after returning from a visit to Japan, where he was wined and dined by members of the Dai Ajia Kyōkai (see II:13). In the article, pointedly titled "Does Japan Desire to Return to Asia?" Hatta predicted the failure of Japanese Pan-Asianism because, in his view, the two conditions necessary to ensure its success—a permanent peace between Japan and China and the achievement of perfect equality between the Asian nations—could not be realized in the foreseeable future. Indeed, notwithstanding his enthusiastic reception in Japan, Hatta regarded Asianism as tainted by fascist tendencies, among which he included Japan's ambition to become the leader of Asia (Gotō 2008: 5f).

In western Asia, hopes for Japanese leadership in the struggle against Western imperialism were growing, but in the end no significant cooperation between Japan and any western Asian nation materialized. Japanese contacts with the Ottoman Empire, official and unofficial, went back to the late nineteenth century. In the first decades of the twentieth century, pan-Islamic activists came to Japan, where (among other things) they cooperated with Japanese pan-Asianists in founding the Ajia Gikai discussed above (cf. Esenbel 2004). During World War II, hopes for Japanese support were strongly expressed throughout the Arab world (cf. Esenbel 2004); they were fueled by the founding of the Greater

Japan Islamic League (Dai Nippon Kaikyō Kyōkai) in Japan in 1938. However, although a number of influential individuals, including Ōkawa Shūmei (II:4) and General Hayashi Senjūrō (cf. Matsuura 2010: 365–75), were sympathetic to the Arab cause, the failure of the Japanese to advance west of India during the course of the war precluded any effective cooperation.

THE "GREATER EAST ASIAN WAR" AND PAN-ASIANISM

The use of pan-Asian ideology to legitimize war and Japanese colonial rule discredited the movement. As a result, Pan-Asianism came to be widely identified as an ideology of colonial rule—specifically, Japan's colonial rule over Asian countries and peoples, which, the Japanese rulers insisted, was more "benevolent" than Western colonial rule because Japanese were fellow Asians. Yet, as much recent research has shown, Japanese colonial rule was equally as oppressive as that of any European power. Just like the European imperialists, the Japanese ruthlessly exploited the territories they ruled. They mobilized their subject populations for the Japanese war effort, and, unlike most Western powers, they made efforts to assimilate the populations of at least some of the colonial territories they controlled (cf. Caprio 2009 for the Korean case). For the populations of Japanese-controlled territories, Japanese colonial rule was not substantially different from Western colonial rule, even if the Japanese proclaimed pan-Asian "brotherhood" and professed to save them from the evils of colonial rule by non-Asians.

Many prominent Asians, however—politicians, diplomats, intellectuals, and writers alike—were forced to choose sides, particularly after the outbreak of the "Greater East Asian War." China, where people were also forced to choose sides, was a special case. For the overwhelming number of Chinese "the war" meant not an "Asian" war of liberation against "the West" but a war against Japanese aggression in which the West was an ally. The war in China had started much earlier than in the rest of Asia: it had broken out in 1931 in northeastern China (Manchuria), spreading to the rest of China by 1937. The different terms to name the conflict that were used by the opposing sides are instructive. While the Japanese term "Greater East Asian War," used for the war against the United States and Britain from December 1941, implied some pan-Asian notion of liberation of the whole region, the Chinese term for the war against Japan rejected the notion that this was a racial war and had anything to do with pan-Asian ideals. It was—and still is—simply the "War of Resistance against Japanese Aggression" (*kangri zhanzheng*).

The Japanese government made concerted efforts to stress the pan-Asian character of the war. Its naming as the "Greater East Asian War" was only a beginning. Numerous government statements during the war emphasized the pan-Asian character of the conflict. However, it should be noted that it was only several months after the outbreak of hostilities that the Japanese government officially included the "liberation of Asia from Western imperialism" in its list of war objectives (Hatano 1996). Pan-Asian propaganda intensified as the war continued. In 1942, the Ministry of Greater East Asia was founded in order to coordinate and strengthen intra-Asian cooperation. As II:27 shows, this move was intended primarily to underline the rhetoric of pan-Asian liberation—but, at this point in the war, "strengthened cooperation" meant, above all, the mobilization of resources for Japan's war effort. The worse the military situation became for Japan, the more the Japanese government tended to draw on pan-Asian rhetoric. In this context, the declaration of the "Assembly of the Greater East Asiatic Nations" issued in 1943 sounds like a last, desperate appeal for pan-Asian unity.[24]

At that time even liberal intellectuals like Hasegawa Nyozekan (1875–1969), seemingly oblivious to the looming disaster ahead, was still insisting that the "Greater East Asian War" must be the starting point for the establishment of "a united cultural sphere [by] the races of East Asia" (quoted in Shillony 1981: 143). In similar vein, Nishida Kitarō (1870–1945), one of Japan's leading philosophers, in 1943 characterized the war as a holy, pan-Asian struggle to liberate and unify Asia:

> The Great East Asian War is a sacred war, because it is the culmination of the historical progress of Asia. . . . The task of the liberated peoples is now to win the war and establish the Great East Asia Co-Prosperity Sphere, in co-operation with the Germans, Italians, and other peoples in Europe, who are engaged in a heroic struggle to create a new order in Europe. . . . Japan will win this war because her people are determined to sacrifice their lives for it. . . . Japan's victory will save Asia and will offer a new hope for mankind. (quoted in Shillony 1981: 112)

So, even though schemes for pan-Asian unity became more and more unrealistic as the fortunes of war turned against Japan, the official espousal of Pan-Asianism by the Japanese government and military resulted in a further wave of publications on Asian solidarity and brotherhood (see II:29 and II:30).[25]

PAN-ASIAN SOLIDARITY AND THE LEGACIES OF PAN-ASIANISM IN THE POSTWAR PERIOD

Japan's surrender and the advent of the Cold War resulted in the disappearance of pan-Asian discourse from the international relations arena. Japanese proponents of Pan-Asianism were purged from office, and pan-Asian associations were disbanded by the occupation authorities. Pan-Asianism was no longer a subject that figured in debates on foreign relations, in Japan or elsewhere. Clearly, there was no room for pan-Asian schemes in the new bipolar world order. This situation did not change even after the estrangement between China and the Soviet Union in the 1950s (culminating in a formal Chinese declaration in 1961 denouncing the Soviet leadership as a "revisionist traitor group") because Japan, once again an important Asian nation, was now closely allied to the United States and thus in effect part of "the West." In the 1960s, however, the emergence of the nonaligned movement (NAM) led to the resurgence of pan-Asian ideals. The NAM was founded in 1961 under the leadership of India's Prime Minister Jawaharlal Nehru (1889–1964), President Gamal Abdul Nasser (1918–1970) of Egypt, and Yugoslav President Josip Tito (1892–1980). However, it was primarily Asian and African countries that played the central role in the activities of the movement, which had its roots in the 1955 Bandung Conference (see II:33). The Bandung Conference and the NAM assumed a firmly anti-imperialist stance and objected strongly to the domination of international relations by the United States, just as the pan-Asian movement before 1945 had opposed (and even fought) Anglo-American world hegemony (cf. Dennehy 2007).

Although Japan did not play a leading role in these developments, in Japan the sense of a pan-Asian "mission" was preserved in other forms. After the devastation wrought by the war had nullified the achievements of the prewar era and, as some suggested, turned Japan into an agricultural economy, intellectuals like Shimizu Ikutarō (1907–1988) felt impelled to proclaim that "now, once again, the Japanese are Asians" (cited in Oguma 2007: 200). Pan-Asian themes also survived in leftist critiques of Western modernity (see II:35) and in the related claims that Japan must side with the oppressed nations of Asia in their resistance to the continuing Western imperialist domination of the non-European world (II:32). Variations on the pan-Asian theme have continued to inform ideas of solidarity, both in left-wing circles and among those who became ultranationalists after giving up hope in the possibilities of socialism, such as the writer Hayashi Fusao (1903–1975; see II:34).

However, postwar Pan-Asianism was tainted by its association with Japanese imperialism and aggression. Indeed it became synonymous with it. For the most prominent political scientist of the postwar period, Maruyama Masao (1914–1996), Pan-Asianism, together with "familism" (*kazokushugi*) and "agrarianism" (*nōhonshugi*), was one of the three fundamental components of Japanese ultranationalism (Maruyama 1964: 40–57). Perhaps because of this association, there was no serious scholarly attempt to deal with Pan-Asianism as a subject of historical inquiry in the 1950s and the 1960s. One scarcely need mention that in Korea and China Pan-Asianism was completely discredited as an ideology of collaboration with the enemy and the colonizers. This was the direct consequence of the use of pan-Asian rhetoric to justify Japanese colonial rule in Korea, and (in wartime China) to justify Japanese aggression and legitimize the Nanjing puppet government (II:23). There are signs, however, that this situation is changing, as indicated by recent efforts by high-level Chinese diplomats to present Pan-Asianism in a more positive light (II:41; Wang 2004).

In Japan, the first serious attempt to grapple with the thorny question of the legacy of Asianism was made by the Sinologist and literary critic Takeuchi Yoshimi (1963a; see also II:35). Takeuchi, who in his youth had enthusiastically embraced pan-Asian ideals, had his beliefs shaken by Japan's defeat. Yet although some aspects of Takeuchi's faith were undermined, he had no doubt that there were positive features that were worth preserving. Pan-Asianism, he never ceased to believe, was much more than mere window dressing for Japan's Greater Asian Co-Prosperity Sphere. In Takeuchi's view, there was a core of pan-Asian ideals that retained validity and therefore needed to be remembered and even cherished. Interestingly, Takeuchi regarded Japan's aggression in China not as a consequence of Pan-Asianism but rather as Japan's "shedding" of Asia (*datsu-A*), a concept that emerged in the 1880s (see I:2) and became highly influential as the antithesis to Pan-Asianism throughout the course of modern Japanese history. From this perspective, Japan's aggression was in effect an application of inauthentic (and therefore culpable) Western methods to Asia and thus had nothing to do with the "Eastern spirit" or Eastern cultural practices or political norms. It was a natural, if deplorable, consequence of the westernization of Japan. This misguided attempt by Japan to depart from pan-Asian principles was corrected, to some extent at least, by the war Japan waged from December 1941 on the colonial powers of the United States, Britain, and the Netherlands. It was little wonder that Takeuchi welcomed this war enthusiastically (see II:35). Takeuchi is difficult to locate on the ideological spectrum. Although he would not classify himself as a rightist, his attempts to restore legitimacy to the discredited term Pan-Asianism were unusual. Those on the left preferred to talk of Asian solidarity, brotherhood, or cooperation, which often overlapped with socialist or communist forms of international solidarity, or the solidarity of the nonaligned movement (see II:33). For the Japanese left, the term "Pan-Asianism" was (and perhaps still is) practically synonymous with Japanese colonialism and aggression.

Yet, whether or not they eschewed the term itself, in postwar Japan the left incorporated pan-Asian elements into its own views. And the continuity between prewar pan-Asian rightists and postwar left-wing circles should not be overlooked in this context. This (at first sight) surprising continuity has only rarely been discussed in previous research.[26] The prewar flirtation with national socialism and Japanism by socialists like Asanuma Inejirō (1898–1960) is well known. It is less widely known, however, that Marquis Tokugawa Yoshichika (1886–1976), one of the major sponsors of the rightist movement in the prewar period and a close friend of pan-Asianists such as Ōkawa Shūmei (II:4), became a benefactor of the newly founded Socialist Party of Japan after the war. It appears that Tokugawa's support for the Socialist Party was motivated to some extent, at least, by pan-Asian motives (for the bizarre details of his support, see Tokugawa 1973: 214). These motives were also apparent in an extraordinary statement by Tokugawa's erstwhile comrade in the rightist movement, Ōkawa, who in 1949 detected a "close resemblance between today's communists and the early Muslims" and wished for "a second battle of Tours-Poitiers" to be fought between the communists and the West, which this time would result in victory for the communists (i.e., Asia) (Szpilman 1998b: 61).

Another right-wing pan-Asianist, Tsukui Tatsuo (1901–1989), well known in the postwar period as an "ultranationalist historian," is known to have lavished praise on communist China (Tsukui 1956). In the mid-1950s, a U.S. counterintelligence report accused Tsukui of bringing a large sum of money from mainland China, funds that were eventually given to the National Diet member and former army colonel, Tsuji Masanobu (1902–1961?), "for safe keeping" ("Rightist Groups in Japan Receive Funds from Communist China," extract from OSI "Counterintelligence Digest," 10 October 1956, 201, File #631 Tsuji Masanobu).

It should be noted that, like Tsukui, the recipient of this unspecified largesse, Colonel Tsuji, who had achieved notoriety during the war, made no secret of his pan-Asian sympathies in the postwar period (for an example of his views, see Tsuji 1950). According to Tsuji, on matters of regional solidarity ideological differences were less important than blood ties. At a gathering of former generals on 20 November 1954, Tsuji is reported as arguing that Japan should work with India to achieve neutrality and with communist China to maintain peace. Noting his friendship with Chinese Communist Party officials such as Zhou Enlai (also Chou En-lai, 1898–1976), he explained that, communist or not, "[a]fter all, they're Asians" (GB-S/C@A, 16 August 1955, Form Nr 137, File #631 Tsuji Masanobu). An American intelligence analyst concluded, "Tsuji, head of the neutralist Self-Defense League (Jiei Dōmei), has long been a vigorous exponent of 'the Asia for Asiatics,' doctrine of the late Ishihara Kanji [II:22]. Like right wing critic Tsukui Tatsuo (INTSUM 4497), who also returned from Communist China, Tsuji considers the ties that bind Asians together stronger than those between Communist China and the

USSR" (File #631 Tsuji Masanobu). A Japanese biographer of Tsuji agreed with this assessment, noting that the former colonel was "harsh on the Soviet Union and soft on communist China" (Sugimori 1963: 216). For members of the Japanese left, Tsuji, as an army colonel blamed for a number of wartime atrocities, was beyond the pale. However, they would no doubt agree with his support for the downtrodden peoples of Asia.[27]

Leftists might find the case of the politician and parliamentarian Utsunomiya Tokuma (1906–2000) even more ambiguous. The son of General Utsunomiya Tarō (1861–1922), commander of the Japanese army in Korea (on General Utsunomiya's pan-Asian views, see Matsuura 2010: 149–52 and note 10 of this introduction), Utsunomiya was one of the founding members of the Liberal Democratic Party in 1955 but cannot be categorized simply as a conservative politician. In the 1980s Utsunomiya emerged as a stern critic of the party he had helped to found but no longer supported, and, on a number of occasions, he appeared to be closely allied with the Socialist Party. He was a fervent proponent of disarmament and ran successfully in elections against the retired Self-Defense Forces general, Kurisu Hiroomi (1920–2004), an advocate of rearmament. In the 1960s Utsunomiya had been a prominent supporter of Algeria's struggle for independence. He went out of his way to support all expressions of "Asian and African nationalism" and never hid his pan-Asianist sympathies (Hayashi 1974: 685–728: see also Matsuura 2010: 847). It could be argued that Utsunomiya's pro-Asian attitudes were inseparable from his anti-Western and, more specifically, anti-American, sentiments.

This same set of attitudes has characterized many on the left, one of whose major criticisms of the Japanese government is its pro-American, pro-Western stance. Most left-wing commentators would never admit to entertaining pan-Asian sentiments, for, as we have seen, in their view Pan-Asianism was irredeemably besmirched by Japan's wartime aggression. But whether they recognize it or not, the political left in Japan is heir to the pan-Asian tradition. This is abundantly clear both from the activities of the Japanese pacifist movement in general and the movement against the Vietnam War (organized by the Citizens' League for Peace in Vietnam; Japanese: Betonamu ni Heiwa o! Shimin Rengō, abbreviated as Beheiren; cf. Hirai 2005) in particular. Numerous statements by members of these movements condemning American imperialism and American aggression have been issued over the years and continue today. The pan-Asian undertones of these criticisms are generally revealed in their appeals to Asian brotherhood and Asian solidarity. This tendency is also seen in gestures made by prominent left-wing politicians such as Doi Takako (1928–), the one-time leader of the Japan Socialist Party, who in 1990 traveled to Baghdad to shake hands with Saddam Hussein (1937–2006);

in statements by activists such as Dr. Nakamura Tetsu (1946–), who has devoted his life to the cause of helping the needy and sick in Afghanistan (II:40); and in lawsuits challenging Japanese logistical assistance to U.S. military activities in Afghanistan, Iraq, and elsewhere. Most recently, in a remarkable example of this tendency to pan-Asian solidarity, in late 2009 the Japanese cabinet, led by Hatoyama Yukio (1947–), the leader of the Democratic Party of Japan in coalition with the Social Democratic Party, halted Japanese military support for American-led operations in Afghanistan and recalled the Maritime Self-Defense Forces from the Indian Ocean.

RECENT DEVELOPMENTS

As stated at the outset, issues of regionalism and regional integration in East Asia have received considerable attention since the 1990s. In Korea, for example, pan-Asian unity is identified as a promising path to avoid domination not only by Japan but also by China. In 2002, for example, former South Korean President Roh Moo-hyun (1946–2009) declared that "the age of Northeast Asia is arriving" (quoted in Suh 2005: 611). At the same time, regional approaches in East Asia, especially since the beginning of the present century, have been an expression of increasing discontent with American-led globalization and a developing unilateral world system. In South Korea, pan-Asianist regionalism is thus "seen as an attractive alternative to Korea's dependence on America" (Shin 2005: 625). South Korean and Japanese interests seem to have converged in these respects. In Japan, from as early as the 1980s, a "New Asianism" (Duus 2001; see also II:36 and Nakagawa 2006 for examples) has begun to resurface, partly as an offshoot of the so-called Asian values debate of the 1980s, a discussion initiated by Malaysia's Prime Minister Mahathir Mohamad (1925–) and the prime minister of Singapore, Lee Kuan-Yew (1923–), supported by the xenophobic populist politician and writer Ishihara Shintarō (1932–), in 2010 governor of Tokyo (see II:37). Despite his frequent "Asian-bashing" outbursts, Ishihara is also known for his advocacy of pan-Asian views—which, essentially, are an expression of his strong anti-Americanism.

In the 1980s these politicians—and others like them—advocated a set of common "Asian values" (always vaguely defined), based on Confucian virtues, as a counter to the universalist claims of liberalism, democracy, and human rights, values that were dismissed as alien to the region and inauthentic for Asians on account of their allegedly Western provenance. However, many Asian politicians and writers, such as the future president of South Korea, Kim Dae-jung (1925–2009) (Kim 1994), strongly rejected the idea of a common set of "Asian" values, and the debate has made little headway since. However, recent work by Chinese scholars suggests an attempt to find some kernel of truth in the legacy of Pan-Asianism with the objective of criticizing "Western" (i.e., United States) policies or the West's claim to the universality of democratic values (see, e.g., Sun 2003). The new trend in Chinese academia to deal more openly with the once completely discredited ideology of Pan-Asianism (see also Wang 2004), in combination with statements by high-ranking diplomats acknowledging the potential of the region's pan-Asian legacy (Wang 2006a and 2006b),[28] arguably reflects a change in attitudes in China.

In Japan, the rise of a "New Asianism" has reflected concrete diplomatic and economic efforts to stimulate regionalist approaches. These efforts were, however, always placed under strain by the strong priority given by the Japanese government to the United States-Japan Security Treaty. Nonetheless, Japan, as a recent study notes, "has been a driving force of Asian regionalism throughout the post-war period," particularly in the economic sphere (Hamanaka 2009: 7). Particularly important in this regard was Japan's involvement in the founding of the Asian Development Fund in 1957 and the proposal for an Asian Monetary Fund in 1997. In addition, Japan has also been relatively active in the ASEAN+3 cooperative network, involving the ASEAN nations plus China, Japan, and South Korea (Hamanaka 2009: 7; see also II:39). But as the acronym indicates, the driving force of this new body is ASEAN—the only effective organization working for regional integration in Asia, which has brought a considerable degree of stability and economic growth to Southeast Asia. Japan also has been rather passive and reactive with regard to the development of a Free Trade Agreement network in East Asia, and, given its continuing dependence on the security treaty with the United States, it remains questionable whether Japan can play a leading role in the integration of the region in the immediate future—notwithstanding the outspoken advocacy of Pan-Asianism by some leading politicians (e.g., Nakagawa 2006).[29]

Nor should one forget the historical legacies of World War II and of Pan-Asianism as an ideology. As late as the 1990s, partly because of the difficulties Japan experienced in coming to terms with its past, writers in Asia as well as in the West warned that Japanese regionalist initiatives could be interpreted as a resurgence of claims for Japan's leadership in East Asia, with the objective of creating "a new version of the Greater East-Asia Co-Prosperity Sphere of World War II" (Johnson 1993: 216). In recent years, the issue of historical memory has become less contentious in Japan, but persistent elements of "retrospective Pan-Asianism"—the rehabilitation of wartime pan-Asian rhetoric to whitewash Japan's wars of aggression and colonial rule in

Asia—continue to hinder attempts to promote regional integration (Kingston 2004: 232–42; Saaler 2005).

On the academic level, however, considerable progress has been made over the past two decades, as witnessed by drafts for an "Asian Constitution,"[30] proposals for an East Asian Common House (II:42) and a myriad of academic conferences dealing with (and not infrequently advocating) regional integration. It is yet to be determined where all this activity will lead in the future. What surely can be said, however, is that attention to the historical legacies of Pan-Asianism and the identification of positive examples of pan-Asian solidarity and regional integration in the past will play an increasingly significant role in the years to come.

RECURRENT PAN-ASIAN THEMES

Pan-Asian styles of thought have always come most to the fore in debates on foreign policy and on Asian identity. If the many varieties of Pan-Asianism had anything in common, it was their opposition to the West: opposition to the West's presence in Asia (i.e., Western imperialism), opposition to Western culture and values, and, conversely, an emphasis on the importance (and in many cases, the superiority) of Asian culture and Asian values. In fact, it could be argued that anti-Westernism was central to Pan-Asianism. In opposition to the "West"—which was, to a large degree, an invented concept—pan-Asian writers constructed their own "Asia." Images of this constructed Asia varied greatly. They changed over time and took particular forms in different places and in the works of different authors. But all pan-Asianists assumed the existence of "one Asia" and based this assumption on one or more of the following categories:

- Geography (Asia, East Asia, the Orient)
- Cultural unity (influence of Indian and Chinese civilization, religions)
- Historical interconnectedness (Sinocentric system, tribute relations, trade networks)
- Racial kinship (the yellow race, races of color)
- The unity of Asian civilization in terms of its values and spiritual character (Confucianism, justice, and benevolence vs. Western materialism and rationalism)
- A common destiny (the fight against Western imperialism and colonial rule)

These are the major themes that the reader will encounter time and again throughout this collection. The idea that geographically Asia forms a unified entity, notwithstanding the relatively recent introduction of the term in the region, was discussed in some detail at the beginning of this introduction. It has to be emphasized again, however, that there was never a consensus on the geographical definition of Asia and that pan-Asian writers constantly revised their definitions of "Asia," blurring geographical exactitude with interpretations that allowed them to extend their definition of Asia even to some European and African nations (see I:25).

The perception and creation of cultural unity, brought to an extreme of simplification in the slogan "Asia is one" (I:7 and I:8), also remains an important theme of pan-Asian writers over the past one and a half centuries—and down to the present day. In 2010, an Internet search (google.com) of the term generates a large number of hits. Although it is clear that any particular assertion of what constitutes cultural commonalities (or differences) is highly arbitrary and subjective, it is important to acknowledge that such a particularized insistence on the existence of commonalities has played an important role in the construction of Pan-Asianism, as the texts reproduced in this collection show.

Recent research has stressed the importance of historical interconnectedness as an authentic foundation for forces encouraging the development of regional integration (cf. Arrighi, Hamashita, and Selden 2003: introduction). The notion of a world system that connected the various states of East and Southeast Asia for centuries, before the imposition of Western-based international law, had sufficient coherence to bind indigenous forces against the threat of external domination. In recent years, these approaches have once again been attracting attention as a reaction to the emergence of a unipolar world order.

Enough has already been said about the incorporation of the Western ideas of race into pan-Asianist rhetoric. References to "racial kinship" were frequent, as the documents in this collection make clear. However, the Western provenance of the concept of race made it highly questionable that such an ideology could serve as the basis for a regional identity—not least since a Pan-Asianism based on racial motives limited "Asia" to East Asia and tended to exclude India, western Asia, and other areas. Further, the ideal of racial equality and the reality of racial discrimination within Asia eventually thoroughly discredited the racial component within Pan-Asianism, particularly in Korea (after 1910) and other territories under Japanese colonial rule.

The complex notion of Asian values—Asian "spirituality" versus the "materialism" of Western civilization—is also highly contested and riddled with contradictions. As we have already noted in the discussion of geographical definitions, the "Asia" of the pan-Asianists sometimes included territories that are generally classified as "Western" countries, such as Germany, Italy, or even Ireland. The 1920s saw a wave of sympathy for the cause of Irish independence in Asian publications, and in the 1930s, Japan allied itself with Germany and Italy—ostensibly since Germany and Italy had chosen to join the fight against "Western" materialism, now limited to Anglo-Saxon civilization.

Notwithstanding the various contradictions generated by any definition of Asia or the West, pan-Asianists have generally regarded "the West" as the alien Other. Time and again, as this collection shows, for pan-Asianists Asia represents the *antithesis* of the West. Indeed, these writers regularly define Asia in terms of the West. This is true of such diverse figures as Okakura Tenshin, Ōkawa Shūmei (see I:7, I:8, and II:4) and, in the postwar period, Takeuchi Yoshimi, Ishihara Shintarō, and Nakamura Tetsu (see II:35, II:37, and II:40). The corollary to this vision of the West as the Other is the assumption that there exists a coherent set of Asian values and that these values, *ex definitione* shared by all Asians, are superior to Western values. This idea is often linked to an emphasis on the antiquity of Asian culture, which is often presented by pan-Asianists as the cradle of civilization, including European civilization. In this connection, much has been made of the fact that all of the major religions of the world, including Christianity, originated in what is geographically considered Asia. On these grounds, it is often argued that only "Asian" civilization has the potential to ultimately save mankind, including the West. In the words of Tagore, "If Asian civilization constituted a great reservoir of spiritual power, and if modern civilization was about to destroy humanity itself, then it must be from a regenerated Asia that man's salvation would come" (quoted in Hay 1970: 64–65). Tagore was an outspoken critic of nationalism in at least some of his writings. There is no doubt that the kind of Pan-Asianism to which he subscribed was "a vision of community that sought to transcend the territorial nation-state and redeem and regenerate the world through Eastern spiritual morality" (Duara 1998: 655).

Nonetheless, others have argued that an affirmation of Asian values is fundamentally misguided, that no single set of moral values is shared by all Asians (e.g., Kim 1994). It can moreover be argued that the East–West opposition is in fact based on an illusion. For, in essence, it is not Asian and Western values that are antithetical to each other, nor is it Asia and the West (comprising Europe and North America) that are in opposition, but rather the forms of society contained in them—modern and premodern. The geographical opposition is not exact: one could no doubt find modern forms of society in Asia and premodern societies in Europe and North America, and all have developed in diverse ways over the last two centuries. We have here a classical conflict between the modern and the premodern masquerading as a conflict between East and West. For a number of reasons, modernity in all its ramifications—secularism, individualism, liberalism, democracy, the decline of traditional morality, the advent of the money nexus and the contract society, and so on—has often been perceived as a specifically Western phenomenon. Likewise, pan-Asianists have tended to see Asian *Gemeinschaft* in conflict with Western *Gesellschaft*. Expanding on these German terms borrowed from the social sciences, some pan-Asianists have regarded the former as a positive collective entity, based on custom, moral, humane, all-embracing, with its members identifying strongly with their community (see, e.g., II:30); the latter they saw as inhuman, soulless, characterized by alienation, individualistic, and atomized, where all transactions are based on money and the contract system (the cash nexus). However, tensions between *Gemeinschaft* and *Gesellschaft* are not specific to the opposition between Asia and the West; rather, they represent the friction or conflict that operates between modern *Gesellschaft* and premodern *Gemeinschaft*. These conflicting impulses, that had riven Western societies (and arguably continue to divide them), were introduced into East Asia in the nineteenth century when the major Western powers extended their influence in the region.

Yet, for all this cultural tension, the material advantages of the West and of modernity in general became obvious to most Asians, except for a very small number of reactionary obscurantists. Western-style modernity was an indispensible condition for success in the nineteenth-century world. For that reason, along with the majority of Asians, most pan-Asianists never rejected modernity as such.[31] Many ancient Asian customs and practices were patently useless in the modern wo·ld, and, under the circumstances, the chief problem that had to be overcome was the antiquated structure of state and society. But was everything distinctive about the East to be denied? Initially there was a tendency to discard the whole culture, lock, stock, and barrel. In an excess of modernizing enthusiasm, some Japanese even wanted to give up their native tongue in favor of English. Needless to say, such proposals were at best impractical. But were there aspects of Eastern tradition still of relevance in this Western-dominated world? Was there nothing that could or should be salvaged? With regard to technology, the answer was clearly no. But in the realm of ethics, morals, and philosophical and religious thought, convincing arguments could be made for the relevance, if not the superiority, of Eastern traditions—arguments that the reader will encounter time and again throughout this collection.

While the meaning—and even the existence—of "Asian values" remains debatable, the notion of commonly held Asian values and a common culture and racial identity, which together constitute the basis of Pan-Asianism, is closely related to the sentiment of a "common destiny" for Asian peoples. This latter notion represents another recurrent theme in Pan-Asianism—one that perhaps retains much of its appeal even today, if recent statements by

Asian governments (e.g., the initiative of former Japanese Prime Minister Hatoyama Yukio; cf. Mulgan 2009) or declarations by transnational organizations such as ASEAN (cf. Association of South East Asian Nations 2009) are anything to go by. It is impossible to gauge whether such sentiments will contribute to the realization of closer transnational cooperation or even regional integration in the future. To be sure, obstacles to regional cooperation in East Asia remain in plenty. They include not only strong expressions of nationalism and the negative legacies of World War II but also the geography and demographics of Asia. Unlike in the case of European countries, the "Other," or the "enemy," for many smaller Asian nations is to be found within Asia, not somewhere outside. While Asia will certainly never be "one," progress will continue to be made in the areas of regional cooperation and integration, and there is no doubt that such developments will contribute to the stability and the prosperity of the region.

NOTES

1. Accessible online at http://www.riccicenter.com/maps/map_world01.JPG. Useful resources (original sources, links to sources, photographs, and so on) can be accessed at http://asianism.japanesehistory.de.

2. Unless indicated otherwise, we follow Takeuchi Yoshimi who regards the terms "Pan-Asianism," "Asianism," and "Greater Asianism" as essentially synonymous. In other words, the variations of "Pan-Asianism" do not necessarily imply any difference of content. It should be noted however that the term "Pan-Asianism" (or any of its numerous synonyms) can stand for a variety of meanings including contradictory ideas, as we show in this introduction.

3. For the concept of "the style of thought," see Mannheim (1953: 74–77).

4. At the time of writing, we have not come across comparable collections in other languages.

5. Notable articles on Pan-Asianism include Norman (1944), Jansen (1980), Hashikawa (1980), Reynolds (1986), Beasley (1987), Nakamura (1991), Hiraishi (1994), Koschmann (1997), Iida (1997), Sun (2000), Hazama (2001), Duara (2001), Duus (2001), Mutō (2003), Kuroki (2005), Shin (2005), and Mark (2006). Further, in 2000, the classic article "Japan's Asianism" (see II:35) by Takeuchi Yoshimi (1963b) was reprinted in book form with a commentary by Matsumoto Ken'ichi (Matsumoto 2000). The bibliography should be consulted for further articles on Pan-Asianism, including those written by the editors and contributors to this volume. A number of important studies that, although not specifically focused on Pan-Asianism, address some important related issues, should not be overlooked. In English they include Goodman (1991), Goto (1997), Shimazu (1998), Karl (2002), Oguma (2002), Esenbel and Inaba (2003), and Duara (2003); in Japanese, Eizawa (1995), Oguma (1995), Furuya (1996), and Yamamoto (2001).

6. In China and Korea, research on Pan-Asianism was discouraged for many years. It was seen as an ideology that was inseparable from Japanese expansionism and imperialism, while its Chinese and Korean advocates were dismissed as traitors who collaborated with the Japanese invader.

7. The acting consul Mizuta Shin regarded this letter, posted in Nice, France, as a case of "extreme anti-Western activism." He thought it important enough to forward to Japanese Foreign Minister Hirota Kōki. Miscellaneous documents relating to problems of ethnic groups: Vol. 2. Gaimushō Kiroku (Diplomatic Records), I.4.6.0.1, Gaimushō Gaikō Shiryōkan (Diplomatic Record Office of the Ministry of Foreign Affairs of Japan).

8. The "Amau Statement" stated that "Japan . . . opposes any joint action on the part of foreign Powers that tends to militate against the maintenance of peace and order in Eastern Asia. . . . Owing to the special position of Japan in her relations with China, . . . it must be realized that Japan is called upon to exert the utmost effort in carrying out her mission and in fulfilling her special responsibilities in East Asia." Cited in United States Department of State: *Papers Relating to the Foreign Relations of the United States, Japan: 1931–1941*, vol. I, pp. 224–29. Washington, DC: U.S. Government Printing Office, 1931–1941. Accessible online at http://digital.library .wisc.edu/1711.dl/FRUS.FRUS193141v01.

9. For a more detailed analysis of the relationship of Pan-Asianism to ultranationalism and the growth of fascism in 1930s Japan, see below; see also Maruyama (1964: 40–57).

10. In a recently published diary, General Utsunomiya Tarō, commander of the Japanese army in Korea from 1918 to 1920, frequently expresses his fervent desire for a "true union of spirits" between Japanese and Koreans. For example, he made a case for such a union in an unpublished document entitled *Daihongan* (My Great Desire), which he distributed to visitors. See Utsunomiya Tarō Kankei Shiryō Kenkyūkai (2007: 225f; see also 255, 296f, 312, 371, and so on).

11. The inherent ambiguity of Pan-Asianism relates to another problem that needs to be addressed, namely, that not all pan-Asianists expressed their ideas in writing. In compiling this collection, we had no choice but to concentrate on written sources. Consequently, the collection includes only texts that contain clear statements of pan-Asian solidarity or Asian unity (even if they do not specifically use such key words as "Asianism," "Pan-Asianism," or "Asian regionalism"). But the problem is that Pan-Asianism was not only an ideology; it was also a movement. Many activists who played central roles in the pan-Asian movement and who regarded themselves as pan-Asianists have left no written record of their views on the subject. Tōyama Mitsuru, introduced in this volume in connection with the Genyōsha, is a case in point, as is Inukai Tsuyoshi. Although his life was dedicated to the pan-Asian cause (see I:25), Inukai, a journalist turned politician with a prolific literary output, has left (to our knowledge) no explicitly pan-Asianist text. Since this is not a collection of general writings by pan-Asianists, Inukai is not included.

12. Max von Brandt (1835–1920), a longtime German diplomat in Japan and China, was well known for the anti-Japanese tone of his writings throughout the late imperial period.

13. As Kuroki (2002: 25) points out, however, at times Ueki also discussed Japanese leadership in Asia—leadership seen primarily in terms of modernization and reform.

14. The editors have been unable to identify the "pamphlets" that Ōyama refers to in his 1916 essay.

15. Liberalism did not necessarily imply hostility to Pan-Asianism. For an example of an early Japanese liberal pan-Asianist, see Ueki Emori above. In the twentieth century, too, some liberals, including Yoshino Sakuzō (1878–1933) and Ishibashi Tanzan (1884–1973), advocated Pan-Asianism; cf. Matsuura (2010: chap. 2).

16. See file FO 371 5350 1-E (1920), Public Record Office, Kew, Richmond, London, for an example of intelligence reports on the movements of anti-British Indians and Japanese pan-Asianists.

17. "Nihonjin to Hoka no Ajiajin" (The Japanese and the Other Asians), *Tokyo Nichinichi Shinbun*, 26 June 1913; "Nihon Minzoku no Dōkasei (Shasetsu)" (The Assimilation of the Japanese Race [An Editorial]), *Ōsaka Asahi Shinbun*, 27 June 1913 (part 1); 28 June 1913 (part 2); "Nihon no Chii" (Japan's Position [in the World]), *Ōsaka Mainichi Shinbun*, 22 July 1913.

18. The idea of "permanent peace," of course, goes back to Immanuel Kant's famous essay *Perpetual Peace*, 1795.

19. The idea pre-dated Woodrow Wilson's "Fourteen Points;" see Archer (2001) and Northedge (1986).

20. The author, Sugita Teiichi, an advocate of Pan-Asianism, had been active in the freedom and People's Rights Movement since the 1870s (see I:26).

21. In a special issue (Kōa Dōmei Kessei Tokugō [The Special Issue on the Founding of the Greater Japanese League for Raising Asia]), the journal *Kōa*, which was destined to become the League's official organ, gave extensive coverage to the proceedings that resulted in the founding of the League and reported the apparently enthusiastic reaction both among political circles and the general public. The issue is accessible online at http://asianism.japanesehistory.de.

22. In Japan, the Confucian Society Shibunkai was founded in 1918. Although Confucianism has been used by pan-Asianists in the service of a revival of Asian values, the Shibunkai advocated Confucianism within a nationalist framework, insisting that it was an expression of "the good ways and beautiful customs of our nation since its founding," traditions that "still exist in our villages" but that had been forgotten in the cities because of modernization, Westernization, and the growth of materialistic attitudes. See Smith (1959: chap. 3).

23. Compilation of miscellaneous documents relating to [the] domestic politics of Britain/Territories and Possessions/India/Anti-Britain Movement, 30 May 1940 to 17 March 1941, Gaimushō Kiroku (Diplomatic Records), A.6.6: Gaimushō Gaikō Shiryōkan (Diplomatic Record Office of the Ministry of Foreign Affairs of Japan).

24. Ironically, the Greater East Asia Conference of 1943 was conducted in English (Shillony 1981: 150). After the expansion of Pan-Asianism's "Asia" into South and Southeast Asia, written Chinese could no longer play the role of a lingua franca and was increasingly replaced with English. This trend away from a narrow focus on East Asia is also apparent in publications produced by the pan-Asian movement. The

turning point came at some time during World War I. For example, the Kokuryūkai (I:10), which until 1908 had published the journal *Tōa Geppō* (East Asian Monthly) in classical Chinese, went to considerable expense in February 1920 to launch the English-language *Asian Review*, intended as a companion journal to the Japanese-language *Ajia Jiron* (Asian Review), published from 1917 to 1921. The Kokuryūkai now saw itself as addressing the entire world, not merely a narrow audience made up of the Japanese and the East Asian elites. In the pages of this glossy monthly the society proclaimed its Japanese-centered pan-Asian program as a regional alternative to Wilsonian universalism. Support for its program came from mainstream figures: Prime Minister Hara Takashi allowed an address of his to be reprinted; Hamaguchi Osachi and a number of other prominent politicians and bureaucrats provided their endorsement. The Japanese government apparently appreciated the "public relations" efforts being made by the Kokuryūkai—several articles from *The Asian Review*, including Hara's contribution, were reprinted in a volume edited by Karl Kiyoshi Kawakami (1873–1949), a publicist in government pay (Kawakami 1921).

25. See also the tables, "Occurrence of terms related to Pan-Asianism in Japanese intellectual discourse," at http://asianism.japanesehistory.de.

26. Research has tended to focus on left-wing defectors to the right, a phenomenon known in Japan as *tenkō* (apostasy); cf. Ishidō (1985) and Steinhoff (1991). Koschmann's article, "Asianism's Ambivalent Legacy," which notes that postwar "left-wing Asianism revived familiar, prewar conceptions of Asian identity" (Koschmann 1997: 104), is a notable exception.

27. Tsuji vanished in mysterious circumstances during a trip to Laos in 1961. His body was never found, and he was presumed deceased by the Tokyo Family Court in 1969.

28. See also a number of Chinese contributions to the booklet *Japanese-Chinese Dialogue* published by Genron NPO in 2006 (e.g., Shi 2006).

29. It is perhaps significant that the article quoted here as Nakagawa (2006) has a different title from Nakagawa's talk reproduced on the Genron NPO website, which does not use the term "Asianism." See http://www.genron-npo.net/world/type/cat159.

30. See "The Draft Charter for an East Asian Community" in *Social Science Japan* 38 (March 2008), also accessible online at http://newslet.iss.u-tokyo.ac.jp/ssj38/index.html.

31. It should be noted that there were considerable regional differences in Asian reactions to Western aggression and to the Asian enthusiasm for Western technology.

Part I

THE DAWN OF PAN-ASIANISM, 1850–1900

This section covers the early development of the notion of Asian solidarity in the second half of the nineteenth century. In this period, the Western powers extended their influence in the region in a series of dramatic events. In relatively quick succession, Britain defeated China in the Opium War (1839–1842) and imposed so-called unequal treaties on the Middle Kingdom; France annexed Indochina; Russia, in its quest to acquire an ice-free port, annexed parts of northeastern China; while the United States forced the opening up of Japan (1854).

Japan was coerced into signing its own unequal treaties with the Western powers that threatened the nation's independence. Western pressure on Asia intensified even more during the so-called Age of Imperialism in the 1870s and the 1880s—the phrase is historians' shorthand for the unbridled scramble by the great European powers to divide up those parts of Africa and Asia that had not yet been colonized. The result was that, by the end of the century, few Asian nations retained their independence, and even this was precarious. Japan had preserved its independence while modernizing at a furious pace, but the success of this modernization was far from assured at this stage. Although China remained nominally independent, divided into "spheres of influence" controlled by various European powers, it was a colony in all but name.

The vulnerability of Japan and other Asian nations stimulated a desire for regional cooperation and solidarity to counter the looming Western threat. It was in this atmosphere that the term "Asia," a word of Western provenance, entered the East Asian lexicon, having been in the process infused with new, emotionally charged connotations. These developments paved the way for the rise of Pan-Asianism as an ideology.

At this early stage, the proponents of Pan-Asianism—which had emerged largely spontaneously and without any governmental support—placed an emphasis on regional cooperation and Asian brotherhood. Although the leadership of Asia by Japan was sometimes stressed, at this stage this emphasis raised no suspicions as to Japanese intentions—either in Asia or in the West. These early forms of longing for regional cooperation and solidarity were vague and rather romantic, and the term "Asianism" itself was hardly ever used during the nineteenth century. The ideal of Asian solidarity was expressed through other terms, such as *Kōa* (Raising Asia) and *Dōbun Dōshu* (Same Culture, Same Race), expressions that reflected a longing for cooperation and intra-Asian fraternity in the face of Western aggression.

Chapter One

The Concept of "Asia" before Pan-Asianism

Matsuda Kōichirō

This chapter traces the development of the concept of "Asia" from the beginning of the Edo period until the appearance of the concept of Asianism (*Ajiashugi*) in the 1880s. Throughout this period, Japanese intellectuals by and large did not accept the concept of "Asia" as symbolizing a common regional and cultural identity. Literature offered a case in point. Although the Chinese classics were widely studied in Japan, this did not necessarily strengthen the sense of a common ground between the two nations. On the contrary, the sophisticated interpretation of the Chinese classics by Japanese intellectuals made them more aware of the *differences*, rather than the similarities, between China and Japan. At the same time, the term "Asia" often connoted the superiority of the Western powers. Admitting to being a part of "Asia" signified submission to the West, which had the power to name countries, regions, and peoples all around the world. Thus, for Japanese intellectuals, "Asia" became a byword for inferiority, one that provoked alarm. The call for closer cooperation between the "Asian" countries, however, was occasionally made during the late Edo period (i.e., in the mid-nineteenth century), but in most such cases the term was a strategic notion framed in the context of Realpolitik rather than a concept based on an idealized unity of "Asian civilization."

The concept of "Asia" was first introduced to East Asia by the Jesuits at the end of the sixteenth and the beginning of the seventeenth century. The Chinese-language world atlas printed in 1602 by Matteo Ricci (1552–1610) was the most important source to transmit the term "Asia," written in Chinese characters, to Japan (see http://www.ibiblio.org/expo/vatican.exhibit/exhibit/i-rome_to_china/images/china01.jpg). As more Western atlases were imported into Japan in the late seventeenth century, the term gained wide acceptance. For example, Nishikawa Joken (1648–1724) used it on a world map, similar to that found in Ricci's atlas, which he included in his books

Nihon Suidokō (Reflections on the Geography of Japan, 1700) and *Kaitsūshōkō* (Reflections on Trade between Civilized and Barbarian Countries, 1708). In Nishikawa's geographical description of Japan, he recognized that Japan was a part of "Asia." Another scholar of the late Edo period, Yamagata Bantō (1748–1821), was highly critical of Indian, Chinese, and Japanese scholars, whom he accused of prejudice and whom he lambasted for their failure to conduct a proper study of foreign countries but praised Europeans who explored the world using scientific methods. Their geographical terminology, he noted, was the result of scientific research. Yamagata found it worrisome that while Westerners freely coined terms like "China," "Japan," or "Asia," the Japanese were incapable of naming even their own country (see source 1).

The term "Asia" was also useful for a group of intellectuals who studied Western geography and were searching for a way of conceptualizing the world that would overturn the Sinocentric world order. Sinocentrism was a problematic issue for Japanese intellectuals in the Edo period. The concept of "Asia" helped them to relativize not only the traditional scheme of the Sinocentric world order but also the modified Japanese version of it. A scholar of Western learning, Maeno Ryōtaku (1723–1830), wrote that "China has had no continuous name as a country since the ancient times of Yao and Shun. The name *Shina* [China] comes from the West" (Maeno 1777).

In the early nineteenth century, the critical problem for Japanese intellectuals was how Japan could survive in a world in which the Western powers were dominant. The Western term "Asia" now needed to be addressed as a symbol of Western power. However, rather than being rejected, it was appropriated by the Japanese. The popularization of the term "Asia" contributed to the development of a national consciousness among Japanese intellectuals rather than creating a sense of belonging to a wider Asian region. A well-known scholar of the Mito school, Aizawa Yasushi (also Seishisai, 1781–1867), argued that dividing the world into several regions and giving them names, such as "Asia," was an arrogant and self-centered practice typical of Westerners—but that such behavior explained their dominance on the world stage. He grudgingly admitted that only the Western countries had the power to name regions and places throughout the world. It made him deeply ashamed that the people of the "divine land" (*shinshū*) of Japan could not rival Westerners in terms of their power to name the world in this way. He warned that "Asia" was no more than a name given by others, and a collective name at that. By being included in "Asia," Japan was being lumped into a general group of "Asian" countries. For Aizawa, this represented a crisis of national identity (see source 2).

A number of Aizawa's contemporaries regarded this crisis not only in terms of military conquest or the threat of colonization but also as a potential moral defeat for Japan. In his diary, the physician Shibata Shuzō (1820–1859) from Sado island, who was also an amateur cartographer, criticized Aizawa, describing him as an inflexible scholar who lamented the lack of an enterprising spirit in the Japanese people but who did nothing to remedy the problem (Tanaka 1996). Moreover, even respected Confucian scholars frequently praised Western civilization for its achievement of benevolent government as judged by Confucian standards. Learning of the Chinese defeat in the Opium War (1839–1842), Yokoi Shōnan (1809–1869) from Kumamoto wrote that China had lost because the Chinese were too proud of their own civilization, which had peaked prematurely. He also pointed out that the Europeans were a brave people who took a strong interest in the outside world because Europe was much smaller and less productive than "Asia" (see source 3).

As early as the late Edo period, there were voices advocating an active cooperation between Japan and China against the Western powers. However, these assertions of Sino–Japanese cooperation were based on a strategic and realistic understanding of the political situation in the region rather than on any romantic ideal of "Asian unity." Hirano Kuniomi (1828–1864), a leading activist in the movement to "revere the Emperor and expel the foreigners" in 1860s Japan, argued for Sino–Japanese cooperation on the grounds that both countries had rejected Christianity (see source 4). Similar views were also held by some political leaders. For example, Katsu Kaishū (1823–1899) wrote in his diary on 27 April 1863 that Japan had to persuade Korea and China to promote the modernization of "Asia" in areas such as naval matters and science (see source 5). These examples, however, do not prove that Aizawa or Hirano presupposed any essential cultural unity between China and Japan. In his widely read *Shinron* (New Theses), Aizawa compared the struggle between the Western powers in East Asia to the Warring States period (403–221 BC) in ancient China. He recognized Japan as a small country situated between two major powers, Russia and China. Aizawa's aspirations, as well as the calls made by Hirano and Katsu for Sino–Japanese cooperation, were based on their understanding of the competition occurring among the Western powers in "Asia."

After the Meiji Restoration of 1868, advocates of cooperation with China continued to raise their voice. Iwakura Tomomi (1825–1883), one of the central figures in the new Meiji government, wrote in 1875 that if China were to be invaded by Russia, it would pose a major threat to Japan, and therefore Japan needed to seek cooperation with China:

> Our imperial country and China are neighbors which are as intimately connected as the lips and teeth. If China were to be absorbed by Russia, it would be like the teeth losing the lips that protect them. Therefore, Japan and China must

strengthen their relations and friendship like the two wheels of a carriage or the two wings of a bird, and thus strive to help each other achieve self-reliance and [preserve] their independence. (Iwakura 1875: 1270)

As these examples of the use of the term "Asia" in nineteenth-century Japan show, the concept functioned in two complementary, if sometimes conflicting, ways. On the one hand, the concept of "Asia" was seen as a useful new tool for acknowledging the global situation without resorting to the Sinocentric world order. On the other hand, "Asia" was regarded as an enforced identity given by the West, a name that represented the weakness and backwardness of the region surrounding and including Japan. These various usages of the term put Japanese intellectuals under a certain amount of pressure in their thinking and writing about the international situation.

Despite these developments, the term *Ajiashugi* (Asianism or Pan-Asianism) was coined only in the 1890s. An early example of its use is found in a journal published by the Seikyōsha, a group of young nationalist intellectuals. In articles published in the journals *Nihonjin* (The Japanese) and *Ajia* (Asia) around that time, a set of arguments that defined the concept of "Pan-Asianism" was beginning to emerge. Using the terms *Ajiashigi*—a predecessor of the later *Ajiashugi*—and *Ajia Keirin* ("Asian policy"), an anonymous contributor to the journal *Ajia* insisted that "the Japanese are the first nation in all of Asia to become civilized" and argued that, as international society is the arena of a racial struggle, "Japan must become the leader of a revolution by the yellow race (*ōshoku jinshu no kakumei*) on the grounds that it combines the intellectual sophistication that goes with civilization with the physical prowess of barbarian might" (*Ajia*, 1 February 1892). In this writer's assertion, it is no longer possible to detect any embarrassment or alarm at Japan's being considered part of "Asia." Even though *Ajia* was critical of Western hegemony, it adopted the East–West dichotomy as a cliché and paid no attention to the question of terminology. The term "Pan-Asianism" thus arose when Japanese intellectuals stopped asking the question, "Why do they call us Asian?"

Source 1 (translation from the Japanese original by Matsuda Kōichirō) Yamagata Bantō (1820), *Yumenoshiro* (A Castle of Dreams), reprinted in Tominaga Nakamoto and Mizuta Norihisa (eds.), *Nihon Shisō Taikei, vol. 43: Yamagata Bantō* (Survey of Japanese Thought, vol. 43: Yamagata Bantō), Iwanami Shoten, 1973, 223, 433.

They say *Daishinkoku* [the Roman Empire] is located near the place where the sun sets and *Fusōkoku* [Japan] is where the sun rises. The name "Japan" originated from this interpretation. [However,] the earth is round. How can it be possible for the sun to rise out of the ground? That is all that is seen by the eyes, so when people see the sun rise in the east and set in the west, they think of the eastern regions as the land of the rising sun and the country to the west as the place where the sun sets. If you travel to the latter lands, you will never see the sun rise or set there; you will merely observe the same phenomenon as is seen here. This is not surprising. The earth is round and not flat. The sun moves across the sky and never in fact rises out of the ground. Therefore, the conventional naming of the lands of sunrise or sunset is obviously the result of fallacious conjecture. . . .

In their travels across the globe, Westerners first encountered three continents: Asia, Europe and Africa. They subsequently discovered two more: America and *mekaranika* [Magallanica: the imagined continent believed to exist near the South Pole]. They call them the five continents. Calling them the "five continents" and giving names to each country is entirely a Western achievement. Accordingly, they call *tenjiku* India, *morokoshi* China and they call our country Japan. What a shame!

Source 2 (translation from the Japanese original by Matsuda Kōichirō) Aizawa Yasushi (1833), *Teiki-ihen* (A Guide to Morals), reprinted in Aizawa Yasushi [Seishisai], *Shinron/Teiki-ihen* (New Thesis/A Guide to Morals), Iwanami Shoten, 1931, 249.

The Western barbarians have allocated names to the continents, such as Asia, Europe and Africa. However, this allocation of names is an outrageous abuse because such names have not been approved by the Emperor of Japan nor are these "universal names" that have been conventionally accepted since antiquity. It is only the Westerners' arrogance that has made them use the term "Asia" and include our divine land [Japan] as part of it. For that reason I will never use the names they have given. In future, when the Emperorization of the world—that is, respect for our Emperor—has spread throughout the globe, all [regional] names will be given by our Emperor according to the appropriate topography. At the moment, as we have no proper regional names of our own to use, we have been forced to use names such as *seiban, hokuteki, nanban* [western, northern, southern "barbarians"]. . . .

Using *soshō* [grouping names of regions] devised by the Western barbarians must be prohibited.

Source 3 (translation from the Japanese original by Matsuda Kōichirō) Yokoi Shōnan (1860), *Kokuze Sanron* (Three Theses on State Policy), reprinted in Satō Shōsuke et al. (eds.), *Nihon Shisō Taikei, vol. 55: Wata-*

nabe Kazan, Takano Chōei, Sakuma Shōzan, Yokoi Shōnan, Hashimoto Sanai (Survey of Japanese Thought, vol. 55: Watanabe Kazan, Takano Chōei, Sakuma Shōzan, Yokoi Shōnan, Hashimoto Sanai). Iwanami Shoten, 1971, 450–51.

China is located in Asia, one of the five continents of the world. It is a great country which faces the sea to the east. In antiquity it created a great civilization. It produces rice, wheat and millet in abundant quantities. No shortage of materials for human needs can be found there. As a result, everybody [in China] from the imperial courtiers down to the lowest commoners have an arrogant attitude and show no interest in trading with foreigners or seeking out goods abroad. They have no desire to increase their knowledge by learning from foreigners. That is the reason China's military forces are so weak and vulnerable to attacks by foreign powers.

Source 4 (translation from the Japanese original by Matsuda Kōichirō) Hirano Kuniomi (1863), *Seiban Sosaku* (Fundamental Measures for Expelling the Barbarians), reprinted in Hirano Kuniomi Kenshōkai (ed.), *Hirano Kuniomi Denki Oyobi Ikō* (Biography and Posthumous Writings of Hirano Kuniomi). Shōzansha, 1980, 54.

In the contemporary world, our country and China are the only countries that remain unconverted to Christianity [Hirano here draws on Aizawa Yasushi's *Shinron*]. In spite of the difference between our history of an unbroken imperial line and their history that is full of revolutions, we are geographically close to each other and the climate of each country is similar. The natural characteristics of both peoples and the color of their eyes and hair are similar. [Japan and China] have had mutual relations since antiquity. Because both countries share common moral values, they are in a strong position to cooperate. If we feed the invaders' horses and supply them with charcoal, that would be tantamount to aiding the barbarians and attacking China. If China were to help the barbarians, it would cause harm to our country. If we examine our situation carefully, it [becomes clear that it] is unreasonable to harm each other, [even if] unknowingly.

Source 5 (translation from the Japanese original by Matsuda Kōichirō) Katsube Mitake, Matsumoto Sannosuke, Ōguchi Yūjirō (eds.) (1972), *Katsu Kaishū Zenshū* (Collected Writings of Katsu Kaishū), vol. 18. Keisō Shobō, 50.

We can see no countries on the Asian continent that are resisting the Westerners. This is because the spirit of all [Asians] has atrophied and they cannot compete with the extensive projects that the Westerners are putting in place. Our country must dispatch ships to the countries of Asia on a mission aimed at persuading their rulers to cooperate with one another, strengthen their naval forces, develop trade and give a boost to science—otherwise we will not be able to resist an invasion by the Western powers. We will begin with Korea, our closest neighbor, and then turn to China.

Chapter Two

The Foundation Manifesto of the Kōakai (Raising Asia Society) and the Ajia Kyōkai (Asia Association), 1880–1883

Urs Matthias Zachmann

The Kōakai, founded in 1880 and renamed Ajia Kyōkai in 1883, was the first pan-Asian society in Japan of any duration, as it existed independently until 1900. The society's activities, although limited in scope and impact, set the pattern for institutional Pan-Asianism in Japan. Moreover, the society's ambiguous position in Sino–Japanese relations and the criticism that it incurred within Japan succinctly illustrate the problems that Pan-Asianism faced from early on.

When the society was founded in 1880, Japan's relations with its neighbors, especially China, did not bode well for the success of the society's primary goal—the cooperation of Asian nations to achieve wealth and power and resist Western imperialism. On the contrary—although Japan had resumed diplomatic contacts and concluded a Treaty of Friendship with China in 1871, subsequent developments very soon showed that Japan was openly challenging China's role as the leading power in East Asia and raised suspicions that it would choose to ally itself with the West in exploiting Asia rather than opting for cooperation with Asia against the West. Thus, in 1874, Japan sent an expedition to Taiwan in an attempt both to reaffirm its old claims to the Ryukyu kingdom and to establish new ones on Taiwan. In 1876 Japan succeeded in concluding a treaty with Korea through an early display of gunboat diplomacy, and in 1879 it annexed the Ryukyu kingdom as Okinawa Prefecture. Given the fact that Ryukyu was one of China's two most important tribute states, it comes as no surprise that the founding of the Kōakai in 1880 took place amidst high diplomatic tensions between China and Japan—tensions that did not let up during the 1880s but on the contrary were superseded by a bitter dispute over Korea, China's other main tribute state. This conflict led eventually to the Sino-Japanese War of 1894–1895.

The Kōakai had a short-lived predecessor, the Shin'akai (Promoting Asia Society), established in 1877 by naval Lieutenant Sone Toshitora (1847–1910). He was allegedly inspired by a 1874 promise by the statesman Ōkubo Toshimichi (1830–1878) to the Chinese politician Li Hongzhang (Li Hung-chang, 1823–1901) to promote Chinese-language schools in Japan as a way of achieving a better understanding between the two countries (Kuroki 2007: 36; see also Tikhonov 2002). As we shall see, modern Chinese-language instruction was to become one of the most important contributions of the Kōakai to institutional Pan-Asianism in Japan.

At its inception, the Kōakai had seventy-seven members, a figure that rose in its early phase to as many as 400 but later declined and, in 1894, for example, numbered 250 (Kuroki 2007). Judging from the relatively high membership fees (1 yen per month), members came from the affluent strata of society. Although the membership was heterogeneous, it included many Foreign Ministry officials in charge of affairs relating to China and Korea as well as activists and sympathizers of the opposition Freedom and People's Rights Movement (*jiyū minken undō*), such as the celebrated writer Suehiro Tetchō (1849–1896), and journalists from the *Chōya Shinbun*. Both traits were combined in the person of Soejima Taneomi (1828–1905), who became foreign minister in 1871 but left the government in 1873 when his call to attack Korea was overruled (Seikanron). In 1874 Soejima had signed with Itagaki Taisuke (1837–1919) a petition calling for the establishment of a parliament, an event that is generally seen as the starting point of the Freedom and People's Rights Movement. In accordance with the society's pan-Asianist goals, its membership included representatives from Asian countries other than Japan. Among them were the first two Chinese ministers to Japan, He Ruzhang (1838–1891) and Li Shuchang (1837–1897); the intellectual and journalist Wang Tao (1828–1897); Korean reformers Kim Ok-kyun (1851–1894) and Pak Yong-hyo (1841–1914); and, at one time, even two diplomats from the Ottoman Empire. Thus, over time, the society registered sixty-six foreign members (Kuroki 2005: 623). It is important to note that, although membership was in practice limited to Asians, the society's Asianism was not of a racist kind. In 1881, it was agreed that Westerners could join the society as long as they supported its goals. This relative indifference to—or even outright rejection of—racial issues was probably another characteristic of Meiji Asianism. Likewise, in accordance with its pan-Asianist goals, in addition to its head office in Tokyo and branch offices in Osaka, Kobe, and Fukuoka, the society also set up offices in the main trading cities of China and Korea. Most notable was the school known as the Tōyō Gakkan (Oriental Academy), which opened in Shanghai in 1884.

The activities of the Kōakai were threefold in character. First, in the early period, members met each month, although these meetings were little more than social occasions and opportunities for Sinophile Meiji intellectuals to exchange poems with their erudite foreign comembers. Second, the society published a bulletin titled *Kōakai Hōkoku* (later *Ajia Kyōkai Hōkoku*), containing news and reports from various parts of East Asia sent in by correspondents stationed in those regions. Some articles were entirely written in classical Chinese, which served as the lingua franca of Pan-Asianists from all East Asian countries. Third and most important, at its inception the society also founded a Chinese-language school (the Kōakai Shina Gakkō) where modern and classical Chinese, as well as Korean, were taught (Sone Toshitora was one of the language instructors). However, as early as 1885, this institution was incorporated into the Tokyo Foreign Language School (Tōkyō Gaikokugo Gakkō). Although the school's achievements were inconspicuous, it produced, among others, the diplomat Odagiri Masunosuke (1868–1934), an important figure in late Meiji Sino–Japanese relations. Moreover, the society's practical focus on language training as a prerequisite for regional integration (and expansion) became a characteristic of institutional Asianism in Japan, a trend most notably illustrated by the Kōakai's successor, the Tōa Dōbunkai (see I:9).

Right from the start, the Kōakai ran into problems over Sino–Japanese relations. Although its declared goal was to promote friendship and understanding between the "core" Asianist countries of Japan, China, and Korea, Chinese diplomats at least met this proposal with coolness and suspicion (Zhang 1999: 117–24). Thus, although He Ruzhang, the first Chinese minister to Japan, was a nominal member of the society, he remained noncommittal about its lofty aspirations and excused himself rather coolly from attending its opening meeting. More to the point, his secretary, the later Chinese reformer Huang Zunxian (1848–1905), despite strong support for the ideal of "raising Asia" in general (Kamachi 1981: 118–24), not only showed no inclination to join the Kōakai but also wrote a letter of protest to his friend Wang Tao in Hong Kong shortly after the society was founded. Wang Tao, who had visited Japan in 1879 and had a number of Japanese friends including Sone Toshitora (Cohen 1974: 103f), had joined the society as a corresponding member and published some positive articles in his newspaper *Xunhuan Ribao* despite private doubts about its real purpose (see Cohen 1974: 103). Following Huang's protest, Wang reconsidered his public stance and published an article, "On the evils of the Kōakai" ("Xingya-hui du qi bi lun," *Xunhuan Ribao*, 16 August 1880), in which he accused the Kōakai not only of utopianism but also of duplicity, as its lofty ideals stood in stark contrast to Japan's behavior in

East Asia. Moreover, he suspected that the extensive language training and information gathering pursued by the society served the purpose not of building friendships but rather of empire building (Zhang 1999: 122–24).

In light of the strained relations between China and Japan at the time, it is no wonder that Chinese diplomats and intellectuals would have eyed the society's activities with suspicion—all the more since most of its leadership had in one way or another been responsible for—or at least deeply involved in—shaping these strained relations. For example, Yanagihara Sakimitsu (1850–1894) and Date Munenari (1818–1892) had tried to force an unequal treaty on China before settling for the equal treaty of 1871; Soejima Taneomi's obfuscating diplomacy had been partly responsible for the escalation of the Taiwan issue in 1874 (McWilliams 1975); Hanabusa Yoshimoto (1842–1917) was the first Japanese minister to Korea after Japan had enforced diplomatic contacts in 1876; and Sone Toshitora had been caught disguised as a Chinese in 1878 while allegedly conducting espionage activities in Fuzhou (Foochow), thereby causing a minor diplomatic incident (Zhang 1999: 122)—to give just a few names. Moreover, another distancing factor reflected one side of human nature, as Japanese Sinophiles were apparently split into rival groups that sought to monopolize the Chinese literati and warn them against associating too closely with the "coarse" fellows of the Kōakai; again, Sone Toshitora seemed to have been the butt of their invective (Zhang 1999: 121f).

Coincidentally, the uneasy relationship between the Kōakai and Chinese diplomats was paralleled by its difficult relations with Japanese politicians. Thus, no high-ranking member of the Satsuma-Chōshū oligarchy ever joined the society. In 1881, for example, president Soejima Taneomi invited Itō Hirobumi (1841–1909) to join the society but received a negative reply (Kuroki 2007: 41). Considering the political leanings of most of the society's members toward the opposition, Itō's reaction comes as no surprise. However, another motive for his refusal may have been that the cautious Itō, who largely shaped Japan's foreign policy over the next two decades and generally pursued a more conciliatory course toward China, was seeking to diminish potential sources of friction by distancing himself from the Kōakai.

However, the Kōakai did not openly advocate an aggressive East Asia policy that swept aside the views of its Chinese and Korean members. On the contrary, some instances speak against this view. Most notably, the name change from the "Raising Asia Society" to the "Asia Association" reflected protests from Chinese members who rejected the name Kōakai as implying the presumptuous notion that a small country like Japan should lead "Asia," including the great empire of China. However, Japan's relative position in relation to China remained a point of contention among the society's Japanese members. The society's leadership tended toward a view of regional integration in East Asia as hierarchical, with Japan as leader, whereas the rank-and-file members entertained a more egalitarian perspective toward China and Korea (Kuroki 2007: 50). As the latter viewpoint disappeared almost completely after the Sino-Japanese War, Kuroki Morifumi has concluded that early Japanese Asianism as embodied in the Kōakai was characterized by this more egalitarian view. However, one could argue that this perspective was merely a reflection of the international situation, as before the war China had in fact been in a much stronger position in relation to Japan.

Finally, it should be mentioned that it was exactly this equality with China that was rejected by an increasingly jingoist Japanese public in the early 1880s and that caused the society's aims to appear dubious, if not downright objectionable, to many people outside Asianist circles. The most famous statement of this rejection was Fukuzawa Yukichi's (1834–1901) editorial "Datsua-ron," which was written at the height of the jingoist frenzy and was prompted by a failed coup d'état masterminded by Kim Ok-kyun, Pak Yong-hyo, and other pro-Japanese reformers in Korea in December 1884. However, the title "On leaving Asia" and the general gist of the text can be traced back to an earlier article by Fukuzawa's associate Hinohara Shōzō (1853–1904) published in the *Jiji Shinpō* in November 1884 (Maruyama 2002; Zachmann 2007). Like Fukuzawa in his article, Hinohara admonished his readers that Japan must dissociate itself from Asia lest the Western powers mistake Japan for a weak country and treat it like the rest of Asia. He concluded his long, rambling piece with the following observation:

> I hear that there are people who for some unfathomable reason have founded a Raising Asia Society (Kōakai), and plan to ally with the countries of Asia to resist Europe at any cost. Why must we revive Asia and resist Europe? Whether the whole Asian continent is crushed, shattered or falls into ruins has nothing to do with us. We have to maintain the independence of our country, Japan, and ensure the welfare of our people. Even if the Chinese Empire is taken over by France and the Indian natives enslaved by the British, as long as Japan does not share the same fate, there is nothing to be sorry about. . . . I hope that, in opposition to the Raising Asia Society, somebody will establish a Leaving Asia Society (Datsuakai). (Hinohara, 13 November 1884)

This was probably the first instance of the term "Leaving Asia," which, in combination with "Joining Europe/the West" (*nyūō*), is often used today to describe Japan's foreign policy direction since the late nineteenth century. However, as the immediate context of the phrase—the founding of the Kōakai—shows, the line between "Raising Asia" and "Leaving Asia" was, in fact, never as clear and distinct as Hinohara (and Fukuzawa) expressed it polemically.

The Kōakai had its heyday in the early years of its existence. Japan's growing conflict with China over Korea soon stifled the activities of the society and turned it into a rather passive organization. After 1883, fewer and fewer Chinese attended its meetings, and the organization soon became exclusively Japanese. In 1900, the society was finally absorbed into the newly founded Tōa Dōbunkai (the East Asian Common Culture Society, see I:9). This society took on many of the characteristics of the Kōakai, albeit under greatly changed political circumstances.

Source 1 (translation from the classical Chinese [*kanbun*] original by Urs Matthias Zachmann)
Foundation Manifesto of the Kōakai (Raising Asia Society, 1880), reprinted in Kuroki Morifumi and Masuzawa Akio (eds.), *Kōakai Hōkoku/ Ajia Kyōkai Hōkoku* (Bulletin of the Kōakai, Bulletin of the Ajia Kyōkai). 2 vols. Tokyo: Fuji Shuppan, 1993.

In our opinion, the situation of Asia today is characterized by the failure of states to rely on each other and of peoples to help each other. Dull and shallow, they attend only to their own welfare. At such a time as this, is there a single high-minded person in the whole of Asia who would not be angry and indignant?

The countries of Europe and America have achieved wealth and power due to their understanding of each other's languages and their intimate knowledge of each other's affairs. Thus, in times of external emergency, they can support each other. Alas, is it so hard for our region to become like them, and so reverse our decline and draw equal with the European and American countries in wealth and power? Of all the countries in Asia, only Japan and China retain the ability to exercise state authority and maintain national independence. The independence of Korea, Vietnam and Siam exists only in name and is otherwise not worth mentioning. Countries such as Burma and India are under direct European rule. This deplorable situation is the reason why a Society for Raising Asia had to be established quickly.

For a long time now, our country has had close contacts with China and Korea. With the countries of Vietnam, Siam, Champa [southern and central Indochina], Luzon [i.e., the Philippines], too, our relations are longstanding, and diplomatic contact and trade have been substantial and important. However, they do not equal those established by the European powers. Thus, until today, our intercourse with China and Korea has lacked genuine trust and friendship—and even more so our relations with the other countries. Therefore, the most urgent task today is to unite worthy men from all over Asia, join our forces, plan together, revive the True Way and halt our decline.

However, to do so, we must first understand the international situation which, in turn, requires linguistic skills. Our country has people who have mastered the European languages, but there are very few who know the languages of China, Korea and other Asian countries. And why is this? Because there are no schools to teach them. Is that not most regrettable!?

As a result, we are now opening a language school in Tokyo to teach people who are interested in Chinese. We will also establish an editorial office in Tokyo, dispatch correspondents to key locations in Asia and inform our society's members in detail about important events in those countries as well as about the society's affairs. In the future, we will also establish schools in Shanghai, China, and in Pusan, Korea, to enlarge our membership. We will learn each other's languages, understand each other other's situation and thus make great progress in finding a common solution. Later, we will gradually extend these initiatives to the other countries of Asia.

High-minded gentlemen, if you leave your recent animosities behind, join this society, support its projects and help to eradicate its defects, then Asia's revival will be near.

Source 2 (translation from the classical Chinese [*kanbun*] original by Urs Matthias Zachmann)
Foundation Manifesto of the Ajia Kyōkai (Asia Association), 1883, reprinted in Kuroki Morifumi and Masuzawa Akio (eds.), *Kōakai Hōkoku/ Ajia Kyōkai Hōkoku* (Bulletin of the Kōakai, Bulletin of the Ajia Kyōkai). 2 vols. Tokyo: Fuji Shuppan, 1993.

Heaven creates mankind [a phrase taken from the classic *Mèngzi*, or *Mencius*] by allowing people to bear and raise offspring and thereby realize their human nature. Whether we have in mind a village, a town or even a state, none is an exception to this reality. Today, of all the countries of the world, China is the largest in the Eastern hemisphere, with Korea lying to its east. Both countries are located very close to us. In antiquity, there was a constant coming and going between us, lasting until the middle ages when the exchange of imperial gifts ceased for a while. However, today, people travel all over the world, and no distance is too great for them. Electricity and the steamship have made our world small and turned it into a single village. Thus, the countries of the Western hemisphere—Britain, France, Germany and America—visit us with foreign goods and their ships are constantly nudging each other on the sea. The people of China, Korea, and even Vietnam, Burma, Champa and Luzon now pursue a friendly intercourse, and there is constant traffic in the region. Thus, the way of the world has greatly changed.

Neighborly relations are a state's most prized treasure. With the countries of the Western hemisphere, we already have a great deal of traffic. Thus, with those in the East which are our natural allies, how can we afford not to improve relations and devise a common strategy to ward off dangers and calamities? However, good relations between neighboring countries are not solely the concern of governments and statesmen, but also of private men of leisure and good taste who come together to exchange poems over a cup of wine. Only when we can talk together in a relaxed atmosphere will we understand each other, and friendships will develop.

A group of high-minded men have understood this already and founded a society in Tokyo called the Raising Asia Society [Kōakai]. Moreover, they have established a school and gathered young people to be trained at a higher level in the languages of various countries, thereby promoting understanding and friendship. However, some have argued that the concept of "Raising Asia" is not broad enough, and we have therefore changed the society's name to the "Asia Association" [Ajia Kyōkai]. This name suggests that we should join our forces and share a common purpose, benefit each other and thereby advance towards strength and prosperity. We will strive to revive the circumstances of the whole Asian continent and, eventually, even catch up with the Western powers. We hope to be more successful in our humanitarian efforts than previously, and we will not betray the purpose for which heaven has entrusted this mission to us.

Chapter Three

The Genyōsha (1881) and Premodern Roots of Japanese Expansionism

Joël Joos

The Genyōsha (Dark Ocean Society) was a right-wing political organization that was active in the Meiji, Taishō, and prewar Shōwa periods. It was founded in Fukuoka in 1881 by a number of men, including Hiraoka Kōtarō (1851–1906), Tōyama Mitsuru (1855–1944), and Hakoda Rokusuke (1850–1888), its first leader. Although it had sprouted from antigovernment elements, from the 1890s on it aligned itself with government policy at home and advocated imperialism and expansionism abroad. This shift was possible because of a flexible founding charter that included three objectives, namely, "to respectfully accept and serve the Imperial House of Japan, to love the fatherland, Japan, and to further the rights of the people." In the first half of the twentieth century, the Genyōsha acquired a sinister reputation as a fascist "secret society" that acted in cahoots with radical army and navy officers and reactionary bureaucrats, as well as gangsters, to harass and even assassinate political opponents. Some have gone to the extreme of drawing parallels between Tōyama and Adolf Hitler (e.g., Norman 1944). The fact that the only civilian executed as a "class A" war criminal after the Tokyo War Crimes Trials (1947–1948), former Prime Minister Hirota Kōki, was a member of the Genyōsha reinforced the impression that the society played a significant role in Japan's pre-1945 expansionism. After Japan's defeat, the U.S. occupation forces outlawed and disbanded the society as a militarist and ultranationalist body. Extreme right-wing groups in the postwar period have continued to honor it as their predecessor.

The Genyōsha, named after the narrow seas that divide Fukuoka in Kyushu from the Asiatic mainland and that are known in Japanese as Genkainada, claims its roots in the 1877 Satsuma Rebellion and in the liberal ideas of the Freedom and People's Rights Movement (*jiyū minken undō*) formed immediately thereafter. The early Genyōsha was highly critical of the Meiji government, particularly its alleged weakness toward the Western powers. Like many other antiestablishment right-wing societies, however, it always drew a clear line between the raison d'état, with which it identified zealously, and more complex political issues, party political infighting in particular, which it professed to abhor. This explains why the Genyōsha attacked (sometimes physically) political leaders, party politicians, liberals, and suchlike but never those representatives of the state the Genyōsha considered nonpartisan and loyal to the emperor. Indeed, whenever a "national" crisis arose, all attention was directed to the foreign foe, while the—invariably—"meek" government policy was criticized.

The liberal banner under which the Genyōsha had been active during its first years was discarded after the suicide of Hakoda in 1888. Under the leadership of Hiraoka, a member of the Lower House of the Diet after 1894, the society gradually assumed a strong statist position. In its "official" history published in 1917, the Genyōsha looked back on this move away from liberalism and people's rights as the "casting aside of a pair of worn-out sandals." However, it is highly likely that opportunistic motives rather than idealism were at play here. For one thing, Hiraoka had acquired a considerable fortune in mining and therefore opposed any radical domestic change. In addition, the Genyōsha's interference in the 1892 Diet elections, in which opposition candidates had been elected (even in Fukuoka) despite the society's often violent attacks, had proven unsuccessful and unpopular. Clearly, the Genyōsha's leaders did not see a bright future in democracy, elections, and party politics.

The postwar reputation of the Genyōsha as a powerful "fascist" organization, however, may be exaggerated. It was not a rigorously organized association with a clearly defined ideology. Its leaders preferred the informality of personal ties. Tōyama Mitsuru, founding member and the de facto leader of the party after the death of Hiraoka in 1906, refused to assume its formal presidency until the day of his death in 1944, leaving that honor to far less famous (and significant) members. The Genyōsha produced a number of offshoot organizations, all of which were short lived and not particularly successful. The Kokumin Dōmeikai (National League), for instance, established in 1900 in cooperation with Prince Konoe Atsumaro and his Tōa Dōbunkai (East Asia Common Culture Association, see I:9), lasted only two years. The Tairo Dōshikai (Anti-Russian Brotherhood) was dissolved less than six months after its founding in the summer of 1903. The Rōninkai (Masterless Samurai Association), a society with a slightly broader base founded in 1908, withered away after ten years amidst the surging tide of the "Taishō democracy" of the 1910s and 1920s. Among these offshoots, the Kokuryūkai, founded in 1901 by Uchida Ryōhei (1874–1937) and Kuzuu Yoshihisa (1874–1958), was the most lasting, active and best known (see I:10).

The Genyōsha's main interest, notwithstanding its subsequent characterization as "fascist," focused on foreign relations, particularly on Japan's relations with Asia. Indeed, "Dai Ajiashugi" (Greater Asianism) is considered to be one of the more representative labels under which to categorize its "ideology," although Genyōsha members did not coin the term (and hardly ever used it). The Genyōsha and its members were to a greater degree engaged in "Asianist" and frequently expansionary activities on the mainland than any other right-wing group. Often acting in blatant disregard of "Western-oriented" government foreign policy and at the risk of infuriating Great Britain, France, and the United States, it supported independence activists from the Philippines (Mariano Ponce, 1863–1916), India (Rash Behari Bose, see I:24), Vietnam (Phan Boi Chau, 1867–1940), and Central Asia (Abdürreşid İbrahim, see I:19); it maintained networks of informants in China and other parts of Asia; it sent spies to remote corners of Asia such as Inner Mongolia to gather intelligence and popular support for the anti-Western (often anti-Russian) cause; it organized volunteer corps to participate in conflicts in Korea (e.g., the Tenyūkyō, or "Heavenly Blessed Heroes," a group of adventurers, most of whom were members of the Genyōsha, participated in civil unrest in Korea in the early 1890s) and China; it advised Manchurian rebels during the Russo-Japanese War (1904–1905); and it played an active part in the Chinese Revolution of 1911–1912.

The society claimed that Japan had a historical mission to honor its status as the "Land of the Gods," as described in Japan's ancient chronicles, and to lead the rest of Asia out of slavery. To this end, as can be seen in the sources reproduced here, the Genyōsha did not hesitate to quote from fiercely nationalist Japanese sources (e.g., Yoshida Shōin's *Yūshūroku* [Prison Records] or Satō Nobuhiro's *Unai Kondō Hisaku* [A Secret Policy against the World Upheaval]), which in the first half of the nineteenth century envisioned a Japan that would not just "liberate" Korea and China but also become a world power by acquiring colonies as distant as India and the Americas. The Genyōsha also legitimized Japan's "mission" in Asia by referring to historical precedents of Japanese interconnectedness with Asia—for instance, in the form of the small state of Mimana, which many Japanese considered to be an ancient outpost of Japanese influence on the Korean peninsula (1st to 6th century AD). As far as the society's "official" history is concerned, no practical guidelines were offered for winning the hearts of the Asian peoples—nothing beyond an unshakable optimism that Asians would hail Japan as their liberator and the determination to crush any resistance. Lacking a structured ideology, it produced no publications of lasting influence.

The reasons for the Genyōsha's initial successes turned out to be the cause of the eventual withering of its influence. While it was involved in a number of terrorist incidents, the society and its offshoots were unable to cope with new political trends. First, the rise of mass democracy in the Taishō period (1912–1926) proved too powerful for the small-scale and informal style of Genyōsha political tactics. Second, Japan's colonial empire had expanded rapidly, becoming in effect much like other colonial empires: there was little room for adventurers in its diplomatic and administrative management of the empire. The annexation of Manchuria in 1931–1932 was the realization of the ideals the Genyōsha had long been advocating. Still, by the time this "dream" was realized by the Japanese Kwantung Army, the society's influence had already declined, and its continuing presence had become largely symbolic.

Source (translation from the Japanese original by Joël Joos)
Genyōsha Shashi Hensankai (ed.), *Genyōsha Shashi* (The Official History of the Genyōsha). Genyōsha Shashi Hensankai, 1917.

SECTION 34: THE PRESENT AND
THE FUTURE OF THE GENYŌSHA

We have already talked about the Genyōsha's past. We have talked about the way in which it has put to public service its great ambitions and grand theories—ideals in the pursuit of which it has abided by its founding charter and been active in many spheres, effervescent as water gushing over rocks in a mountain stream, sending off sparks like stone striking metal. It has not surrendered to the threat of forceful oppression. It has feared neither power nor influence. At times it has espoused democratic theories, and then again lent its ear to appeals for stronger government control. In all of this, however, it was merely adapting to the trend of the times. Not once has it betrayed its own ideals as given in the founding charter [of the Genyōsha]. . . . Some commentators have argued that the Genyōsha initially championed people's rights, and was the first to demand the establishment of a Diet. They have pointed out that Fukuoka Prefecture is known, just like that of Okayama, for being the cradle of constitutional government, thanks to the activities of the Genyōsha. The same commentators, however, have gone on to lament that, notwithstanding the Genyōsha's contributions in initiating constitutional rule, it has shifted direction toward a statist discourse. [They regret] that it has lent its weight to intervention in elections and that, while in the prefecture of Okayama Inukai [Tsuyoshi, 1855–1932] is doing his utmost for the sake of constitutional government, the prefecture of Fukuoka has forsaken it. All of this fills them, they tell us, with regret and indignation.

What they say may be true, but even so, all these appeals for more popular rights or for the development of constitutional rule were made in hopes of the growth of state power, of the enhancement of national prestige. Such being our goal, we have to adopt workable and desirable means to that end. Past choices, even when excellent, must sometimes be abandoned and changed. Some things cannot be changed, others can. At the foundation of all our activities lies national prestige. We do not, however, exclude the possibility that modifications may need to be made. It is because the Genyōsha was hoping that popular rights would contribute to the development of the state that we advocated these rights. Once the Constitution was promulgated and the Diet established, the popular rights parties failed to realize that the state was being surrounded on all sides by formidable enemies, and increasingly looked down upon by foreigners. They remained absorbed in futile debate. Thus the Genyōsha cast away the theory of popular rights like a pair of worn-out sandals. This time it decided to rely on a statist doctrine, and strove to fend off foreign enemies by preparing the country for military action and strengthening its army. The essential aim of the Genyōsha is not to engage in political conflict, but to prepare itself for dealing with major events on the foreign affairs front. How could those men who go wherever our country's changing fortunes require them, spare the time to mull over niceties such as the honor of having initiated constitutional rule? Such is the situation.

Initially, the [future founders of the] Genyōsha had [in 1877] violently opposed the Meiji government by staging an armed revolt against it [reference to a revolt in Fukuoka in support of the Satsuma Rebellion in the South of Kyushu, which was soon crushed by government troops]. Fighting the leaders of the *han* cliques (*hanbatsu*), the Genyōsha did all it could to reform the government. While belonging to the violent strand of [domestic] opposition, it was also hawkish on foreign policy issues. When it mobilized in response to the outbreak of the Satsuma Rebellion, however, the main force of this violent opposition died in battle. Still, the survivors continued to attack the government, stubbornly refusing to discard their ideals of political reform. As soon as they realized that democratic theory was the most practical way of attacking the government, they devoted their entire energy to that cause. However, when it came to foreign policy, they remained true to the will of Ochi [Hikojirō] and Takebe [Shōjirō], without ceding an inch. Compared to a political faction that takes internal policy as a priority, the Genyōsha does indeed take a vociferous stance as a hawkish group. It has dealt some severe blows to the enemy fortress of the cliquish tyranny, and brought it down.

When it finally saw that domestic order was being restored, it gradually started shifting to activities abroad. The dispatching of its members to Shanghai for study, or for extensive exploration work in Manchuria and Korea, has nothing to do with scholarly diligence or travelling for pleasure. Its sole purpose is to prepare for the day when the state will get itself involved in some [foreign] incident. The Genyōsha has sent missions to Korea, and has attempted to initiate great changes on the peninsula; it has given shelter to Korean exiles; and it carried out an attack on [Foreign Minister] Ōkuma [Shigenobu] in Kasumigaseki [in 1889]. It has also been involved in the foundation of the Tenyūkyō [see commentary]; Uchida [Ryōhei]'s reconnaissance tour of Europe and Asia; the foundation of the Kokumin Dōmeikai, the Tairo Dōshikai and the Manchurian volunteer corps; the offering of shelter to Chinese exiles, and assistance to the [Chinese] revolution—all of which demonstrates the commitment of the Genyōsha to the national interest, particularly in the sphere of foreign affairs.

Aah, let Imperial Virtue be established in every place where horses' hoofs can venture, and let its light enlighten all places that are covered in darkness, just as It illuminates the stem of our vessel wherever it is headed. Putting its modest forces on the line, the Genyōsha will always strive to do its bit for the advancement of the state. Could any of its efforts fail to be devoted to the Magnificent Splendor of Our Emperor?. . . . For the sake of His Splendor we shall devote ourselves to the Great Way of the Divine Wish, to the learning of the wise men of the past and to those who take our future to heart.

When we examine our ancient sacred texts, we find this written in the *Kojiki* ["Records of Ancient Matters," a collection of ancient Japanese myths compiled in the eighth century]:

> . . .The small country shall become vast, the steep-hilled land stretching out flatly. Far shall His land reach, as if 80 nets had been thrown out and hauled in. He shall be the Divine Ruler, and all shall things come toward Him, goods will be brought to Him, in great quantity before the Divine Ruler. As mountain ranges they will be laid out in front of Him. His deeds are extraordinary, and all will hear and see. And thus will be His world, [the creation] of the Heavenly Imperial Grandchild. The whole world will come under His rule, unshaken as granite, eternal as bedrock.

These words are the true proof that our imperial lineage has been charged with the great task of founding the country and the grand mission of unifying the world. It is in them that we find the bold plans and heroic undertakings that the Japanese people (*minzoku*) are to carry out. Bold and heroic indeed are the plans and undertakings that have already been laid out for us! Now they must be executed with appropriate courage. Could anyone considering the maritime history of Japan's ancient past fail to be overwhelmed by the intrepidity of our Japanese ancestors? And look, in the present day we have made attack after attack on the Korean peninsula, on the northern frontiers, in Manchuria and Mongolia, in the Bohai Sea [also Gulf of Pechihli] area, in the archipelagos of the Southern Pacific. Indeed, the virtuous splendor of these feats has rivaled that of our ancestors.

Already during the Tokugawa era, the early modern period of national isolation [from the 1630s until 1854], one man was writing about Japan's policies regarding Manchuria and Mongolia, about unifying the world. In his [*Unai*] *Kondō Hisaku* [1823], Satō Nobuhiro [1769–1850] wrote:

The best way of invading other countries is to start with those areas that are weak and easy to conquer. Among the nations of the world, the territory that is the easiest to attack and conquer from our Imperial Land is China's Manchurian region. Separated from our San'in and Hokuriku, Dewa and Matsumae regions by a sea that is approximately 800 *li* [1 *li* = approx. 4 km] wide, it clearly cannot be too hard to stir up their forces. . . . Therefore, while it may be hard to tell when our Imperial Land shall achieve the conquest of Manchuria, there is no question that the day shall come when Manchuria shall fall into Japanese hands. In that case, we shall not only acquire Manchuria, but the whole land of China will be ripe for the taking. We shall acquire the Central Asian regions too, and surely we should also consider [taking] Korea and China as well.

In his *Sangoku Tsūran* [An Illustrated Description of Three Countries], in which he discusses the geography of Korea and the Ryukyu and Ogasawara archipelagoes, amongst other places, [the geographer] Hayashi Shihei [1738–1798] notes that "it is my intention that, should Japan's valiant warriors ever set out on an expedition and enter these three lands, they will have memorized these maps to put them to good use."

In the first volume of his *Shinron* [New Theses, 1825], Mito's Aizawa Yasushi [Seishisai, 1781–1863] states:

I let my humble thoughts dwell upon the Divine Land—the realm where the sun rises, where spirits are high, where the grandson of the sun goddess rules as supreme emperor since time immemorial. From the origin of time, he has been the leader of the earth and is to rule over all the countries of the world. It is a truly pleasant prospect that it cannot be long before he will reign over the whole universe, and there will be no limits to his benevolence. But today, Western barbarians are striding over the four seas with their filthy feet and trampling all nations. We have observed their steps, and wonder where they find the brutality to strive to overcome nations that are superior to their own.

In his *Yūshūroku* (Prison Records) [1854], Yoshida Shōin [1830–1859] states:

We must prepare ourselves immediately for military action, we must equip warships, we must increase the number of our guns. Lords of domains should be freed from their feudal duties and no time should be lost in conquering Kamchatka and

Okhotsk, and in winning the Ryukyu Islands. All the lords should assemble at the imperial court, launch an attack on Korea, acquire booty and present it to the court. When we once again prosper as in olden times, we should carve up Manchuria for ourselves in the north and take hold of Taiwan in the south. We should exhibit sufficient vigor to carry on and take possession of the Philippines. Following that, we shall take care of the people and raise valiant warriors. We shall guard ourselves carefully and fortify the border regions. Would this not be considered the most effective way of defending our country?

These are indeed his words, and more of the same is found in his *Gokuzechō* [Prison Notes]: "In the meantime we must nurture our national forces, subdue those regions that are easy to conquer—Korea, Manchuria and China—and get compensation for the losses we are suffering in trading with Russia and America by taking this land in Manchuria and Korea."

Hashimoto Sanai [1834–1859] advocated a similar policy: "All things considered, it will be very hard for Japan to maintain its independence. This can only be achieved by annexing Manchuria and Kamchatka and Korea. In fact, there is little hope of success unless we can gain control of some territories in the Americas or the Indian interior."

And Hirano Jirō [Kuniomi, 1828–1864], sage and fellow member of the Genyōsha, urged the following course in his *Kaiten kanken saku* (Personal Opinions and Plans for Prodigious Efforts):

First we have to restore our protectorate in Mimana [a reference to an ancient state in the south of the Korean peninsula that presumably had close relations with states on the Japanese archipelago], opposing the three [ancient] Korean kingdoms [Silla, Baekje, and Goguryeo]. Thus we shall restore our past dominance [in Korea]. Then we shall attack Bokkai [Balhae or Bohai, an ancient/early medieval kingdom in the north of Korea and Manchuria, 698–926] for its refusal to pay tribute, set up camps there for our generals and troops and assemble a commercial fleet. Then when we reach Dinghai [a city on the island of Zhoushan] and Hong Kong, we shall investigate the customs of the barbarians and send special detachments of Korean ground troops; we shall thus subdue that unruly bunch, chasing them as falcons chase sparrows—straddling huge warships, we shall trample the hoards of barbarians. We shall overturn the present world order and turn the "resplendent center" [China] into vile barbarians; we shall bring heaven down and put the earth on top, we shall punish and kill in every region. Shall the Imperial Benevolence not then burst forth in limitless profusion?

Thus our ancestors already had the courage and the vision. Should we then bow down before a world full of uncertainty and fear? In our view, Korea has already come back to us, along with Manchuria—the first steps have been made, and the doors have been opened to our exploitation and expansion in the south. How then could we not push forward?

Chapter Four

Kōa—Raising Asia:
Arao Sei and Inoue Masaji

Michael A. Schneider

Kōa (literally "raising Asia") is one of the key concepts in the pan-Asianist lexicon. It is, however, an ambiguous term, implying both an enlightened and a prospering Asia while reserving the task of raising Asia in one country's hands: Japan. The term became associated with the pan-Asianist movement with the founding of the Kōakai (Raising Asia Society) in 1880 (see I:2). The translated selection here, written at the height of the Sino-Japanese War (1894–1895), shows that staunch advocates of *kōa* could not resist attaching significance to Japan's leadership role. The author of the passage, Arao Sei (Kiyoshi, 1859–1896), and his disciple and biographer, Inoue Masaji (1876–1946), are emblematic of the movement (see Nagami 1942 for an outline of Inoue's life). They were young, interested in language study, and eager for travel and adventure in Asia. They believed that education about Asia and commercial development constituted the two pillars of any *kōa* policy. No matter how fervently they believed other Asian societies would benefit from Japanese policies designed to raise Asia, they also were convinced that Japan must be the leader of Asia. For this reason, much of the early rhetoric of *kōa* was easily recycled within official justifications for Japan's war in China in the 1930s, with Arao's disciple Inoue supporting that cause.

As an early spokesman for *kōa*, Arao Sei occupies an important, if occasionally mythical, position in the history of pan-Asian thought. Not only did he offer persuasive rhetoric on behalf of the movement, but he also worked to create institutional bases to support his rhetoric. Arao was born to a high-ranking samurai family in central Japan. He received extensive education in foreign languages before entering the Military Academy, from which he graduated in 1882. Rising in military rank, he eventually was attached to the General Staff as an interpreter and spy. In 1887, he famously used the cover of bookstore manager in Hankou (Hankow), China, to carry out his surveillance activities.

While there, he became convinced that the task of raising Asia demanded serious Japanese study of Chinese language and society in order for trade relations to move forward. To this end, in 1890, Arao established the Institute for Sino-Japanese Commercial Research (Nisshin Bōeki Kenkyūjo) in Shanghai. Since key individuals within the Institute went on to help establish the East Asian Common Culture Academy (Tōa Dōbun Shoin, see I:9), Arao's Institute is regarded as the direct forerunner of the latter, more famous school. Arao contracted bubonic plague and died in Taiwan at age thirty-eight, with, according to legend, the words "The East . . . the East" on his lips.

Inoue Masaji has the unusual distinction of appearing at the fringes of many important events in modern Japanese history but almost never playing a central role in them. Born Adachi Masaji in Kagoshima, he aspired to a naval career. He quit naval school in 1894, however, when a reorganization of the naval schools closed off any possibility of Masaji climbing to the upper command ranks. He wandered back to Kyushu, consulting with friends in the Liberal Party (Jiyūtō) and the Genyōsha (see I:3) about his future. These conversations eventually put him in contact with Arao. In 1895, he spent eight months as a close disciple of Arao, engaging in intense study of Chinese language and discussion of Asian issues. In the same year, Masaji married Inoue Hide and assumed the family name of Inoue (see II:28). Arao helped Inoue secure an appointment as an interpreter in the Taiwan Government-General, launching his career as an Asian specialist. After a few years in Taiwan and China, he returned to study at Waseda University and participated in the launching of several pan-Asian societies such as the Tōakai (East Asia Society, 1898), the Kokuryūkai (1901, see I:10), and the East Asian Common Culture Society (Tōa Dōbunkai, see I:9). He would spend the next twenty years serving in various governmental and semigovernmental posts while traveling in Taiwan, Korea, China, central Asia, and Europe. He gradually developed an interest in Southeast Asia and achieved financial success through investments in a Malay rubber plantation. By the 1920s, Masaji had turned away from Asian development and began espousing internationalist views consistent, in his mind, with Japan's evolving needs as an economically expanding power. He headed a government-supported effort to send Japanese emigrants to central and South America to alleviate Japan's alleged population problem. He also served one term (1924–1929) in the Diet without party affiliation. The Manchurian Incident in 1931 reignited his interest in the continent. He spent the last fifteen years of his life writing books on his early years in the *kōa* movement in hopes of inspiring a renaissance of youthful activism and commitment to Pan-Asianism. Among Inoue's many writings was a 1910 biography of his teacher, in which Inoue summarized Arao's pan-Asian views and rationalized the 1910 Japanese annexation of Korea as necessary for pan-Asian resistance to Western colonialism. In this passage, Inoue quotes Arao's views on *kōa* as articulated during the Sino-Japanese War, about a year before Arao's untimely death.

Source (translation from the Japanese original by Michael A. Schneider) Inoue Masaji (1910), *Kyojin Arao Sei. Tsuketari Jūni Resshiden* (The Giant Arao Sei. Including Lives of Twelve Patriots). Sakura Shobō, 145–57.

ARAO SEI'S VIEWS ON THE KŌA POLICY [1895]

The two continents of Europe and Asia are distinguished by Western and Eastern culture. White and yellow constitute two fundamentally different races. The so-called Eastern Advance of Western power must surely mean a clash between the two. Therefore, the frailty of Korea should be deeply lamented, not for what it means for Korea, but what it means for our country. The senility of the Qing dynasty [Ch'ing, 1644–1911], whatever it means for them, should be sharply deplored for what it means to us. We must stand together as three countries and rely on each other, staking our domestic order and national prestige before the whole world, in order to show reverence to the supreme morality of our Imperial Ancestors. We must aid those who are enfeebled, assist those who have become relics, and thus reverse the decline of East Asia. There is no more urgent task than to spread our influence, chastise the European beast, and block their extravagant demands. This is truly a long-term commitment of the state, a task of great urgency that we cannot neglect for even a single day. . . .

How should we do this? It is said that there is nothing better than being in accord with the will of Heaven, and no better words than those spoken in accord with the will of Heaven. Only by assisting those who are feeble and making them strong, only by restoring those that are antiquated and making them vigorous will our Empire's mission and the [current] undertaking be in accord with Heaven's will. When we send troops to Korea to bolster its independence, it is to fulfill our mission. When we send a punitive force and try to chastise the hubris of the Qing Court, we are working to achieve our mission. Virtue must triumph over vice, and the vigorous must prevail over the decrepit. . . . Once the end of hostilities is announced and Qing understands our true aims, even the ignorant Qing must surely recognize that our plan to promote Korean independence and prosperity is the first step in securing the peace and prosperity of East Asia. When this truly occurs, not only will they no longer view us as an enemy, but rather will assist us and collaborate in this great Eastern enterprise. Not only will we achieve our aim of assisting Korea, but moreover we will arouse the Qing and incite radical reform there. In this way, through extraordinary resolve and perseverance, they can rid themselves of a century's worth of evils. Were they to restore their wealth and power as the center of the continent, clarify their administration and education, and open the paths of employment and promotion, they would dramatically capture the world's attention for enhancing their national prestige and prosperity while also leading a resurgence of their human talents and institutions.

Chapter Five

Tarui Tōkichi's *Arguments on Behalf of the Union of the Great East,* 1893

Kyu Hyun Kim

Tarui Tōkichi (1850–1922), the author of *Arguments on Behalf of the Union of the Great East* (*Daitō gappōron*), was an activist, journalist, and, later, politician whose career was devoted to the causes of antigovernment activism, continental expansionism, and socialism.

Tarui was born on 25 May 1850 in Reianji Village (today's Gojō City, Nara Prefecture) to the household of timber merchant Tarui Yōsuke. By his late childhood, his father's business seems to have gone into decline as a result of the flooding of the Yoshino River. As a youth Tarui was attracted to the "Revere the Emperor and Expel the Barbarians" (*sonnō jōi*) movement, inspired by the proimperial (i.e. anti-Shogunate) terrorist activities of the loyalist group Tenchūgumi (1863). He moved to Tokyo following the overthrow of the Tokugawa Shogunate and the Meiji Restoration of 1868, but instead of seeking a job in the new government, he enrolled in the private academy run by Inoue Yorikuni (1839–1914), a well-known Kokugaku (nativism) scholar. In 1875, Tarui and a group of like-minded young journalists founded *Hyōron Shinbun*, a journal highly critical of the new government. Two years later, the Satsuma Rebellion under Saigō Takamori spurred Tarui to travel around the northeastern region of Japan in an effort to recruit volunteers to rise up against the government. Little came of these efforts, however.

In 1879, Tarui embarked on a fanciful trip to locate a deserted island near the southern coast of Japan off the Korean peninsula, allegedly with the intention of establishing a political base from which to attack the Korean court—an action that he hoped would lead to the formation of a reformist government in Korea. After nearly three years of fruitless wandering, Tarui returned to political activism in Japan and founded the Tōyō Shakaitō (Oriental Socialist Party) in Nagasaki in 1883. Although its membership was small, Tarui and other party leaders immediately became the target of government suspicions. Within a month of its formation, the party was ordered to disband. Later—ostensibly to "aid" Kim Ok-kyun (1851–1894), the Korean reformist exiled in Japan—Tarui, Tōyama Mitsuru of the Genyōsha (Black Ocean Society, see I:3), and other advocates of adventurism abroad hatched various clandestine schemes to intervene in Korean politics. These machinations eventually ensnared Tarui in the so-called Osaka Affair (1885), along with the renowned champion of the Popular Rights Movement, Ōi Kentarō (1843–1922). Tarui was arrested, but he pleaded not guilty to the charge of aiding Ōi's party to prepare explosive devices, and was acquitted.

Arrested again in 1887 for joining a populist campaign opposed to Foreign Minister Inoue Kaoru's (1836–1915) plans to revise Japan's unequal treaties with the Western powers, Tarui was pardoned by the Meiji Emperor on the occasion of the promulgation of the Imperial Constitution in 1889. In 1892, he won a seat in the newly created Imperial Diet. A year later he published *Daitō gappōron*. Tarui is nowadays best known for this work, written in classical Chinese (*kanbun*), which since its first publication has appeared in several editions, including a translation into modern Japanese (in Takeuchi 1963a). By the mid-1890s Tarui's political career appears to have petered out—although the second edition of *Daitō gappōron* came out only one month prior to the annexation of Korea in 1910, endorsing Japanese policy there. Afterwards, he tried his hand at various business ventures, including mining interests in Manchuria and Korea and investment in the development of Mongolia, but none of them seems to have been successful. He died in 1922 in poverty and mostly forgotten by the public.

The life and thought of Tarui Tōkichi has never experienced the revival of interest in postwar Japanese academic circles akin to that accorded, say, to Ueki Emori (1857–1892)—although, like Ōi Kentarō, his credentials as a pioneer of socialism kept his star from fading into total obscurity. Tanaka Sōgorō's book *Tōyō Shakaitō-kō* (Tanaka 1930), which is focused largely on Tarui's role in the introduction of socialist thought in late nineteenth-century Japan, remains the most detailed biographical study of Tarui. The noted Marxist historian Hirano Yoshitarō (1897–1980) championed Tarui Tōkichi as one of the Asianist visionaries who anticipated the ideology of the Greater Asian Co-Prosperity Sphere (see II:30), used to justify the Pacific War as the struggle for the liberation of Asia from Western colonial domination (Hirano 1945).

In contrast, in his influential essay on Asianism, the noted Sinologue Takeuchi Yoshimi (1910–1977, see II:35) denounced the ideology underlying the Co-Prosperity Sphere as a charade, distinguishing it from early forms of Pan-Asianism as represented by the writings of Tarui. While acknowledging that Asianism in Japan ultimately embraced expansionism and the promotion of war against fellow Asians, Takeuchi nonetheless found hints of egalitarian solidarity in Tarui's campaign for the union of Japan and Korea (Takeuchi 1963b; see also II:35). On the other hand, Hatada Takashi, a specialist in Korean history, while acknowledging the germ of egalitarian solidarity among Asian peoples in Tarui's thought, rejects the view that this could have served as a counterideology to the Meiji state's imperialist designs; he points to the *Daitō gappōron*'s unconditional acceptance of the Treaty of Ganghwa (Kanghwa, 1875), enforced by Japan's gunboat diplomacy, as an act of "benevolent guidance" (Hatada 1969).

To some extent, it is not surprising that the *Daitō gappōron* has given rise to such divergent interpretations since the text is hardly a model of coherent argumentation. Indeed, his contemporaries noted that Tarui's life showed a pattern of ideological inconsistency. Despite his close association with activists from the Popular Rights Movement, for example, one of his earliest appeals to the Meiji government rejected democratic elections as a means of constituting the national legislature (Tanaka 1930: 82). Tarui begins *Daitō gappōron* with a general discussion of the historical evolution of nation-states, a process through which the superiority of independent, sovereign nations with constitutional governments over other forms of political community has in his view been unquestionably demonstrated. Here, his language and ideas fit quite well with the mainstream views espoused by the Popular Rights Movement in the 1880s—characterized by unquestioning support for the idea of historical progress from barbarism to civilization, an emphasis on the "independent spirit of the people" as the determining qualification for building a nation-state, and "despotism" as an absolute evil to be overcome by any means.

Having established that Japan had successfully transformed itself into a constitutional state, Tarui delineates his main point—that Meiji Japan should form a union (*gappō*) with Chosŏn Korea, a country still under monarchical rule and having only recently gained "independence" (via Japan's intervention) from Qing (Ch'ing) China. He painstakingly refutes potential objections to such a union. Yes, Tarui acknowledges, the Korean court is weak, its politics chaotic and the Korean people ignorant and lacking in the spirit of independence. However, none of these problems is insurmountable. If the Koreans were to live with the Japanese under the same roof, they would have much to learn from them, and their customs, habits, and predispositions would be improved accordingly. They would soon be able to make a positive contribution of their own—for instance, as superb soldiers protecting their borders against Russian aggression, given their large physiques and physical strength (Tarui 1975: 120).

Tarui, however, has few concrete proposals on the mechanics of a Japan–Korea union. After listing European and American examples of the federal system of government—from ancient Greece to Germany, Switzerland, and the United States—he merely notes that matters relating to the union between Korea and Japan should be recorded in a federal constitution, that there should be provisions for its amicable dissolution, and that such a union would be consistent with the global trend toward larger alliances of sovereign nations, perhaps one day resulting in a world government. In the final section of *Daitō gappōron*, Tarui expands his argument to propose an alliance between a unified Japan–Korea and China—an important step toward the construction of a pan-Asian federation he dubs the "Great East (Daitō)." In the terminology he uses, Tarui is careful to distinguish union (*gappō*) from alliance (*gasshō*)—a term apparently derived from a classical Chinese reference to the alliance of six states against Qin Shi Huang (259–210 BC) during the Warring States period (476–221 BC). The same term was also adopted by some later pan-Asian writers (see introduction). In other respects, however, Tarui is inconsistent in his naming of the unified Japan and Korea, as well as the larger entity proposed to incorporate Japan, Korea, and China—he regularly employs the term "Eastern Nation" (*tōkoku*), for instance, to designate Japan–Korea in contradistinction to Qing China.

In this section of the book, Tarui draws heavily on concepts of race and ethnicity as well as on social Darwinist notions of conflict and competition as engines of progress. At one point he chastises the Chinese for giving the cold shoulder to the Japanese, who are of the "same race," in favor of the British. His argument for a Sino–Japanese alliance is also marked by a certain geopolitical mind-set, stressing the strategic advantages Qing China could gain with Japan as its ally against the might of the British and Russian naval forces.

Takeuchi is probably correct in claiming that Tarui (along with other former Popular Rights activists with a strong Asianist bent) genuinely struggled to formulate a type of political relationship based on solidarity and fraternity and thus should not be dismissed as a mere stooge of the Meiji imperialists. The real question, however, is whether such a formulation was ever successful. If Tarui's *Daitō gappōron* is to serve as evidence, we must conclude that the enterprise was a failure.

The issue is not, as is sometimes construed, whether Tarui's intentions were good—whether he was genuinely idealistic and not concealing the cold calculations of Realpolitik behind talk of "international public law (*bankoku kōhō*)," that is, Western-style international law. The real issue is that Tarui's text lacks any attempt to understand the perspective of the Koreans. His repeated emphasis on the equality of Japan and Korea cannot disguise the unquestioning supremacy of Japan as an *a priori* assumption. Tarui simply states that Koreans should be grateful for the chance to claim Japan as their own country—a nation far superior to Korea in terms of climate, the fertility of the land, and the beauty of the landscape, not to mention Japan's international status and the superior qualities of its government (Tarui 1975: 122). Despite the text's stated purpose of persuading Koreans of the necessity for union, it makes little effort to regard them as active subjects; a few "exceptional" individuals like Kim Ok-kyun notwithstanding, Koreans are seen as "uncivilized people in need of Japanese help" to achieve modernization and political autonomy. In Tarui's text, Koreans come packaged in racial stereotypes ("big bodies, fit for soldiering"), notions reinforced through unflattering comparisons with Western modernity. In other words, *Daitō gappōron* is essentially a monologue: an inward-looking text of reflection and strategy building by a Japanese political activist seeking the means to strengthen his fledgling modern nation by finding the least morally objectionable and costly way of "dealing with" the "Korea problem." It is hardly helpful, whether in terms of the perspectives of the 1890s or today, to view the possibilities inherent in the Japan–Korea relationship of that era exclusively as the "Korea problem."

Source (translation from the classical Chinese [*kanbun*] original by Kyu Hyun Kim)
Tarui Tōkichi (1893), *Daitō Gappōron* (*Arguments on Behalf of the Union of the Great East*), reprinted in *Fukkoku Daitō Gappōron* (Chōryō Shorin/ Wakatsuki Shoten, 1975); the translation into modern Japanese by Takeuchi Yoshimi (in Takeuchi 1963a: 106–29) has been consulted.

INTRODUCTION

From the East rises the Sun. It is the source of growth and harmony. The Guardian of the East is the Blue Dragon. Its Virtue is Benevolence. In terms of the quarters of the day, it corresponds to the morning. In terms of the four seasons, it represents spring. The Five Elements originate from the East. So do the Seven Constellations. If we divide the Earth into East and West, the Western hemisphere contains North and South America, two great continents, whereas in the Eastern hemisphere reside three great continents, Asia, Africa and Europe. Asia is located to the east of Europe and Africa, and Japan and Korea in turn are at its easternmost limits. This is the reason why Japanese and Koreans are endowed with temperaments rich in generosity and love, as well as with a spirit of directness and innovation. It is only natural that their characters and customs are free from the autumnal gloom typical of the Northwestern peoples. Japan has always cherished harmony and indeed established it as its major principle of statecraft. Korea has done the same with benevolence. Harmony means sharing the needs of others; benevolence is the virtue of treating others as one treats oneself. Given this, friendship between Japan and Korea should arise naturally out of their respective temperaments, and nothing should be able to stop it.

Then why is it that such a relationship of friendship between Japan and Korea remains unrealized? A Westerner once claimed, "A nation is a person without the physical form." Immature youngsters cannot grasp the feelings of love between man and woman. Such is the case with nations as well. Without attaining a certain level of enlightenment, true feelings of friendship cannot arise between nations. Even if the general atmosphere is favorable, their peoples cannot dispel mutual suspicion and unease. This is why Japan and Korea are still estranged from one another. . . .

Today, the world is going through a constant process of renewal. A trip of a thousand *li* takes only a day to complete, while messages can be delivered from one country to another in a matter of moments. An immeasurable distance during ancient times is, today, nothing more than a stone's throw. Countries with mutually incompatible customs in ancient times can, today, become close associates. The territories of Japan and Korea are as close to each other as the lips are to the teeth, while their respective attributes are like the two wheels of a cart. Their feelings toward each other are like those of siblings, while their moral relationship resembles that of close friends. Moreover, the two nations are moving into the realm of enlightenment. Why should we still be suspicious of each other? The dawning light of Eastern Civilization already shines upon these two nations, yet they have not quite awakened from their confused dreams. Those who cling to the old habits have not understood the duties of those living in the present era. They must work toward fulfilling their duties by pursuing cooperation and mutual aid between the two nations. One finger cannot grasp an object. One leg cannot walk on its own. If we truly seek to enlarge our knowledge and enter into the realm of enlightenment, there is no better way [to achieve this] than by both nations binding themselves to an agreement and becoming a single united entity. . . .

CHANGES IN THE WORLD ORDER

The origins of human society are to be found in the coming together of barbarous peoples. Likewise, the current competition among powerful nations is a sign of the forthcoming unification of the world into a single nation. Today, the White race is the one possessing poisoned talons and sharp fangs. It aspires to be the First Emperor of Qin [the dynasty that first unified China in 221 BC] in today's world. We, the Yellow race, in comparison, are merely satisfied with being relegated to the position of the Six Nations [of pre-Qin China]. What can I say about this situation? I say we should not be satisfied with the status of the Six Nations. We must actively develop plans to overcome this new Qin. . . .

FUNDAMENTALS OF NATIONAL POLITICS

. . . In order for a state (*kokka*) to be a complete entity, it must possess four essential elements: territorial boundaries, fixed residences for its people, institutions of governance, and autonomous sovereignty. The lack of any of the above elements disqualifies an area from being a state. . . . Sovereignty refers to a state's ability to deal with both internal and external affairs on its own, without subordinating itself to the dictates of another state. Autonomy or independence refers to the ability of a state to fully claim its sovereignty. Even if a state pays tribute to another, as long as its sovereignty is intact it should be considered independent. Conversely, if a state is not bound to a tributary relationship but is forced to rely on another nation to exercise its rights, it is only semi-independent. This is one of the basic rules of international relations. . . .

Our country, Japan, has reflected on the history of the world and established a constitutional government for itself. Its administration has been put in proper order, and its culture is flourishing. Yet, even now, we Japanese are not always free from suffering and shame. This is because our abilities are not sufficiently advanced, nor has the power of our nation yet grown strong enough. For a people, there is no greater source of suffering than poverty. For a nation, there is no greater shame than being insignificant. The suffering and shame felt by the Korean people, still living under monarchical despotism, are familiar to us Japanese. If we can share these same feelings with the Koreans, what could stop us from being their sympathetic allies? . . .

Take a look at the Western nations, by way of comparison. Those who refer to the most powerful nation in today's world always point to Britain. Britain consists of a union of three countries. Those who refer to the most morally upright government point to the United States of America. The United States is likewise formed of forty-four states [*sic*]. It is only natural that people hate oppression and love freedom. A Western saying goes, "Freedom is the wind that blows down from the mountains of Germany." Not surprisingly, Germany is a constitutional federation as well. The Korean government is like a field of grain eaten by worms and overrun by weeds. It goes without saying that a union (*gappō*) with our constitutional government will eliminate their accumulated vices and ultimately guarantee the safety of the country and the happiness of its people. A union is achieved through the mutual harmony (*kyōwa*) of two nations. A union of constitutional governments, in particular, is energized by the sense of honor and superior morality of both parties. Among all forms of government, therefore, nothing is better and more beautiful than a constitutional federation. . . .

ADVANTAGES AND DISADVANTAGES OF A UNION

There are those in Japan who would object to a union between their own nation and Korea. They cite many reasons. First, they argue that Korea is poor and weak. Uniting with Korea would mean loss of wealth and prestige for the Japanese. Second, Korean culture remains underdeveloped: its industry has not thrived and the education of its people has failed to advance. To form a union with such a country is akin to making friends with an ignorant person. Third, Korea shares a border with Russia and Qing China. Any union with Korea would result in Japan having to pay for the defense of the border regions. Fourth, leading Korea into a state of enlightenment may well benefit the Koreans but will be a thankless burden for the Japanese. Fifth, Korea is cursed with a harsh and unpredictable climate, prone to droughts, flood and poor harvests. Japan will have to provide relief and rescue operations for these annual disasters once the two countries join together. Sixth, there is at present no political order in Korea, and its government is likely to experience a major upheaval in the immediate future; Japan will end up being entangled in it once it has merged with Korea. Seventh, Koreans lack the spirit of independence, and uniting with them will introduce elements of weakness into the Japanese character.

While all these critiques contain grains of truth, they ignore the obvious advantages of the union. Although Korea may be poor, it is around half the size of Japan. Its poverty results from the evils of its institutions. After union with Japan removes these drawbacks, Koreans will recover their ability to gain wealth for themselves. Examples from the past of poor nations which have reversed their fortunes are too numerous to mention. We must not allow our current prejudices to discount future possibilities. A nation's lack of cultural sophistication, as well as the stagnation of industry and education, are all matters subject to change. It was not long ago that we were ourselves pupils of the Korean literati, acquiring from them the knowledge on which our current success is based. For us to lead them toward enlightenment now would be nothing more than returning the favor—an act further justified by the fact that, half of the time, teaching is itself learning. The defense of the Korean territories is not only necessary for their own protection, but also critical for us. If Korea were to be invaded by another nation, we would not stand idly by, even if we had not yet formed a union with them. . . . Again, if the Koreans were to be struck by famine and death by starvation became commonplace, Japan would have to come to their aid, even if no formal union existed. A more rational course would be for Japanese and Koreans to jointly explore means of protecting the latter from natural disasters. Such action will ultimately reduce the cost of relief operations and add to the wealth of both [nations]. It is true that Korea shows signs of rebellion and other political troubles. However, such difficulties are always man-made. Reforming the political system through a union will result in the natural disappearance of these problems. The lack of a spirit of independence is merely a symptom of living in a small and weak nation. Joining us will make Korea strong and great again. In such circumstances, it is only natural that the spirit of independence will emerge among the Korean people.

A union with Korea will greatly benefit trade relations with Russia and Qing China. This is the first advantage of such a union. Koreans are large-bodied and physically strong. Trained by our military, and taught to use our weapons, they would defend us from the Russian bandits. This is the second advantage. In any case, Japan and Korea are geographically close. There is no good reason for remaining separate from one another. Now, some Japanese have been clamoring for a military expedition to Korea (*seikanron*). Subjugating Korea through warfare would not only result in the depletion of national strength on our part, but would also give rise to feelings of vengeful resentment by the Koreans. Despite being well aware of this, some continue to advocate this path, afraid that some other nation might occupy Korea in Japan's stead. The outcome of a peaceful union would be so much more favorable than any military conquest. By means of the grand public act known as a union, we could obtain Korea without employing military means. The Koreans, too, would gain Japan without any fighting. The lives of many soldiers would be spared, with only the glory of a single general diminished. All the resources set aside for war could now be used to develop Korea. Korean resentment would be replaced by a deep feeling of gratitude. How can anyone say that this union would not be beneficial to Japan?

I am not yet aware of Korean opinion regarding a union with Japan. Considering the current state of affairs in Korea, the notion would probably be rejected outright. At one time, the Koreans put up a manifesto in each province stating, "Foreign invaders must be met with armed struggle. Those who advocate peace are traitors." With an attitude like this, any discussion of a union with a foreign nation is likely to fall on deaf ears. However, the real meaning of these statements is that a foreign enemy must be fought, and a foreign friend given a friendly welcome. Japan is certainly not an enemy of Korea. We have no reason to fight Korea. How could seeking peace with Japan then be regarded as treason? . . . In terms of its climate, the fertility of the soil, the beauty of the landscape and international status, Japan is far superior to Korea. To be united with such a nation can only benefit Koreans. When we consider the standard of government, there is simply no comparison between the two nations. The benefits that would result from the union for the Koreans are too great to enumerate adequately. . . .

WHY QING CHINA SHOULD FORM AN ALLIANCE WITH THE EASTERN NATION [THE UNITED JAPAN AND KOREA]

. . . A federation can only work if the participant nations maintain their independence, and their peoples participate equally in the greater government of the united national entity. The union between Japan and Korea must follow this principle. Any union with Qing China should also be nothing less than this. However, in the case of China, this is not feasible. If the Qing court were to form a union with the Eastern Nation [the united Japan and Korea], it must give not only Han Chinese but also Tartars, Mongolians and Tibetans independent status, so that they can participate in federal politics on an equal basis. . . . Otherwise, the principle of equal participation will be undermined, resulting in movements for secession among the aggrieved parties. In the current situation, it is clear that the present Qing court will never allow the independence of these ethnic groups. Given that this is not the right time to seek union with Qing China, we should proceed to build an alliance (*gasshō*) with it, in order to defend our dignity against other races. . . .

If Qing China rejects the path of friendship with the Eastern Nation, both parties will fall prey to terrible consequences. Westerners recognize two powerful nations in East Asia: Japan and China. It is fortunate that Japan and China exist in East Asia to maintain the dignity of the Yellow race. Without them, the White race would have violated the whole of Asia and made slaves out of our yellow-skinned brethren, just as they have done with the African blacks. . . . Sadly, the Qing court has been forced to endure intolerable indignities from the British ever since the Opium War. Australia and Canada levy poll taxes on the Chinese upon entry to their ports. And yet the Qing court does not question these practices. It simply defies commonsense: why would the Qing court show such friendliness to the British, an alien race, and such hostility to the Japanese, who belong to the same race as them? . . .

Provided that Qing China comes to share our objective [to liberate Asians from the domination of the white race], then together we can plan the colonization of the islands of the South Pacific, showering the indigenous peoples with the benefits of civilization. Within only a few decades, we will come to form a great federation of the Yellow race. Then, we, the Yellow race—blessed with fertile soil and many times more numerous than the White race—will become the most formidable force in the world.

Chapter Six

Konoe Atsumaro and the Idea of an Alliance of the Yellow Race, 1898

Urs Matthias Zachmann

In the New Year issue of 1898, the popular magazine *Taiyō* (The Sun) published a short piece titled "Dō-jinshu dōmei, tsuketari Shina mondai kenkyū no hitsuyō" (An Alliance of the Same Race and the Necessity of Studying the Chinese Question), authored by one of the most illustrious figures of late Meiji society, the president of the House of Peers and principal of the Gakushūin, Prince Konoe Atsumaro (1863–1904). In the first part of this article, Konoe evoked the apocalyptic vision of a final battle between the "white" and the "yellow" races, which the latter—including Japan—could survive only by forming a racial alliance. In the second, much shorter part, Konoe argued for the necessity of gathering intelligence and strengthening personal ties with the political elite in China. Today, the article is celebrated for its idea of a racial alliance and, in fact, has almost assumed canonical status as a text of Japanese Pan-Asianism. However, considering the circumstances of its origin, the immediate reception of the text, and Konoe's further conduct, it is safe to say that the pragmatic program of the article outlined in the latter part was much more characteristic of (institutional) Japanese Pan-Asianism than the visionary first part of the document.

The international background for Konoe's text was formed by two major developments—the so-called Triple Intervention of 1895, in which Russia, Germany, and France prevented Japan from annexing the strategically important Liaodong (Liaotung) peninsula as spoils of its victory in the Sino-Japanese War, and the Far Eastern Crisis of 1897–1898, which began with Germany's occupation of Jiaozhou (Kiaochow) and Russia's taking possession of Port Arthur (present Lushun) and Dalian (Dairen), the two most important bases on the Liaodong peninsula. These events led to momentary tensions among the Western powers, but the situation was resolved by Britain and France securing their own share of concessions on Chinese soil in

1898. Apart from obtaining a nonalienation commitment for Fujian (Fukien) province, the Japanese government held back in this scramble for concessions and, much to the real or feigned indignation of the opposition, also failed to protest against the Western powers' rapacious conduct. At the same time, the crisis had the effect of facilitating a rapprochement between China and Japan that, however, the Japanese government, the Foreign Ministry, and the military were intent on keeping on an informal level lest the Western powers should suspect a potentially threatening alliance between China and Japan that, in turn, would jeopardize Japan's relations with the West and prevent its recognition as a free and equal member of the comity of nations.

Konoe's was certainly not the only voice among the clamor of protest that, in this situation, called for a racial alliance of Asian nations against the Western powers. However, his was certainly the most prominent and contentious expression of this idea. Despite his young age of thirty-four, Prince Konoe owed his high standing to the illustrious lineage of his family and his proximity to the emperor. In fact, he was marked out for the premiership by the emperor, a position he would probably have attained had not death intervened at the age of forty. However, in the short time between the publication of this text in 1898 and his death in 1904, Konoe emerged as the leading figure in the Japanese pan-Asianist movement and, later, as the leader of pro-British and anti-Russian activism.

The immediate circumstances of the text can be traced through entries in Konoe's diary. Thus, on 25 November 1897, shortly after Germany's occupation of Jiaozhou became known in Japan, Toyabe Sentarō (Shuntei, 1865–1908), an editor of Taiyō, asked Konoe for a contribution to the magazine. On 9 December 1897, Toyabe visited the prince again, and together they drafted the text, Konoe dictating it to Toyabe. At around the same time, in August 1897, Konoe had two conversations that probably provided the intellectual stimulus for the two separate parts of the article. The first of these was with his new secretary, Ōuchi Yōzō (1874–1944), who had just come back from the United States, where he had studied law and politics. During the interview, as Konoe recorded, they talked about the "Eastern Question (Tōhō mondai) and the projects he [Ōuchi] is going to carry out." Decades later, Ōuchi recalled that, in this interview, he wanted to impress Konoe with the new ideas he had brought back from his studies abroad, especially with the notion of an ultimate racial contest (jinshu kyōsō) between East and West and "race (reesu) antagonism" in the Pacific (Ōuchi 1934: 145). Ōuchi had even written an essay on the subject and wanted to publish it. Curiously enough, Ōuchi recalled that at the time, Konoe had rejected the idea, insisting that there was only a "competition of cultures" and nothing else and even warning Ōuchi that no such thing should be published. There is always a possibility that Ōuchi fabricated this story after Konoe's death to take the brunt of the censure that the article elicited from the public, as we shall see; however, if this was not the case, Konoe very quickly changed his mind and published the idea of "race antagonism" under his own name.

Less problematic is the intellectual source of the second part of the article. On 26 November 1897, just a day after Konoe had been asked to write an article for *Taiyō*, he received a visit from Shiraiwa Ryūhei (1867–1942), a minor railway entrepreneur in China who was a disciple and devoted follower of Arao Sei (Kiyoshi) (see I:4). Shiraiwa had returned a few months earlier from China, where he had observed the political situation and recent attempts at reform. As a China hand more interested in Sino–Japanese economic coop-eration in a gradually developing political environment rather than in drastic political reform, Shiraiwa favored working with influential local politicians such as the governor-general of Hubei (Hopei) and Hunan, Zhang Zhidong (Chang Chih-tung, 1837–1909). Thus, it is very likely that the person who, in the second part of Konoe's text, is described as "somebody who has lately come back from China" and who comments extensively on the Chinese political situation, extolling especially Zhang as China's hope, is, in fact, Shiraiwa Ryūhei.

The two parts of Konoe's article met with different responses in Japan. Konoe's idea of a racial alliance elicited harsh protest. The newly launched magazine *Tenchijin* (Heaven, Earth, and Man), for example, severely criti-cized Konoe's "poetic" but pernicious sentiments in favor of China: rather than elevating China to a superior level of civilization, a racial alliance would invariably drag Japan back into the quagmire of Oriental stagnation (*Tenchijin*, 2 February 1898, 7–11). Ōkuma Shigenobu (1838–1922) in the same issue of the magazine derided the concept of a racial alliance as a "stu-pid idea" (*guron*) and, instead, strongly argued for an alliance with Britain. Finally, even *Taiyō* had to concede that the real criterion for alliances was strategy, not race.

However, even more damaging was the article's reception abroad. Konoe's thesis became known throughout Europe, and even local German news-papers published accurate accounts of it. For example, Nakamura Shingo (1870–1939), one of Konoe's most devoted followers who was studying law in Heidelberg at the time, sent Konoe news clippings from local and national newspapers and warned him about the negative impression that his article had created in Europe (Konoe Atsumaro Nikki Kankōkai 1968–1969, 2:47–52). Hence, in Europe, Konoe's name came to be invariably associated with the idea of an anti-Western racial alliance. For the Japanese government, the at-tention that the article received as an official statement by one of the most distinguished public figures in Japan seemed so damaging that it saw no other way than to publicly distance itself from Konoe. In Paris, the Japanese minister in France, Kurino Shin'ichirō (1851–1937), publicly declared that Konoe was "well known in Japan for the eccentricity of his political ideas. He is very young, very fanatical, has always sided with the opposition and belongs to the small chauvinist party which is hostile to foreigners. For the very reason of his noble birth and his family ties, the government has always treated him with the utmost respect and he is indeed the President of the House of Peers. However, one should not . . . overestimate his political influence" (Konoe Atsumaro Nikki Kankōkai 1968–1969, 2:49f). Thus, given a choice between slandering the emperor's protégé and prospective future prime minister and jeopardizing Japan's standing with the Western powers, the Japanese government chose the former as the lesser evil.

In addition, Konoe's text was also circulated in China. A translation appeared under the title "The Theory of a Same-Race Union" (*Tongzhong lianmeng-shuo*) in the Shanghai-based newspaper *Subao* in May 1898. Although the translation on the whole renders Konoe's arguments faithfully, the translator clearly tried to make it more palatable to Chinese readers. Thus, the most damning remarks on China are glossed over, and China's difficulties are presented merely as a temporary impasse. Moreover, the deliberate omission in the translation of Zhang Zhidong's name suggests that the translator was of a different political stripe. In fact, although the *Subao* was owned by a conservative, its contract authors had nationalist, revolutionary sympathies. How the paper's Chinese readership reacted to Konoe's proposition remains unknown.

Konoe soon seemed to have regretted his blunder and repeatedly recanted the idea of a racial alliance. Thus, already during his conversation with the exile Kang Youwei (1858–1927) in November 1898, Konoe made the famous (if somewhat tautological) declaration that "East Asia is the East Asia of East Asia" (*Tōyō wa Tōyō no Tōyō nari*) but immediately added that this should be understood as a sort of East Asian Monroe Doctrine—that is, in a geostrategic, not racial, sense. (By coincidence, 1898 was also the year of the Spanish-American War, which was seen in Japan as a parallel to the East Asian situation; hence, the Monroe Doctrine would become a catchphrase of Japanese Pan-Asianism; see I:28.) However, even more explicitly, Konoe disavowed his original idea on the occasion of the founding of the East Asia Common Culture Association (Tōa Dōbunkai), also in November 1898. As president of the new society, Konoe published an essay in the inaugural issue of the society's organ *Tōa Jiron* (The East Asian Times) in which he declared, "Today, I no longer claim that, because our empire and China share a common culture and a common race (*dōbun dōshu*), our empire should volunteer to shoulder China's fate by itself. I say that we should merely consider our own empire's destiny, decide an appropriate policy with a sense of urgency, respond to the opportunities and watch the changes around us, act with swift determination and thereby secure the advantages of the moment" (Konoe 1898b: 6). The newly founded Tōa Dōbunkai (see I:9) adhered closely to Konoe's new political pragmatism regarding China and concentrated on those objectives that Konoe, probably on Shiraiwa Ryūhei's advice, had proposed in the second part of his original text—gathering intelligence and creating personal networks with the Chinese elite. In fact, together with Konoe, Shiraiwa had been instrumental in founding one of the society's predecessors, the Same Culture Society (Dōbunkai), in June 1898 (Reynolds 1989: 224). In this sense, Konoe's vision of a pragmatic China strategy proved much more durable than his vision of a pan-Asianist racial alliance.

Source (translation from the Japanese original by Urs Matthias Zachmann) Konoe Atsumaro, "Dōjinshu Dōmei, Tsuketari Shina Mondai Kenkyū no Hitsuyō" (An alliance of the same race and the necessity of studying the Chinese question). *Taiyō*, 24:1 (1 January 1898), reprinted in Konoe Atsumaro Nikki Kankōkai (ed.), *Konoe Atsumaro Nikki*, supplement. Kajima Kenkyūjo Shuppankai, 1969, 62–63.

A SAME-RACE ALLIANCE AND ON THE NECESSITY OF STUDYING THE CHINESE QUESTION

In recent times, our brilliant victory in the [Sino-Japanese] war has made the Japanese proud in their hearts, and their contempt for the Chinese has become more and more extreme. In particular, the Japanese who reside in the various parts of China treat the Chinese with the same attitude as Western people display towards the Chinese. They believe that "Japan is the only civilized country in East Asia, and a more advanced country than China." Now, it is true that Japan is more advanced than China in that it has established civilized institutions and has a civilized education system. Therefore, it is very well placed to guide China and assist it by means of its advanced civilization. However, if we are mightily pleased with ourselves and boast of being such an advanced country, if we mock the Chinese people and put them to shame and, in return, earn their hostility, apart from the fact that such behavior runs counter to the generosity expected of an advanced country, does it not also create a massive impediment to the advancement of our China policy, and will the trouble this stores up for the future not also be very great? As I see it, in the future East Asia cannot avoid becoming a stage for a contest between the races (*jinshu kyōsō no butai*). Even if fleeting considerations of foreign policy should produce a different environment, this will yield no more than a temporary result. The final outcome will be a contest between the yellow and white races (*kōhaku ryō-jinshu no kyōsō*), and in this contest the Chinese people and the Japanese people will be placed in the same position, being both considered as the sworn enemy of the white race (*hakujinshu no kyūteki*). Those who are considering a long-term strategy will do well to consider these facts.

If we think about it, the policies of the European powers in recent times have been principally formulated to accomplish the subjugation of other races. Whether it is their strategy in Africa, or the colonization of Australia and the South Seas, or the opening up of South America—all these ventures bear evidence of racial subjugation. However, from the beginning the penetration of the Western powers into these undeveloped areas was characterized by an extreme imbalance of power. Thus, conquest was easy, just like felling a rotten tree or kicking someone who is down. This was almost tantamount to taking over uninhabited territory and does not represent the situation where we could speak of a contest between races. The European powers in this case vied with one another over the extent of their conquests and occupations, without investing much effort into subjugating the natives. Consequently, any such contest must be seen as one between the powers themselves, originating in European politics, rather than as a contest between races. This is the situation today. However, the position of the [Western] powers regarding the yellow race differs significantly from their attitude towards other undeveloped countries. On the one hand, they look down upon the countries of the yellow race, but at the same time they are deeply suspicious of the yellow race. In particular, seeing the prowess of the Japanese in the Sino-Japanese war, they have suddenly come to realize the difficulties of continuing to look down upon the yellow race, and, on the contrary, they are even showing signs that they fear it very much. In terms of material civilization, the yellow race is still lagging far behind the European powers and can, of course, in no way compete with them on this point. However, when it comes to the question of superiority in physical power and mental ability, this point cannot be so easily decided. After all, this is what the Europeans frequently say, too. Therefore, there is simply no way that the [Western] powers can confront the countries of the yellow race with the same attitudes they display when subjugating other undeveloped regions.

Some people say that the time for the partition of China (*Shina bunkatsu*) has come. Whether or not the [Western] powers intend to divide up China is a separate question which I will not discuss here. However, even if we assume that the danger of a partition of China is not immediately pressing, I believe that the process has already been set in motion and all the countries of the yellow race must set themselves to devise a strategy for the protection of their race. In other undeveloped regions, the [European] powers do not need to form alliances in response to racial competition, but in China they cannot exercise their powers as freely as they would in other undeveloped regions. Each power can easily subjugate such regions using no more than its own resources. However, if any country wished to subjugate China on its own, this would no doubt be much less easy than taking over some uninhabited territory. Therefore, the day on which the division of China becomes a reality will be the moment when an alliance between the [Western] powers comes into existence. The moment these powers form an alliance and divide up China, the final contest between the yellow and white races will have begun and, in this final confrontation, will the Japanese alone be able stay outside this dramatic struggle of racial competition?

I grieve at the frivolousness of the Japanese who, in unison with the Europeans, recklessly strike up the tune of China's demise (*midari ni Ōshūjin to gassō shite Shina bōkoku o utau keifu*). In principle, the fate of the government in Beijing need not unduly trouble the Japanese. However, the survival of the Chinese is certainly not somebody else's business, and touches on the vital interests of the Japanese. Therefore, the Japanese must make it a habit to treat the Chinese in a friendly manner, advance their progress through offers of help and guidance, concentrate on promoting their development and thus find ways of dispelling their suspicions and allaying their hostility as much as possible. Then the Chinese, too, will gradually draw closer to us and will find a heart to trust us, and in the process, I predict, an unspoken contract about the protection of [our] race will come to bind the two peoples.

A person who has recently returned from China told me: "As always, the government in Beijing stubbornly persists in its ignorance, and its hubris and conceit have not changed at all since former times. Not only has it not learnt from its defeat and shows no indication of reforming the civil and military systems, but, not yet having awakened from the old dream of China as the center of the world, apparently it is also oblivious to the danger which the state presently faces. However, powerful people outside Beijing have finally seen through the machinations of the tripartite alliance [*sangoku dōmei*, i.e., Russia, Germany, and France] and see that the retrocession of Liaodong has brought even greater misfortune for their country. The willingness of the Beijing government to fulfill the demands of Russia without the slightest resistance causes them no small grief. Zhang Zhidong is among those who are most unhappy about the situation. He is most intent on reforming China and talks about again setting up a partisan newspaper to alert the government and the people to what is happening [Zhang Zhidong financed the founding of the reformist newspaper *Shiwubao* in Shanghai]. His influence, too, is not to be underestimated. However, people living around Shanghai especially fear the ambition of the three powers, and their affinity with the Japanese grows stronger by the day." I believe that what this person says is not far from the truth. After all, this is what I foresaw as the inevitable course that matters would take a long time ago.

Therefore the Japanese now must take care about their response and determine a long-term policy through careful attention to the true nature of the Chinese Question (*Shina mondai*). They absolutely must not yield to the persuasions of the great powers and as a result lightly decide to turn their back on China. The important task today is, first of all, to study the Chinese Question. If we want to take this task seriously, all of us—whether politicians or other interested parties (*yūshika*)—should visit China, mingle with the country's elite and so reconcile the differences between the two countries. Or people should observe the customs and beliefs [of the people in general] while exploring the interior and thereby learn to understand the Chinese and conditions in China. It is not unusual for Japanese to visit Europe and become knowledgeable in European affairs, but scarcely anyone visits China to become well-informed in Chinese matters. Now, attempting to solve the Chinese problem without a proper knowledge of China would be extremely dangerous. Given this situation, how could I be free of concerns for the future?

Chapter Seven

Okakura Tenshin: "Asia Is One," 1903

Brij Tankha

Okakura Tenshin's (1863–1913, also known as Kakuzō) writings represent an early attempt to search for and define Japan's past. Asia, for Okakura, becomes the frame that represents the colonial order, and Japan's successful transition to modernity points the way for the liberation of Asia. Okakura's explorations do not present a tightly articulated agenda but partake of the ambiguities and contradictions inherent in the situation he faced. His contribution lies not only in defining the artistic heritage of Japan and linking Asia through Buddhism and art but also in laying the boundaries of what it means to be Japanese. In effect, even as Okakura talked of a common Asia, he was, through a shared aesthetic past anchored in Buddhism, as well as through the progress of Japanese history, identifying the intellectual inheritances and heroes that created modern Japan. His analysis of Japanese and Asian history contributed to the intellectual discourse and became the core of ideas subsumed under the rubric of Pan-Asianism that played and continue to play a vital role in shaping the way the Japanese define themselves and their relationship to the Asian region.

In 1873, Okakura entered the Kaisei Gakkō (after 1877, Tokyo Imperial University), where, in addition to Western philosophy and foreign languages, he also pursued his interests in Chinese philosophy and Japanese art, in which Ernest Fenellosa (1853–1908) played an important role. After graduating in 1880, he joined the Ministry of Education, where he established his power and influence in crafting the government's art policies.

In his capacity as a Ministry of Education official, Okakura undertook many trips to identify and catalog Japanese art, a process that helped in identifying "national treasures." In the 1890s, he traveled to China, where he carried out extensive surveys of Chinese art and wrote widely on Chinese culture.

Back in Japan, Okakura was appointed as the head of the Tokyo Fine Arts Academy (Tokyo Bijutsu Gakkō) in 1890 as well as the head of the art section in the Tokyo Imperial Museum. Meanwhile, he and Fenollosa launched the art history journal *Kokka* (State Flower). By the age of twenty-seven, Okakura had reached a powerful position in which he shaped government policy and played a crucial role in contributing to the formation of wider intellectual debates. The books, in English, that brought him an international reputation were written after he resigned from his position at the Academy in 1898. The notes for *The Awakening of the East* were written in English during Okakura's stay in India (December 1901–October 1902). It was a powerful indictment of Western imperialism and the "White Peril" (*hakka*), but by the time it was published in Japanese in 1940, the intellectual climate had changed, and Okakura's ideas were used in ways that may have been contrary to his intentions.

Okakura Tenshin's cultural critique of Western civilization found its expression both in the books he wrote in English (*The Awakening of the East, The Ideals of the East,* and *The Awakening of Japan*) and in his activities as an art historian and art administrator. These need to be placed in the context of contemporary Japanese writing, as they are part of a process of creating a body of professional knowledge to establish Japanese credentials in the West, a process supported by the state. In this process, Okakura was but one of many Japanese who traveled abroad, not only to Europe but also to Asia, to trace the roots of Japanese culture and to establish a firm academic basis to identify the lineaments of this culture and the basis for its superiority and its equivalence with the West. These writings also served to "explain" Japan to the outside world. It is significant that Okakura's English books were written mostly during or shortly after his trip to India, but his long stay in the United States did not lead to any major publication in English.

Okakura, famous for his proclamation that "Asia is one," distinguishes between the Orient and Asia, as can be seen in source 1 here. The Orient for him represented all that was backward and decayed, namely, India and China, while Japan was developed and Asiatic. How did he explain Japan's strength and the reasons why it alone could represent Asia? For him, Japan was historically uniquely placed, for it represented the best in Asian civilization, as Japan's "Indo-Tartaric blood was itself a heritage which qualified it to imbibe from two sources, and so mirrors the whole of Asian consciousness" (Okakura 1920: 4–5).

Okakura also argued that Japan's unique position derived from its Imperial house and its unbroken lineage. These two elements, the Imperial House and a protected insularity, allowed Japan to preserve the traditions of Asia and made Japan into a "museum of Asiatic civilisation" (Okakura 1920: 7). But what made Japan strong was the "expenditure of thought" that it had spent in assimilating ideas and culture from other parts of Asia. This experience, more than anything else, had given Japan an intellectual strength that allowed it to "face the terrible exigencies of modern existence." A similar sentiment was voiced by the Nobel Prize for Literature laureate poet Rabindranath Tagore (1861–1941), who saw Japan's strength in its aesthetic discipline.

Japan, because it has preserved its independence and is the repository of Asian culture, has, he argued, a responsibility to lead Asia. "The task of Asia today," he wrote, "then becomes that of protecting and restoring Asiatic modes. But to do this she must successfully recognize and develop consciousness of these modes" (Okakura 1920: 224). This was the task of developing the modes of Asian consciousness that Okakura set for himself. He sought to make of himself a "man who can ponder and dream at pleasure—a highly cultivated man" (Okakura 1981: 184). He defines these modes in the following manner: for India, the religious life is the essence of nationality, China is a moral civilization, and Japan has the spiritual purity of the sword soul. He wrote that "in our history lies the secret of our future" (Okakura 1920: 131). Asia having been equated with Japan, it became the destiny of Japan to formulate the program for defining Asiatic modes of consciousness, identifying the essential characteristics of each part of the Orient, and integrating these within the framework of Japan.

Even though he titled his book *Ideals of the East,* Okakura was in search of what he defined as reality, for even as Asia needed to return to its traditions, these modes of consciousness could be developed only through an understanding of the actual. He wrote, "We have wandered among ideals, let us awaken once more to the actual" (Okakura 1940a: 131). Opposition, therefore, had to be based on an understanding of the power of the Western countries.

How is one to understand the power of European civilization and its hold over the world? Okakura saw this as the central question around which Asia can be reborn. European civilization, he argued, despite its powerful position in the world, was based on narrow principles and so was in a historically inferior position. Yet, despite this inferiority, it had emerged as a powerful force, and this was because of nationalism. The lack of sufficient land in Europe, Okakura argued, had led to the development of a very strong sense of nationality that allowed the Europeans to overrun the East. Further, he asserted, Asian civilization was one of tolerance, but this tolerance proved a weakness, as it prevented effective resistance to Western aggression (Okakura 1940a: 157–58).

Western countries established their superiority so that "steam and electricity in encircling the globe impose the London tailor and the Paris milliner in every continent,—symbolic of the single garment which their genius of combination weaves for all their race" (Okakura 1940a: 137), but mutual isolation has prevented Asian countries from comprehending their common plight. "It's wonderful how little we know of each other," he writes (Okakura 1940a: 144). Asia derives its knowledge today from European sources so that "a Fifth Avenue scandal causes greater excitement amongst us then a rebellion in Honan, a Boulevard accident a deeper emotion than the defeat of Arabi Bey."

It is, he argues, European technology that allows the unification of the nation-state and asserts that "their very language, in which I am enabled to appeal to you, that signifies the unification of the east" (Okakura 1940a: 160). How did he see the regeneration of Asia? The importance of national strength for Japan's successful modernization is often stressed as underlying his thinking, but in the *Awakening of the East*, even though it was a poetic ode to the nation, written under the spell of the radical nationalism then prevalent in Calcutta, he underlined that each nation must develop its strength through an understanding of its history and culture and that this will provide the basis for a pan-Asian alliance. Japanese leadership was not the crucial element. The essential factor was individual national strength and strength defined not in military or even economic terms but in culture and ideas, what today would be called soft power. The idea that the nation was a powerful force able to resist colonial domination and patriotism took on a different coloring in the Japanese environment as Japan's empire expanded, but at the time Okakura was writing, the revival of national strength was the main aim of independence movements fighting colonial rule (see the source reproduced here).

Okakura Tenshin died in 1913, and the way his writings were used later has come to color interpretations of Okakura's thought, but Okakura can hardly be blamed if the Patriotic Association for Japanese Literature (Nihon Bungaku Hōkokukai) used his phrase "Asia is one" to commemorate 8 December 1941, the day of the Pearl Harbor attack (Kaneko 2002: 1).

Some scholars have accused Okakura of espousing a vision of Asia within Japan's imperial project, but they have done so only by glossing over his call for resistance to the West, a call that was for preserving, sustaining, and developing alternative modes of conceptualizing the world based on an awareness of cultural and philosophical traditions. Okakura's project carried the ambiguities and limitations of his time, but it would be wrong to dismiss it merely as a justification for Japanese leadership (and domination) of Asia. Orientalism and Western colonialism often seem to be given an absolute power that molds and shapes all debates, but Okakura's writings and his engagement with Indian nationalists point to the importance of another circuit of engagement.

Source 1 (English in the original)
Okakura Kakuzō [Tenshin], *Ideals of the East with Special Reference
to the Art of Japan,* London: J. Murray, 1920 (originally published in
1903), 1–5, 16.

Asia is one. The Himalayas divide, only to accentuate, two mighty civilisations, the Chinese with its communism of Confucius, and the Indian with
its individualism of the Vedas. But not even the snowy barriers can interrupt
for one moment that broad expanse of love for the Ultimate and Universal,
which is the common thought-inheritance of every Asiatic race, enabling
them to produce all the great religions of the world, and distinguishing them
from those maritime peoples of the Mediterranean and the Baltic, who love to
dwell on the particular, and to search out the means, not the end, of life. . . .

For if Asia be one, it is also true that the Asiatic races form a single mighty
web. We forget, in an age of classification, that types are after all but shining
points of distinction in an ocean of approximations, false gods deliberately
set up to be worshipped, for the sake of mental convenience, but having no
more ultimate or mutually exclusive validity than the separate existence of
two inter-changeable sciences. . . . Arab chivalry, Persian poetry, Chinese
ethics and Indian thought, all speak of a single Asiatic peace, in which there
grew up a common life, bearing in different regions different characteristic
blossoms, but nowhere capable of a hard and fast dividing line. Islam itself
may be described as Confucianism on horseback, sword in hand.

Or, to turn again to Eastern Asia from the West, Buddhism—that great ocean
of idealism, in which merge all the river systems of eastern Asiatic thought—is
not coloured only by the pure water of the Ganges, for the Tartaric nations that
joined it made their genius tributary, bringing new symbolism, new organisation, new powers of devotion, to add to the treasures of the Faith.

It has been, however, the great privilege of Japan to realize this unity-in-
complexity with a special clearness. The Indo-Tartaric blood of this race was
in itself a heritage which qualified it to imbibe from the two sources, and so
mirrors the whole consciousness. The unique blessing of unbroken sovereignty, the proud self-reliance of an unconquered race, and the insular isolation which protected ancestral ideas and instincts at the cost of expansion,
made Japan the real repository of the trust of Asiatic thought and culture. . . .

Source 2 (English in the original)
Okakura Tenshin, *The Awakening of Japan,* edited with notes by Hiroshi
Muraoka. Kenkyūsha, 1940 (originally published 1904), 6–7, 186, 188–89.

Great was the difficulty involved in the struggle for a national reawakening, a still harder task confronted Japan in her effort to bring an Oriental nation to face the terrible exigencies of modern existence. Until the moment we shook of it off, the same lethargy lay upon us which now lies on China and India. Over our country brooded the Night of Asia, enveloping all spontaneity within its mysterious folds. Intellectual activity and social progress became stifled in the atmosphere of apathy. Religion could but soothe, not cure, the suffering of the wounded soul. The weight of our burden can never be understood without a knowledge of the dark background from which we emerged to the light. . . .

Since the earliest dawn of history our national patriotism and devotion to the Mikado shows a consistent tenacity of ancient ideals, while the fact that we have preserved the arts and customs of ancient China and India long after they have become lost in the lands of their birth is sufficient testimony to our reverence for traditions. . . .

The expenditure of thought involved in synthesizing the different elements of Asiatic culture has given Japanese philosophy and art a freedom and virility unknown in India and China. It is thus due to past training that we are able to comprehend and appreciate more easily than our neighbours those elements of Western civilization which it is desirable that we should acquire.

Source 3 (English in the original)
Okakura Tenshin, *The Awakening of the East*, with notes and an introduction by Akira Asano, Seibunkaku, 1940, 3–4, 12–13, 18–19, 23–26, 62–63.

Brothers and sisters of Asia!

We have wandered long amongst ideals, let us awaken once more to the actual. We have drifted on the river of apathy, let us land once more on the cruel shore of reality. We have isolated ourselves from one another, in pride of a crystalline, containedness. Let us dissolve ourselves now in the ocean of common misery. The guilty conscience of the West has often conjured up the spectre of a Yellow Peril, let the tranquil gaze of the east turn itself on the White Disaster. I call you not to violence but to manhood. I call you not to aggression but to self consciousness. . . .

They speak much of Chinese diplomacy,—woe to the nation that has to rely on its tongue, not the sword. They speak much of Indian subtlety,—woe to the nation that has to mask its thought in words, instead of casing the body in mail. They speak of Arabian faith,—woe to the nation that waits for providence and marches not with God. . . .

The imitation and worship of Europe has at last become our natural regime. The gilded youths of Calcutta or Tokio who flaunt the newest London fashions with all the sadness of the ridiculous, are only an expression of the pervading idea. They seek in dress that protective colouring which our fashionable scholars seek in the borrowed phrases of modern philosophy. Sanskrit is barbarous if not Germanic, the Taj a blot if not Italian. . . . Gowri-Shankar did not exist till Everest discovered the Himalayas. Tibet was a myth before Landor invented Lhasa' . . .

Shameful as it is our impression of neighbouring countries is mostly derived form European sources, and are naturally coloured with their interpretation, if not indeed intentionally distorted . . . , above all the exuberant imagination of the literary traveller clothe the east in colours bizarre in their abomination, absurd in their inhumanity. . . .

But what does the West know of the East? The Europeans claim to oriental scholarship is shadows indeed! Who in Oxford or Heidelberg can compete with a second rate pundit in his knowledge of Brahmanical lore? Who of Berlin or Sorbonne can compare with a third-rate mandarin in his grasp of Confucian classics? . . .

Each nation must seek within itself the seed of its regeneration. The Pan-Asiatic Alliance is in itself an immense force but the individual factors must feel their own strength. . . . History must be written so presenting our past glories and our present woes that every student shall burn with the longing to avenge and save. Songs must be sung by the people through which the cry of shame and revolt may rise. . . . The spell of white prestige must be completely broken that we may learn our own possibilities and resources. . . .

Chapter Eight

Okakura Tenshin and Pan-Asianism, 1903–1906

Jing He

Okakura Tenshin (1863–1913, also known as Kakuzō) was born in the treaty port of Yokohama to a merchant family of samurai origins. At Tokyo Imperial University, he met his future mentor, Ernest Fenollosa (1853–1908), and started his lifelong dedication to the nationalistic art movements of the Meiji period. An art bureaucrat in the Ministry of Education from 1890, he helped organize and operate Japan's first modern museums, played important roles in committees organizing expositions and exhibitions of Japanese art overseas, served as head art historian for the official compilation of Japanese imperial art history, and became the first principal of Tōkyō Bijutsu Gakkō (Tokyo School of Fine Arts). Although Okakura's influence waned after 1898 as a result of a personal scandal, he maintained a notable level of authority and influence in the Meiji art world, society, and bureaucracy.

Okakura traveled overseas numerous times, to Europe, China, Korea, India, and the United States. In the last decade of his life, he further cemented his position as a pioneer in the promotion of Japan and Japanese culture overseas through his famous English-language publications *The Ideals of the East* (1903), *The Awakening of Japan* (1904), and *The Book of Tea* (1906). He was a celebrated public speaker in the United States, acquired many Chinese and Japanese artworks for American galleries during his tenure as an adviser and later curator at the Boston Museum of Fine Arts, and came to be regarded in the West as one of the most important living authorities on East Asian art and art history.

Okakura has exercised a substantial influence on modern cultural commentators, and changing patterns in their approaches to him reflect some important aspects of twentieth-century intellectual history. While in the last years of his life he was constantly challenged in Japan as the spokesman for state-sponsored art campaigns and academism, at the same time he was celebrated in the West as, following World War I, European intellectuals turned to Eastern spirituality to look for solutions to modern cultural crises. In prewar Japan, his nationalism—emphasizing Japan's artistic and spiritual superiority and its leadership mission in the new world order—had made him a leading voice in nationalist discourse. After Japan's defeat, he was accused posthumously of being an imperialist and a war criminal; he was not rehabilitated and recognized as an author of the Meiji canon until the 1960s.

Characterized by his famous line "Asia is one," Okakura's Meiji version of Pan-Asianism revealed a distinctive way of thinking in the modern Japanese construction of national identity. The historical position accorded to pan-Asianist Okakura, like that of nationalist Okakura, reflects the ideological contortions by means of which later Japanese intellectuals and political activists legitimized their own positions and agendas. Nonetheless, Okakura's Pan-Asianism was more than a political slogan that made a sudden appearance in *The Ideals of the East*—the impact of which in the Japanese context should not be overestimated. Long before his assertion that "Asia is one" in 1903, Okakura's concept of Asia had emerged in his lectures on Japanese art history (1890–1893), in which he not only examined the art of East Asia but also referred to the art of India, Assyria, and Arabia. These lectures revealed Okakura's deep unease with Ernest Fenollosa's neo-Hellenistic position in the Hōryūji Debate in 1888, in which the Hōryūji was romanticized as a Japanese expression of the Greek style after Alexander the Great (356–323 BC) and the city of Nara as "the museum of central Asia." Okakura's ideas matured during his journey to China in 1893 shortly before the outbreak of the Sino-Japanese War (1894–1895) and offered a strong challenge to the neo-Hellenistic narrative of the history of world civilization. He not only emphasized Eastern influences on the West in mutual cultural exchanges and from multiple sources but also boldly placed Arabic cultures under the influence of medieval Chinese civilization in order to deny Hellenism's parenting role.

Okakura was equally as concerned with Japan's interests and security in East Asia as both the advocates of *Nisshin teikeiron* (the argument for Sino–Japanese cooperation) of the 1870s (and later) and the proponents of *Datsua-ron* (the "leaving-Asia" movement), which peaked in the 1890s. Okakura's definition of Asia was directed primarily to the need to influence Japan's image in the West. To him, the creation of an Asian identity was not the chief priority, even though it was part of his "one-Asia" concept, which addressed both Western colonizers and Japan's Indian brethren suffering under Britain's colonial rule. Okakura's "one Asia" was designed primarily to redefine Japan's leading role and central position in the rigid political, cultural, and racial hierarchies of Asia and the world. In his Asia, both China as the embodiment of philosophy and India as the personification of religion were inferior and subordinate to Japan, which stood for the fine arts at the top of the Asian triangle. The Arabic cultures' historical connections with Hellenism were questioned and twisted to suit his own ideas. Modern India needed Asian support to free itself from British rule. China was to be dehistoricized, as its Confucian political institutions and cultural glories remained only in antiquity. China was to be disempowered by undermining its centrality in the modern Asian order, as it lacked the cultural values and real power to participate in international politics as a viable nation-state. The modern nation-state of Japan, as "the museum of Asia," must be the leader of Asia in a newly mapped world order.

Intended primarily to facilitate the construction of a Japanese art historical and cultural canon, Okakura's Pan-Asianism nonetheless served modern Japan's political campaign for *national* identity no less than any other contemporary articulations of what Asia should be. His definition of Asia probably had the broadest geocultural range of all the major pan-Asian advocates of his time; it therefore enabled him to focus on much larger spheres of involvement for Japan than merely the East Asian region. Okakura's ideas depicted Asia as a religious, aesthetic, and humanistic community to Western audiences even before the post–World War II boom in Eastern spirituality but also attracted Japanese intellectuals in the 1930s who saw "an inevitable connection between cultural particularism, nationalism, and political forms of revolt against the West" (Doak 1994: xxv).

Okakura's Pan-Asianism was met with controversy in his own time. His admiration for classical China and his denigration of modern China created considerable confusion (although these views were shared by other Japanese *kangaku* [Chinese learning] intellectuals; cf. Tanaka 1993: 17–20). In the 1930s and 1940s, when his influence was at its height after his works had been published in Japanese (*The Book of Tea* in 1929, *The Ideals of the East* in 1938, and *The Awakening of the East* in 1940), both the pacifist and the romantic sides of Okakura were engaged with China. His passion for Chinese art, his cautious and intellectual approach to Sino–Japanese conflict, and his strong stand against Japan's hard-nosed China policies all set him apart from the hostile and aggressive Meiji politicians. However, the roles that Okakura assigned to Japan, of China's "museum" and civilizing agent, demonstrated his strong colonial mentality. In the case of India, he found allies like Rabindranath Tagore (1861–1941) and Swami Vivekananda (1863–1902) in Bengal (1901–1902) and inspired nationalist Bengalis across the generations with his popular nationalist slogans. However, Okakura placed India at the bottom of the Asian triangle in order to support a superior and dominant Japan and facilitate his anti-Hellenist Japan-centrism as part of an official nationalist campaign on behalf of the Meiji state. He launched a harsh critique of modernity while simultaneously reconstituting the historical origins of Japanese modernity in terms of Asian cultural traditions. In general, Okakura's pan-Asianist proposals demonstrated the contradiction between his theory and practice. On the one hand, he appreciated the Western appraisal of a spiritually sophisticated Japan and responded to it enthusiastically, utilizing Western scholarly vocabulary and racial, essentialist conceptions about both West and East to serve his anticolonial ideology. On the other hand, the ideological framework and structure of his theories and concepts showed that he had been intellectually enslaved by Western epistemic and ethical principles.

Like that of many other pan-Asian advocates, Okakura's Pan-Asianism is also characterized by a racial agenda that he applied to both the new Asian and the international orders he proposed. After 1893, when he developed a racial perspective on Chinese ethnic diversity, the East–West conflict was reduced in his mind to a naked racial confrontation. Okakura believed that international relations, in both Asia and beyond, would in the future be subject to the efficacy of racial regroupings. The "white race" could be successfully countered only when the "yellow" hegemony, led by Japan, had become established; Japan enjoyed a superiority that was rooted in the refined details of daily life and flourished in the political, ideological, and institutional realms.

Most interestingly, Okakura's racial agenda was also a gendered discourse. His genderization of Japanese art of different historical periods can be traced back to his Japanese art history lectures of the 1890s and runs throughout his English writings from the 1900s. During his time in Boston in the 1900s, Okakura modified his concept of gendered racial relationships by reinforcing the Taoist notion of dualism in order to calm the American outcry over the Yellow Peril exacerbated by Nitobe Inazō's (1862–1933) masculine image of the Eastern Warrior in *Bushidō* (1899). As illustrated in *The Book of Tea*, he made Japan a feminine metaphor for the art of life and the ideal of humanity in order to counter the image of a masculine, rational, materialistic, modern West. Moreover, Okakura placed the ultimate mission of saving humanity in the hands of the Goddess Niuka (Nǚ Wa), a female savior of the chaotic universe in ancient Chinese myth, by emphasizing her victorious role in the final creation of a universal Oneness. He declared the inevitable triumph of femininity over masculinity as well as the victory of art and humanity over capitalism and materialism. The role and ultimate victory of Niuka also symbolized Japan's unique mission and power both in Asia and worldwide.

Source 1 (English in the original)
Okakura Kakuzō, *The Ideals of the East, with Special Reference to the Art of Japan.* London: J. Murray, 1903.

THE RANGE OF IDEALS (1903)

ASIA is one. The Himalayas divide, only to accentuate, two mighty civilisations, the Chinese with its communism of Confucius, and the Indian with its individualism of the Vedas. But not even the snowy barriers can interrupt for one moment that broad expanse of love for the Ultimate and Universal, which is the common thought-inheritance of every Asiatic race, enabling them to produce all the great religions of the world, and distinguishing them from those maritime peoples of the Mediterranean and the Baltic, who love to dwell on the Particular, and to search out the means, not the end, of life.

Down to the days of the Mohammedan conquest went, by the ancient highways of the sea, the intrepid mariners of the Bengal coast, founding their colonies in Ceylon, Java, and Sumatra, leaving Aryan blood to mingle with that of the sea-board races of Burmah and Siam, and binding Cathay and India fast in mutual intercourse.

The long systolic centuries—in which India, crippled in her power to give, shrank back upon herself, and China, self-absorbed in recovery from the shock of Mongol tyranny, lost her intellectual hospitality—succeeded the epoch of Mahmoud of Ghazni, in the eleventh century. But the old energy of communication lived yet in the great moving sea of the Tartar hordes, whose waves recoiled from the long walls of the North, to break upon and overrun the Punjab. The Hunas, the Sakas, and the Gettaes, grim ancestors of the Rajputs, had been the forerunners of that great Mongol outburst which, under Genghis Khan and Tamerlane, spread over the Celestial soil, to deluge it with Bengali Tantrikism, and flooded the Indian peninsula, to tinge its Mussulmaan Imperialism with Mongolian polity and art.

For if Asia be one, it is also true that the Asiatic races form a single mighty web. We forget, in an age of classification, that types are after all but shining points of distinctness in an ocean of approximations, false gods deliberately set up to be worshipped, for the sake of mental convenience, but having no more ultimate or mutually exclusive validity than the separate existence of two interchangeable sciences. If the history of Delhi represents the Tartar's imposition of himself upon a Mohammedan world, it must also be remembered that the story of Baghdad and her great Saracenic culture is equally significant of the power of Semitic peoples to demonstrate Chinese, as well as Persian, civilisation and art, in face of the Frankish nations of the Mediterranean coast. Arab chivalry, Persian poetry, Chinese ethics, and Indian thought, all speak of a single ancient Asiatic peace, in which there grew up a common life, bearing in different regions different characteristic blossoms, but nowhere capable of a hard and fast dividing-line. Islam itself may be described as Confucianism on horseback, sword in hand. For it is quite possible to distinguish, in the hoary communism of the Yellow Valley, traces of a purely pastoral element, such as we see abstracted and self-realised in the Mussulmaan races.

Or, to turn again to Eastern Asia from the West, Buddhism—that great ocean of idealism, in which merge all the river-systems of Eastern Asiatic thought—is not coloured only with the pure water of the Ganges, for the Tartaric nations that joined it made their genius also tributary, bringing new symbolism, new organisation, new powers of devotion, to add to the treasures of the Faith.

It has been, however, the great privilege of Japan to realise this unity-in-complexity with a special clearness. The Indo-Tartaric blood of this race was in itself a heritage which qualified it to imbibe from the two sources, and so mirror the whole of Asiatic consciousness. The unique blessing of unbroken sovereignty, the proud self-reliance of an unconquered race, and the insular isolation which protected ancestral ideas and instincts at the cost of expansion, made Japan the real repository of the trust of Asiatic thought and culture. Dynastic upheavals, the inroads of Tartar horsemen, the carnage and devastation of infuriated mobs—all these things, sweeping over her again and again, have left to China no landmarks, save her literature and her ruins, to recall the glory of the Tang emperors or the refinement of Sung society.

The grandeur of Asoka—ideal type of Asiatic monarchs, whose edicts dictated terms to the sovereigns of Antioch and Alexandria—is almost forgotten among the crumbling stones of Bharhut and Buddha Gaya. The jeweled court of Vikramaditya is but a lost dream, which even the poetry of Kalidasa fails to evoke. The sublime attainments of Indian art, almost effaced as they have been by the rough-handedness of the Hunas, the fanatical iconoclasm of the Mussulmaan, and the unconscious vandalism of mercenary Europe, leave us to seek only a past glory in the mouldy walls of Ajanta, the tortured sculptures of Ellora, the silent protests of rock-cut Orissa, and finally in the domestic utensils of the present day, where beauty clings sadly to religion in the midst of an exquisite home-life.

It is in Japan alone that the historic wealth of Asiatic culture can be consecutively studied through its treasured specimens. The Imperial collection, the Shinto temples, and the opened dolmens, reveal the subtle curves of Hang workmanship. The temples of Nara are rich in representations of Tang culture, and of that Indian art, then in its splendor, which so much influenced the creations of this classic period—natural heirlooms of a nation which has preserved the music, pronunciation, ceremony, and costumes, not to speak of the religious rites and philosophy, of so remarkable an age, intact.

The treasure-stores of the daimyos, again, abound in works of art and manuscripts belonging to the Sung and Mongol dynasties, and as in China itself the former were lost during the Mongol conquest, and the latter in the age of the reactionary Ming, this fact animates some Chinese scholars of the present day to seek in Japan the fountain-head of their own ancient knowledge. Thus Japan is a museum of Asiatic civilisation; and yet more than a museum, because the singular genius of the race leads it to dwell on all phases of the ideals of the past, in that spirit of living Advaitism which welcomes the new without losing the old. The Shinto still adheres to his pre-Buddhistic rites of ancestor-worship; and the Buddhists themselves cling to each various school of religious development which has come in its natural order to enrich the soil.

The Yamato poetry, and Bugaku music, which reflect the Tang ideal under the régime of the Fujiwara aristocracy, are a source of inspiration and delight to the present day, like the sombre Zen-ism and No-dances, which were the product of Sung illumination. It is this tenacity that keeps Japan true to the Asiatic soul even while it raises her to the rank of a modern power.

The history of Japanese art becomes thus the history of Asiatic ideals—the beach where each successive wave of Eastern thought has left its sand-ripple as it beat against the national consciousness. Yet I linger with dismay on the threshold of an attempt to make an intelligible summary of those art-ideals. For art, like the diamond net of Indra, reflects the whole chain in every link. It exists at no period in any final mould. It is always a growth, defying the dissecting knife of the chronologist. To discourse on a particular phase of its development means to deal with infinite causes and effects throughout its past and present. Art with us, as elsewhere, is the expression of the highest and noblest of our national culture, so that, in order to understand it, we must pass in review the various phases of Confucian philosophy; the different ideals which the Buddhist mind has from time to time revealed; those mighty political cycles which have one after another unfurled the banner of nationality; the reflection in patriotic thought of the lights of poetry and the shadows of heroic characters; and the echoes, alike of the wailing of a multitude, and of the mad-seeming merriment of the laughter of a race.

Any history of Japanese art-ideals is, then, almost an impossibility, as long as the Western world remains so unaware of the varied environment and interrelated social phenomena into which that art is set, as it were a jewel. Definition is limitation. The beauty of a cloud or a flower lies in its unconscious unfolding of itself, and the silent eloquence of the masterpieces of each epoch must tell their story better than any epitome of necessary half-truths. My poor attempts are merely an indication, not a narrative.

Source 2 (English in the original)
Okakura Kakuzō, *The Book of Tea*. London: G. P. Putnam, 1906.

. . . Teaism is a cult founded on the adoration of the beautiful among the sordid facts of everyday existence. It inculcates purity and harmony, the mystery of mutual charity, the romanticism of the social order. It is essentially a worship of the Imperfect, as it is a tender attempt to accomplish something possible in this impossible thing we know as life.

The Philosophy of Tea is not mere aestheticism in the ordinary acceptance of the term, for it expresses conjointly with ethics and religion our whole point of view about man and nature. It is hygiene, for it enforces cleanliness; it is economics, for it shows comfort in simplicity rather than in the complex and costly; it is moral geometry, inasmuch as it defines our sense of proportion to the universe. It represents the true spirit of Eastern democracy by making all its votaries aristocrats in taste.

The long isolation of Japan from the rest of the world, so conducive to introspection, has been highly favourable to the development of Teaism. Our home and habits, costume and cuisine, porcelain, lacquer, painting—our very literature—all have been subject to its influence. No student of Japanese culture could ever ignore its presence. It has permeated the elegance of noble boudoirs, and entered the abode of the humble. Our peasants have learned to arrange flowers, our meanest labourer to offer his salutation to the rocks and waters. In our common parlance we speak of the man "with no tea" in him, when he is insusceptible to the seriocomic interests of the personal drama. Again we stigmatise the untamed aesthete who, regardless of the mundane tragedy, runs riot in the springtide of emancipated emotions, as one "with too much tea" in him.

The outsider may indeed wonder at this seeming much ado about nothing. "What a tempest in a tea-cup!" he will say. But when we consider how small after all the cup of human enjoyment is, how soon overflowed with tears, how easily drained to the dregs in our quenchless thirst for infinity, we shall not blame ourselves for making so much of the tea-cup. Mankind has done worse. In the worship of Bacchus, we have sacrificed too freely; and we have even transfigured the gory image of Mars. Why not consecrate ourselves to the queen of the Camelias, and revel in the warm stream of sympathy that flows from her altar? In the liquid amber within the ivory-porcelain, the initiated may touch the sweet reticence of Confucius, the piquancy of Laotse, and the ethereal aroma of Sakyamuni himself.

Those who cannot feel the littleness of great things in themselves are apt to overlook the greatness of little things in others. The average Westerner, in his sleek complacency, will see in the tea ceremony but another instance of the thousand and one oddities which constitute the quaintness and childishness of the East to him. He was wont to regard Japan as barbarous while she indulged in the gentle arts of peace: he calls her civilised since she began to commit wholesale slaughter on Manchurian battlefields. Much comment has been given lately to the Code of the Samurai,—the Art of Death which makes our soldiers exult in self-sacrifice; but scarcely any attention has been drawn to Teaism, which represents so much of our Art of Life. Fain would we remain barbarians, if our claim to civilisation were to be based on the gruesome glory of war. Fain would we await the time when due respect shall be paid to our art and ideals.

When will the West understand, or try to understand, the East? We Asiatics are often appalled by the curious web of facts and fancies which has been woven concerning us. We are pictured as living on the perfume of the lotus, if not on mice and cockroaches. It is either impotent fanaticism or else abject voluptuousness. Indian spirituality has been derided as ignorance, Chinese sobriety as stupidity, Japanese patriotism as the result of fatalism. It has been said that we are less sensible to pain and wounds on account of the callousness of our nervous organisation!

Why not amuse yourselves at our expense? Asia returns the compliment. There would be further food for merriment if you were to know all that we have imagined and written about you. All the glamour of the perspective is there, all the unconscious homage of wonder, all the silent resentment of the new and undefined. You have been loaded with virtues too refined to be envied, and accused of crimes too picturesque to be condemned. Our writers in the past—the wise men who knew—informed us that you had bushy tails somewhere hidden in your garments, and often dined off a fricassee of newborn babes! Nay, we had something worse against you: we used to think you the most impracticable people on the earth, for you were said to preach what you never practiced.

Such misconceptions are fast vanishing amongst us. Commerce has forced the European tongues on many an Eastern port. Asiatic youths are flocking to Western colleges for the equipment of modern education. Our insight does not penetrate your culture deeply, but at least we are willing to learn. Some of my compatriots have adopted too much of your customs and too much of your etiquette, in the delusion that the acquisition of stiff collars and tall silk hats comprised the attainment of your civilisation. Pathetic and deplorable as such affectations are, they evince our willingness to approach the West on our knees. Unfortunately the Western attitude is unfavourable to the understanding of the East. The Christian missionary goes to impart, but not to receive. Your information is based on the meagre translations of our immense literature, if not on the unreliable anecdotes of passing travelers. It is rarely that the chivalrous pen of a Lafcadio Hearn or that of the author of "The Web of Indian Life" enlivens the Oriental darkness with the torch of our own sentiments.

Perhaps I betray my own ignorance of the Tea Cult by being so outspoken. Its very spirit of politeness exacts that you say what you are expected to say, and no more. But I am not to be a polite Teaist. So much harm has been done already by the mutual misunderstanding of the New World and the Old, that one need not apologise for contributing his tithe to the furtherance of a better understanding. The beginning of the twentieth century would have been spared the spectacle of sanguinary warfare if Russia had condescended to know Japan better. What dire consequences to humanity lie in the contemptuous ignoring of Eastern problems! European imperialism, which does not disdain to raise the absurd cry of the Yellow Peril, fails to realise that Asia may also awaken to the cruel sense of the White Disaster. You may laugh at us for having "too much tea," but may we not suspect that you of the West have "no tea" in your constitution?

Let us stop the continents from hurling epigrams at each other, and be sadder if not wiser by the mutual gain of half a hemisphere. We have developed along different lines, but there is no reason why one should not supplement the other. You have gained expansion at the cost of restlessness; we have created a harmony which is weak against aggression. Will you believe it?—the East is better off in some respects than the West!

Strangely enough humanity has so far met in the tea-cup. It is the only Asiatic ceremonial which commands universal esteem. The white man has scoffed at our religion and our morals, but has accepted the brown beverage without hesitation. The afternoon tea is now an important function in Western society. In the delicate clatter of trays and saucers, in the soft rustle of feminine hospitality, in the common catechism about cream and sugar, we know that the Worship of Tea is established beyond question. The philosophic resignation of the guest to the fate awaiting him in the dubious decoction proclaims that in this single instance the Oriental spirit reigns supreme. . . .

The Taoists relate that at the great beginning of the No-Beginning, Spirit and Matter met in mortal combat. At last the Yellow Emperor, the Sun of Heaven, triumphed over Shuhyung, the demon of darkness and earth. The Titan, in his death agony, struck his head against the solar vault and shivered the blue dome of jade into fragments. The stars lost their nests, the moon wandered aimlessly among the wild chasms of the night. In despair the Yellow Emperor sought far and wide for the repairer of the Heavens. He had not to search in vain. Out of the Eastern sea rose a queen, the divine Niuka, horn-crowned and dragon-tailed, resplendent in her armor of fire. She welded the five-coloured rainbow in her magic cauldron and rebuilt the Chinese sky. But it is told that Niuka forgot to fill two tiny crevices in the blue firmament. Thus began the dualism of love—two souls rolling through space and never at rest until they join together to complete the universe. Everyone has to build anew his sky of hope and peace.

The heaven of modern humanity is indeed shattered in the Cyclopean struggle for wealth and power. The world is groping in the shadow of egotism and vulgarity. Knowledge is bought through a bad conscience, benevolence practiced for the sake of utility. The East and the West, like two dragons tossed in a sea of ferment, in vain strive to regain the jewel of life. We need a Niuka again to repair the grand devastation; we await the great Avatar. Meanwhile, let us have a sip of tea. The afternoon glow is brightening the bamboos, the fountains are bubbling with delight, the soughing of the pines is heard in our kettle. Let us dream of evanescence, and linger in the beautiful foolishness of things.

Part II

THE ERA OF IMPERIALISM AND PAN-ASIANISM IN JAPAN, 1900–1914

This part focuses on Japanese reactions to and participation in imperial rivalry in East Asia in the two decades prior to the outbreak of World War I. During this period, a rapidly modernizing Japan became the first non-Western power to acquire a colonial empire. It acquired Taiwan following the Sino-Japanese War (1894–1895), although its claims in mainland China were thwarted by the Triple Intervention of Russia, France, and Germany. Japan made further strides as an imperial power when, in the aftermath of the Boxer Rebellion (1900), in which it sided with the Western powers, it obtained indemnities and special privileges in China. As a result of its victory over Russia in the war of 1904–1905, Japan increased the size of its colonial empire even more spectacularly by turning Korea into a protectorate and acquiring southern Sakhalin as well as special rights in Manchuria.

An alliance concluded with Great Britain in 1902 had prevented another "triple intervention" following this war. Japan's military victories, its alliance with the leading imperial power, and its successful negotiations to obtain a revision of its unequal treaties combined to make Japan a fully fledged member of the "imperialist club." Naturally, Japan's imperial ambitions conflicted in many ways with pan-Asian claims.

The official position of the Japanese government in this era was one of rejecting pan-Asian ideals and policies (see I:12), but this stance encountered considerable opposition within Japan. The government was criticized on numerous grounds, but, as the documents in this part reveal, the argument that Asia was "in [imminent] danger" and that Asian nations needed to cooperate in order to survive was the one most often proposed.

It is true that some of the most vocal critics of the government's rejection of a pan-Asian policy, such as Prince Konoe Atsumaro (I:9), were themselves members of the ruling elite. But these were exceptions. In general, as the example of Miyazaki Tōten (I:11) illustrates, pan-Asianists in the late nineteenth and early twentieth centuries were characterized by their lack of government connections and by an overriding concern to promote regional cooperation by forging direct links with their fellow Asians.

Chapter Nine

The Foundation Manifesto of the Tōa Dōbunkai (East Asian Common Culture Society), 1898

Urs Matthias Zachmann

In the years 1897–1898, only three years after the Sino-Japanese War, China and Japan began gradually to move toward a rapprochement. The renewed and intensified encroachments of the Western powers on Chinese territory estranged Chinese politicians from Russia and compelled them to seek support from Japan, albeit reluctantly. Japanese government agencies, especially the Army General Staff and the Ministry of Foreign Affairs, were happy to oblige for their own reasons, and close cooperation ensued on an informal level, involving assistance to China's modernization program and academic exchanges. On the nongovernmental level, the international situation in East Asia led to the formation of a number of groups with an interest in forming cultural and political ties across the region. In November 1898, two of these groups merged into the East Asian Common Culture Society (Tōa Dōbunkai). The society was to become the most important pan-Asianist organization active on the continent until 1946—although the use of the term "pan-Asianist" to describe it is somewhat debatable, as we shall see here.

The two groups that formed the nucleus of the new society were of a rather hybrid or even—in terms of ideology and objectives—incompatible character (Sakeda 1978). The East Asian Society (Tōakai) had been founded in the spring of 1898 by politicians from the Shinpotō (Progress Party), members of the *Nippon* group (*Nippon* was a leading journal at the time), and students from Waseda and Tōkyō Imperial University. Among its prominent founding members were the politicians Inukai Tsuyoshi (1855–1932) and Hiraoka Kōtarō (1851–1906), who was also a prominent member of the Gen'yōsha (see I:3), and journalists Kuga Katsunan (1857–1907), Miyake Setsurei (1860–1945), Fukumoto Nichinan (1857–1921), and Ikebe Sanzan (1864–1912). The society advocated a hard-line foreign policy, consistently attacking the government for its "weak-kneed" stance. The society supported political reform in China and decided at its first meeting that it would accept the membership of the Chinese reformers Kang Youwei (1858–1927) and Liang Qichao (Liang Ch'i-Ch'ao, 1873–1929), who were to play a significant role in the so-called Hundred Days' Reform in China in 1898. This early support for Chinese reformers is most likely due to the fact that one of Kang Youwei's students, Xu Qin (1873–?), who had come to Japan to open a Chinese school in Yokohama called the Datong Xuexiao, happened to be a founding member of the Tōakai.

The second predecessor of the Tōa Dōbunkai was the Common Culture Society (Dōbunkai), founded in June 1898 and headed by the president of the House of Peers, Prince Konoe Atsumaro (1863–1904, see I:6). The society's name was an abbreviation of the phrase "same culture, same race" (*dōbun dōshu*), which, in the context of Sino–Japanese relations during this period, was often cited to invoke the romantic notion of cultural and biological links between the two countries. Konoe had invoked the notion as early as January 1898 in his essay calling for a "same-race alliance and the necessity of studying the Chinese Question" (see I:6). However, Konoe's later advocacy of an Asian Monroe Doctrine overlapped with the thinking of pan-Asianist advocates of a strong Japanese foreign policy. Nonetheless, the majority of the Dōbunkai's members were, in fact, of a pragmatic and even anti-ideological temperament. The society was founded largely on the initiative of the "China adventurers" Munakata Kotarō (1864–1923), Ide Saburō (1862–1931), Nakanishi Masaki (1857–1923), and Shiraiwa Ryūhei (1867–1942)—all members of the Shanghai-based Itsubikai (probably best translated as "The 1895 Society," as it was founded shortly after the Sino-Japanese War), a group of former disciples and students of Arao Sei (1858–1896), the cofounder of the Nisshin Bōeki Kenkyūjo (Research Institute for Sino-Japanese Trade; see I:4). Faithful to the teachings of Arao, this group carried on his mission of gathering information on China and creating personal networks as a means of furthering economic and strategic cooperation with and penetration of China. Consequently, the mission statement of the newly founded Dōbunkai stressed the necessity of studying "practical problems" in Sino–Japanese relations, emphasized its political neutrality in terms of party politics, and declared that its sole aim was to promote mutual understanding between "gentlemen" on both sides and to aid the development of trade and commerce between the two countries.

Given these differences, the merger of the two societies in November 1898 was less a matter of personal inclination (although there was a certain overlap) than one of financial necessity. Both societies needed government funding, and, considering the limited resources of the Foreign Ministry hitherto expended on "public diplomacy," it was only sensible that the two societies should apply jointly for any funding (in fact, this course was also suggested by then prime minister Ōkuma Shigenobu). Negotiations went smoothly, and the two societies merged as early as late October 1898. The following year, largely because of the influence of Hiraoka Kōtarō, the Diet granted the Foreign Ministry a substantial secret fund, half of which provided the financial base of the Tōa Dōbunkai.

Apart from the members already mentioned here, the new Tōa Dōbunkai included such diverse figures as Miyazaki Tōten (1871–1922, see I:11) and Hirayama Shū (1870–1940), both close associates of the Chinese revolutionary leader Sun Yat-sen (1866–1925; see II:5) and Japanese advocates of Chinese revolution but also Ariga Nagao (1860–1921) and Tachi Sakutarō (1874–1943), both eminent international lawyers and influential advisers to the Foreign Ministry over many years. The diversity of membership and views was evident from the first days of the new society. At the inaugural meeting of the new Tōa Dōbunkai in November 1898, members decided on a manifesto, translated here, and the following four principal goals of the society:

- To preserve the integrity of China (*Shina o hozen su*)
- To aid China's advancement
- To investigate the current state of affairs in China and decide on appropriate action
- To raise public awareness

In late 1898, the assertion that Japan should contribute to the "preservation of China's integrity" (in contrast to the division of China, *Shina bunkatsuron*) reflected the opinion of the majority of the Japanese public. It is important to note that this concept precluded an alliance of equal partners, as it envisaged Japan in a protective and leading role. Consequently, Konoe, as the new president of the society, in the inaugural edition of the society's organ *Tōa Jiron* (The East Asian Times), revoked his earlier notion of a "racial alliance" and made it clear that Japan should not shoulder China's problems through a simple appeal to such slogans as "same race, same culture" but should help China as a way of realizing Japan's own interests.

Nonetheless, opinions in the society differed widely as to the proper means of achieving this aim and of aiding China's advancement. This showed early on in the case of the Chinese reformers Kang Youwei and Liang Qichao, who had fled to Japan after the dismal failure of the Hundred Days' Reform movement in September 1898. Before long, Kang's presence in Japan became an embarrassment for the Japanese authorities, who came under considerable pressure from China and especially from Governor-General Zhang Zhidong to hand Kang over or extradite him. The Itsubikai members had long favored working with influential local politicians such as Zhang and distrusted the reformers around Kang as inexperienced and radical. In the end, they won the day against the former Tōakai members who had supported reform, and Konoe declared his willingness to help persuade Kang Youwei to leave Japan for America. The Foreign Ministry funneled travel money through the Tōa Dōbunkai to Kang, who departed for Canada in March 1899. Thus ended, successfully, the Tōa Dōbunkai's first "official" assignment (Zhai Xin 2001).

Subservience to government needs and a single-minded focus on nonideo-logical, professional support for Japan's role in China characterized the Tōa Dōbunkai's later development. This was remunerated by funding from gov-ernment sources, and, after 1923, the society was also guaranteed receipt of specially assigned revenues from the indemnity funds from the Boxer upris-ing of 1900. The lion's share of this money went to the single most important (and successful) project ever undertaken by the Tōa Dōbunkai, the East Asia Common Culture Academy (Tōa Dōbun Shoin). This facility for "training young China hands" (Reynolds 1989) was set up in 1900 in Nanjing but soon moved to Shanghai. There Japanese students enrolled in a three- to four-year training program (including a field trip assignment) to acquire the linguistic and technical skills needed to operate in China as entrepreneurs or intel-ligence agents (or both at the same time). In this way they would fulfill the society's third goal of "investigating the current state of affairs in China and deciding on appropriate action." Many of the more than 5,000 Japanese stu-dents who passed through the Tōa Dōbun Shoin worked in Japan as (military) interpreters, mediators, and managers for government agencies, thus prepar-ing the ground for their China operations. The Tōa Dōbun-kai also repeatedly attempted to train Chinese students—an endeavor that was, however, much less successful, especially after the outbreak of Chinese nationalism in 1919.

Another goal was "raising public awareness." In Japan, this was done through the society's own publications such as the *Tōa Jiron* (later *Shina, China*), in-depth studies of conditions in China, or sympathetic newspapers and magazines such as *Nippon* (Japan) and *Nipponjin* (The Japanese). How-ever, more to the point, this effort was also directed at the *Chinese* public through Chinese-language newspapers such as the Itsubi-kai organ *Yadong Shibao* (The East Asian Times) and other supportive newspapers. Again, these operations had their heyday in the late Meiji period, especially in rela-tion to the Russo-Japanese War, but continued into the Taishō period and peaked again after 1931 (Nakashita 1996).

The Tōa Dōbun-kai's last president was Prince Konoe Fumimaro (elected in 1936), the eldest son of Atsumaro. He committed suicide in 1945 to avoid being prosecuted as a war criminal by the International Military Tribunal in the Far East (Tokyo Trials). The society as such ceased to exist in 1946, but successor organizations such as the Kazankai (Kazan Society; Kazan was Konoe Atsumaro's pen name) continue to the present day. Moreover, members of the Tōa Dōbun Shoin, together with other returnees from universities in the Japanese colonies, founded Aichi University in 1947 (Reynolds 1989).

Source (translation from the Japanese original by Urs Matthias Zachmann) Manifesto of the East Asian Common Culture Society (Tōa Dōbunkai shuisho). *Tōa Jiron* 1 (December 1898), 1.

Contacts between Japan and China go well back in time. Our cultures are related and their customs and religions are the same. Emotionally, we are as close as brothers; strategically, we are as near to each other as the lips and teeth. Based on the impartiality of heaven's laws and grounded on the justness of humanity, gifts have passed back and forth between our emperors since ancient times, unaffected by change. Is this [relationship between Japan and China] anything like those enjoyed by neighboring powers, which form fleeting alliances and rob each other incessantly? However, who would have thought that, in recent years, heaven would show no compassion and that brothers would be fighting each other. The [European] powers have exploited this discord and the situation is becoming more and more difficult every day. Alas, is not the most urgent task today to forget all these mistakes, reject all hatred and ward off further contempt? At this time, both governments, acting from above, must perform the requisite public duties, honor the traditional rites and increasingly strengthen the contacts between the two countries. Acting from below, the tradespeople of both countries must act faithfully for the common good and must steadily improve relations with each other. The elites of both countries must become a firm rock amidst the swirling waters, associate with each other in perfect sincerity, and expound the Great Way— and in so doing help those above, lead those below and achieve strength and prosperity for both our countries. This is the reason that we founded the East Asian Common Culture Society. We ask those gentlemen from both countries, who have been born in these lands and aspire to great things in these times, to endorse this statement, join this society and thereby unite their powers.

Chapter Ten

The Kokuryūkai, 1901–1920

Sven Saaler

The Kokuryūkai was a political association (*seiji kessha*) founded in Tokyo in February 1901 by fifty-nine men under the leadership of "continental adventurer" (*tairiku rōnin*) Uchida Ryōhei (1874–1937), nephew of Genyōsha cofounder Hiraoka Kōtarō (1851–1906) (see Hatsuse [1980] for details on Uchida, Saaler [2008b] for details on the Kokuryūkai, and I:10 for details on the Genyōsha). At the time of the foundation of the Kokuryūkai, Uchida was already widely known for his activities on the Asian continent. He had been a member of the Tenyūkyō ("Heavenly Blessing Heroes"), a small group of adventurers who had supported the Donghak (Tonghak) rebellion in Korea in the 1890s (Kiyofuji 1981). Subsequently Uchida had lived for several years in Vladivostok, officially as a judo instructor but actually to gather intelligence about Japan's main rival at the time—Russia. And, finally, he had traveled alone through Siberia to Moscow and in this way earned a reputation as a man of action and a firsthand expert on Asian affairs.

Other influential figures in the formation of the Kokuryūkai included another Genyōsha cofounder, Tōyama Mitsuru (1855–1944; see I:3), leading people's rights activists such as Nakae Chōmin (1847–1901) and Ōi Kentarō (1843–1922), as well as party leader Inukai Tsuyoshi (1855–1932), who later became a symbol of "Taishō Democracy" and prime minister. All of them joined the society as "supporting members," while the full members belonged to a younger generation—the generation of Uchida.

Notwithstanding its close ties to the early Freedom and People's Rights Movement (*jiyū minken undō*)—a dozen members of the Liberal Party (*Jiyūtō*), which had been dissolved in 1898, were among the founding members of the Kokuryūkai—historical dictionaries usually characterize the Kokuryūkai as a statist (*kokkashugi*) or right-wing expansionist (*uyoku shinryakushugi*) association, but it is also frequently linked to Pan-Asianism.

The *Kokushi Daijiten* (Large Dictionary of Japanese History) describes the Kokuryūkai as "an influential nationalist organization that advocated and propagated Greater Asianism (*Dai Ajiashugi*)." The society's pan-Asiatic reputation is based, first of all, on the foundation statement of the society (see source 1) as well as on its name—Kokuryū (in Chinese pronounced Heilong) is the Chinese name for the Amur River, and the Amur River basin was the area favored by the society as the target of future Japanese expansion. The English name "Black Dragon Society," chosen by the Kokuryūkai itself and sensationalized in the United States during World War II, is a literal translation of "Amur" into English—Kokuryū literally means "Black Dragon."

In addition, Kokuryūkai members also undertook a variety of activities that can be summarized under the lofty ideal of "Asian solidarity" and that contributed to the society's pan-Asian reputation. Just as Uchida had done, many of them had spent years on the continent, some of them as members of the aforementioned group Tenyūkyō. Many of them had supported revolutionary movements in Korea and China, engaged in espionage in the Russian Far East, and aided various Asian independence movements. In China, Uchida, in close cooperation with Miyazaki Tōten (see I:11), had supported the revolutionary movement of Sun Yat-sen (see II:5), and in the Philippines, Uchida and his friends planned to support the anti-American uprising of Emilio Aguinaldo (1869–1964). Most of the Kokuryūkai members were at the same time members of other societies such as the Genyōsha or the Tōa Dōbunkai (East Asia Common Culture Association; see I:9), to which some twenty of the Kokuryūkai's founding members belonged.

Finally, the Kokuryūkai openly advocated Pan-Asianism in a number of publications, as the sources reproduced here demonstrate. The first time the association used the term "Pan-Asianism" (or alternative expressions like "Greater Asianism" or "All Asianism"), however, was sixteen years after its founding, when the inaugural issue of the association's journal *Ajia Jiron* (Asian Review) stated,

> The threat that the White people (*hakujin*) pose to the Yellow people (*ōjin*) is now imminent. . . . The Japanese Empire, as the last [independent] representative of Asia, is the only one that can face and fight the West as the backbone of the Yellow race (*ōshoku minzoku*). . . . We need to formulate a comprehensive foreign policy . . . , implant the idea of Greater Asianism, the great achievement of the foundation of our country, in the minds of the people, and bring about a comprehensive solution to the East Asia problem based on this [Asian]ism. (*Ajia Jiron* 1:1, July 1917, 3)

In later publications, this statement was frequently repeated (see, e.g., source 3). Interestingly, the English-language journal of the association, *The*

Asian Review, published between February 1920 and November 1921 and directed at a foreign, above all Western audience, failed to mention the term "Asianism" in the "Editorial Foreword" of its inaugural issue—an omission also made by Uchida Ryōhei in his contribution "The Asian Review and the Kokuryukai" (*The Asian Review* 1:1, 1920, 1–5). Be that as it may, what contributed to the reputation of the Kokuryūkai as *the* pan-Asian organization par excellence much more than the explicit use of pan-Asian rhetoric is the fact that, in later years, its members became the historians of Pan-Asianism in Japan and naturally placed the association at the center of the historical narrative (see source 3). In the 1930s, the association compiled a three-volume "unofficial history" of the pan-Asian movement in Japan—the *Tōa Senkaku Shishi Kiden* (Biographies of Pioneer East Asian Patriots [Kokuryūkai 1966b], originally published in 1933–1936). It also published a two-volume biography of Saigō Takamori (1828–1877), the Meiji Restoration leader whom many later pan-Asianists considered an early exemplar of Japanese activism on the Asian continent; the two-volume *Nikkan Gappō Hishi* (Secret History of the Union of Japan and Korea [Kokuryūkai 1966a] first published in 1930), praising the Japanese annexation of Korea in 1910 as a great achievement of the pan-Asian movement; and the pictorial *Nikkan Gappō Kinentō Shashinchō* (Photo Album of the Monument to the Union of Japan and Korea [Kokuryūkai 1934]), celebrating a memorial that had been built by the Kokuryūkai to mark the thirtieth anniversary of the annexation of Korea.

From an initial fifty-nine, Kokuryūkai membership expanded to more than 300 within a few months and reached almost 1,000 in the 1920s. In the first ten years of the association's existence, most of the Kokuryūkai's members came from Kyushu, with members from Fukuoka making up the vast majority, followed by Saga and Kumamoto. But, in contrast to the Genyōsha, which is often regarded as the Kokuryūkai's parent body, supporters from all over Japan flocked to join the Kokuryūkai, while the membership of the Genyōsha remained limited to Kyushu (Kan 1984: 93).

The Kokuryūkai exerted a much greater influence than the size of its membership implied. The society was actively engaged in promoting its views on politics and society, partly through personal contacts but also through publications. Unlike the Genyōsha, right from its inception in 1901 the Kokuryūkai published a journal that made its research on Asian affairs available to a wider readership. The first incarnation of the society's journal was simply called *Kaihō* (Bulletin). After only two numbers, it was banned by the government because of the "immoderate tone" of its editorials on foreign policy. The early journals published by the Kokuryūkai—*Kaihō*, its successor *Kokuryū*, and *Tōa Geppō* (East Asian Monthly)—served as outlets for the findings of the association's research on East Asian affairs. *Tōa Geppō* was published in classical Chinese (*kanbun*) in order to serve as a forum to exchange ideas between Japanese, Chinese, and Korean pan-Asianists. Only the later *Ajia Jiron* (Asian Review) and the English-language *Asian Review* can be characterized as publications serving, above all, the purpose of political agitation (Saaler 2008b). Apart from these periodicals, Uchida Ryōhei penned numerous memoranda that he frequently forwarded to Japan's top politicians and bureaucrats, some of whom trusted his opinions. Uchida's high reputation as an expert on Asia was recognized when the colonial administration of Korea employed him as an adviser in 1907 and when Chinese leader Sun Yat-sen hired him as an adviser on foreign affairs in 1913. Because the Kokuryūkai received some funding from the Japanese government and the army, some of its publications were explicitly devised to brief the nation's diplomats and military leaders. The *Kokuryūkai Mankan Shinzu* (Kokuryūkai's New Map of Manchuria and Korea [Kokuryūkai Honbu 1904]) was a best-seller, and the *Seiro Annai* (A Guide to Conquering Russia [Kokuryūkai 1904])—proved extremely useful to the Imperial Army in its preparations for the coming war with Russia.

The Kokuryūkai was at its most active around the time of World War I, when it reached the peak of its influence (see Saaler 2008b). Part of the association's popularity derived from its advocacy of racial equality and its vociferous opposition to racial exclusion legislation of the type passed in the United States in 1924, which banned Japanese and Chinese immigration to the United States. In 1920, after the failure of the Japanese delegation to secure the inclusion of a racial equality clause in the Charter of the League of Nations (Shimazu 1998), one of the many smaller offshoots of the Kokuryūkai, the League for the Equality of Races (Jinshu Sabetsu Teppai Kiseikai, lit. Association for the Abolition of Racial Discrimination; see source 4; see also I:26), spearheaded demonstrations against Western racism. In general, the Kokuryūkai agitated strongly against the League of Nations, considering its foundation as nothing more than a device for the Anglo-Saxon powers to preserve the unjust status quo (see source 3 and I:32 on Konoe Fumimaro for a similar view). Thus, anti-Westernism, as a result of a perceived rise of anti-Japanese racism in international relations, gradually replaced the society's initial anti-Russian attitudes. At the same time, the growing political, economic, and military strength of Japan led to stronger claims for Japanese leadership—the claim for leadership of the Japanese race, the *Yamato minzoku*, and the insistence on a "Japanese mission" (see source 2) as one of the core facets of Pan-Asianism as advocated by the Kokuryūkai and related organizations. The initial claim for Asian solidarity was eventually replaced by imperialist designs under the cloak of pan-Asian rhetoric and, at times, the rhetoric of universal brotherhood and "world peace" (see source 3)—which the association also drew on in its attacks on the Western powers.

During the first decades of its existence, the Kokuryūkai was not considered in Japan—as most historians view it today—to be a right-wing or particularly extremist association. This is indicated by the large number of companies that financed the society by advertising in the Kokuryūkai's journals. All the major companies of the day were represented in the advertising columns of *The Asian Review* and *Ajia Jiron*—firms such as the Mitsui Bank Ltd, the Mitsubishi Bank Ltd, the trading houses Mitsui Bussan Kaisha Ltd and Suzuki Shōten, the Bank of Korea and the Bank of Taiwan, the shipping company Nippon Yūsen Kaisha Ltd, and the South Manchurian Railway Company (Minami Manshū Tetsudō KK).

However, from the late 1910s, in an atmosphere marked by the polarization of political debate into prodemocracy and antidemocracy camps, the Kokuryūkai's tone grew increasingly extremist, and the society turned more and more violent. The Kokuryūkai campaigned vociferously against advocates of democratization such as Yoshino Sakuzō (1878–1933) and branded progressive newspapers as "traitors to the nation" (*hikokumin*) (Saaler 2008b). At the same time, the Kokuryūkai was losing support—the old political and bureaucratic allies were gone, but the society failed to mobilize alternative sources of support and eventually proved unable to cope with the new era of mass society and mass mobilization. A "Memorandum to Expand the Kokuryūkai" written by Uchida Ryōhei in 1924 (Kokuryūkai Honbu 1924) apparently had little effect, and thus, in 1931, Uchida and his close associate Kuzuu Yoshihisa (1874–1958) founded a new party designed to attract a larger membership—the Dai Nihon Seisantō (Great Japan Production Party). However, this group also failed to become a major political force before (or even after) Uchida died in 1937. The Kokuryūkai as well as the Dai Nihon Seisantō were banned and disbanded by the American occupation forces as "ultranationalist societies" in 1946.

In the early stages, the Kokuryūkai engaged, above all, in action, and, like most other pan-Asianist organizations, it failed to put its pan-Asian ideals down in writing. Although its members were pan-Asianist in their sentiment and outlook, the Kokuryūkai made no effort to clearly and explicitly *define* Pan-Asianism as an ideology; hence, it is difficult to find any specific texts on the subject among its earlier publications. However, the sources reproduced here give proof of a strong interest in Asia from the time of the founding of the society; they bear witness to a strong anti-Western, anticolonialist, and particularly anti-Russian attitude, to a strong fear of further Russian expansion in the Far East, but also to feelings of Asian solidarity (source 1). Not until the time of World War I, however, do we find explicit pan-Asian rhetoric in the Kokuryūkai's publications. The sources reproduced below also show that the Kokuryūkai itself was the main propagator of its reputation as an important and pioneering pan-Asian organization. Although the society did not use the terms "Pan-Asianism," "Asianism," or "Asian solidarity" before World War I, in 1917 the society suddenly started describing itself as "a long-standing advocate of Pan-Asianism" (*Ajia Jiron* 1:1, July 1917, 3). The aforementioned publication of *Tōa Senkaku Shishi Kiden* in the 1930s, as well as later statements made on the occasion of the anniversaries of the founding of the society, further bolstered the self-made image of the Kokuryūkai as the leading actor in the pan-Asian movement in modern Japan.

Source 1 (translation from the Japanese original by Sven Saaler)
Kokuryūkai Sōritsu Shui (Foundation Gist of the Kokuryūkai) (1901), reproduced in Uchida Ryōhei Monjo Kenkyūkai (ed.), *Kokuryūkai Kankei Shiryōshū* (Collection of Sources Relating to the Kokuryūkai), vol. 1. Kashiwa Shobō, 1992, 2–3.

Germany, Russia, Britain and France have been constantly increasing their presence and expanding their influence. They have been sailing the oceans, climbing the mountains, fighting their way over a thousand miles, and have finally reached the shores of our Orient (*waga tōyō*). Furthermore, although this development has contributed to the increasing ills of Korea and the weakness of China, nobody seems worried—people [in Japan] close their eyes and are only concerned with their own security, enjoying the safety of the day. What kind of era do we live in? But it is also pointless to become indignant. Thoughtful men must first investigate the situation of the world, make the facts public, openly explain [Japan's] strengths and weaknesses, and make [Japanese] interests clear. . . . This will inevitably to lead to the formulation of a Grand Strategy for the next hundred years.

Russia has revised the Peking Treaty with China, annexed the Ussuri region and built a railroad 10,000 miles long [the Trans-Siberian railway]; it has colonized the land, sent in settlers and steered the development [of Siberia]. In so doing, it has given the world the biggest shock for more than 400 years, and recently it has gone so far as to build a naval base on Liaodong [the Liaotung peninsula], strengthen its military presence [in the Orient] and advance south into Manchuria. . . . The Russians have also started up a railway in the north[ern part of Manchuria], established a naval base in the South [Port Arthur], and gained control of all three of the Eastern provinces [Manchuria]. . . . The other Powers have closed their eyes and have not hindered Russia's actions. Rather, they too have become interested in partitioning China: Germany has established a sphere of influence in Shandong [Shantung], Britain in Guangzhou [Canton], and France in Yunnan—and the various Powers have made no attempt to restrain each other.

It is in the context of this situation that we have to weigh the merits and demerits of expelling the Powers from the Orient, and make it clear that our country is in imminent danger. [First,] we need to conduct a thorough examination before we can actively pursue our chosen political course. Our politicians can only deal with simple concepts, they are short-sighted and will only take small forward steps; they feel indignation and become excited for no reason, they attribute perseverance to their actions, they call themselves determined, but they easily make sudden retreats, and are deaf to the need to strengthen our position in Korea and China, both of which are weak. . . . It is unnecessary to repeat the fact that we are connected to Siberia, Manchuria and Korea by a close relationship which has lasted more than one hundred years, but public opinion is oblivious to this. And even today, at a time when a grave crisis is approaching, nobody speaks out about it—how is this possible? We think it is because they [the politicians] have not [investigated and] made public the situation of the land and people in China and Korea. Even when we were poor and had nothing, for many years we slept under the open sky along the Amur River; we experienced hardships at the foot of Mount Changpai [Baekdu], we lived undercover on Liaotung [peninsula] and, through these experiences, we investigated the people and their customs and observed that they have not lost their desire for independence. We have established the Kokuryūkai to examine the world situation, because we are angry about the present state of affairs and our aim is to draw up a long-term policy plan [to remedy it].

We plan to present the results of our study and thereby raise the popular awareness of the people. To fulfill our aims, we will pursue further research on the spot, rather than in a strictly academic setting. We will conduct research on politics, but also on customs, the people, agricultural production, geography and other topics relating to these regions [Siberia, Manchuria, and so on]. We will collect the findings of our research and analyze them, and then we will select projects that are really necessary for the present and future [welfare of our country]. If we push forward with devotion and persistence, we can establish a long-term policy which without doubt will lead to the consolidation of our position [on the continent]. We hope that all thoughtful people will praise our sincerity, cooperate with us and understand our objectives.

Source 2 (translation from the Japanese original by Sven Saaler)
Uchida Ryōhei (1918), "Jo" (Preface). Kokuryūkai Shuppanbu (ed.), *Ajia Taikan* (Overview of Asia). Kokuryūkai Shuppanbu, 1918, 1–4.

Asia is the world's oldest civilization. Three thousand years ago, when the present European countries were inhabited by rude barbarians, the civilization of India was already shining brightly all over the world. As was the civilization of Persia. As was the civilization of Asia Minor. As was the civilization of China. . . . After the sixteenth century, the West[ern Powers] began to advance eastward and . . . most of Asia lost its political destiny [i.e., independence]. At that time, when international conflict was poised at a crossroads, it was only the Yamato race (*Yamato minzoku*), representing all the Asian nations (*minzoku*), which resisted the advance of the Western Powers into the East and, fighting furiously, stood solid as a rock. . . .

The Great European War was their suicide as a civilization. . . . We cannot say whether European civilization is really going down a dead-end street at present. However, as a consequence of the European War, the Asian nations have settled down and now have to awaken to their Asian roots, to awaken spiritually, awaken in a cosmopolitan manner. . . . The Great European War is the great opportunity for an Asian revival (*Ajia fukkō*), and whether this opportunity is going to be seized or not depends only on how the Asian nations decide [their own fate].

Our Kokuryūkai has been a leading advocate of Pan-Asianism (*Dai Ajiashugi*) for many years. Looking back over the Great European War and the present changes in the world, we have compiled the "Overview of Asia" (*Ajia Taikan*) . . . and we hope that it will contribute a little to the realization of Greater Asianism. . . . Today, we publish this book in the hope that it will be an important turning point in the [process of the] awakening of the Asian nations (*Ajia minzoku*).

May 1918
Uchida Ryōhei

Source 3 (English in the original)
Uchida Ryōhei, "The Asian Review and the Kokuryu-kai." *The Asian Review*, 1:1 (1920), 3–5.

The Asian Review and the Kokuryu-kai
By Ryohei Uchida, President of the Kokuryu-kai

"The Asian Review" is intended to be a medium for making the outside world understand our political opinions. Therefore, on the occasion of this initial issue, we feel called upon to try to dispel some misunderstandings from which we have suffered from foreign critics since the foundation of the Kokuryu-kai.

The aspiration of the Kokuryu-kai is to ensure lasting peace in the world, at least in this part of the world, which it wishes to be saved from any ruffle of disturbance—a peace in which justice and humanity reign supreme, the ideal of civilization, but not a patched-up peace in which everything is stagnant and calm on the surface alone, nor a false peace which is used by aggressive nations as a cloak to hide their dire designs. This is the national policy of Japan which has undergone no change during three thousand years. The Japanese nation worships AMATERASU OKAMI, the *avatar* of mercy and benevolence. . . .

The valour and chivalry shown by the Japanese in wars with China [1894–1895] and Russia [1904–1905] are now matter for historical study. Since the facts are before the world, critics are at liberty to pass their own judgment. In these wars members of the Kokuryu-kai were closely involved; but no charge is farther from the truth than that the association is Jingo [jingoistic] with land grabbing ambitions.

It is true that previous to the war with China [1894–1895], members of the Kokuryu-kai organized an association "Tenyukyo," and extended aid to the Korean people who had been struggling hard to throw off the shackles of Chinese interference as well as of the maladministration of the Korean Government.

Further is it true that during the war they gave invaluable assistance to the Japanese army. . . . It is hardly necessary to mention that the Japanese, including the Kokuryu-kai members, had no aggressive designs, as has been recognized by the intellectuals of the world.

But alas! The aftermath of the war did not redound to the credit of the European nations, but cast a shadow on their own moral prestige. Japan emerged victorious from the war, but she was forced by the triple intervention of Russia, Germany and France [1895] to conclude a loser's peace. In these circumstances, who wonders that the Japanese began to feel uneasy about the Far Eastern situation?

It is a well-known fact that Russia . . . had aggressive designs on the Far East. . . . The Kokuryu-kai members were not meant to sit content with easy-chair discussion. They concentrated their efforts on actual investigations in Korea, Manchuria and Siberia . . . and in 1898 they came to the conclusion that it would be impossible to avoid war with Russia if the safety of the Far East was to be maintained. . . .

Thus, the Kokuryu-kai was formally organised in January 1901, for the purpose of formulating a plan to ensure lasting peace for the Far East, by making our people familiar with the actual state of affairs in Korea, Manchuria, and Russia. In September of the same year, the Japono-Russian Society (Nichiro-Kyokai) was founded at our instance. It was intended as an organ of rapprochement between Japan and Russia after the war. . . .

As for the annexation of Korea in 1910, the Kokuryu-kai had used every means in its power to accelerate it in pursuance of the desires of the "Isshin-kai," an association having 1,000,000 Korean members. . . .

The Kokuryu-kai has also paid due attention to the development of China. . . . [I]n 1911, when a revolution broke out in China we organised an associa-tion, the "Yurinkai," . . . and gave assistance to the Chinese revolutionaries. All the time, we were making a close study of the China question. In 1913, we organised another association called the "Taishikenkyu-kai" for the purpose of studying all questions pertaining to China. Further, in order to settle the Manchurian and Mongolian questions, we merged our associations . . . and founded a federated association, the "Taishi Rengo-kai." . . .

The Kokuryukai publishes the Japanese edition of the "Ajia Jiron" (Asian Review) in order to give the Japanese people general information about Asia and to help them to define their attitude. . . .

The world, which has been harrowed by the great cataclysm of the War has its vision confused. It cannot help feeling very uneasy about its future. But the contention of the Kokuryu-kai is backed by history, sincerity, and substantial power. Whatever slander and whatever vilification ambitious propagandists may hurl against Japan in their attempts to eliminate her influence from the Far East, this influence grows stronger than ever, and the contention of the Kokuryu-kai remains firm as a mountain. After all, Asia is for the Asiatics. History, manners, customs and human nature cultivated in this part of the world for the past five thousand years can be understood only by the Asiatics. And who but Japan should venture to undertake the task of harmonizing this Oriental civilization with Occidental culture and thereby ensuring peace for the world? And the reason we promote a magazine in a foreign language is to give publicity to this aspiration of the Japanese nation.

Source 4 (English in the original)
"Universal League for the Equality of Races, Foundation Manifesto." Paul Richard, *The Dawn over Asia*. Madras: Ganesh & Co. Publishers, 1920, 89–97.

LEAGUE FOR THE EQUALITY OF RACES

The Origin of the League

The League for the Equality of Races was born of the war—of that war in which all the races mingled their blood; the proudest calling to their help the most humble; in which all the cultures were confounded—these rising, those sinking—in which all the peoples inflicting on each other a common ruin, all men in a mutual slaughter came to understand their strong solidarity and learnt that a durable peace and the safety of all depend on their respect for each other—on Equality:

The League for the Equality of Races first took birth in Japan. At the moment when there met what was thought to be the Conference of Peace at Paris, thirty-seven great Japanese associations, representing all the forces of the nation, assembled with the intention of supporting the claim made by the delegates at the Conference in the name of the oppressed races of the world.

At its first meeting, the League thus formed, under the Presidency of M. Teiichi Sugita, Member and former president of the House of Peers, addressed to the Peace Conference the following message:

(abridged [see I:26])

General Object of the League

To proclaim the principle of Democracy as between the races; the equality of rights, the right to equality, not only of the individual in the Nation, but of the peoples and races in Humanity.

To assure respect for human dignity in every man, whatever be his race or colour—and thereby the progress of all the races of the more advanced as of the more backward; enlightening the pride of the former, the humility of the others; elevating all above that real barbarism which consists in the want of mutual understanding and fraternity.

For Asia

To serve the moral and material unity of Asia by offering to her peoples and her races a basis of permanent agreement and common interests.

To prepare, by the development of inter-asiatic relations, the League and the Congress of the nations of Asia.

To favour by the free growth of the races of Asia their harmonious relations with the other races of the world. . . .

Declaration

In the name of History which all times and all races have written—history that shows us all the families of men mounting and descending, across the Dawns and the Evenings of time, and taking by turns the lead of human Progress;

In the name of Science, daughter of all the civilisations of the earth, light of all, that brightens and grows in each, and teaches that the races of men are made one from the other, for never in the course of ages have they ceased to exchange their thoughts, and to mingle their blood;

In the name of the Religions, to which all the races give their saints, revealers and guides, in the name of the religions which say to us:

. . .

In the name of Humanity, multiple and one, whose whole body feels the injury done to a single one of its members, in the name of Humanity rich by the diversity, strong by the solidarity of its races; progressing in the progress of them all and in all the free development of their forms;

In the name of Human Peace—for without mutual respect there is no peace;

In the name of Reason—which tends towards Unity, and of the Soul—which lives by love,

WE DECLARE AND PROCLAIM. THE
UNIVERSAL EQUALITY OF THE
HUMAN RACES.

Chapter Eleven

Miyazaki Tōten's Pan-Asianism, 1915–1919

Christopher W. A. Szpilman

Miyazaki Torazō (1871–1922), known subsequently also as Tōten, was born on 23 January 1871 into a family of *gōshi* (peasant samurai, yeomen) in Kumamoto Prefecture (for his life, see Watanabe Kyōji 2006) . He attended the Ōe Academy run by Tokutomi Sohō (see I:28), where he was stirred into revolutionary fervor by accounts of the French Revolution. He was receptive to such ideas no doubt because his eldest brother, Hachirō (1851–1877), had been killed by government troops while taking part in the Satsuma Rebellion of 1877. An antiauthoritarian sentiment certainly ran in the family. His brothers, Tamizō (1865–1928) and Yazō (1867–1896), were prominent in the people's rights movement and it was natural for Miyazaki, when he went to study at the Tokyo Vocational School (Tokyo Senmon Gakkō, predecessor of Waseda University) in 1886, to get involved in politics. In 1887 he converted to Christianity but, disenchanted, abandoned his new faith after two years. Instead, he developed a passion for a revolution that would liberate Asia from the yoke of the white man. This soon became his raison d'être.

In pursuit of this new goal, Miyazaki traveled to Shanghai in 1891, but his plans to participate in a revolutionary movement against the Qing (Ch'ing) dynasty, whose continuing existence he believed was antithetical to effective Asian resistance to Western aggression, came to nothing, as he was forced to return to Japan when his modest funds ran out. But this setback did nothing to cool his enthusiasm for the cause of Asian liberation. Temporarily shifting his attention away from China, he now focused on the promotion of Japanese immigration to Siam, which, he assumed naively, would somehow spearhead the liberation of Asia. After a number of years in Siam, however, the project failed. Back in Japan, Miyazaki, divorced by his wife and alienated from his closest family, led a lonely existence in dire poverty. Things improved in 1897, when the foreign minister, Ōkuma Shigenobu (1838–1922), paid for a second trip to China out of the ministry's secret funds. In China, Miyazaki got to know members of the Chinese Revolutionary Party, including Sun Yat-sen (see II:5). Impressed by Sun, he redoubled his efforts for the cause of toppling the Qing dynasty while remaining faithful to his wider pan-Asian ideals. In 1899 he was involved in gun-running to anti-American guerillas in the Philippines; in 1900 he tried to bring unity to the fragmented Chinese revolutionary movement. In 1905, together with Sun Yat-sen and other Chinese exiles in Tokyo, he founded the Chinese Revolutionary League (Tongmenghui or T'ung-meng-hui; Japanese: Chūgoku Dōmeikai) and in 1907 assumed the editorship of the *Kakumei Hyōron* (Revolutionary Review), a monthly founded to promote the cause of the Chinese Revolution.

After 1900, financial difficulties forced Miyazaki to put his revolutionary activities on the back burner. He became a *naniwa-bushi* (ballad reciter), performer, and writer. In 1902 he published his autobiography, *Sanjūsannen no Yume* (My Thirty-Three Years' Dream), which brought him fame but little money. A moving record of the trials and tribulations of his youth, the work expresses the romantic, idealistic outlook that underlay his Pan-Asianism, as the following passage indicates:

> People may say, "an ideal is an ideal and cannot be realized." But I believe that ideals must be realized. What cannot be realized is fantasies. . . . I do believe in the brotherhood of man and for that reason I abhor the present situation of might being right (*jakuniku kyōshoku*). I subscribe to the theory that the world is one single family. For that reason I detest international competition that is raging at present. (Miyazaki 1902: 37; English translation, *My Thirty-Three Years' Dream*, 1982)

In the last decade of his life, Miyazaki was plagued by bad health. His sudden collapse in 1913, when he was taking part, along with Sun Yat-sen, in the so-called Second Chinese Revolution, put an end to his active involvement in Chinese politics—although he subsequently made frequent trips to China to visit old friends. In 1915 Miyazaki ran as a candidate in the Japanese general elections. He failed to get elected in spite of being endorsed by such diverse pan-Asian figures as Tōyama Mitsuru of the Genyōsha (see I:3), Inukai Tsuyoshi (1866–1932), and Professor Terao Tōru (1859–1925) of the Law Faculty, Tokyo Imperial University. In the last few years of his life, he eked out a living by writing columns in newspapers. He died in 1922, aged fifty-two, his health destroyed by many years of alcohol abuse and bad diet.

Miyazaki's contacts in pan-Asian circles were extensive. He was especially close to Uchida Ryōhei of the Kokuryūkai (see I:10), Tōyama and Inukai. All these men supported Miyazaki financially at one time or another. Miyazaki was also in touch with radical pan-Asianists of the younger generation, notably Kita Ikki (see I:27). He knew the Indian independence activist and pan-Asianist Ras Behari Bose. Among the Chinese, Miyazaki was a close friend of Sun Yat-sen, Huang Xing (also Huang Hsing, 1874–1916), and other revolutionaries. As mentioned previously, Miyazaki devoted his life to the ideal of the liberation of Asia from the yoke of imperialism. His credentials as a pan-Asianist are not in doubt. Yet it is difficult to find a short text that encapsulates his pan-Asian ideals, partly because he was not a systematic thinker but preferred to "muddle along" on an ad hoc basis. A well-developed sense of fairness and justice, not logical consistency, was his guide.

Nevertheless, his election manifesto, dated February 1915 and reproduced here, summarizes his pan-Asian views accurately. It is significant that in this document Miyazaki uses the term Pan-Asianism—one of the earliest examples of this expression used in a positive sense. Two things must be borne in mind when assessing the manifesto. First, as an election campaign statement, the views expressed in it may have been modified so as avoid alienating Tōyama, Inukai, and Miyazaki's other supporters. Second, it was written during World War I. Both these factors account for the unusually—for Miyazaki—"gung ho," militaristic tone of this statement. Nevertheless, certain continuities inherent in Miyazaki's Pan-Asianism can be detected. For example, his hostility to Japan's Western allies comes across clearly. Miyazaki called for a military buildup to defend Japan (and Asia) against what he believed to be an imminent onslaught by the Western powers that would begin once the war in Europe was over. This follows logically from his general hostility to imperialism including the Japanese variety (although, in this instance, he softened his stance on Japanese imperialism, of which he was eloquently critical elsewhere).

The call for the formulation of a fundamental China policy by Japan reflects another continuity—Miyazaki never wavered in his conviction that the liberation of Asia was contingent on the success of reform in China. In other words, he believed that the liberation of Asia was impossible without first successfully reforming China. It is thus possible to argue that, as in the case of Kita Ikki, his dedication to China stemmed from wider pan-Asian concerns.

Although the election statement contains nothing that pan-Asianists such as Tōyama or Terao would consider objectionable, it would be wrong to assume that there was nothing to distinguish Miyazaki from such reactionaries or that, by 1915, Miyazaki had become a rightist. On the contrary, in his other writings Miyazaki continued to be highly critical of Japanese foreign policy, Japanese militarism, and the colonial administration of Taiwan and Korea (e.g., Miyazaki 1971: 132). Nor did he mince words regarding the domestic scene. On at least one occasion he called on the Japanese people to rise and topple the military cliques—an outcome which would not only improve Japan's stance toward China, but also toward the world (Miyazaki and Onogawa 1971: 135).

After World War I, Miyazaki stressed the need for "Asian solidarity" (*renkei*). From this position, he opposed Japan's membership in the League of Nations—he preferred Japan to establish an Asian league based on "true humanity and righteousness." Paul Richard's (see I:29) influence is clear here; he attended lectures given by Richard and praised the ideas expressed by the Frenchman (Miyazaki and Onogawa 1971: 128–29).

In spite of these later influences and contacts with Kita (who sent him a Lotus Sutra with a personal dedication) and other radicals, Miyazaki was a representative of an early form of Pan-Asianism that had little in common with the variety that arose in the 1920s among a generation of younger men such as Kita, Ōkawa, and Kanokogi (see chaps. 27, 36, and 46). It is difficult to suspect his motives, for clearly his heart was in the right place. His friendship for Chinese revolutionaries was not subordinated to his patriotism; for Miyazaki, China almost always took priority over Japan.

Yet for all his earnestness, his version of Pan-Asianism contains within itself the reasons why his efforts frequently ended in failure. Miyazaki was a dreamer. In contrast to Tōyama, Uchida, or Ōkawa, he disdained interest in practical matters. Where others profited from their pan-Asianist associations, Miyazaki spent all his and his family's money on the cause and died in abject poverty. His impracticality to a large degree explains his failure to realize any of his goals. The list is long. Take, for example, the 1899 scheme to smuggle weapons into the Philippines that ended in tragedy when the dilapidated ship carrying them sunk with considerable loss of life. His Siamese venture is also a case in point, as is his attempt to reconcile Sun Yat-sen and Kang Youwei, which also ended in failure, with Miyazaki being arrested by the British on the absurd suspicion of being a hired assassin. Yet his impracticality, guilelessness, and naïveté—his complete lack of self-interest and calculation—make him a universally attractive figure. He appeals to the modern reader, just as he appealed to Chinese revolutionaries like Sun Yat-sen, who genuinely liked and trusted him.

Miyazaki's impracticality reflected the fact that there was something distinctly romantic and premodern about him. He represented a reaction to the havoc wrought on the lives of the masses by westernization and to the destruction of the *Gemeinschaft* of the East, which was idealized especially by those who, like him, could hardly remember what Japan had really been like in the Tokugawa period. Like a true samurai, he disdained materialism, money, and moneymaking. Asianism was a dream in which he tried to find solace from the daunting realities of modern Japanese life.

Source 1 (translation from the Japanese original by Christopher W. A. Szpilman)
Miyazaki Tōten, "Rikkōho Sengen" (Election Manifesto, 1915), reprinted in *Miyazaki Tōten Zenshū* (Complete Works of Miyazaki Tōten), vol. 2, Heibonsha, 1971, frontispiece.

DECLARATION OF CANDIDACY BY MIYAZAKI TORAZŌ, A CANDIDATE FOR THE LOWER HOUSE OF THE DIET

The Great War in Europe is an upheaval unprecedented in the annals of history. They [i.e., the Europeans] swooped down on Asia like wolves and jackals, and the only thing that prevented them from using all their might was their fear of destroying the mutual balance of power within Europe—even if, ironically, the present upheaval is entirely the result of this [very breakdown]. This upheaval has now reached an extreme, the war is at its climax. Although it is impossible to predict exactly when peace will be restored, there is absolutely no doubt that, when it comes, financial exhaustion will cause enormous political difficulties in the [European] states. There is a saying that one flood is always followed by another. In Europe after the Great War there will be a clash of imperialism and non-imperialism and, if imperialism does not perish, it is easy to see that the starving tigers [of Europe] will turn around on their heels and fight over scraps of meat in the Orient. It is obvious which of these alternatives, imperialism or non-imperialism, will prevail. Then it will be up to Japan to lay down its great foundation—which is the great policy of national defense—and, through achieving a comprehensive solution to the Chinese question, establish the basis for Pan-Asianism (*Dai Ajiashugi*). There is no time to lose. This is a golden opportunity.

The gist of my candidacy is simple and clear. It is summed up in my determination to do everything I can at this time within my limited ability to find a fundamental solution to our China policy. I pledge to involve myself in making Pan-Asianism a reality and will try to repay a tiny fraction of the debt of gratitude I owe to the state. In obedience to the spirit of the Constitution, my desire is to see the establishment of constitutional government. That is why I hate the politics of compromise and detest cliquish politics, the kind that goes on behind closed doors (*yoriai*). Given the situation we are facing, I believe that proposals to reduce armaments are foolish. That is why I am delighted that today's political parties are not advocating such foolish proposals. However, if I regret anything, it is that the current call for total conscription and for two extra army divisions, the demand to extend military service by one year—although they all recognize the need for strengthening the military—are the result of egoistic intentions that fall short of the study and careful consideration required, and turn the question of national defense into matter for political strife.

For that reason, everything boils down to this. The government has its private motives; the political parties have their own policies. Wild arguments—the result of the clashing agendas of the government and party policies—occur because the state is regarded as of secondary importance. People see this and talk of cabals or coteries, which is surely no exaggeration. This is why I espouse a strictly impartial position and am not affiliated with any party.

However, Japanese party politics is in a period of transition at present. How can we expect much from the parties? Only as regards the China question, which I consider the most urgent of all urgent questions, will I help those with whom I agree and attack those with whom I disagree. That is all. When it comes to the foreign policy of the present cabinet, its policies on China, on Europe and on America are all wrong. For the people to accept this on trust is to accept humiliation, to be made a laughing stock. There is no need to say that the true significance of the Anglo-Japanese Alliance is that [Japan] has become a lackey of Britain. There is no need to state that [the current policy of preserving] the territorial integrity of China serves only to curry favor with Yuan Shikai [Yuan Shih-k'ai, 1859–1916].

There is no need to repeat here that a solution to the American problem will not be found by exchanging compliments. Faced with a grand design that is fundamentally misconceived, there will be no golden opportunity other than the present one. That is why I am running in this election in spite of my lack of ability.

February 1915

Source 2 (translation from the Japanese original by Christopher W. A. Szpilman)
Miyazaki Tōten, "Tokyo yori" (From Tokyo, 1919), *Miyazaki Tōten Zenshū* (Complete Works of Miyazaki Tōten), vol. 2, Heibonsha, 1971, 128.

. . . There is a good reason that, at the present world peace conference [in Paris], Japan has fallen into isolation, alienated from the Western powers. This is because the principles that control Japan follow the so-called gospel of the sword, in imitation of German militarism, and it was these principles that Japan has been applying to China and Korea.

But, if anything, this is a natural outcome. The Western Powers, which pride themselves on their Christianity, look down on us as alien beings; they pretend to be sheep but have the greed of tigers and wolves in their hearts, and are ready to pounce whenever an opportunity arises. Things are now the same as before—no, they are in fact much worse than before. It is possible that their goal is to deprive Japan of its freedom of movement. . . . But if this is so, how is the Japanese nation to act? Is there enough determination in the people to continue the policy of statism (*kokkashugi*), no matter what? Would we not give it up, even if we were on our backs?

Or should we preserve harmony with the Western Powers and, assuming higher moral ground than they, propose, as Dr Richard says, an Asian federation (*Ajia renmei*) based on a thorough-going humanitarianism? Should we not give freedom to Korea and Taiwan? Moreover, should we not change our China policy and, benefiting from [Chinese] friendship, help all the weak countries [of Asia]; and, having organized a federation on principles of equality, should we not resist the Whites . . . ?

Chapter Twelve

Pan-Asianism, the "Yellow Peril," and Suematsu Kenchō, 1905

Sven Saaler

In 1981, Diet member Aoki Kazuo (1889–1982)—a former minister for Greater East Asia (*Daitōa daijin*, 1942–1944)—noted that in prewar Japan, Pan-Asianism had never been adopted as official government policy but, as a slogan, had always been restricted to the private sphere (*minkan*; quoted in Yamamuro 2001: 573). Indeed, no statement issued by a prewar Japanese government actually contained the terms "pan-Asian" or "Asianism." Aoki's statement must be seen as an expression of Japanese fears of being perceived, in the West, as a potential leader of a pan-Asian league—a rhetoric that goes back as far as the Meiji period (1868–1912), when Japan was developing into a so-called first-rate power (*ittōkoku*) and was in desperate need of friendly relations with the much stronger Western powers. Japan's military strength had to some degree been recognized after its victory over China in 1894–1895. However, China at that time was considered weak and in decline, and it was only Japan's victory in the war against Russia, the world's military superpower of the time, in 1904–1905 that established Japan's reputation as a first-rate power—and eventually led to the recognition of Japanese equality with the great powers (*rekkyō*) of the West, at least in diplomatic terms. This recognition was manifested in the promotion of the diplomatic representatives of Germany, France, and Britain in Japan to fully fledged embassies—a status granted only to first-rate powers.

But the Russo-Japanese War was not merely a military conflict. It also was a "propaganda war," with Japan undertaking "a calculated press campaign to persuade the West that Japan was its equal and deserved a place among the more enlightened nations of the world" (Valliant 1974: 415). At the same time, Japan worked to prevent an outbreak of anti-Japanese sentiment in Europe and the United States, to avert fears of a "Yellow Peril," and to pre-empt the development of "a new crusade" (Matsumura 1987: 28) against the non-Christian newcomer in international relations—Japan. To that end, Japan sought to "manipulate the press" (Prime Minister Katsura Tarō) through the "encouragement" of pro-Japanese journalists in Western countries, payments to journalists and editors, and even attempts to purchase entire newspapers (Valliant 1974: 423–31).

The notion of a Yellow Peril in international relations—the development of an anti-Western alliance or league of Asian peoples, possibly under Japanese leadership—was voiced for the first time after Japan's victory over China in 1895. The European press and politicians started talking of an "awakening of Asia" and a possible threat to Europe—that is, European supremacy and colonial rule—in the form of a combination of the "Chinese masses" (the influence of Malthusian theories can be seen here) with "Japanese military strength and modern [i.e., Western and, at the same time, borrowed] technology." German Emperor Wilhelm II (1859–1941) even gave these fears a visual expression—the notorious Knackfuss painting of 1895. In Japan, these "visions" of a Yellow Peril were closely observed (cf. Saaler 2008a).

It is not surprising that, less than ten years after the Knackfuss painting made its appearance, senior politicians in Japan expected the specter of the Yellow Peril to resurface in Europe—particularly if Japan won the war with Russia. In order to head off the resurgence of such fears—or rather hysteria—the Japanese government decided to dispatch Kaneko Kentarō, a friend of the president of the Privy Council and former Prime Minister Itō Hirobumi, to the United States, and Suematsu Kenchō, Itō's son-in-law, to Europe (Nish 2005). Both were instructed that, "since fear of the 'Yellow Peril' is deeply rooted in the thinking of Europeans and Americans, and as Russia is stirring up such fears everywhere, we must prevent a further outbreak" (Matsumura 1987: 25–26; Valliant 1974: 422). In England, Suematsu gave a number of speeches (Suyematsu 1905) emphasizing that Japan had gone to war in self-defense against Russia, not to combat Western influence in East Asia (Matsumura 1987).

In his speeches, one of which is excerpted here, Suematsu time and again reassured his audience that Japan had not the slightest interest in leading a pan-Asian coalition against the West. He reassured his audience that Japan was no threat to Europe since Japan had chosen the side of the "Occident" in order to pursue security and wealth. At the same time, Suematsu also extended his characterization of peace-loving Asians to the Chinese—potential partners of Japan in any pan-Asian union in the eyes of those afflicted with Yellow Peril hysteria. As a diplomat, Suematsu's statements embodied the official views of the Japanese government. They expressed a realistic foreign policy under which a pan-Asian league with an anti-Western agenda was simply beyond the realms of possibility.

During the Russo-Japanese War, the activities of Suematsu and Kaneko achieved some success, as Russia failed to mobilize support from other countries against Japan on the basis of racial premises. However, after the war, talk of the Yellow Peril and allegations of renewed Japanese plans for a pan-Asian league frequently resurfaced and continued to play a role in international politics. As a direct consequence of the Russo-Japanese War, Japan was recognized as a member of the great powers' club. However, in Japan, disillusionment with the West, due to continuing racial prejudice against the Japanese that fueled fears of a future "racial war," began to intensify after 1905 (cf. Saaler 2008a). And with the rise of the various Asian independence movements after 1905—which were at least partly inspired by Japan's victory over Russia—the idea of a pan-Asian alliance became a viable notion for the first time.

Surprisingly however, Western newspapers, such as the *Times* of London and the *New York Times*, remained silent on Japanese pan-Asian ambitions during these years. Rather, it was in the context of Sino-Japanese rivalry, which intensified after 1919, that fears of a Japanese-led Pan-Asianism began once again to play a role in the Western media. This development was encouraged by China and fueled by a number of strongly anti-Japanese Western writers, such as Thomas F. Millard, who ran his own journal in China, *Millard's Review*, and who also wrote for the *New York Times*. An early example of an alleged pan-Asian bias in Japanese foreign policy is found in the *New York Times* in 1919—a story based on an appeal by China to the U.S. Senate accusing Japan of plotting such a scheme (*New York Times*, 15 June 1919, 7). According to the Chinese note, a settlement of their differences at the Paris Peace Conference, where China and Japan were arguing over the ownership of the former German possession of Shandong, was being obstructed by Japan's pan-Asian ambitions. "The Chinese question involves the issue of whether the manpower and resources of China are to be developed in the interest of the world and human progress or are to be exploited and used for selfish Asiatic ends. . . . China arraigns Japan as a power whose soul is mediaeval, but whose methods are Prussian in their ruthlessness and efficiency" (*New York Times*, 15 June 1919, 7).

At this point, to be sure, Western countries were aware that a pan-Asian league was still beyond the reach of Japanese Realpolitik. In 1921, shortly before the Washington Conference, the *New York Times* reported that, as a consequence of Japanese–American frictions (over the question of Japanese migrants to the United States), "renewed talk of Pan-Asiatic combinations" was being heard once again. However, in the writer's view, this kind of "talk" had little substance:

Various writers have fancied this sort of gossip as good newspaper copy; indeed by long quotations from exotic and fanatical propaganda popular books have been constructed. . . . [T]hey overlook the fact that the differences and antagonisms within Asia are vastly greater and more numerous than those in Europe or South America. Yet who would speak seriously of a Pan European movement as a political factor of immediate or vital importance? . . . Above all, the notion of a Pan-Asiatic movement neglects the fundamental factor of religion. Only when spiritual union . . . becomes possible can such movements have importance. (*New York Times*, 12 February 1921, 81)

Throughout the 1920s, Japan's need for cooperation with the West continued to rule out the possibility of an anti-Western pan-Asian league led by Japan, and Western diplomats and media knew that very well. Not even the "Asian Peoples Conferences" of 1926 and 1927 (see II:8) could change this fundamental perception. It was only in the 1930s, when Japan adopted some aspects of a pan-Asian policy—and particularly after the founding of Manchukuo (see II:16), which was legitimized through pan-Asian rhetoric—that the West began to regard Pan-Asianism as a serious threat.

Source (English in the original)
Baron Suyematsu (Suematsu Kenchō), *The Risen Sun*. London: Archibald Constable & Co., 1905, 269–97.

CHINESE EXPANSION HISTORICALLY REVISITED

Looking at a map of the world, one will at once see how vast is the Chinese Empire. There was a time when it was even more vast than at present. The expansion of China is an important subject in history, but its limit was reached long ago. . . . The area of the original centre of China was very limited, but its sphere of influence and activity gradually spread, generation after generation, as its civilization developed and extended to the surrounding regions. . . . The one peculiarity of this extension is that, roughly speaking, it has not been the result of aggressive conquest. China has always been on the defensive, and it is the surrounding peoples who have always assumed the offensive against her. The conquests China has made have in reality been the effect of the influence of her civilization. . . .

The limitation of Chinese expansion has become more marked since the advent of Western civilization in the Far East. China is surrounded by this new force on all sides and her attitude is constantly one of defence. A little time ago I read in an American review an article written by a Chinese diplomatist. He made a remark somewhat in the following words:

Our motto is, "Do not do unto others what you would not have others do unto you," but your motto is "Do unto others as you would have others do unto you"; in other words, we are negative, but you are positive. In consequence of this your people often force other people to do what you yourself like without inquiring whether those other people want it to be done or not. It therefore often results in your doing things against the wish of other people, and often with mischievous results.

This seems to be about the correct description of the feeling of the Chinese as against the rest of the world. China has her moral notions, which are by no means lacking in refinement. It is well for outsiders not to despise the Chinese too much, or, rather, it is desirable that they should be treated with proper consideration. If they are so treated, they will always prove themselves to be a good nation with which to maintain peaceable and beneficial intercourse.

Of late, there has been much talk about the Yellow Peril, or the possibility of a Pan-Asiatic combination; this appears to me, as I have said so often elsewhere, nothing more than a senseless and mischievous agitation. How can China rise up alone, and become a source of peril in this form to the rest of mankind? [emphasis added]. From what I have said in this paper it will be plainly seen that it is a matter of the greatest improbability. It is therefore in this respect all the more desirable that the mass of Chinese cotton be left alone. We have a proverb saying, "Even a small insect has a soul," and another saying, "A rat in despair might bite a cat." These proverbs mean that too much persecution should not be inflicted even upon weak objects. Therefore I can say that even such peaceful people as the Chinese should not be treated without due consideration for their feelings.

As I have shown already, China has not been and is not of her own seeking an aggressive nation. It is not only so with the ruling classes—in other words, with those who conquered China and became Sinicized—but with the nation itself at large, which has been imbued with the same spirit and the same ideas throughout all time, so that they have become its distinguishing and permanent attributes. The very basic principle of Chinese civilization is essentially pacific [peaceful]. . . .

Then, again, there are some who accuse Japan as the probable organizer of the Pan-Asiatic peril [emphasis added]. Peace-loving as the Japanese also are, the characteristics, notions, and feelings of the Japanese and Chinese are not so different that there is no possibility of their complete amalgamation in one common cause; and what is true with regard to the Chinese holds even more true with regard to other Asiatic peoples.

Japan aspires, moreover, to elevate herself to the same plane and to press onward in the same path of civilization as the countries of the West. Even in every-day matters one likes to choose good company, so as not to estrange one's best friends. *Can anyone imagine that Japan would like to organize a Pan-Asiatic agitation of her own seeking, in which she must take so many different*

*peoples of Asia into her confidence and company—people with whom she has
no joint interests or any community of thought and feeling?* [emphasis added].
And what of the risks Japan would wantonly incur were she to dare to attempt
such an enterprise in the face of the most powerful nations of the earth? . . .

Let us view the matter from another standpoint, and I trust I shall be excused if I allow myself to be extremely candid. In Europe and on its borders
there are many States, some of them well advanced, some rather backward.
Would it be practicable for all these States to form themselves into one compact body in organized offensive combination against an outside Power, say
America? I venture to assert that, even with the intelligence and ability of
the advanced nations of Europe such a union of interests and strength would
be quite impossible. How, then, could it be expected for one moment that
the various peoples of the East, with their varying degrees of intelligence,
their conflicting interests, and their old-standing feuds and jealousies could
ever have cohesion enough to range themselves under one banner against the
powers of the Occident? And if they could do so, is it to be imagined that
Japan would enter upon so quixotic an enterprise as to place herself at the
head of so unmanageable a mob? At the very first onset of a Western military
force, the untrained masses would take to flight, and Japan would find herself
alone, to bear the consequences of her folly. In Japan we have profited by our
military studies to the extent that we comprehend the value of a thoroughly
homogenous force. Could any conceivable agglomeration of Asiatic troops
be termed a homogenous body, and could such an agglomeration be made, by
any means known to man, into a compact force fit to associate with a highly
trained and thoroughly experienced army such as Japan now possesses, even
were she prepared to sacrifice everything for the very dubious privilege of
placing herself at their head? Turn for an instance to India. There we have an
example of a vast population immeasurably more numerous than the white
element which rules it, yet split up into so many States and sects and castes
that combination always has been and must be completely out of the question.
Has any one seriously supposed that England has to fear a peril there, such as
might be conceivable were union among the many divided peoples at all possible? What is the history of the one attempt to overthrow British rule? [The
author here refers to the Sepoy rebellion of 1857.] That of its utter failure owing to lack of combined effort; of a mutiny of a comparatively small number
of troops checked by the fidelity of other regiments who refused to assist in
the rising, owing to personal and tribal difference and caste prejudices. Is it
not notorious that these Indian races have not only no cohesion but downright
antagonism, notwithstanding that they are alike subjects of a conquering nation? Is there any likelihood of these Indian natives and other Asiatic peoples
being organized into a compact and united force, as some mischievous writ-

ers suggest? If this argument can fairly be applied as regards organization into an effective fighting force of the Asiatic peoples, how much stronger does it become when the matter is considered in the political sense! The peoples of the East are, some of them, politically independent; others are under the sway of one or other European Power. To combine them in a single undertaking would be a task utterly impracticable and unpromising. *Japan has already cast in her lot with the Occident, and in the eyes of many Asiatics it is to be remembered the Japanese are no less "Yang-Kwai" (foreign devils) than the Occidentals* [emphasis added].

In addition, and with the same candour as before, let me say that Japan has herself chiefly to consider. While she does not for one instant wish it to be thought that she looks down with contempt upon other Oriental nations—which she does not—they, for reasons of their own, have not chosen to accompany her along the path of progress, and actually regard her as something of an apostate. Can she by any stretch of the imagination, be suspected of a willingness to permit her own future to be jeopardized by pausing in her own advance in order to join them in what she fully realizes could only be an enterprise foredoomed to disastrous failure? Moreover, no Occidentals need imagine that Japan would particularly welcome the creation of a strong Power on the Continent of Asia in close proximity to her own shores. To me it seems that the charge of organizing a Pan-Asiatic League which is now and then brought against Japan, if taken seriously, would only be to subject her to utterly unjust persecution, quite unworthy of the civilized nations of the world. It would be like turning round upon an apt pupil whom one had one's self trained and encouraged and brought to the world's notice—rather against its own original inclinations and wishes—and that on the mere ground that the pupil belonged to a different set from one's own, and had grown a trifle more quickly and become more robust than one had expected when one first took him by the hand and led him forth into new paths.

Japan took up the cudgels in the present war with Russia, as I have elsewhere shown, and as it is by this time, I hope, perfectly understood, with no other motive than the defence of her own interests. Whenever it [i.e., the war with Russia] may come to a conclusion she will, as heretofore, seek to establish peace on a sure and sound foundation, having no objects in view that are not consistent with a pacific policy. She has sought throughout, and will continue to seek in the future, the benefits which accrue from this line of action, and it is in pursuance of these principles that she has endeavored to associate herself with the aims and objects of Western nations. Her people cannot, if they would, change the tint of their skins, and if, after all her efforts, she is to be ostracized merely on the score of colour, she will be obliged to regard it as harsh treatment, far exceeding anything that she had a right to expect from the chivalry and enlightenment of the nations of the Occident. At all events, I cannot imagine what material advantage those Occidental Powers who profess to be friendly with Japan can achieve by driving her to desperation by means of those ungenerous and, let me say, unmanly accusations. When this war ends, we shall devote ourselves to the arts of peace; and I may add that we can hardly expect that, no matter in what form the present contest may terminate, circumstances will permit of our embarking upon hostilities in other directions. I can positively declare, in the name of Japan, that when this struggle reaches its conclusion she will honestly and faithfully pursue a policy of peace.

Chapter Thirteen

Hatano Uho: *Asia in Danger,* 1912

Renée Worringer

The text titled *Asia in Danger* represents pan-Asian attitudes of the early twentieth century in its anti-Western content and recounting of European misdeeds in Asia as much as through the text's dissemination across the Asian continent itself—through translation from Japanese language into Ottoman Turkish. This treatise was originally written by a Japanese activist and early convert to Islam named Hatano Uho (1882–1936), a graduate of the East Asia Common Culture Academy (Tōa Dōbun Shoin; see I:9) in Shanghai that was established around 1900 "to train young Japanese for business and government service related to China" (Reynolds 1986: 945). His training and experience there clearly had a profound influence on him, the imprint of which will become apparent on reading his ideas and analysis of what was plaguing Asia in 1912. Hatano was very politically aware of the system of global alliances in play at this time, and he astutely speculated in the text about what might happen if a pan-Asian union of some sort were to be established. The front matter of the booklet includes photos of atrocities committed against Asians at the hands of their European colonial overlords to remind Asians of Western barbarity.

Hatano associated with Mohammed Barakatullah (1854–1927), the Indian political activist resisting British control of India who, following stints in Britain and America, found himself in Japan after being appointed professor of Hindustani at Tokyo Imperial University in 1909. Barakatullah also published an English-language magazine in Japan titled *The Islamic Fraternity* that espoused pan-Islamic ideas. True to his mission, he proselytized Islam among the Japanese as well, and Hatano Uho, an assistant editor of the journal, was one of the first Japanese converts to Islam around 1911, along with his wife and her father (Baron Hiki Kentarō, 1854–1922). Hatano, who subsequently came to be known as Hasan U. Hatano, penned *Asia in Danger* at that time. The Japanese government would later terminate Barakatullah's teaching appointment and suppress publication of *The Islamic Fraternity* because of his anti-British stance (the Anglo-Japanese Alliance signed in 1902 proved too valuable to the Japanese), but he and Hatano published and attempted to smuggle another pan-Islamic paper called *El-Islam* into India to continue the mission of the former publication (it was also suppressed in 1913).

The translation of Hatano's *Asia in Danger* into Ottoman Turkish (as *Asya Tehlikede*) expands the narrative of pan-Asian networking: Hatano's political treatise was published as a twenty-four-page Ottoman pamphlet in Constantinople in 1912. It was distributed by the Islamist *Sebilürreşat* bookstore, and from the Ottoman capital it was circulated throughout the empire among the reading public (the copy obtained in my research was located at the National Library in Cairo, Egypt). The translation had been produced by another Japanese convert to Islam, Mehmet Hilmi Nakawa, and a Tatar Muslim exile from Russia named Abdürreşid İbrahim (see I:19). Nakawa was a Russian-speaking member of the right-wing Kokuryūkai (Amur River Society; see I:10). İbrahim had traveled extensively across the Islamic world before, in 1908, arriving in Japan, where he was deeply involved with Barakatullah and Hatano in the same pan-Asian, pan-Islamic circles (while also serving as a correspondent in Japan for the Ottoman paper *Sebilürreşat*, drafting several articles detailing his experiences). Nakawa likely translated *Asia in Danger* into Russian and then İbrahim from Russian into Ottoman Turkish.

İbrahim spent his life promoting Pan-Islamism and resisting "Western" imperialism wherever he encountered it—against Russians in his native country by organizing Muslims politically to demand participation in the Russian Duma and publishing a pan-Islamic newspaper in Arabic called *al-Tilmīdh*; by traveling in Ottoman lands with another Japanese convert and operative, Omar Yamaoka, to give pan-Asian, pan-Islamic speeches in local political clubhouses in the cities; by assisting in the establishment a Muslim–Japanese cooperative called the Asian Congress (in Japanese Ajia Gikai [Asia Righteous Society]) in Japan in 1909 with fellow Asianists (Aydin 2007b: 83; Worringer 2006); by participating in pan-Islamic Ottoman resistance against the Italian invasion of Tripoli (Libya) in 1911 and, during World War I, working within the Ottoman–German effort to turn Muslim prisoners of war from Russia against their former empire; or much later in his life, when once again from Tokyo, he produced anti-Western war propaganda for the Japanese that was to be disseminated among the local population in the East Indies in the 1940s. İbrahim's involvement with the Hatano text in 1912 is as a conduit for this pan-Asian, pan-Islamic thought; he and these other Asian activists demonstrate a particular moment in the history of global politics:

they are a collective of international anti-Western resistance hailing from various places in Asia, many of whom converged in Japan and all of whom had in mind a new vision for the world that required Asians and Muslims to set aside their differences and support one another in the interest of resisting colonialism and forging their own destinies.

Of course, this plea for pan-Asian solidarity had its paradoxes and contradictions. The most glaring dilemma for a pan-Asian union in the early twentieth century was the imperialist nature of the Japanese Empire itself, particularly in East Asia. By 1912 the spirit of the Meiji era that had begun with the 1868 Restoration had given way to a Japan more concerned with securing colonial possessions to buffer its islands economically and strategically. The Meiji emperor had passed away in this year, marking the finality of Meiji idealism's end; Japan had already officially annexed Korea, Formosa, and the Liaodong (Liaotung) peninsula until 1910. Even more ironic was the insistence by the Japanese officials who had attempted to negotiate a formal alliance with their "Asian brother" on Russia's other flank, the Ottoman state, that the Sublime Porte grant capitulatory privileges to Japan, on a par with what European powers had been guaranteed. The Japanese government demanded to be viewed as equals to the Western Powers and to be treated accordingly; Ottoman statesmen, weary of the detrimental effects of these seemingly irreversible provisions on their empire, stood their ground and unassumingly resisted Japanese demands for more of the same while politely continuing to negotiate. As a consequence of this difference of opinion, a formal alliance was never signed between Japan and the Ottoman Empire; however, both governments appeared to be showing solidarity with one another from a publicity standpoint.

Hatano takes the Japanese government to task over these issues in his treatise. He implores the Japanese government to recognize China's fledgling republic and to stand firm in insisting that Mongolia and Tibet be properly administrated according to the wishes of the local people while fully aware of Japanese imperial aims in Manchuria. He also scolds the Japanese diplomats who, tempted by Western notions of power, failed to reach an agreement with the other "citadel" in Asia, the Ottoman Empire, thus neglecting to look after the Japanese national interest. Perhaps most ironically, the Ottomans at the helm in the first decades of the twentieth century sincerely desired inclusion in the concert of Europe as an empire that, though it had been abused in the past as a "Sick Man of Europe," was nonetheless an integral member of European politics that should be respected. Thus, Ottoman officials viewed any alliance with Japan as secondary to their need for European acceptance, and they considered very carefully in private discussions the ramifications a treaty with the Japanese might have for their future relations with Western powers. In other words, Ottoman Pan-Asianism, as supported by the state, had limits too.

Ultimately, pan-Asian ideologues like Hatano, Barakatullah, and İbrahim recognized Japan's ability to lead Asia in this anti-Western movement, as Japan was militarily and economically the only Asian power capable of defeating a Western power in a modern, technological war (as they did in 1905 against the Russians). Japan could play great power politics and win. But this was at the expense of the very anti-imperialist principles Japan claimed to be representing, and it created hostilities within Japan between the political state and ideological movements, such as those espousing pan-Asian solidarity. The political enmity that developed between the Japanese government and Barakatullah with his pan-Islamic ideology is reflected in the state's decision to ultimately silence Barakatullah so as not to jeopardize its relations with Britain. Hatano's criticism of Japanese officials in their dealings with the Ottoman Empire demonstrates the rift that had opened up between pan-Asian aspirations and Japanese political realities in the twentieth century.

The following translation of *Asia in Danger* introduces readers to the vastness of lands, peoples, and ideas that are included under the generic label of "Pan-Asianism"—eliciting such questions as where the boundaries of Asia were understood to lie in 1912, who was in contact with one another, and what pan-Asian intellectuals hoped to accomplish in uniting Asia as one. What is of particular interest is the way in which *Asia in Danger* captures the nuanced distinction to be made between the Japanese state and Japanese political movements in the prewar era. The Japanese government sometimes promoted pan-Asianists in the early twentieth century, and at other times they were at odds with one another, with differing goals. But the combination of a powerful modern Japan and an anti-Western enthusiasm for Pan-Asianism seemed to yield the worst of both of these forces rather than the best of them: instead of a pan-Asian, anticolonialist Japan from the 1920s on that secured independence for fellow Asians, we see the emergence of an ultranationalist, colonialist Imperial Japan that dominated East Asia until the end of World War II. The voices of an idealist pan-Asian solidarity were drowned out.

Asia in Danger begins with an assessment of the potentially detrimental consequences for Japan if Asia were to be parceled up by Western powers like Britain and Russia (with the tacit approval of the United States) and how it was that Asia came to be "in danger." Hatano cites as evidence telegraphs received from Shanghai and Peking in 1912 that describe Russian policies such as forcing Mongolia to borrow only Russian money for necessary provisions and allowing Russia complete freedom of action there, compelling China to sign a concession for the establishment of a railway line, Britain's demand that China not interfere in the Tibetan administration, and so on. In light of this, the author says, "Every Asian says it is imperative that no more time can be wasted in securing a [pan-]Asian alliance; to neglect this is absolutely unacceptable." In the second section of the treatise, subtitled "The Necessity of a Pan-Asian Alliance [Umum-ı Asyalıların İttifaakı]," the author quotes a Japanese scholar named Suchio (probably a garbled version of Itō Chiyū), who wrote on the famous samurai Saigō Takamori and what he described as Saigo's resistance to America and Britain forty years earlier. Saigō, according to Suchio, supposedly suggested that governments in the Far East should form a pan-Asian alliance of sorts. To this Hatano enthusiastically retorts, "What a great idea!" The author also refers to Dr. Sun Yat Sen's (see II:5) views about Japan and his position that, despite Japan's occupation of Manchuria, they are still China's best treaty option; though American and British policies are not bad, Japan is a better choice because "the Japanese are a nation that possesses the greatest material forces on the globe" (Hatano 1912: 9–12).

Hatano launches into more detail concerning the need for a pan-Asian alliance, the ways in which to achieve this union, which countries should be involved, and what their roles in a pan-Asian union would entail. He finishes the treatise with a grave indictment of the Japanese state that contains an implicit call to overthrow the government if it does not carry out the nation's wishes. Despite Hatano's insightful reading of the colonial situation in Asia and the need for Asian solidarity to combat European imperialism, his idealism and dedication to "defending Asia" at times leads him to some far-fetched conclusions—for example, when he calls Kaiser Wilhelm a "prudent manager" of the Triple Alliance. Nonetheless, Hatano's plea to establish a pan-Asian union proved attractive to plenty of intellectuals all across the Eurasian continent.

Source (translation from the Turkish version by Renée Worringer)
Hatano [Uho], *Asya Tehlikede* (Asia in Danger). Translated from Japanese by Mehmet Hilmi Nakawa and Abdürreşid İbrahim. İstanbul: Ahmed İhsan ve Şürekası, 1912.

. . . If Europe were to decide to forge an agreement with America, and, in relation to the Far East question, partition China, Japan must realize how much it would be affected by this. If such a military might were to threaten Japan, in order for Japan to rely upon its own armed forces, it would be necessary to gradually increase their preparedness to the point that the Japanese nation's strength would necessarily be taxed. Besides this, American and European commercial goods would be in competition with Japanese commerce, subjecting us to [further] difficulties. In short, China's partition by the Europeans would be, so to speak, Japan's downfall.

Some men are able to surmise a partly correct opinion about Japanese sentiments, were China to be partitioned. In reality the Japanese would be able to invade Southern Manchuria. But even if they were to occupy Southern Manchuria, Japanese interests could not be assured to their desired degree. Just the opposite—the probability of harm is not far-fetched. Therefore I can reiterate that, to say "partition of China" is to say "Japan's downfall." Observing and taking into consideration Russia's political stance which it is following vis-à-vis Mongolia, it is obvious that Russia's goal is to occupy Mongolia. Apart from this, the policy that Britain is pursuing concerning Tibet compels us to cry out "Asia in Danger." This is not an empty threat; it is exactly the truth. In this regard, the facts that we will set forth consecutively will completely support these assertions of ours. . . .

It is possible to say that in order for a total alliance of Asia, foundations can be established and capitalized upon, one by one. In that regard, the Japanese government must immediately and without hesitation seize the opportunity to forge a Sino-Japanese alliance; after that, it would strive for alliances with Ottoman, Afghan, and Siamese states. Just the same, as it learns of a union such as this, Persia [Acemistan] would extend its own hand and take part [in the union]. And junior members of the Indian government would soon start sending secret envoys, perhaps joining without hesitation. Coming to the East Indies (Java), there too enlightened men who grasp the aim are not few; they would immediately extend their hands to us in support. In order to form an alliance such as this, before all else, an extremely able and insightful leader is necessary. It is not possible at any time to establish a sound alliance as long as governments are always in competition with one another. The Triple Alliance [of Germany, Austro-Hungary, and Italy], considered relatively sound, is under the administration of a prudent [manager] like Wilhelm. As for the Triple Entente [Britain, France, and Russia], it does not possess a reliable leader.

3: AN ALLIANCE OF ASIAN PEOPLES
[ASYA AKVAMININ İTTIFAKI]

An influential historical event like the Russo-Japanese War in Asia did not occur by chance. All white European races had always treated Asian people with contempt up until the Russo-Japanese War; and Asians had believed themselves to be creatures compelled [to accept] Europe's insults. Then when the Japanese forces achieved victory, and at that time all the peoples of the East who had been content with this life, they were immediately, and continuously from this moment onwards, satisfied with this situation. They lifted their heads, which had for centuries hung low, and said to the Europeans: "The foundation of civilization is ours; Asian civilization is rich; as for Europe, it is our pupil."

Since that time all Easterners find themselves feeling the most sincere sense of friendship towards the Japanese. All Asian peoples are nourishing the hope that they can govern themselves under the protection of Japan.

In the year 1911 one of the Sultans of the Malay Archipelago fled to Japan, complaining of injustice at the hands of the Dutch [colonial] authorities. And another one sent an official envoy to Japan secretly and wanted arms in order to defend themselves. There is absolutely no doubt that in general Easterners are not hesitating to come together under the banner of "The Rising Sun."

. . . From one of our distinguished Tatar brothers. . . . The honorable individual had come and had taken an extremely important step. He asked for Japan's assistance in order to restore his own nation's political existence [this most likely refers to Abdürreşid İbrahim]. That is to say: if the Japanese government would, in all earnestness, take upon itself to assume leadership and would make the effort to establish an Asian union, in three to five years [they] would be able to secure the greatest victory.

First of all, we will consider what an agreement and rapprochement with China could yield there: if the Japanese government wants to establish a secret treaty with China, above all else the Japanese government must recognize the Republic of China and at a later time warn China that, concerning the issues of Mongolia and Tibet, it has to be made to formally protest in the most absolute way [Russian and English policies there]; it must endeavor to secure the comfort of the Mongols and Tibetans.

In addition, if the Japanese government itself were to publicly announce that the Russian and British states were interfering in Tibet and Mongolia's issues and infringed upon the reconciliation in the Far East, neither Russia nor Britain could act at all. They would have to stay silent.

Certainly when Japan takes steps like this it should adequately ensure its own military strength and war munitions. Nevertheless it is certain that (praise God) our military forces, land and naval, will prevail over both Russia's and Britain's.

In reality if Russia would have been able to muster all its land forces against Japan, it would have been able to resist to a [better] degree. But by being overextended in the Balkan crises and in Persia's political affairs, Russia was unable to muster even 500,000 soldiers in the Far East, whereas in order to threaten Japan, at least 500,000 soldiers permanently stationed in the Far East would be necessary. That is to say Russia absolutely cannot go to war with Japan.

As for Britain, henceforth the era of Britain's greatness has passed and it has grown old; it has become merely a bygone power that can be remembered in the pages of history. In order to protect the North Sea, Britain has had to summon its fleet which was in the Mediterranean. Seized by complete weakness, it sought refuge in cooperation with France's navy; under these circumstances it was able to succeed in signing a treaty. And how much trouble [Britain] endures in order to be able to protect India. In short, Britain could not go to war against the Japanese for hundred years.

Let's suppose that Russia, Britain and France sign an offensive and defensive alliance; Russia postpones for a time the policy that it is pursuing in Persia, disregarding temporarily its position vis-à-vis Turkey, to the point that Russia abandons France against Germany and Austria, and Britain entrusts all its power to France; were they to send a great portion of their own naval force to Japanese waters (because another [force of this sort] could not stand against our might)—even in that case our land and naval forces would meet these two "strangers" with complete satisfaction.

In reality as long as Germany does not experience weakness and so long as India does not escape [Britain's] grasp, Britain cannot declare war on the Japanese. Unless Britain participates, Russia would not be able to make war on anyone in any case.

Supposing the impossible, that America were to unite with the Triple Entente, still they could not threaten Japan. It is more accurate [to say] that there is no state in the world today that is in a position to be able to go to war against Japan. We wonder: Why doesn't Japan's government take advantage of the opportunity and immediately undertake the means to unify Asia, to assure eternal peace and tranquility?

4: HOW IT CAN BE POSSIBLE TO ESTABLISH ASIAN UNITY

1) China

China's republic has already been founded. Now Japan's government must confirm this. It is possible that if it were to re-establish an imperial monarchy at some point, Japan could ratify this too.

It has no significance for Japan whether China becomes an imperial monarchy or a republic. As for what is the important thing for us, it is that the Chinese have a permanent, genuine friendship with the Japanese.

Today the Japanese government must not miss the opportunity, after signing a secret agreement with the present Chinese government, to promise also to cooperate with military force when required. And China, relying upon Japanese military power, should exert [their] influence over the Mongolians and Tibetans and invite them into an Asian union.

And if desired, secure independent or autonomous administrations for the Mongolians and Tibetans, on condition that it not be to the level that they seek refuge under the protection of Britain or Russia. If everyone were to embrace union with sincerity, certainly Allah will bestow success. Because Allah deems good the voice of sincerity. And there's no doubt at all that the Mongolians and Tibetans will accept genuine advice.

In recent times Chinese Muslims are unifying and have established a lot of organizations in order to secure their own progress. They even invited all Chinese to [sign] an agreement, they published declarations, and in the declarations they invited all Chinese people to join in an alliance.

2) The Ottoman Empire

Japanese-Ottoman unity possesses more importance than a union with China. [This is] because Japan and the Ottomans are each like a citadel on Asia's two sides. If these two states were to conclude a genuine alliance, they could prevent every type of European activity in Asia, in spite of the present state of affairs in which the Ottomans currently find themselves in a distinctly inferior position in the view of Europeans.

The Ottomans have sought an association with Japan for some time; unfortunately whenever they undertake negotiating an agreement, every time they are subjected to the opposition of the Christian powers, who seek in others' misfortune their own benefits, and who especially do not desire any progress among Muslims.

Unfortunately, Japan's diplomats who "don tophats" and who are mindful of this [European] opposition, would not venture to sign a treaty, the Japanese state not wishing to hear of European objections. Had [the Japanese] wanted to reach an agreement with the Ottomans without [insisting on] the Capitulations and according to international law, the Ottomans would have consented to it without hesitation, and they would have restored the greatest patron for the unity of Asia. If we [Japanese] had been able to think with our own heads about our own [potential] advantages and seen the task with our own minds, the Ottomans could have been a pillar of support for our political life. When required, we [by means of the Ottomans] could have kept Russia busy in Europe and Britain busy in the Mediterranean. But since we could not think with our own heads, we are not able to benefit from opportunities like this.

3) Afghanistan

. . . Currently a sincere Muslim who is patriotic and loves his country to the utmost degree is someone like the extremely smart and experienced Afghan

Emir Hacibullah Khan. In the recent Ottoman-Italian war, Hacibullah Khan gathered together his own nation and delivered a speech. And in his speech he expressed very moving words for the East. The Afghan Emir is a man of complete earnestness, truly heroic and bold, and innately intelligent. The Afghan people will be an extremely great nation able to play a role in the future.

If the Japanese government were to send a particular individual to the Afghan Emir that would invite [Afghanistan] into the union, His Excellency the aforementioned would not only accept, but he would even be able to provide significant assistance in this regard. This is because this man is one of the East's greatest personas.

4) Persia

. . . At a glance, Britain and Russia are about to devour Persia. In reality it is merely a question of time before Persia will collapse. Iran can preserve its territorial integrity with a bit of vigilance. If Japan were to dispatch someone to Persia, it [Persia] would hasten to accept the news of such a union with complete satisfaction. Iran occupied an extremely important place in the annals of history. Nonetheless even a nation of such historical traditions would, when on the verge of collapse, rally itself immediately, with a bit of assistance, to secure the greatest advantage.

5) India

(abridged)   .

6) Indochina

After the Russo-Japanese war, the government of France began to worry about Indochina cooperating with Japan. Although the degree to which Indochina attracts their attention does not seem to denote its importance, France attributes more importance to Indochina than to Marrakesh.

A reporter from the newspaper *L'issue de Chine* says that: currently there are quite a few groups of men pursuing the notion of armed rebellion in Indochina; in the midst of these are the pro-republican Annamese who occupy the greatest position. The [Ch'ing] Chinese dynasty that had persisted for centuries, possessing its great traditions, was annihilated, and with the influence of China's rebellion which succeeded all at once in establishing a Republic, the Annamese republican partisans took up arms immediately, setting their sights on establishing an Annam Republic.

The aforementioned group prepared actions and thorough plans with very good programs; though quite a few men had decided to assassinate government officials in an operation [to be carried out] on a specific day, [the plot] became known to the government and they have been arrested. After this the government of France is taking extremely serious and detailed precautionary measures.

7) Siam

No doubt lovely Siam would agree to Japan's aforementioned proposal [of an Asian union]. France could not even threaten Japan at all, if [Siam] agreed in principle to this.

8) East Indies [Java Cezairi]

As for [the East Indies], there are so many reasons for Japan to intervene [there]. To say a word about them is even too much. The adversity of Dutch oppression has caused the Javanese people to endure every kind of misery. Because every Japanese possesses a lot of information about them, I choose to be silent.

9) Turkestan

Coming to the people of Turkestan whose courage has been diminished by Russian oppression, they, who are the most uninformed, have yet to nourish an appetite whetted by [a desire for] complete sovereign independence. Humanity and civilization's most brilliant episodes in Turkestan's history were come across by chance. Anyway, they are not yet familiar with captivity. Their past, their graves, are ahead of them.

Four years earlier a respected individual who came to Japan had given us the most accurate information about Turkestan, and had inspired the most significant and most correct ideas especially concerning the issue of an Asian union. At that time they published his ideas day after day in our newspapers and they continued for months. In this case there can be no doubt that Turkestan would be open without hesitation to the idea like this.

10) Japan

Behold it is Japan which is most final, and foremost in this issue. The basis of the matter is very simple and easy. But as for the problem, that is that the current Japanese government, needing to assume a leadership position in this matter, has not been able to venture to strive for this without hesitation. In Japan today in the beginning of the year in which we find ourselves, our men who possess their own ideas and who act according to their own ideas, are few. Essentially, the most important point is that. In which case if government officials do not want to understand that issue, the nation must make them understand, or must bring to power men who will understand. This is my final word for the Japanese.

Chapter Fourteen

Nagai Ryūtarō: "The White Peril," 1913

Peter Duus

In the summer of 1943, Nagai Ryūtarō, a former leader of the Minseitō Party, addressed an audience of Japanese religious leaders on the theme "Asia is one." "The English and the Americans profess the principles of democracy," he told them, "and they claim to be rebuilding the world through democracy, but in fact Anglo-American democracy is the money politics of a cabal of financial combines who provide the government and the political parties with secret funds and election expenses. In a drive to secure dominant control over the world's resources by invading smaller countries and exploiting ethnic minorities, these financial combines have finally plunged the world into a great conflict. Claims to be rebuilding the world through democracy made by those who ought to be condemned for upsetting world peace are like claims by a criminal that he is a policeman protecting law and order. I believe that there is no greater threat to the whole human race." His words were greeted with applause. He had struck a chord heard over and over during the "Greater East Asia War," which had begun in 1941: that Asians were threatened not by Japanese liberators but by "white imperialists" who had exploited them.

Nagai was a paradoxical, perhaps anomalous, advocate of Pan-Asianism. Not only was he a devout Christian who read the Bible every day, but he championed liberal causes such as universal manhood suffrage, social welfare programs, recognition of labor unions, and greater rights for women after he had entered politics in the 1920s (see, e.g., Nagai 1920). Indeed, he is identified with the emergence of "Taishō democracy" (for Nagai's career, see Duus 1970, 1971; Minichiello 1984).

Born in 1881 the son of an impoverished former samurai of the Maeda domain, Nagai encountered Christianity at two missionary schools, first at Dōshisha Middle School, then at Kansei Gakuin, where he converted to Unitarianism in 1901. As a student in the Faculty of Politics and Economics of

Waseda University, a citadel of Meiji middle-class liberalism, Nagai came under the influence of Abe Isoo, a Christian Socialist. His religious outlook was heavily influenced by the humanitarian message of Christianity, and he thought of Jesus as a champion of the underprivileged who challenged the privileges of the wealthy and powerful. In his Waseda yearbook he proclaimed his commitment to *keisei saimin* ("easing the people's suffering through statecraft.")

With Abe's help, Nagai secured a Unitarian scholarship to study at Manchester College, begun as an academy for non-Anglican dissenters at Oxford University, where he studied the politics and policies of the Liberal leader William Gladstone. As a student at Waseda, Nagai's eloquence as an orator had attracted the attention of Ōkuma Shigenobu, the university's founder. On his return home he became a professor of colonial studies at Waseda and the editor of *Shin Nihon* (New Japan), a monthly opinion magazine that served as a vehicle for publicizing Ōkuma's political views. He became known as a "little Ōkuma," and in 1917 he stood as a candidate for the Imperial Diet from his hometown of Kanazawa. He lost the election but ran again successfully in 1920.

While educated in institutions suffused with liberal reformism, Nagai, like many other political leaders in the 1930s and 1940s, came of age at a time when Japan emerged a major military and diplomatic power. As he often said, echoing the words of his mentor Ōkuma, Japan was no longer simply a "Japan for Japan" but had become a "Japan for the world." Nagai did not measure Japan's new status simply in terms of its military victories or its Realpolitik successes, nor did he see Japan's colonial expansion as incompatible with liberal institutions at home. Rather, he urged Japan, like the Western nations, to "contribute to world civilization" by becoming a "center for civilizing forces" to whom other peoples could turn for guidance. In a sense, this too echoed Ōkuma's pan-Asianist notion that Japan, as a benefactor of Chinese influence in the past, had an obligation to protect the Chinese from further Western incursions on their sovereignty and to lead them toward "civilization."

Nagai's conception of Japan's national mission was also shaped by his experience abroad as a student in England, where he encountered racial discrimination for the first time. He had expected all Englishmen to understand the "ideals of Carlyle and Milton, Byron and Tennyson," but instead he found English students teasing him about whether rain fell sideways in Japan. In a letter to Abe Isoo, he wrote that his experience in England left him indignant at "white attitudes toward Orientals" and that he was filled with "an earnest faith in the survival of the Japanese race." As a Christian he believed that all men, whatever their innate abilities or virtues, were of equal moral worth, and he was disappointed that the English and later the Americans did not honor these ideals either in their public policy or in their private lives.

After his return to Japan, Nagai was a vocal critic of Anglo-American foreign and domestic policy. In speeches and essays, for example, he attacked the Oriental exclusion movement in the United States not simply as an affront to Japan but as morally indefensible, and he criticized military American interventions in Latin America as evidence of the predatory character of American foreign policy. Like Konoe Fumimaro (regarding Konoe; see I:32), he dismissed Allied propaganda during World War I, especially the Wilsonian worldview, as high-sounding but hypocritical rhetoric that had little to do with the real character of the war: a struggle of the Anglo-American imperialists to rein in Germany when it upset the status quo. As a Diet member in the 1920s, he defended the Shidehara policy of cooperation with the Anglo-American powers in Asia, but he continued to criticize the "moralism" of American foreign policy as well as its embrace of "Monroeism" in Latin America—and he also expressed regret that concessions made to China at the Washington Conference came about not as an expression of Japan's goodwill toward China but as a response to pressure from the English and Americans.

His 1913 essay on "The White Peril"—an ironic play on "The Yellow Peril," an ethnophobic vision publicized in a painting commissioned by Kaiser Wilhelm II—reveals the vehemence of his feeling that the nationalistic power struggles, the racial discrimination, and the colonial exploitation pursued by the Europeans and Americans betrayed the ideals that he had learned from the West. His linkage of Japan's national mission with a crusade against "white imperialism" remained intact from his early years as a public intellectual throughout his career as a politician and political leader. The sentiments in his 1943 speech differed little from those in the essay he wrote thirty years earlier. But what distinguished his use of the term "white imperialism" from that of many contemporaries is that it sprang from a commitment to the value of human equality rather than to a narrow chauvinism or racial resentment. For Nagai the wartime catchphrase *hakkō ichiu* ("the eight corners of the world under one roof") did not mean imperial domination of the world but rather establishment of "universal brotherhood" among all humankind. As he said in another wartime speech, the only way to construct a "new world order" of peace in Asia and the rest of the world was "to regard man as a noble spiritual being given life by the great universal spirit, to regard all men as brothers regardless of color . . . or property, to establish a new order capable of achieving their co-existence and co-prosperity, and thereby to realize everywhere the great spirit of *hakkō ichiu*." Nagai died in 1944 shortly after Allied bombing raids began to hasten a defeat that revealed how sadly the brutal realities of Japan's military expansionism had betrayed his vision of Japan's national mission.

Source (English in the original)
Nagai Ryūtarō, "The White Peril." *The Japan Magazine* 1913, 39–42.

THE WHITE PERIL

By Professor Ryutaro Nagai
(Waseda University)

WHEN Buckle wrote his history of Civilization the Crimean War was at its height, and the whole of Europe was being regaled by the press with pictures of blood and carnage. To solace the wounded sensibilities of the public, Buckle contended that in modern times wars were necessary as the inevitable defence of civilized states against the aggression of half civilized or savage nations, but he congratulated his countrymen on the conviction that the time was now past when one civilized people could take up arms against another for purpose of mere aggression.

Who could have thought that immediately after this, civilized France would have gone to war with Austria; and that the combined forces of Prussia and Austria would have invaded Denmark and calmly appropriated Sleiswick and Holstein? Not very long afterwards came the conflict between France and Germany, two highly civilized white nations. Then we have such unedifying spectacles as the war between America and Spain, and the seizure of the South African Republics by the British. In addition to this most of the nations of Europe have been carrying on a system of appropriating the lands of the more uncivilized races too weak for self defence. The extent of territory taken by the white races in this way during the nineteenth century totals nearly 10,000,000 square miles embracing a population about 135,000,000. And it will be seen that even within the comparatively short space of time since 1860 the white races have taken nearly 10,000,000 square miles of land and enforced their rule over many millions of the darker skinned races! . . .

In the face of all this we have been treated by the white races in recent years to tracts, treaties and newspaper articles galore on what they are pleased to call, "The Yellow Peril." Surely, in comparison with the white races, there is no indication of any peril of yellow aggression, at least. We do not mean to condemn aggression independently of circumstances; for, there might be the duty of interfering for the sake of opening up the resources of a people and thus promoting their wealth and happiness. Mr. Leroy Beaulieu [1843–1916] says that the human race may be classified as 1. Civilized Christian peoples; 2. Civilized Non-Christian races; 3. Half-civilized people; 4. Savage tribes. The former, he holds, have the right and obligation to lead the latter two classes to civilization, just as parents have the right and the duty to educate their children. According to this theory it would be unjust to reproach any nation for intruding upon a barbarous race to impose upon it civilized conditions. But the difficulty is that most of such interferences do not appear to be for any benevolent purpose, the motive being, for the most part, simply aggressive. On the authority of their own historians we are forced to convict the Spanish invaders of South America as bent chiefly on rapine and plunder of a very murderous kind, the number of people killed in 50 years being estimated at upwards of 10,000,000. In Mexico alone the number killed is calculated at 4,000,000. This does take into account the terrible decimation of territory, leaving destruction everywhere in the wake of murder. In some cases the native tribes were furnished with arms and set fighting with one another so as to bring about self-destruction. Is it not a fact that many tribes have been wiped out by the white races? Others have been driven out from their ancient habitations, as witness the Kaffirs in South Africa. These are all conspicuous facts that do not lie. If it be said that such things belong to a past age of civilization, we point to the conduct of the Belgians in the Congo, where under the plea of protection and development of territory, heavy taxes have been imposed on the miserable natives, and the refusal to comply with arbitrary exactions visited with the crudest of punishments, even to the cutting off of hands and otherwise-mutilating the bodies of the victims. What are the yellow races to say to all this, especially in the face of complaints against the yellow peril? Can we be regarded as either unreasonable or unnecessarily offensive if we incline to the conviction that the peril is rather a *white* one?

Our American friends, who talk more about Freedom and Equality than most other nations, have nevertheless many hard things said of them by their own citizens in regard to their treatment of the Indians and Negroes. At any rate it would be difficult to parallel in any country in the East such savagery as the lynching and burning of negroes. According to the census of 1909 the negroes of 12 southern states made up 40% of the population; yet out of $32,000,000 spent in common school education in those states, only $4,000,000 went to the education of the coloured people, less than twelve and one half per cent of the total. Nor are conditions better in India, if we are to believe the accounts given by Englishmen themselves of the treatment of natives there. . . . Even the public conveniences are classified as for foreigners and natives; so that even the beggar and the outcast with white skin can be better accommodated than the most refined Indian gentleman. . . .

Now in the face of all this who can say that the yellow and otherwise coloured races are not in some peril from the white races? When I was on my way home from Europe there were some Englishmen on board the steamer, engineers on their way to posts in the Orient. Among these foreigners there seemed to prevail a very unpleasant degree of race-prejudice. Of their conduct toward the Chinese on board it is difficult to speak with due restraint. Once during the passage through the sultry heat of the tropics a Chinese gentleman of position came on deck to take a nap on a rattan chair. He had hardly got to sleep when he found himself wound round with coils of line and being dragged about the deck on his chair. This gentleman afterwards said to me: "Suppose the position were reversed, and it was a white man that was so treated, what would they say?" And then he went on to say that it was so everywhere, the white man always treating his yellow brother with contempt.

At the present time Australia is endeavoring to induce immigrants to settle in that country. Agents of the Commonwealth advertise endless acres of fertile land only awaiting people to occupy them. Even the passage money of prospective settlers is being advanced or paid by the government. The immigrants are promised every assistance in settling down, even to the loan of the necessary funds. Their children will be educated free in the national schools. Then the notice is conspicuously given that *only white people will be admitted.* . . . Practically the same attitude prevails in British South Africa, Canada, and the United States. Asiatics can enter only with the greatest inconvenience. . . .

Now from the point of view of the yellow races all this seems most arrogant and unfair. To seize the greater part of the earth and refuse to share it with the races who are hardly pressed for territorial space at home, even when the privilege is highly paid for by hard labour, is so manifestly unjust that it cannot continue. . . . In Australia, South Africa, Canada and the United States there are vast tracts of unoccupied territory awaiting settlement, and although the citizens of the ruling powers refuse to take up the land, no yellow people are permitted to enter. . . . Thus the white races seem ready to commit to the savage beasts and birds what they refuse to entrust to their brothers of the yellow race. Even a yellow fisherman gleaning the sea along some solitary island coast is watched and apprehended for encroaching on the white preserves. Surely the arrogance and avarice of the nobility in appropriating to themselves the most and the best of the land in certain countries, is as nothing compared with the attitude of the white races toward those of a different hue.

Suppose the conditions were reversed and the yellow races were thus territorially in the ascendancy! Suppose we enforced the same policy in, say, Korea or Manchuria! Well, I should not like to be responsible for the consequences. What an outcry there would be against "violation of equal opportunity" and the monopolization of natural resources. Well, the present attitude of the white races may be *white*, but it certainly is not Christian. Did not Christ say: "Do unto others as you would that they should do unto you?" How can the white races have the face to demand equal opportunities in the Far East when they have denied them to the Far East in the West? It is a misfortune that we are not sufficiently Christianized to set about Christianizing the west in this particular! We do not pretend to be Christians, but we believe in doing unto others that we would have them do unto us!

Viewing the matter seriously, for it is a very serious matter indeed, it ought to be said that every defiance of justice must in the long run provoke revolt. Just as in the labour world, if the capitalist is unfair in his division of profits and the labourers are ground down, they will not forever submit, so in the international world, unless justice obtains between race and race, there will be trouble. In the case under review, then, who will be responsible for the trouble? If one race assumes the right to appropriate all the wealth, why should not all the other races feel ill-used and protest? If the yellow races are oppressed by the white races, and have to revolt to avoid congestion and maintain existence, whose fault is it but that of the aggressors?

We freely admit that the yellow races cannot boast of any superlative innocence or achievement, though we furnished most of the religious inspiration and motive of the world. We have in some respects much to learn in the way of further advancement along modern lines. There are amongst us glaring deficiencies in culture and conspicuous inefficiencies of mechanical contrivance. But in morals we can compare favourably with those nations to whose aggression and greed we have with reluctance been obliged to allude. If our immigrants be honestly compared with those of other nations, we have nothing to fear. The average yellow immigrant entering the United States is found to possess a larger amount of capital than those from other countries. As nations the yellow people have never waged war of any kind on the white races, nor in any manner provoked them to jealousy or resentment. When we fight, it is always in self-defence. The white races preach to us, "peace, peace," and the futility and waste of armamental expansion; while all the time they are expending vast sums on armies and navies, and enforcing discrimination against us. Now, if the white races truly love peace, and wish to deserve the name of Christian nations, they will practice what they preach, and will soon restore to us the rights so long withheld. They will rise to the generosity of welcoming our citizens among them as heartily as we do theirs amongst us. To cry "peace, peace," without rendering us justice, is surely the hollowest of hypocrisy. Any suggestion that we must forever be content to remain inferior races, will not abide. Such an attitude is absolutely inconsistent with our honour as a nation and our sovereign rights as independent states. We therefore appeal to the white races to put aside their race-prejudice and meet us on equal terms in brotherly cooperation. This will convince us of their sincerity more quickly than a thousand proclamations of peace and goodwill, while denying us sympathy and fair-play. Words and attitudes without charity are "as a sounding brass and a tinkling cymbal."

Part III

ASIAN RESPONSES TO IMPERIALISM AND JAPANESE PAN-ASIANISM, 1900–1922

This part introduces voices from Asian countries (other than Japan) that were raised in reaction both to the threat of Western imperialism and to the kind of Pan-Asianism advocated by Japan encountered in the previous part. In the face of the Western threat, ideas of pan-Asian cooperation circulated throughout Asia from the late nineteenth century. Advocates of such cooperation saw it as a possible strategy for resisting continued Western intrusion. In Korea, which had ceased to be a Chinese dependency in 1895 after China lost the war against Japan (1894–1895), the idea of Asian solidarity (sometimes expressed in the slogan "Easternism") gained some popularity in the ensuing decade. Korea faced growing Russian pressure, and some writers argued that, now that China's weakness had been exposed, Korea should ally itself with Japan in order to defend its independence. But, after Japan's victory over Russia in 1905, which resulted in Korea becoming a Japanese protectorate, Asianism was swiftly rejected as an illusionary notion that could only assist the expansionist aims of Japan.

Following the Opium Wars, the Boxer Rebellion, and other internal upheavals, China was likewise forced to reconsider its foreign policy options. Although the Chinese remained skeptical of Pan-Asianism, they nevertheless agreed that some kind of transnational cooperation was needed if Asia was to avoid complete colonization by the Western powers. But after Japan increased its pressure on China during World War I, particularly with the so-called 21 Demands of 1915, Chinese suspicions of the ideology reached new heights.

Pan-Asianism was more appealing to writers and activists from countries that were not threatened directly by Japan. The Indian R. B. Bose and the Tatar Kurban Ali, both introduced in this part, were enthusiastic advocates of cooperation with Japan. They were keen to obtain Japanese support for the national independence movements that they represented in the hope of forming organizations that they regarded as part of a transnational or pan-Asian network of cooperation opposing Western imperialism.

Chapter Fifteen

Sŏ Chaep'il: Editorials from *Tongnip Sinmun* (The Independent), 1898–1899

Kim Bongjin

Sŏ Chaep'il (Philip Jaisohn) was born in 1864 in Bosŏng County in North Cholla province in the southwest of the Korean peninsula into the family of a local magistrate. As a teenager, Sŏ was already imbued with modern political ideas associated with the reformist leader Kim Ok-kyun (1851–1894). He passed the civil service examination, becoming a junior official in 1882. The following year, he was sent to Japan, where he studied both at the Keiō Gijuku (the predecessor of today's Keiō University) and the Military Academy. Having graduated from the academy, Sŏ returned in 1884 to Korea, where he was involved in the Kapsin Coup, a radical attempt to overturn the old regime. After the failure of the coup, Sŏ and his comrades were forced to flee to Japan (Sŏ Chaep'il Kinyŏmhoe 2003).

As the group received no support from the Japanese, in 1885 Sŏ went to San Francisco, where he worked for a time as a laborer. The following year, he enrolled at the Harry Hillman Academy in Pennsylvania having obtained financial support from a wealthy American. It was at that time that he started using the name "Philip Jaisohn." In 1889, he went on to study medicine at Columbian College (the present George Washington University), supporting himself by translating Chinese and Japanese medical books into English. He received his medical degree in 1892, having become a naturalized U.S. citizen in 1890.

In 1895, Japan defeated China in a war that had been fought mainly on the Korean peninsula. Immediately after the war, a new Korean cabinet was formed that consisted mainly of reformers who looked to Japan as a model of modernization. As a result of these political changes, those involved in the Kapsin Coup, including Sŏ Chaep'il, were pardoned. At the end of the year, Sŏ returned to Korea, where he threw himself into efforts aimed at popular political education. On 7 April 1896, he launched a daily newspaper,

171

the *Tongnip Sinmun* (The Independent), printed in the Korean *hangul* script without using any Chinese characters, aiming to make the paper accessible to the lower classes and women. To promote the Korean cause abroad, he also published an English-language version (*The Independent*) between 1896 and 1898.

The preservation of national independence was Sŏ's principal political goal, and to this end he advocated neutrality in foreign relations so as to protect Korea from the unwanted attention of China, Russia, and Japan. He also took an interest in Asian solidarity or Asianism, which he expressed in a number of editorials in the *Tongnip Sinmun*. But these pieces on Asian solidarity were rare, suggesting that he doubted whether a union between Korea, Japan, and China was realistic or, rather, that he was suspicious of the aggressive ambitions of Japanese Asianism, as can be seen in the sources reproduced here, particularly in the editorial of 9 November 1898.

On domestic issues, Sŏ stressed the importance of education, industrialization, and awareness of hygiene. The *Tongnip Sinmun* was also particularly critical of misconduct by government officials, an approach that elicited a negative reaction from the conservatives. Under the aegis of the Independence Club (Tongnip Hyŏphoe), a political organization founded on his initiative by the Korean Ministry of Foreign Affairs in July 1896, Sŏ organized the All-People's Congress (Manmin Kongdonghoe), a public forum for debating political issues. The Congress was led by young reformists and soon began establishing chapters nationwide. In 1898, however, the conservatives accused Sŏ and the Independence Club of seeking to replace the monarchy with a republic, and the Korean government expelled him while disbanding the Independence Club and arresting its leaders.

Back in the United States, Sŏ worked for many years as a medical researcher at the University of Pennsylvania and later became a successful printer and stationer. However, after learning of the nationwide protest against Japanese colonial rule in Korea known as the March First Movement (1919), Sŏ organized the First Korean Congress of Korean residents in America, which took place in Philadelphia. Convinced of the need to inform the American public of the situation in Korea and to obtain the U.S. government's support for Korean independence, he also founded the League of Friends of Korea with branches in twenty-six American cities. He also operated a Korean Information Bureau and published a political journal, *Korea Review*.

The cause of Korean independence proved to be expensive. In 1924, Sŏ was declared legally bankrupt and was forced to take up the medical profession again to make ends meet. During World War II, he volunteered as a medical officer in the U.S. forces, buoyed by the belief that an Allied victory would bring freedom to Korea.

Sŏ returned to Korea after Japan's defeat in 1945 as chief adviser to the U.S. military government, which controlled the southern part of Korea. Turning down petitions by many Koreans, however, he refused to run in South Korea's first presidential election and decided in 1948 to go back to the United States, where he died in 1951.

In the sources reproduced here, Sŏ warns his countrymen of overly relying on foreign support and pleads for the establishment of closer ties with Korea's Asian neighbors—nations of the same "yellow race," that is, China and Japan. However, as the first source shows, Sŏ remained a patriot rather than a strong advocate of Asianism or Asian solidarity.

Sources (translations from the Korean originals by Kim Bongjin)
Sŏ Chaep'il: Editorial, *Tongnip Sinmun*, 31 March 1898.

A member of the Independence Club, Yun Ki-jin is highly respected for his allegiance to and faith in the country, his patriotism and love for this nation of 12 million people. At the time this letter was sent to the Independence Club, Mr. Yun was in charge of Okku (*Chungch'ŏng Pukto*) prefecture. As his letter was received there with admiration, it is published here for the benefit of all the people of the Korean Empire.

We, the members of the Independence Club, do not entertain any ambitions for political office or for the acquisition of wealth through reliance on others. Nor do we attempt to gain a reputation and commit wrongful acts by deception. Rather, we profess to preserve our right to remain independent and sovereign, to oppose oppression by others, to love our own country with sincerity, to enlighten our brethren, and to be respected as one of the most advanced peoples in the world.

It is true that a nation can be regarded as sovereign by acquiring its own rights. Our country, however, is too obsessed with the old teachings of Confucianism to realize the value of modern learning and strategies for making a nation wealthy.

After concluding the treaty with Japan in 1876, we began the process of enlightenment. However, we were not content with having to depend on other nations to settle our own affairs, even though our national independence was still intact. Although we felt comfortable employing the British and the Japanese, when the Russians began to assume important positions in the government and the military, the whole nation felt threatened. . . .

Although the Eastern countries should strive to cooperate with each other to defend themselves against Russia, the Chinese only dream whereas Koreans are heedless and besotted with drink. Distracted by the maintenance of traditional social class distinctions, Koreans, lacking their own power and strategy, are so thoughtless as to bring in the Russians. If the Koreans continue depending on Russia, their sense of satisfaction may not last for very long, for in the end it will only lead to selling out the nation and ruining the country.

Then, consider this, members of the Independence Club! There is no point in Koreans simply assuming high political rank for the sake of their country. The result will be deplorable. Some of our members in the Club have obtained high rank, some have wealth, and others are highly educated in the fields of agriculture, manufacturing, and commerce. Under the aegis of our ancestor kings, our country has prospered. If our country prospers, we can prosper; if our country is ruined, we too will be ruined. . . .

Now our Club will gain glory through loving our country and people, and our nation will recover its right to stand up as an independent country in the world by overcoming the barbarian customs that have benefited common people such as peddlers and the Tonghak Party. We are pleased to wish our king enduring glory and our long-lasting patriotism. We hope that our fellow members will maintain an unwavering determination to look after national affairs as we would oversee our own affairs, and contribute to the development of the nation so that it achieves the status of a highly developed country.

Sŏ Chaep'il: Editorial, *Tongnip Sinmun*, 7 April 1898.

A foreign proverb asserts that "blood is thicker than water." What this means is that a person, however close he may be, can never be dearer to us than the relatives who share our blood. This principle applies not only to interpersonal relations, but also to international relations. States may be cooperative and fair to each other in time of peace—yet, in times of conflict and dispute, countries inevitably fall to fighting each other. . . .

Our brethren gathered in the one nation may not always be so friendly, but they will protect me in times of crisis. Therefore, everybody has their own obligations and sense of justice. Politicians should never forget their duties: politicians who forget their special duties and the demands of justice will harm themselves as well as the nation. For a nation to be independent and sovereign, its citizens should care for and help one another while going through difficult times. If the people and their government are at each other's throats, when they forget their own obligations and sense of justice, threatening each other's lives, the whole nation will perish.

People should love their own family more than a family of strangers; people should love their own parents and siblings more than those belonging to other families; people should love their own neighbors more than the neighbors of strangers; people should trust their own government more than foreign governments; people should love their own people more than other peoples; people should love their own king more than other kings. And it is evident that this same moral code applies to every nation.

In international relations, every nation considers this obligation to some degree. Although the European countries are now fighting and competing against one another in their region, if the Asian or American countries were to invade European countries, the Europeans would cooperate among themselves in order to cope with any threat from the Asians or Americans. . . .

Korea, Japan, and China exist in one Asia and because their race (*chongja*) is the same; their bodies and hair are similar, they use a common script, and even have many customs in common. These three nations in the East, then, should cherish, protect, and help each other, and at the same time, learn Western knowledge and education, in order to fight against Europeans. Although the East is in danger of becoming a Western colony, China does not pay attention to this grave situation and is asleep. China is being stripped of its territory and people, making the whole of Asia very dangerous and risky.

Korea should not sleep like China and must learn day and night. The king and ministers must cooperate with each other to make fundamentals of the nation firmer and more independent. By doing this as well as associating with Japan, Korea can make China civilized [enlightened] and preserve the East, making the independence of three countries sustainable. If Korea becomes like China, Japan will not be able to stand alone. If Korea and China both fall apart, Japan will not be able to take on the European powers alone.

Sŏ Chaep'il: Editorial, *Tongnip Sinmun*, 9 November 1899.

In general terms, the goal of the Westerners is to destroy religion other than their own, oppress other races, and occupy the higher ground alone. The Westerners have invaded the North and South American continents, destroyed the red race, and built their own society in its place. All the natives have perished. They also invaded the African continent, enslaving black people or working them to death and stealing all the fertile land.

The brown races of the Asian continent have also become subject to the Westerners. Only the yellow race of Korea, Japan, and China is still resisting, but in recent days the Russians and other Westerners have been . . . bearing rapidly down on the South and the East like a hurricane. Alas! How perilous is the destiny of the yellow race! Is it true that the danger of relegation to an inferior status is just around the corner? It cannot be true. Why not? Because the Japanese have provided us with a lesson, we can presume the future of the yellow race.

The Westerners despise Eastern countries and races, denying them equal status. Even though the political structures and institutions of Japan were equal to those found in the most advanced countries in the West—and were even superior to those of Spain and Italy—the Western countries still refused to revise their unequal treaties with Japan. Only after Japan acquired strong weapons, Westerners could not but recognize the equal status of Japan, which reflected the capacity and knowledge of the yellow race. Therefore it is time to praise Japanese not only for what they have accomplished for Japan but for [all of] the yellow race of the East.

Despite the differences among them, the Western countries cooperate with each other against the yellow race of the East. . . . Why then have the peoples of the yellow race of the East failed to cooperate with each other and fallen prey to the Westerners' strategy of divide and rule? People cannot look down on others without doing the same thing for themselves. If an Easterner remains unenlightened and let himself be enslaved by the Westerners, he will be guilty not only in the eyes of his own people but also of the whole yellow race of the East, regardless of his social status. Now I declare that all the yellow race, my dear brethren, recover sovereign equal rights following in the footsteps of the Japanese.

Japan is now the leader of all the yellow race of the East, a model of the domestic development in political and legal affairs, and a great wall to fight against foreign robbers. Having successfully revised its treaties with the Western countries, Japan should lead other brethren of the yellow race, make light of its own national interests, aspire to greater purposes, protect the whole East, and preserve the peace in the region with long-term strategy. This is the duty bestowed by God.

Chapter Sixteen

Zhang Taiyan and the Asiatic Humanitarian Brotherhood, 1907

Yuan P. Cai

Zhang Binglin (Chang Pinglin, more usually known by his pseudonym Taiyan) was born in 1869 into a landed gentry family in China's Zhejiang (Chekiang) province. His family had a long-standing tradition of classical Confucian scholarship and involvement in the imperial civil service; both his elder brothers were awarded imperial degrees. Zhang Taiyan was deeply versed in the Confucian canon and produced numerous commentaries on classics such as *I-Ching* (The Book of Changes). He is remembered not only as an erudite classical scholar (and the teacher of modern China's most celebrated writer, Lu Xun, or Lu Hsün) but also as a noted revolutionary involved in the Wuchang uprising and the founding of the Chinese republic. The contemporary historical assessment of Zhang Taiyan has been affected by his antagonistic relationship with Sun Yat-sen (see II:5), who has assumed a semimythical status as the father of the republic. Their relationship deteriorated drastically in 1907 after Sun accepted secret funds from the Japanese government in exchange for leaving Japan under pressure from the Manchu Court. One of the least examined areas of Zhang's life, however, are his pan-Asian sympathies and writings (on Zhang in general see Wong 1989).

Zhang Taiyan became involved in politics in 1895 following the Sino-Japanese War. He joined the editorial team of the reform-oriented newspaper *Shiwu Bao* (Contemporary Affairs), founded by Kang You-wei (1858–1927). He showed signs of pan-Asian sympathies in one of his earliest articles titled "Asian Countries (Japan and China) Should Be as Close to One Another as the Lips and Teeth," in which he enthusiastically advocated the case for mutual dependence and assistance between China and Japan. Zhang regarded tsarist Russia as the common enemy of both China and Japan that threatened the survival of both countries. More startling still, he rationalized Japan's occupation of Port Arthur (present Lushun) during the Russo-Japanese War as an act of self-defense in the collective interest of both countries. One can discern very little difference between Zhang's position and that of contemporary Japanese pan-Asian expansionists on this issue.

In a petition to the elder statesman Li Hongzhang (Li Hung-chang, 1823–1901) in 1898, Zhang strongly advocated a pan-Asian alliance between China and Japan. He rationalized such an alliance with a mixture of pragmatic Realpolitik and Spencerian notions of racial struggle. It should be noted that Zhang, whose views on race were molded by social Darwinism that was fashionable among Asian intellectuals at the time, subscribed to the concept of survival of the fittest in a highly competitive world. In his address to Li, he vividly described a deep racial bond between China and Japan and argued that, at a time of Western imperialist expansion, Japan and China must share a common destiny. The confrontations between China and Japan were brushed aside as benign fraternal disputes that posed no threat to a future relationship. He also believed rather naively that the bad relations between China and Japan were the fault of the Japanese government and that the Japanese people through their parliamentary representatives would eventually force the government into an alliance with China. In addition to his pan-Asian rhetoric, Zhang also made his case based on more pragmatic concerns. Urging Li to cede Weihaiwei (Weihai) to Japan to form a convenient wedge between the Russian-occupied Port Arthur and the German-held Jiaozhou (Kiaochow) Bay on Shandong (Shantung) peninsula, he dismissed Weihaiwei as a "scrap of rotten flesh" that the Chinese could feed to Japan (Tang Zhijun 1977: 55). He also argued that it was much cheaper to employ Japanese advisers than the more expensive Western ones.

It is important to note that Zhang Taiyan was not alone in his support for a pan-Asian alliance between China and Japan at the time. Modern Chinese historiography has persistently painted Japanese Pan-Asianism in an overwhelmingly negative light, as nothing more than sugar-coated Japanese imperialism. It is easy to understand such a sentiment given the atrocities committed subsequently by the Japanese army in China. However, it seems that for emotional reasons, many Chinese historians are tempted to commit the fallacy of interpreting past events with the benefit of hindsight. There is substantial evidence to suggest that many influential figures from both ends of the political spectrum in China at the turn of the twentieth century supported a pan-Asian alliance. For example, both a constitutional reformer like Kang You-wei and the ultraconservative Prince Regent of the Manchu court expressed their admiration for the Tōa Dōbunkai led by Prince Konoe Atsumaro (see I:9 and I:6).

Following the failure of the short-lived reform movement in China in 1898, Zhang became one of the many hundreds of reformers exiled to Japan. During his exile, he made a decisive break with his erstwhile companions in the reform movement through a number of devastating attacks on the conservatism and monarchism of Kang You-wei and his followers. At one time, he went back to Shanghai, where, in the safety of a foreign concession, he threw himself wholeheartedly into the Republican camp by staging a ceremony in which he cut off his queue. After a brief imprisonment in a foreign concession, he was forced to seek exile once again, and after he went back to Japan in 1906, he assumed the editorship of *Min Pao*, the official organ of the Chinese Revolutionary League (Tongmenghui or T'ung-meng-hui; Japanese Chūgoku Dōmeikai). At that time, he befriended Indian nationalist exiles living in Tokyo who were also subsequently associated with Ōkawa Shūmei (see II:4) and other radical pan-Asianists. His new friendships spurred his interest in Indian history, culture, and Buddhist philosophy. This gave a religious undertone to his pan-Asian ideas. Zhang wrote a commemorative essay on his meeting with two Indian revolutionaries. In it he wrote that "I was completely overwhelmed by sadness after I had heard the Indian revolutionaries' bleak account of India's abysmal condition" (Zhongnan Diqu Xinhai Geming Shi yan Jiuhui 1980: 79).

On 24 April 1907, Zhang Taiyan was invited to attend a function in Tokyo to commemorate Shivaji, the Raja of the Marathas who led a Hindu revolt against the Mogul ruler in 1659. Zhang regarded him as a precursor of the Indian independence movement and made explicit reference to the need to follow in the footsteps of Shivaji in pursuing India's struggle for national liberation from British imperialism. During the celebration, one of the Japanese guests of honor, former and future prime minister Count Ōkuma Shigenobu (1838–1922), commented, "His Britannic Majesty has been reigning over India with incomparable benevolence and love" and called on Indians "not to blame the British for their ills, nor to resort to violence, but instead concentrate their energies on social reform." Before this episode took place, Ōkuma had been regarded as very sympathetic to the cause of oppressed Asian peoples. This comment came as a great shock and disappointment to Zhang, who had written only days before that a tripartite relationship between China, India, and Japan was like the structure of a fan, in which three distinct but mutually necessary pieces reinforce each other. Specifically, he likened China to the wooden framework, India to the folded paper, and Japan to the threads holding the framework and paper together. But after listening to Ōkuma's speech, he realized with despair that, for Japanese statesmen, the Anglo-Japanese Alliance (1902) was more important than any pan-Asian sympathies.

Zhang Taiyan and his Indian revolutionary friends denounced Ōkuma's comments in the strongest possible terms and branded as traitors Japanese who sided with white imperialists to humiliate their own kind. Outraged by what they perceived as Japanese intransigence, Zhang and other Asian revolutionaries decided to form an alliance to throw off the imperialist yoke (without official Japanese support). Thus, the Asiatic Humanitarian Brotherhood (Chinese: Yazhou Heqinhui; Japanese: Ashū Washinkai) was founded in 1907 (see Tang 1991). Its stated goal was to free oppressed Asian peoples from the tyranny of Western imperialism. Zhang was elected president of the society. Among its founding members were noted Chinese intellectuals such as the romantic poet and translator Su Manshu (1884–1918); the first secretary-general of the Communist Party of China, Chen Duxiu (Ch'en Tu-hsiu, 1879–1942); and Indian nationalists. There were also participants from other colonized Asian countries such as Korea, Annam, Burma, and the Philippines. Japanese participants included some of the leaders of the early socialist movement, such as Kōtoku Shūsui (1871–1911).The founding of this society caused quite a stir among the large Chinese student population in Japan at the time.

Zhang used *Min Pao* as the principal platform from which to propagate ideas of Asian solidarity. In numerous articles he denounced the barbarity of British, French, and American imperialists and urged all oppressed Asians to work together to achieve national liberation. He wrote angrily that, for example, "under the French occupation, taxes have been levied on births, funerals, begging and cleaning toilets, and people have been executed for crossing borders, destroying public notices or attending public gatherings. These cruelties are without precedent." Other exiled Asian nationalists were also invited to contribute to the publication. Korean nationalists published two pieces, "An Address to the Korean Nation" and "An Address to Our Foreign Compatriots," that expressed great sympathy with the fate of colonized fellow Asian peoples.

One of the most important documents in Zhang's pan-Asianist writings is the Charter of the Asiatic Humanitarian Brotherhood. It systematically outlines the goals and organizational structure of the association and was originally published in three languages: Chinese, Japanese, and English. The society's goal was stated explicitly as the "struggle against imperialism to regain independence for Asian peoples who have their lost their sovereignty." Especially significant was the fact that the charter required members of the society to assist each other in their revolutionary struggles with all the means at their disposal.

It is important to note that a Sino–Indian alliance replaced a Sino–Japanese partnership as the centerpiece of the pan-Asian writings and activities of Zhang Taiyuan shortly after the founding of the association. Like many Chinese pan-Asianists, he had admired the success of the Meiji Restoration and its modernization efforts and harbored the hope that Japan would play a crucial part in China's own revival. Many Chinese had crossed the sea to seek the secrets of success in Japan, but they had become gradually disillusioned and alarmed by Japan's increasingly aggressive ambitions in East Asia and especially in China. By 1907 Japan was viewed no longer as a reliable Asian ally but increasingly as an imperialist power even more dangerous than the Western powers. Zhang was personally shattered by his experience at the function to commemorate Shivaji referred to previously. The new association made it unambiguously clear in its charter that, in order to be eligible for membership, members must denounce imperialism and aid their fellow Asians in their struggle. Zhang no doubt wrote this with Japan in mind for, as he saw it, Japan, though an Asian country, had abandoned its Asian neighbors and had joined the imperialist club.

Another interesting aspect of Zhang's Pan-Asianism is its strong religious and cultural undertones, no doubt influenced by his strong personal interest in the study of Sanskrit and Indian philosophy and culture. He wrote that the basis for any Asian revival would be a Sino–Indian alliance and that this partnership would be greatly strengthened by cultural cross-fertilization, especially in the area of religion. He argued that the religions of Asia should be used as weapons to strengthen the moral fabric of fellow Asian nations and to expose the "falsehood" of Western religion. In 1908, Zhang expressed his desire to travel south to India to further his study of Sanskrit. He wrote that the popularization of this language in China would not only benefit the spread of Buddhism but also greatly increase the chances of realizing a pan-Asian alliance.

Following Zhang's break with Sun Yat-sen, his career was marked by continued criticism of the new Republican national government and support for an anti-Japanese crusade following the Mukden Incident in 1931. In the final years of his life, he vehemently opposed the policies of appeasement and non-confrontation with the Japanese and launched a barrage of criticism against the Nanking government's incompetence in resisting the foreign invaders. He lectured extensively on the topics of national salvation and traditional culture and encouraged the Chinese to take up arms to resist impending national disaster. Zhang Taiyan died in 1936, aged sixty-seven. On his deathbed, he forbade his children to accept any official post from foreign invaders if China were to be conquered. He was mourned nationwide as a great patriot and classical scholar and was given a state funeral despite a lingering resentment in official circles over his outspoken criticisms of the government.

The Asiatic Humanitarian Brotherhood lasted for only about sixteen months after its foundation in April 1907. Its premature dissolution was largely due to the intervention of the Japanese government. At the request of the Qing (Ch'ing) government, *Min Pao* was banned in Japan. It was not only an important revolutionary Republican publication but also an influential platform for the propagation of pan-Asian ideas among exiled Asian nationalists in Japan. Though the society achieved little in terms of lasting influence, it nevertheless showed that Pan-Asianism was a potent ideal entertained by leading Chinese intellectuals at the turn of the twentieth century as a possible cure for China's ills.

Source (translation from the Chinese original by Yuan P. Cai)
"The Charter of the Asiatic Humanitarian Brotherhood," reprinted in Zhongnan Diqu Xinhai Geming Shi yan Jiuhui (ed.) (1980), *Xinhai Geming Shi Cong Kan* (Materials on the History of the Xinhai Revolution), vol. 1. Beijing: Zhinghua Shuju, 83–84.

PREAMBLE

In the Asian countries, India has the religion of Buddha and the philosophy of Sankara, China has the teaching of Confucius, Mao-tzu, Lao-tzu, Zhuan-tzu, and Yang-tzu and, in distant Persia, there are the worshippers of fire known as the Zoroastrians. These races have maintained their distinctive identities and have rarely encroached on their neighbors. The Southern Islands (the Malay Peninsula and its environs) were influenced by Sanskrit culture, and there is little need to mention the influence of Chinese culture on the countries of the Eastern Sea (Japan and Korea). These cultures have all lived in relative harmony, with very little mutual aggression and according the greatest respect to moral virtue.

Since the previous century, the Europeans have been expanding eastwards. The power of Asia is declining. It is not only a matter of political and military strength, but people are increasingly losing their self-confidence and becomingly materially obsessed, and learning is also in terminal decline. India was lost first and then China fell to the Manchus. Various Malay races have been enslaved by the Whites, and Vietnam and Burma have also been taken over. The Philippines, which had been initially occupied by Spain, was annexed by America after a brief interlude of independence. Only Siam and Persia are able to maintain a semblance of independence, and even that is decaying rapidly.

In ancient times, there were thirty-six countries in the Tianshan Mountain region—but they were destroyed by nomadic Turkic tribes and their peoples exterminated. Our Chinese, Indian, Annamese, Burmese and Filipino brethren have vowed not to follow in the footsteps of these nations and have established the Asiatic Humanitarian Brotherhood to fight imperialism in order to preserve our various races. In the future when we rise up against the Western barbarians, people from both East and South will unite in their efforts and we will have all the strength of bundled reeds. We will form a fraternal alliance that will revive the fortunes of our Brahmanism, Confucianism and Daoism and expose the immoral falsehood of the West. While we cannot assemble all our brethren now, we can first unite India and China, the two most ancient and largest lands in the East. If these two countries can achieve independence, they will be able to form a protective shield over Asia and many countries will be the beneficiaries. All Asian races who share a firm belief in national independence should unite, and we extend our warmest welcome to them.

NAME

The name of the society shall be the Asiatic Humanitarian Brotherhood.

OBJECTIVE

The objective of the society is to fight against imperialism and to achieve the independence of Asian peoples who have lost their sovereignty.

MEMBERSHIP

All Asians, except those who advocate imperialism, shall be admitted regardless of whether they are "Nationalists," "Republicans," "Socialists" or "Anarchists."

OBLIGATIONS

All the Asian countries have either been invaded by outsiders or enslaved by other races; the situation is absolutely deplorable. The duty of the society is to offer mutual assistance to its members and help each one achieve independence and freedom.

If a revolution breaks out in one country, members of all the Asian countries must provide assistance, whether directly or indirectly, to the best of their abilities.

All members must put aside their previous differences, communicate regularly, and show mutual respect and love, with deepening understanding and affection for one another, to further the interests of the association. Members must regard it as their duty to recruit those who sympathize with the goals of the association and who can assist it. New branches must be formed throughout the world, to the best of our ability.

ORGANIZATIONS

All members shall meet once a month.

Each member shall keep a list of the names and addresses of all members.

New members will be introduced before the meeting commences and will have their names recorded. A record of the activities of the association will be published. Letters and reports from members in different countries will be read out aloud during meetings, and these communications will also be reported to all our branches. Some (as yet unspecified) membership dues will be levied to cover the operating expenses of the association, but these will be limited to the costs of stationery and postage.

The posts of chairman and secretary shall be left unfilled, in order to reflect the egalitarian nature of the association and the spirit of mutual respect. All members shall enjoy equal rights and privileges and are expected to contribute equally to the association. According to the aims of the association, all members shall be treated with respect regardless of their national origins.

The association's headquarters will be in Tokyo, with branches in China, India, Korea, the Philippines, the United States and other countries; letters will be sent to the permanent addresses of branches for the sake of convenience and also to inform isolated members of the activities of the society.

Chapter Seventeen

Aurobindo Ghose: "The Logic of Asia," 1908–1909

Brij Tankha

Aurobindo Ghose was born into a prominent middle-class family in Bengal. His father, a doctor, sent Aurobindo to England for his education, wanting him to be brought up without any Indian influence. Money was limited and life difficult, but Ghose was talented and managed to obtain a senior classical scholarship to Cambridge University. Graduating at the top of his class from King's College, he passed the difficult Indian Civil Service (ICS) examination with distinction; but, already disinclined to work for the British, he famously refused to sit the compulsory riding examination and so failed to enter the ICS.

Ghose returned to India and worked in the princely state of Baroda, where his interests turned increasingly to learning about India. He knew seven European languages but no Indian language, so he taught himself Sanskrit, Bengali, and Hindustani. He continued to publish poetry, which he had been doing from an early age. Critical of British rule and dissatisfied with the moderate policies of the Indian National Congress, he built connections with leading nationalists such as Lokmanya Tilak (1856–1920), who argued for *swaraj* (self-rule), and resistance groups in Bengal.

In 1905 Bengal was partitioned, an act that convulsed the state, and Ghose took leave from Baroda to take an active part there. He was invited by Bipin Chandra Pal (1858–1932), a prominent advocate of complete autonomy from Britain, to help him edit the radical newspaper *Bande Mataram*, which became the voice of the radicals. In 1907 the editors were prosecuted by the British government on charges of instigating violence, but Ghose was not jailed, as the prosecution failed to prove he was one of them.

Ghose went on to found an underground party, Jugantar, to prepare the ground for independence. In 1908 he was among those tried in the Alipore bomb case for instigating the attempted assassination of a British magistrate known for his severe judgments against nationalists. Ghose was acquitted, but the case caught the popular imagination and made him a widely known and admired figure. However, Ghose continued to face police harassment and finally sought refuge in the French colony of Pondicherry, where he gradually abandoned active politics for spiritual pursuits.

Although Ghose's writings touch on a variety of issues, his early political writings were grounded in a wider perspective on Asia. He saw each Asian civilization as having long-term historically based characteristics; he noted that it was not only Japan that was able to transform itself but also China and that the only reason that India could not advance in equal measure was because it was enslaved by the British. He argued that Asian nations had sources of strength that were superior to those of the European nations and, therefore, that their ability to resist and transform themselves was correspondingly greater. To understand these particular Asian sources of strength, it was important to recognize that the political ideals of the West were not the mainsprings of the political movements of the East. These were the distinctive products of a very different history (Ghose 1972a: 757–60).

According to Ghose, the real strength of Asia derived from two separate sources: the Islamic ideal of equality and the divine unity of man and spirit as expressed in the Vedanta (literally, "appendix to the Vedas," used to describe a group of philosophical traditions concerned with the self-realization understood as the ultimate nature of reality). The failure of European democracy, he wrote, lay in the fact that it was based on the notion of rights. A movement for Asian democracy, he argued, could succeed only if it discarded the illusion that it must follow Europe and forget its own past. It could not abandon its own past, he suggested, "for it is the *dharma* of everyman to be free in soul. It is this ideal that differentiates the soul of Asia from that of Europe."

Ghose's vision of Asia extended from Japan in the East to encompass China, India, Persia, and Turkey and other countries in western Asia. He argued that the Japanese had a "patriotic spirit and imitative faculties" but went on to say that the strength of the Chinese lay in the "grand deliberation, the patient thoroughness, the irresistible organization of China" (Ghose 1972b: 812–17). It was the Indian genius that earned his most fulsome praise, however, for he saw in it "an all-embracing intellect, her penetrating intuition, her invincible originality"; he concluded that if "the genius of Japan lies in her imitation and improvement, that of India [lies] in origination" (Ghose 1972c: 842–45). He also noted in his comments on the constitutional movements in Persia and Turkey that the strength of these two countries lay in "the preservation of their national individuality and existence while equipping themselves with the weapons of the modern strength for survival" (Ghose 1972e: 247–48).

Ghose regarded each Asian nation as having distinctive cultural characteristics even while sharing common features that bind them into a single Asian civilization and that to make the difficult transition from colonial rule to independence it was necessary for small groups of enlightened people to take the lead—partly because the masses were insufficiently mature and partly to more effectively counter the political threats the new governments would face from the colonial powers (Ghose 1972d: 230–31; 1972e: 247–48).

Even though he supported national independence in general, Ghose was ambiguous when it came to the question of Korea. Writing about Itō Hirobumi's assassination by a Korean in 1909, he bemoaned the death of a great man and asserted that "Korea will gain nothing by this rash and untimely act," for Japan "will grind the soul out of Korea until it is undistinguishable from Japan." He noted that while a subject nation must attract sympathy, the Koreans lacked "the strength of soul to attain freedom" (Ghose 1972e: 256).

Ghose saw India as crucial to the British Empire and, therefore, to European relations with Asia. He argued that Europe must accept India as a mediator between a resurgent China and Japan—but, if it failed to do so, then India would ally with those two countries to fight and ultimately dominate Europe. The first blow to Europe had been struck against Russia in 1904–1905, and the second would be struck against Britain in India. The Sino-Japanese Alliance, as Ghose called it, would first expel Britain from India and then "will form an alliance to expel Europe from Asia, Africa, Australia" (Ghose 1972b: 812–17). In Ghose's vision of the future we can see an ideal of Asian liberation that is found in many pan-Asian writings from this era.

Source 1 (English in the original)
Ghose, Aurobindo, "Asiatic Democracy," Bande Mataram, 16 March 1908, Sri Aurobindo Birth Centenary Library (ed.), *Bande Mataram Early Political Writings*, Vol. 1 (Sri Aurobindo Ashram Trust, Pondicherry 1972), 757–60.

When the ideals of liberty, equality and fraternity were declared at the time of the French Revolution and mankind demanded that society should recognize them as the foundation of its structure, they were associated with a fierce revolt against the relics of feudalism and against the travesty of the Christian religion which had become an integral part of that feudalism. This was the weakness of European Democracy and the source of its failure. It took as its motive the rights of man and not the dharma (or duty) of humanity; it appealed to the selfishness of the lower classes against the pride of the upper; it made hatred and internecine war the permanent allies of Christian ideals and wrought an inextricable confusion which is the modern malady of Europe. . . .

The movements of the nineteenth century in India were coloured with the hues of the West. Instead of seeking for strength in the spirit, [there was] the appeal to the rights of humanity or the equality of social status at an impossible dead level which Nature has always refused to allow. Mingled with these false gospels was a strain of hatred and bitterness, which showed itself in the condemnation of Brahmanical priestcraft, the hostility to Hinduism and the ignorant breaking away from the hallowed traditions of the past. What was true and eternal in that past was likened to what was false or transitory, and the nation was in danger of losing its soul by an insensate surrender to the aberrations of European materialism. Not in this spirit was India intended to receive the might opportunity which the impact of Europe gave to her. When the danger was greatest, a number of great spirits were sent to stem the tide flowing from the West and recall her to her mission; for, if she had gone astray, the world would have gone astray with her. Her mission is to point back humanity to the true source of human liberty, human equality, human brotherhood. When man is free in spirit, all other freedom is at his command; for the Free is the Lord who cannot be bound. When he is liberated from delusion, he perceives the divine equality of the world which fulfils itself through love and justice, and this perception transfuses itself into the law of the government and society. When he has perceived this divine equality, he is brother to the whole world, and in whatever position he is placed he serves all men as his brothers by the law of love, by the law of justice. When this perception becomes the basis of philosophy, of social speculation and political aspiration, then will liberty equality and fraternity take their place in the structure of society and the Satya Yuga (The Age of Truth). This is the Asiatic reading of Democracy, which India must rediscover for herself before she can give it to the world. . . . It has been said that Democracy is based on the rights of man; it has been replied that it should rather take its stand on the duties of man; but both rights and duties are European ideas. Dharma is the Indian conception in which rights and duties lose the artificial antagonism created by a view of the world which makes selfishness the root of action, and regain their deep and eternal unity. Dharma is the basis of Democracy which Asia must recognize, for in this lies the distinction between the soul of Asia and the soul of Europe.

Source 2 (English in the original)
Ghose, Aurobindo, "The Asiatic Role," *Bande Mataram*, 9 April 1908, ibid., 842–45.

Something is wanting which Europe cannot supply. It is at this juncture that Asia has awakened, because the world needed her. Asia is the custodian of the world's peace of mind, the physician of the maladies which Europe generates. . . . When Greek and Roman had exhausted themselves, the Arab went out from his desert to take up their unfinished task, revivify the civilisation of the old world and impart the profounder impulses to the pursuit of knowledge. Asia has always initiated, Europe completed. The strength of Europe is in details, the strength of Asia in synthesis. When Europe has perfected the details of life or thought, she is unable to harmonise them into a perfect symphony and she falls into intellectual heresies, practical extravagances which contradict the facts of life, the limits of human nature and the ultimate truths of human existence. It is therefore the office of Asia to take up the work of human evolution when Europe comes to a standstill and loses itself in a clash of vain speculations, barren experiments and helpless struggles to escape from the consequences of her own mistakes. Such a time has now come in the world's history.

In former ages India was a sort of hermitage of thought and peace apart from the world. Separated from the rest of humanity by her peculiar geographical conformation, she worked out her own problems and thought out the secrets of existence as in a quiet Ashram from which the noise of the world was shut out. Her thoughts flashed out over Asia and created civilization, her sons were the bearers of light to the peoples; philosophies based themselves on stray fragments of her infinite wisdom; sciences arose from the waste of her intellectual production. When the barrier was broken and nations began to surge through the Himalayan gates, the peace of India departed. She passed through centuries of struggle, of ferment in which the civilisations born of her random thoughts returned to her developed and insistent, seeking to impose themselves on the mighty mother of them all. . . . To her they were reminiscences of her old intellectual experiments laid aside and forgotten. She took them up, re-thought them in a new light and once more made them part of herself. So she dealt with Greek, so with the Scythian, so with Islam, so now she will deal with the great brood of her returning children, with Christianity, with Buddhism, with European science and materialism, with the fresh speculations born of the world's renewed contact with the source of thought in this ancient cradle of religion, science and philosophy. The vast amount of new matter which she has to absorb is unprecedented in her history, but to her it is child's play. Her all-embracing intellect, her penetrating intuition, her invincible originality are equal to greater tasks. The period of passivity when she listened to the voices of the outside world is over. No longer will she be content merely to receive and reproduce, even to receive and improve. The genius of Japan lies in imitation and improvement, that of India in origination. The contributions of the outside peoples she can only accept as rough material from her immense creative faculty.

Chapter Eighteen

Sin Ch'ae-ho: "A Critique of Easternism," 1909

Kim Bongjin

Sin Ch'ae-ho was born on 7 November 1880, the grandson of a Korean court official. He was educated in the traditional Korean way, with no exposure to Western thought, and received a doctoral degree from the Confucian academy, Sŏnggyungwan, in 1905. He was appointed a teacher in the same school, but, because of his strong nationalist feelings, he resigned his position after Japan had declared a protectorate over Korea (see Sin 1981, 1984).

Sin Ch'ae-ho used his literary reputation to support the Patriotic Enlightenment Movement and, in August 1909, wrote an editorial titled "Tong'yangjuyi" (A Critique of Easternism) in the *Taehan Maeil Sinbo* (Korea Daily News), in which he warned the Korean people of the dangers of Easternism. In this piece, which is reproduced here, he criticizes the idea of Pan-Asianism as a tool of Japanese expansionism and imperialism in the guise of Asian solidarity. He dismisses the idea of East Asia, regarding it merely as a "geographical expression."

After Japan had annexed Korea in 1910, Sin Ch'ae-ho sought exile in China. He helped set up the Qingdao (Tsingtao) Council in exile and also organized the New Korea Youth Society in China in 1915. He was briefly associated with the Shanghai Provisional Government of Korea in 1919. Later he became interested in anarchism and was involved in the drafting of the Manifesto of the Korean Revolution (*Chosŏn Hyukmyong Sŏnŏn*, 1923).

Sin Ch'ae-ho was arrested in Taiwan (Jilong) in May 1928 when, traveling on a false Chinese passport, he was engaged in smuggling counterfeit currency to fund the activities of the Eastern Anarchist Association. In 1930 he was sentenced to ten years in prison. He died in prison in 1936.

Sin is known as the founder of the nationalist historiography of Korea (see Choi 2004) and is often referred to as "Korea's greatest historian," both in South and in North Korea. In his books *Toksa Sillon* (A New Reading of History, 1908) and *Chosŏn Sanggosa* (The Early History of Chosŏn, 1924–1925), he set out the first linear national history of Korea based on ethnic (*minjok*) lines. He is also famous for his claim of a Manchurian connection with the grandeur of Korea's ancient past.

Source (translation from the Korean original by Kim Bongjin)
Sin Ch'ae-ho, "A Critique of Easternism," *Taehan Maeil Sinbo*, 8 August 1909.

What is Easternism? Some say that its goal is to defend the East against the incursions of the Western powers, based on cooperation among Eastern countries. Who is making this claim? First of all, it is the traitors to our nation. They have given up the fatherland to foreigners and agreed to enslave their own brethren. They defend themselves with lies as follows: "This is the time of great conflict between the yellow race of the East and the white race of the West." . . . They argue that it is all right to give up the country—not to Westerners, but to Easterners, so as to better resist the West. If we sell our country to the Westerners, they say, then we will be guilty [of treason]. But, if the sellers and buyers are both Easterners, it is like trading between ancient Chinese dynasties, so we are not guilty. Such people are merely indulging themselves in illogical explanations and confused defenses—and now Easternism is being advocated by these same crazy people.

Second, there are those who flatter foreign countries. Their only interest is their own wealth and political power so they behave like flies and dogs, even when foreigners steal all kinds of legal and economic rights from us. They think that only flattery will bring benefits. Greedy, they are not satisfied with taking small things. What they ultimately want is to wipe out the national soul (*kukhon*). . . . Using this strategy, they invent weird tactics to destroy the soul of their own country.

They also tell people, "Forget your own country and serve Japan." But even small, ignorant children who hear this argument will rise up to punish them with the sword. Thus all their arguments will be in vain. Trying to ward off the inevitable punishment, they invented the idea of Easternism using a vicious logic involving a string of evils. When we are angry at Japan for depriving Korea of its rights, they tell us that "All Eastern countries are one, and you should not be upset." When we are infuriated by Japanese exploitation, they lie to us: "All of the yellow race is one, so you should not complain." They are trying to make people forget about nationalism by making them intoxicated with Easternism. It is these bandits who have been propagating the slogan of Easternism.

The third [group using this argument] are confused and ignorant. They have no noble thoughts of domestic sovereignty and are constantly influenced by the outside world. They always follow the fashions set by others, but without original ideas of their own. Lacking any clear sense of right and wrong, they follow what others follow; they attempt to civilize themselves when others are doing the same. They insist that "Sages also follow the current of the times." Such people were born by chance, and nowadays are flirting with the idea of Easternism. Intoxicated with notions propagated by the government, they merely repeat the concept of Easternism without adding any soul of their own.

Sin Ch'ae-ho, "A Critique of Easternism (continued)," *Taehan Maeil Sinbo,* 10 August 1909.

These people are constantly talking to each other and lecturing on Easternism. Following these presentations, they get some people to agree with them, interpreting the meaning of Easternism for themselves. Our people—twenty million people without a proper education—are tempted to follow this satanic spell. They have come to regard any Eastern country as a potential partner even if they are an old enemy, and any [members of the] yellow race as brethren even if they are foes.

Some people confuse us by such statements as these: "As I was born here, I love my country. . . . [However,] Since we belong to the yellow race in East Asia, we should love the [other members of the] same race. Our nation, located in the East, cannot exist without the East." . . .

People, listen to *my* words. "If one were to argue that the day would come when we began trading with the planets Venus and Mercury, then we humans on the Earth would admit the unity of all mankind, strengthen our military to defend the world, and educate our children to compete with other planets; were such a day to come, then we would regard all races including yellow and white as one, and East and West as a single part of a larger Earth." . . .

Today, competition among states is becoming more ruthless. To retreat even a little means extinction. Even though the enemy may be weak, we will still be seriously wounded. Regardless of the national crisis that we now face, how can we ever take seriously this absurd idea, giving credibility to fanciful dreams of scenarios that *might* take place thousands of years from now? What if the Poles were now to agree to Europeanism, expressing admiration for it and forgetting the tragedy of the loss of their fatherland, only to call for a coalition with the West? I would respond, "It is unacceptable."

When your own family is in distress, when your relatives are being killed and the thief is still in your midst, how can you simply think about getting on with your daily life—and not of how to get rid of the thief? It is absurd. Alas! If indeed we *could* save our family by uniting with others, we might seriously consider that possibility. But now that is out of the question. In this context, cooperation has nothing to do with saving my family, and you would simply be a fool to discuss your affairs with vicious thieves.

Having said this, if the Koreans, at a time of ruthless struggle among states, were to become confused by Easternism, forgetting about nationalism, then they would only be uselessly worrying about competing with foreigners. And if the Koreans, without giving any thought to getting themselves out of this miserable situation, still insisted on the need for Easternism, they would be like the Poles talking about Westernism.

The nation is the master, and the East is nothing more than a geographical expression. But observing the advocates of Easternism, they regard the East as the master and relegate the state to the status of a mere concept. They leave the destiny of the state to the whims of fortune, and want rather to preserve Asia. How foolish they are! Would it then be acceptable if Korea and the Korean nation (*minjok*) were to perish utterly, and only the yellow race be preserved? It is absurd!

Some people say that the advocates of Easternism are not enamored of the East, they are merely seeking to take advantage of Easternism to save the nation. But I am now telling you: "No Korean can save the nation by resorting to Easternism. But there are foreigners who are trying to rob us of our patriotism by exploiting Easternism. So we must be vigilant!"

Chapter Nineteen

Abdürreşid İbrahim:
"The World of Islam and the
Spread of Islam in Japan," 1910

Selçuk Esenbel

Although there were many pro-Japanese Muslim figures known for their sympathy to Japanese pan-Asianist ideals between the Russo-Japanese War of 1904–1905 and World War II, the life and works of Abdürreşid İbrahim (1853–1944) most fully represent the multifaceted character of the rapprochement between Japanese Pan-Asianism and the Muslim pan-Islamist and nationalist currents evident during those years. A member of the Tatar community, a major Turkic group within Russia, Abdürreşid İbrahim began his working life as a journalist and gained fame as a political activist against tsarist rule. Ibrahim's publications were popular in the Turkish-speaking world of Russia and Ottoman Turkey and offered Japan as an alternative to a hegemonic European/Western modernity, influencing the emergence of public admiration for the harmonizing of Japanese spiritual values with the astute adaptation of Western knowledge to modernize the Japanese state.

The famous Turkish poet and novelist Mehmet Akif (Ersoy) (1873–1936), who wrote the lyrics of the national anthem of the Republic of Turkey, was a good friend of Ibrahim and shared his views on Islamic modernism. In Akif's epic poem *Safahat* (Passages), Ibrahim is presented as delivering a sermon from the pulpit of the Suleymaniye Mosque in Istanbul about the problems facing the world. After criticizing Russian despotism, the ignorance of Chinese Muslims, the superficiality of the extreme westernizers among Tatar intellectuals, and wealthy elites, in the poem Ibrahim extols the virtues of the Japanese nation as the closest to the ideals of Islam. "Ask what kind of nation are the Japanese. They are so amazing that words fail me. I can only say so much: the religion of the faithful [Islam] is there. Its spiritual generosity has spread, only its shape is the Buddha. You should go forth and see the purity of Islam in the Japanese! Today, those short children of a great nation are equally exceptional in upholding the principles of Islam—they only lack the ability to declare the faith" (Akif 2003: 154).

Ibrahim was born in Tara in the Tobolsk province of the Russian Empire. His family was of Bukharan origins and had the hereditary *akhond* status reserved for religious leaders in the Muslim communities of Central Asia and China. Ibrahim was educated as an *imam* (cleric) and was later to serve as a *kadi* (judge) in Orenburg, an important position in Russia's judicial bureaucracy established for Muslims in the eighteenth century.

Pursuing his education in Russia as well as in the religious seminaries of Mecca and Medina in the Ottoman Empire, Ibrahim spent his early years traveling back and forth between the Ottoman Empire and Russia, primarily to escape the attentions of the tsarist authorities. Ibrahim was a member of the reformist camp known among Russian Muslims as *cedidism* (the new reformists). These reformers advocated the creation of a modern civilization appropriate to Muslim sensibilities through the adoption of positive tenets of contemporary Western civilization and opposed the *kadimism* (traditionalism) of religious conservatives who were skeptical of westernization. His intellectual approach to reform in Islam was the foundation of his admiration for Japan's modernization as a suitable model for reforming the social and family traditions of the Muslim world (Kanlidere 1997: 33–52).

According to later U.S. intelligence reports, Ibrahim had formed a close friendship with Colonel Akashi Motojirō (1864–1919), the Japanese military attaché in Russia, as early as the eve of the Russo-Japanese War in 1904. After war broke out, Akashi moved to neutral Sweden, from where he masterminded Japanese intelligence activities in Europe (Akashi 1988). The Office of Strategic Services reports claim that Akashi supported Ibrahim's activities against the tsarist authorities financially (Office of Strategic Services, 1944: 15–16, 25–26, app. 63, 80; Akashi 1988). Although Akashi's own accounts of this period do not refer to Ibrahim, circumstantial evidence of his intimate connections with Japanese army officers, including members of the General Staff, suggests the validity of the claim.

Though there is no clear evidence, we can surmise that Ibrahim first visited Japan during his extensive travels in the period immediately following the Russo-Japanese War. It was at that time that he began his "fateful marriage" to Japan's pan-Asianist groups and started collaborating with like-minded civilian organizations and military authorities in Japan. The account of his mature life starts with his official visit to Japan between 17 November 1908 and 15 June 1909 under the auspices of the Kokuryūkai (see I:10), headed by Uchida Ryōhei (Esenbel 2004).

Ibrahim's visit to Japan inaugurated a lifelong career of cooperation with the leading pan-Asianist figures in Japanese politics and with several high-ranking military officers. While in Japan, he took part in the founding of the Ajia Gikai (Asian Congress), participated in meetings of the Tōa Dōbunkai (East Asian Common Culture Society) of Prince Konoe Atsumaro (see I:9 and I:6), and regularly met with officers from the army's General Staff. Ibrahim was joined by other Muslims with backgrounds similar to his own, such as Mouvli Barakatullah (1856–1927) and Ahmad Fadzli Beg (1874–?), both anti-British nationalist activists who had briefly found Tokyo to be a haven for Muslim political activism. During his return journey to Istanbul, Ibrahim spread his newly formed ideology of Japan as a friend of Muslims in China and the Dutch East Indies, networking on behalf of the Kokuryūkai. Ibrahim also accompanied Omar Yamaoka Kōtarō, a Kokuryūkai member whom he had met and converted to Islam in Bombay, in the first pilgrimage by a Japanese Muslim to the holy cities of Mecca and Medina.

Ibrahim's return journey in 1909 from Japan to Istanbul indicates a new momentum, demonstrating his new role as the global networker for Japan among Muslims in Asia—reflecting the recent interest of the Japanese authorities in exploiting the admiration for Japan among Muslims in the Near East following the Russo-Japanese War.

Ibrahim was no longer welcome in secular Turkey after the founding of the republic in 1923 because of the Kemalist revolution's staunchly secular and pro-Western policies. He was kept under house arrest in central Anatolia, where he was probably contacted by Japanese military attachés and other diplomats and invited to return to Japan. After his second and final arrival in Japan in 1933, Ibrahim's career took a new turn of collaboration at an advanced age. He began working with groups with pan-Asianist views within the Japanese army and Foreign Ministry to develop publicity and propaganda materials promoting Japan among Muslims in the Near East and Asia.

The marked pan-Asianist orientation of Japanese foreign policy following the 1931 invasion of Manchukuo and Japan's growing diplomatic isolation after its walkout at the League of Nations encouraged a renewal of Islamic studies and Islamic affairs in Japan. Beginning with the governments of the 1930s, several prime ministers can be identified as pan-Asianists. They include Inukai Tsuyoshi, a party politician known also as a pan-Asianist who was assassinated by militarist radicals; Kokuryūkai member Hirota Kōki; General Hayashi Senjūrō; Prince Konoe Fumimaro (see I:32 and II:17); and especially Baron Hiranuma Kiichirō (1867–1952; see II:21). Under such leadership, in the 1930s Japanese military and Foreign Ministry officials took active steps to develop a Japanese Islamic Policy, *kaikyō seisaku.* Ibrahim and other Muslim political figures and intellectuals were invited to Japan to form a Muslim collaborationist community in support of Japan's continental expansion. The 1930s also witnessed a large-scale dumping of cheap Japanese goods onto

Middle East markets, taking advantage of the international economic depression that had severely truncated traditional exports from Europe to countries such as Syria, Egypt, and Iraq under French and British mandate governments. The Japanese entry into the oil politics of the Middle East marked an important new phase of this rapprochement.

Ibrahim's second visit to Japan represented this engagement in Islamic policy by the Japanese government to meet the new demands of Japan's international relations. Ibrahim soon became the foreign head of the Dai Nippon Kaikyō Kyōkai (DNKK), the Greater Japan Islamic League, which was founded in 1938 with the support of the Foreign Ministry, the army, and the navy as the official arm of Japan for promoting Islamic studies and introducing Japanese culture to the Muslim world, the development of mutual trade ties, cultural exchanges, and policy research. The DNKK undertook propaganda work and worked hard to obtain the Diet's recognition of Islam, which it received in 1939—although somewhat ambiguously—as one of the country's officially authorized faith communities (on a par with Buddhism, Shinto, and Christianity), an arrangement deemed necessary for Japan's continental policy. Ibrahim was also appointed as the official *imam* of the Tokyo Mosque, which had been built with contributions from the local Tatar Muslim community and support from the Japanese authorities and opened in 1938. General Hayashi Senjūrō, who had supported the Japanese occupation of Manchuria in 1931, became the president of the DNKK, with Ibrahim as its Muslim head.

Ibrahim died in 1944 and was buried in the Muslim section of Tama Cemetery in the suburbs of Tokyo in an official ceremony attended by resident Muslims and Japanese dignitaries. He had spent his final years in Japan primarily working for the Japanese military authorities in public relations exercises aimed at Muslim countries and producing propaganda aimed at the Muslims of Southeast Asia. With the outbreak of World War II, the Tokyo Mosque became part a training ground for a new breed of young Japanese Muslim agents who served in the vanguard of the Japanese military invasion of the South Seas (Esenbel 2004: 1166).

An enigmatic figure who spent most of his life engaged in a constant political struggle for the freedom of the Turkic peoples in Russia and the emancipation of Muslims under colonial rule, Ibrahim made his mark for his advocacy of constitutional rule and the modernization of Islam. His interaction with both major and minor figures on the Japanese pan-Asianist scene effected the development of a Japanese-oriented pan-Islamist discourse that stimulated Japanese pan-Asianists to cooperate with Muslims and Islamic movements as a new revolutionary force. Yet, in the final analysis, his diaspora émigré status as a political intellectual with a mission to aid the cause of Muslim awakening and emancipation had compelled Ibrahim to become a collaborator with imperialist Japan.

In addition to the newspaper articles on Japan that he began publishing in Istanbul, Ibrahim's book *Alem-i Islam ve Japonya'da Intisari Islam* (The World of Islam and the Spread of Islam in Japan), published in 1910–1911 in Istanbul in Ottoman Turkish, reveals the full scale of his argument in favor of Japanese collaboration with Muslims and the mission to convert the Japanese to Islam. *Alem-i Islam* is Ibrahim's account of this journey to and from Japan; it recounts his experiences and exposes his views on the strengths of modern Japan, setting out the basic argument for Muslim rapprochement with the ideals of Pan-Asianism. The work, which is written in a straightforward, fluent narrative style, gives an engaging account of his activities in Japan, including interviews with such prominent figures as Count Ōkuma Shigenobu (a supporter of Muslims), Prince Itō Hirobumi (a neutral skeptic), Uchida Ryōhei and Tōyama Mitsuru and midlevel activists in the Kokuryūkai, sympathetic members of the Japanese aristocracy, and the renowned journalist Tokutomi Sohō (I:28).

Ibrahim's short essay on "The Future of the Japanese from the Perspective of Religion" (translated here) was written as the conclusion to the first volume of *Alem-i Islam*, marking the point at which he had left Japan and embarked on his long public relations journey through Asia. The selection offered here represents the main tenets of the argument, which subsequently became the core polemic employed by Japanese pan-Asianist publications of the 1930s in Japan and abroad to explain why Japan should befriend the suffering Muslims of the East and practice an Islam-based policy in the Muslim communities of China, Central Asia, Russia, and Southeast Asia. In this essay, Ibrahim sets out his classic argument on the need for Muslims to work toward converting the Japanese to Islam or at least having Islam recognized as a religion by the authorities in Japan. Ibrahim sought to convince the Japanese of the political and economic advantages of cooperating with Muslim causes and hopefully convert to Islam. This argument was based on the demographic reality of 300 million Muslims in the Middle East, China, Indonesia, and India who would become a natural market for Japanese goods and constitute an "Islamic international" that would support Japan's political aims against Chinese nationalism and the established European empires in Asia. His depiction of a fertile pan-Islamic hinterland for Japan was heavily grounded in the global concerns of the day—nationalism, anti-imperialism and anticolonialism, all challenges to modern Western civilization—which could be exploited to Japanese advantage.

Ibrahim's book was also the first publication to recount the circumstances of the inauguration ceremony for the Ajia Gikai (see also I:13) that entailed the gift of a land deed from the Tōa Dōbunkai for building a mosque in Tokyo and the signing of a joint Japanese–Muslim document pledging commitment to the pan-Asianist alliance with Islam and underlining the role of Ibrahim as a symbol of this purpose. The intellectual and political affiliations between these two circles linked by Ibrahim are revealed in later Japanese publications of the 1930s. The second version of the 1909 oath taking is found in a Japanese pan-Asianist publication of the 1930s. After Ibrahim's return to Japan in 1933, Wakabayashi Nakaba (Han), an Islam expert who supported the militarist policies of the late 1930s and was a close associate of Ibrahim, published a photograph of Ibrahim and the leadership of the Kokuryūkai with the handwritten scroll of the oath, similar to that in the original 1909 Ottoman Turkish book, in his popular work *Kaikyō Sekai to Nihon* (The World of Islam and Japan), published in 1938. Wakabayashi's book can be seen in the context of 1930s propaganda justifying a pro-Islamic policy in the service of Japan's pan-Asianist claims and arguing that the roots of such a policy go back to the 1910s—a claim that was not completely false, although the agendas of the Japanese and Muslim actors in this pact would shift considerably over time (Esenbel 2007).

A much more prominent intellectual figure in prewar Asianism, Ōkawa Shūmei (see II:4), in his major publication on the need for a pro-Islam Japanese policy (Ōkawa 1943), also based his arguments on the political, demographic, economic, and historical factors that made it logical for Japan to cooperate with Muslims in the making of modern Asia. Ōkawa's views were very similar to Ibrahim's original argument. Ōkawa saw the anti-imperialist currents in Asian Islam as a powerful force that could act as an Islamic international supportive of Japan's plans for the emancipation of Asia. The demographic argument (300 million Muslims), the ethnic argument (Eurasian and African Muslims of many nations as a lobby and market for Japan), and the economic argument for Japanese trade in Muslim markets are all repeated. However, there was one important point of difference. An advocate of Islamic studies in Japan during the 1930s, Ōkawa, who took lessons in classical Arabic from Ibrahim in order to read the Koran, saw this rapprochement as being in the interests of empire and as a strategy to gain ground in the Dutch East Indies in particular. By contrast, while Ibrahim had developed his original argument based on the political economy of Japan's interests in Asia, it was advanced for the sake of ultimately converting the Japanese to the "honor" of knowing Islam—a religious motive, which is understandably coming from one who styled himself as an Islamic missionary. Ibrahim's role as an advocate of a shared Islamic and Japanese pan-Asianist vision contributed to the development of a similar discourse among Japanese, who nevertheless shifted the weight of the argument for rapprochement to serve purely political visions of an Asian awakening that would serve the Japanese Empire (Ōkawa 1943: 1–13).

Source (translation from the original Ottoman Turkish by Selçuk Esenbel) Abdürreşid İbrahim, *Alem-I Islam ve Japonya'da Intisari Islamiyet* (The Future of the Japanese from the Perspective of Religion). Istanbul: Ahmed Saki Bey Matbaasi, 1328 (1910), vol. 1, 453–56.

THE FUTURE OF THE JAPANESE FROM
THE PERSPECTIVE OF RELIGION

This question is worthy of serious consideration, as today the missionaries of all the great powers are working with great enthusiasm. They assume that a hundred years from now the Japanese will be totally converted to Christianity. If only it could happen! Such a result is certainly being assumed. It has been 46 years since the missionaries first came to Japan. At the time, the Japanese were living in total ignorance. They had nothing to show in the name of science, education, or national strength. If a million people had converted as a result of the labors undertaken after spending millions of liras during such a time of disunity, we could have found their [i.e., the missionaries'] hopes justified. However, it is doubtful that the Japanese will become Christians from this point on. They cannot be compared to the Ethiopians.

For many reasons, I have come to the conclusion that the Japanese will receive the honor of knowing Islam.

First, the customs, morals and lifestyle of the Japanese are appropriate to beautiful Mohammedan morals, with no detectable differences between them; hence, if a Japanese person and a Siberian Muslim were travelling together, it would be impossible to tell which was Japanese and which was not. In particular, relations between husbands and wives are absolutely in step with Islamic teachings on proper behavior in this regard. A woman does not act in any way without her husband's permission. Furthermore, she asks her husband's permission to visit her father's home; a woman is fully in charge of the home and is obliged to obey her husband.

Second, the national morality of the Japanese is their only capital. In general, the Japanese are proud of their national morals and are willing to make sacrifices of all kinds in order to protect them. On the one hand, Christianity has started to corrupt their morals. Those who have accepted Christianity have mostly succumbed to bad morals. The Japanese have fully realized that as corruption spreads it will disturb the economic stability of nations. They will prepare themselves with every kind of sacrifice and with all their power to prevent this happening. The only way to avoid this outcome is the acceptance of Islam. Morality cannot be preserved unless one embraces religion, as has been proved through countless experiences. Buddhism cannot serve this purpose. Therefore, the most certain and expedient shortcut is the path of Islam. They will not hesitate at all from entering this path. It requires some degree of effort on our part to achieve this end because, today, there is no [easy] way of informing the Japanese of the truth of the religion of Islam. They do not know Arabic or Turkish, and there are no books in foreign languages that explain the truth of Islam in suitable terms.

On the one hand, European missionaries are spending great amounts of money and are not shy about publishing material in Japanese attacking the great religion of Islam—a situation which invariably creates an atmosphere of low self-confidence and invites doubt.

If our clerics (*ulema*) could try a little harder, and if the Japanese work with effort and patience, Islam will spread with great speed. I have always promoted this approach, which is irrefutable—there is no other way.

Apart from the above, there are a good number of political reasons for the Japanese to accept Islam. If the Japanese accept Islam, Muslims in China would undoubtedly be a ready market for Japanese products. Half of the population of Manchuria are Muslims. When the Japanese accept Islam, they will be able to occupy these areas without lifting a sword. In addition, the islands of the Indian Ocean will cooperate with the political aims of the Japanese, for 20 million Muslims are ruled by a small country like Holland. These Muslims are always ready to throw themselves into the bosom of the Japanese—the only way for them to be free of Dutch oppression is to seek asylum with Japan.

The future advancement of the Chinese is a very important issue for the Japanese as well, for if the Chinese manage to achieve significant progress the Japanese will face greater and greater difficulties. At the same time, the 100 million Muslims within China will be loyal friends to the Japanese and their ideological servants. Hence, from this perspective, the spread of Islam in Japan will provide a great political advantage to the Japanese.

There are many other aspects to be considered. There are about 30 million Muslims within Russia, which is a great enemy of the Japanese. And even if we do not take into consideration the India factor, the area covering the Malay Peninsula and Singapore which constitutes the southern part of Asia includes seven Muslim emirates that will be grateful for Japanese support.

Therefore, if we think in terms of all of these elements, if a guide can be assigned to the *ulema* who will be invited to Japan and if those who are sent there have some political talent, without doubt Islam will attain a very important position in Japan and all those who are in positions of responsibility will serve to spread this notion.

If such a political approach is not taken, religion will have no importance for the Japanese, because it is obvious after even a little consideration that it will never be possible to convince the Japanese on spiritual grounds alone.

Naturally, our scholars might well ask, "If the Japanese grant no importance to religion, why should we want to have them convert?" Such a question might indeed spring to mind. But those familiar with politics will have no hesitation in recognizing the importance of the spread of Islam in Japan. Yes, in the beginning their reputation alone will be sufficient—even if they acknowledge that "we have accepted Islam" only as a form of words. It will change the status of all Muslims with respect to the political environment of Europe.

I myself have greatly desired that the Japanese become familiar with Islam and, while I was in Japan, I gave a great deal of careful thought to the question and indeed saw some degree of success. If our Muslim *ulema* make some effort in this regard, undoubtedly the prospects will be very bright. Furthermore, even if in the beginning it will be connected with politics, I have the utmost confidence that, if we can show them the truth, the result will be a very firm and staunch Muslim identity in the future.

At the same time, today there are some very distinguished men who have been conferred with the honor of Islam, and there are always people who will convert with seriousness and sincerity. But the important point is to find a way for senior government officials to turn toward Islam. The real accomplishment is to have Islam accepted as an official religion. If one works with careful preparation, all these things can be realized.

Chapter Twenty

An Chung-gŭn: "A Discourse on Peace in East Asia," 1910

Eun-jeung Lee

An Chung-gŭn (also rendered Ahn Choong Kun or An Jung-geun, 1879–1910), who assassinated the Japanese elder statesman Prince Itō Hirobumi, resident-general in Korea from 1905 to 1909, in Harbin in 1909, was a young Korean intellectual and independence fighter. In 1907, he left Korea for Manchuria and the Russian Far East, where the Korean independence movement had its bases. Before he was executed in 1910 for his assassination of Itō, he had begun writing a book with the title *Tongyang pyŏnghwaron* (A Discourse on Peace in East Asia), which he did not complete. The manuscript, discovered in 1979, consists only of the preface and a few pages of the first chapter. However, in spite of its brevity, the manuscript shows a deep understanding of the international situation of his time and the complexity of the problems facing East Asia.

Tongyang pyŏnghwaron is based on An's belief that Japan has betrayed the idea of an East Asian community founded on peace and solidarity. He argues that the Koreans and the Chinese supported Japan in the war against Russia because the Japanese Emperor had explained in his declaration of war in 1904 that Japan was going to war to preserve peace in East Asia and to protect Korean independence. Furthermore, for An, this was a war between the "white race" and the "yellow race," which necessitated China and Korea to form a united front with Japan and explained why both Chinese and Koreans, at first, rejoiced in the latter's victory. Indeed, as An saw it, Japan would not have been able to win the war without support from China and Japan. After the war, however, Japan broke its promises and made cooperation in East Asia impossible. This situation, An argued, proved dangerous for East Asia because it was in need of greater regional solidarity in order to protect itself against Western expansion. Japan's failure to acknowledge this necessity and its continuing attacks on countries of the same race, he insisted, would, at some point in the future, inevitably result in a catastrophe both for itself and for Asia as a whole. In An's thinking, Itō Hirobumi, the Japanese resident-general in Korea after 1905 and thus the all-important symbol of Japanese colonial rule in Korea—and Japan's betrayal of Asia and the idea of Asian unity—had to be assassinated in order to protect East Asia from such a catastrophe. Without him, An hoped, East Asia would be able to build a peaceful community built on true equality.

Reading An's text, it becomes clear how strongly the editorial line of nationalist newspapers like *Tongnip Sinmun* (The Independent; see I:15), *Hwansŏng Sinmun* (Imperial Capital News), and *Cheguk Sinmun* (Imperial Post) had influenced him. He himself admitted that these newspapers had shaped his political thinking. Before the Russo-Japanese War (1904–1905), the idea of Asia as a political community was quite commonly expressed in the political columns of these nationalist Korean newspapers (see I:15). Their editorials focused on the need to "civilize" Korean society and presented Japan as a model. Koreans, too, these editorials argued, should be proud of Japanese accomplishments since the Meiji Restoration of 1868 because the Japanese had shown the world that East Asians were able to successfully "civilize" themselves. The Koreans, Japanese, and Chinese were one "race" and thus should form a political community to resist invasion by the Western powers. In these editorials, East and West were presented as a dichotomy that had its origin in the differences of race, reflecting contemporary notions of the classification of mankind into races. The editorials argued from a social Darwinist position that East Asia must win an ongoing "struggle of the races" without questioning the idea of racial classification, on which this social Darwinist view was based. From this perspective, Korean newspapers urged solidarity among the three East Asian countries and demanded that Japan show real leadership. "The heavens planned to revive East Asia's good fortune by enlightening Japan and making it [East Asia's] leader. However, if Japan, out of selfishness, scorns China and Korea and fails to share its technology and expertise, it will be difficult to avert disaster in this region. Japan must give deep thought to this." (*Hwangsŏng Sinmun*, 12 April 1899: 1).

Such statements could be misunderstood as the acceptance in Korea of Japanese "Asianism," but actually the Korean elite's way of thinking was still based on their traditional worldview. Even though they had absorbed the tenets of social Darwinism and acknowledged that Japan and not China was now the most civilized country in East Asia, they tended to believe that a "more civilized" country should help a "less civilized" one when the latter was ready to learn. This belief was based on the traditional East Asian worldview, which divided the world into the cultivated *hua* and the uncultivated barbarians, or *yi*. However, the words "cultivated" and "civilized" diverged from their traditional sense. "Cultivation" was linked to moral and spiritual issues, while "civilization," above all, was identified with institutional and material matters.

When the members of the Korean elite realized that Japan's regional leadership did not mean support for China and Korea—countries still undergoing the "civilizing process"—but instead involved the exercise of its own power and the protection of its own interests, they were shocked. They had accepted in good faith the Japanese assertion that the Sino-Japanese War (1894–1895) had been fought to make Korea an independent sovereign state. As late as 1899 (and even later), they believed that the three countries of East Asia were a "one-family house." As such, they ought to unite together against the West in order to maintain peace in their joint region. Therefore, when the Russo-Japanese War broke out in 1904, it would have been logical for these Korean intellectuals to back Japan as an Asian (or Eastern) power in its struggle with Russia, a Western power. Although some still believed that Japan fought the war against Russia for the sake of Asia, the establishment of a Japanese protectorate over Korea in 1905 dispelled any such hopes. Thus, Korea's reaction to the outcome of the Russo-Japanese War differed sharply from that of other non-European countries. While many in India and even as far afield as Egypt celebrated the defeat of a European power by a non-European nation, Koreans were disappointed and disillusioned with Japan and eventually turned against it.

Nevertheless, the colonization of Korea by Japan could not be prevented. As a result, the idea of Asia as a political community lost its appeal in Korea, and Japanese Pan-Asianism was rejected. When An murdered Itō Hirobumi in 1909, his act was also an expression of the disappointment and anger that the Korean people felt toward Japan. In *A Discourse on Peace in East Asia*, An had intended to formulate a new perspective on East Asia, including some astonishing and farsighted proposals, such as the establishment of a joint Sino–Korean–Japanese bank and a common East Asian currency as well as a joint military force—ideas that, much later, were to lie at the heart of (Western) European integration. Although An failed to finish his work, *A Discourse on Peace in East Asia* offers important insights into the thinking of Korean intellectuals at the beginning of Japanese colonial rule in the early twentieth century.

Source (translation from the Korean original by Eun-jeung Lee)
An Chung-gŭn (1910), "Tongyang Pyŏnghwaron" (A Discourse on Peace in East Asia). Reprinted in Ch'oe Wŏn-sik and Paek Yŏng-sŏ (eds.), *Tongasia, Munje-wa Sikak* (East Asia, Problems and Points of View). Munhak-kwa Chisŏngsa, 1997, 205–15.

It is a clear-cut principle that [a nation] will be successful if it is united, while it will fail if it is in conflict with itself. Today the world is divided into East and West, with different races engaged in a daily contest. They put greater emphasis on the improvement of modern technology and machinery than on the development of agriculture and commerce. Thus, new electric weapons, flying machines, submarines and so on are invented continuously. These are all things which hurt human beings and destroy useful things.

Young men receive military training and are sent off to war. Many have sacrificed their precious lives. There is no end in sight of the streams of blood and the soil covered with their corpses. What horrible pictures are these? All men and women love life, but not death.

From ancient times the peoples of the East have devoted themselves to literature and, if necessary, rallied to the defence of their countries. They have never attacked any part of Europe. . . .

For several centuries now, many countries in Europe have forgotten virtue entirely, acting only by means of violence and fostering rivalries against one another. They have no feeling of shame. Among them, Russia is the worst.

Russia's violence and brutality can be seen in the West as well as in East Asia. Its evil and guilty ways stink to high heaven and have made God and mankind furious. That is why heaven has allowed Japan, a small island state in the Eastern Sea, to inflict a resounding defeat on Russia on Manchurian soil. Who could have dreamt of something like this ever happening? . . .

If [during the Russo-Japanese War] the people of Korea and China, in an act of vengeance, had spurned Japan and supported Russia, such a great victory [as Japan's] would not have been possible. . . . The peoples of China and Korea . . . supported the Japanese Army wholeheartedly and provided it freely with information on geography, transport and so on. Why? There are two reasons for it.

When the war between Japan and Russia broke out, in the declaration of war the Japanese Emperor stated that its purpose was "to preserve peace in the East and to secure the independence of Korea." This was as clear as daylight. Therefore the inhabitants of China and Korea, both wise and ignorant, believed these words. This is the first reason. At the same time, the conflict between Japan and Russia could be seen as a contest between the yellow and the white races. As a result, any enmity [toward Japan] evaporated overnight. [The Chinese and Koreans] together [with the Japanese] are one large race, a mass of people who love one another. This corresponds to a universal human principle. It is the second reason . . . that this representative of the white race, which has done so much harm over the centuries, was defeated in a single war. It was a rare event in this world and well worth celebrating. The reason why the intellectual elites of China and Korea did not hesitate to celebrate with Japan was that they interpreted Japan's emergence on the world stage as one of the most significant moments in world history.

After this surprising victory, Japan subjugated Korea, its closest neighbour inhabited by a weak and docile race, imposing an [unequal] treaty upon it and occupying it. Thus the peoples of the world became distrustful of Japan and its declaration of war and famous victory lost all their lustre overnight. Japan is now considered to be even more brutal than Russia. . . .

If Japan fails to change its political strategy and if oppression continues to increase daily, then the Chinese and Koreans will no longer endure the humiliations inflicted upon them by the people of the same race, but will prefer defeat at the hands of another race. The consequences are clear. The oppressed inhabitants of China and Korea will jointly and voluntarily collaborate with the white people.

If things go that far, why should the sincere and the upright, and the angry and oppressed among the hundreds of millions of people of the yellow race in the East just sit idle and wait for a tragedy to happen—for the whole East to be burned to cinders? How could this be right? This is why I fired the first shot in Harbin in the righteous struggle for peace in the East [by assassinating Itō Hirobumi]. This is the reason I am on trial in Dalian [Dairen]. What I have written here is my point of view on peace in the East. I hope that you will come to see the seriousness of the situation with your own eyes.

February 1910

PROPOSALS

1. Japan must turn Port Arthur (Lushun) into a military port, to be administered jointly by the three nations (China, Korea and Japan). The three countries will send representatives and organize an Oriental Peace Conference. Funds are to be collected by the conference members and added to the respective government budgets. As a result, several hundred million people in these three countries will join together in a common cause.

2. To create sound financial foundations, the three countries involved need to establish a joint bank and issue a common currency.

3. The three countries must organize a joint military force and educate them [the officers of this corps] in at least two languages. This will nurture friendship towards the neighboring states and strengthen brotherly feelings.

4. Korea and China must further trade and industrial development under Japanese guidance.

Chapter Twenty-One

Benoy Kumar Sarkar:
The Asia of the Folk, 1916

Brij Tankha

Benoy Kumar Sarkar (1887–1949), a pioneer of sociology in India, was born in 1887 in Malda, Bengal. A precocious and brilliant student, he entered Calcutta University at the age of thirteen, graduating in 1905 with a double degree in English and history. He received his MA the following year. A nationalist committed to social service, he was active in the self-rule movement as well as the National Education movement in Bengal. Between 1914 and 1925, he traveled extensively, supporting himself by teaching, lecturing, and writing. He acquired fluency in several European languages, writing in Italian and German, and knew Bengali, Sanskrit, Hindi, and English as well.

Sarkar had an astonishingly wide range of interests. He wrote important books on economics, sociology, and religion and, in addition, founded several organizations, such as the Bengali Institute of Sociology, the Bengali Asia Academy, the Bengali Dante Society, and the Bengali Institute of American Culture. In 1925 Sarkar became a lecturer in the Department of Economics at the University of Calcutta, where he continued to teach until the end of his life. In 1947 he was promoted to full professor and head of department. He died on a trip to the United States in Washington, D.C., in November 1949.

Sarkar outlined his pan-Asian ideas in a Bengali-language book titled *Varttaman Jagat* (The World Today, 1914–1925), based on his extensive travels in Europe, the United States, Hawaii, Japan, Korea, Manchuria, and China. He developed these ideas further in *The Futurism of Young Asia* (Sarkar 1922), where he argued that "Young Asia," as he called it, was born in 1905 after the defeat of Russia by Japan. It was only the political climate that came into being after World War I, when the right of nations to self-determination was proclaimed, as well as the diplomatic restructuring that followed in Europe that had allowed the new Asia to grow. In this book, Sarkar was critical of the dogma of a "superior race" and the idea of the "white man's

211

burden" and argued that it was foreign control that had a debilitating effect on nations and prevented progress. Sarkar took the example of China to show that, as a result of internal dissension and military weakness, China was de facto controlled by foreigners. On this basis, he argued that the first premise for establishing peace in Asia was the expulsion of the West, and, for this purpose, military strength was of great importance. Sarkar, like Aurobindo Ghose (see I:17), čame to adulthood during the tumultuous years of the Bengal partition in 1905, but his ideas took a different turn—he rejected the Europe–Asia dichotomy, as well as the notion of racial differences, to stress rather the importance of the medieval–modern dichotomy. The West was not an equal and homogeneous space, he argued, nor did the East lack its own secular, life-affirming traditions. He emphasized that Euro-America had been equally as "primitive" or "unscientific" until the end of the eighteenth century and pointed out that modern ideas were new and equally revolutionary for Europeans as well as Asians. Sarkar advanced what today would be called a critique of Western Orientalism, asserting that it was based on double standards and prejudice. He argued that the spread of industrial civilization would bring about an economic convergence, with the result that all countries would ultimately develop and achieve parity (see the source reproduced here).

"Young Asia," Sarkar argued, was born of the contact with the modern West and the idea of progress; industrialization and antipathy to foreign domination, intervention, and coercion were helping to shape it. These new ideas of the East drew their inspiration from earlier achievements in culture, economics, and politics, but they were also a product of modern scholarship and Western education. This process had begun in Asia around 1850. However, while modernization had gotten under way around the same time in the various Asian countries, the rates of growth were different, with Japan following close to Euro-America but with India lagging behind. One major point of these extensive comparisons was to underline his belief that all societies followed the same path to development—so that sociological research and policymaking should focus on how to hasten this process.

In seeking an Asian unity, Sarkar argued against basing it on cultural practices or trade links. In his *Chinese Religion through Hindu Eyes*, he argued that to see China and Japan as Buddhist, while Buddhism in India was dead, was historically wrong. First, religion in India had changed between the fourth and sixth centuries when Chinese pilgrims came to India and took back Buddhist teachings, and, second, Buddhism and Hinduism could not be viewed as essentially different. His study of folk religion in the three countries showed that the local gods—*Avalokiteswara* or *jizō*—worshipped in China and Japan were the same as those in India, especially as to their functions. He argued that the creative energies of the people had transformed religion into a secular activity for the realization of happiness on earth. The conclusion he drew was that the rituals shared by Buddhism and Hinduism point to the importance of polytheism in Asian psychology. Polytheism, for Sarkar, was far more rational than Western monotheism, and he argued in support of republicanism in politics and polytheism in religion.

Sarkar's book was reviewed by the English-language *Journal of the Indo-Japanese Association*, published in Tokyo, in 1917:

> Our countryman Mr. Okakura wrote The Ideals of the East, which began with the sentence, "Asia is one." But according to him the unity of Asia consisted in the religion, literature, art, and philosophy of Buddhism. We have now received a copy of "Chinese Religion Through Hindu Eyes" by Professor Sarkar of Calcutta. The book is a "study in the tendencies of Asiatic Mentality." The author says that "even without Buddhism Asia would be one." "The unity rests on a common psychology supplying a fundamental basis. It is this psychological groundwork that makes Asiatic Unity a philosophical necessity in spite of ethnological and linguistic diversities."

Sarkar concluded that there were shared commonalities in Asian cultures that had to be understood through a comparison of religious practice. He thus saw the process as dynamic, with a complex flow of cross influences rather than as a one-way process of transmission of a set of fixed ideas. The cultural unity of Asia was based on a dynamic and people-centered unity— not on idealized conceptions of grand traditions. However, with the spread of an industrial civilization, these practices were in a process of change and ferment. The changes so initiated were creating not only regional but also global links and transforming ways of thinking. He saw that Asia was being united in new ways even as the old isolation was breaking down. Thus, even in matters of religion, there was an exchange of ideas: people were becoming familiar with hitherto unknown or foreign religious practices (see the source reproduced here).

These developments led Sarkar to conclude that Asian unity was not based on relative and changing elements but rather was to be found at a more fundamental psychological level. His analysis of folk religions showed that polytheism was a binding concept that linked the whole Asian region.

Source (English in the original)
Sarkar, Benoy (1916), *Chinese Religion through Hindu Eyes. A Study in the Tendencies of Asiatic Mentality* (originally published in Shanghai in 1916, reprinted by Oriental Publishers & Distributors, Delhi, 1975), 245–80.

Neither historically nor philosophically does the Asiatic mentality differ from the Euro-American. It is only after the brilliant successes of a fraction of mankind subsequent to the Industrial Revolution of the last century that the alleged difference between the two mentalities has been first stated and since then grossly exaggerated. . . .

The Gods and Goddesses of the Purana and Tantras are the joint products of all these factors; so, too, are the Gods and Goddesses of Buddhist China and Buddhist Japan. The present day deities of the Hindus owe their parentage to the Mahayanic cult of medieval Hinduism and are historically descended from the Gods of "Northern Buddhism" in the same way as the pantheons of modern Japan and China continue the tradition of the "Hinduism of the Buddha-cult."

Thus both philosophically and historically, Neo-Hinduism and Sino-Japanese Buddhism are essentially the same. The Vaishnavas, Shaivas and Shaktas of India should know the Chinese and Japanese Buddhists as co-religionists. Similarly the Sino-Japanese Buddhists should recognise the neo-Hindus of India as Buddhists. . . .

When Japan entered upon the scene the Indo-Chinese world was expanded by the addition of a third member. The triple alliance of culture thus affected was the *San-Goku* [Japanese for "three countries"]. Every Japanese thought in terms of the three regions, not of his native land alone. It was not enough, according to their conception, for any person to attain the highest position only in Japan. The most ambitious among them must have his worth recognised by China and India too. An international or Asiatic standard of science or *Vidyas* governed the aspiration of all Japan. *San-Goku* is thus a suggestive technical term contributed by the Japanese to the literature of world international science.

It has to be observed that, culturally speaking, the heart of this Concert of Asia was Hindustan, *Tienchu* or *Tenjiku i.e.* Heaven; but geographically, the heart was China. This "middle kingdom" may or may not be in the middle of the whole world as the Chinese believed it to be; but it was surely the centre of *San-Goku*. . . .

THE THREE-FOLD BASIS OF ASIATIC UNITY

Asiatic unity is, therefore, one. This unity rests on a common psychology supplying a fundamental basis. That foundation of Asiatic consciousness may be said to consist in three conceptions:

First is the conception of the *Tao* [Dao], the *To*, the *Michi*. The Chinese, the Japanese and the Hindus consciously as well as unconsciously govern their life-relations according to a postulate. They have a living faith that there is an Eternal order, a *sanatana* way, regulating the course of the diverse members of the Universe (including Nature and Man). The Cult of World-Forces is the common bed-rock of Asiatic spiritual institutions manifesting itself in and through a rich diversity.

Second is the conception of Pluralism. The Chinese, the Japanese and the Hindus are essentially pluralists in religious beliefs. Their pluralism is a corollary to their cult of the World-Forces or Nature Powers. These eight hundred million people are fundamentally polytheists. . . .

One of the great superstitions of the modern age has been the glorification of so-called monotheism.

Monotheism has been awarded by scholars the place of honour in the schedule of religious systems. It is supposed to be the ideally best system. Students of comparative mythology and comparative religion have, therefore, managed to detect in their favourite Indo-Aryan lore grand conceptions of monotheistic faith. Asiatic scholars also in their anxiety to be abreast of the modern spirit have fallen an easy prey to this superstition. . . .

Nothing can be further from the truth. A preconceived theory or the imagination of closet-philosophers cannot give the lie to facts.

Not only in Asia, but all over the world, man has ever been a polytheist. Monotheism is a psychological absurdity. . . .

It is a fact that man is a pluralist in every worldly field. He is a pluralist in all his social relations—economic, political and even domestic. In governmental matters no man nowadays believes in one man rule. The economist has declared: "There is a limit to each want, but there is no limit to the *variety* of wants." . . .

The third basis of Asiatic mentality is the spirit of toleration or the "conception of peace and good-will to all mankind." Toleration follows as a matter of course from conceptions of Pluralism. . . . What Socialism is in the economic sphere, what republicanism is in the political world, that is Polytheism or the Cult of the many in matters spiritual or religious. Each has its motto, the individualistic doctrine of *laissez faire*, non-intervention, or creation of opportunities for all.

The synthesis between the one and the many, the spirit and the matter, the transcendental and the positive, the infinite and the finite, the universal and the particular, on the one hand; and the toleration and encouragement of diversities, angularities, discrepancies and inconsistencies, on the other, these are the outcome of this triple foundation of Asiatic consciousness. . . .

It is this psychological groundwork that makes Asiatic Unity a philosophical *necessity* in spite of ethnological and linguistic diversities. This unity is thus more fundamental than has been hitherto recognized by historians. The intercourse between the members of the *San-goku* established by Buddhistic missionizing or by commercial activity and diplomatic relations has only supplied additional connecting links. But the chief point to be noticed is that, Buddhism or no Buddhism, international relations or no international relations, the three nations of Asia have had a common mentality. That commonness is deeper than what can be supplied by actual comings and going—in fact, *absolute*, as contrasted with the *relative*, which is born of political or commercial contact. The *relative* unity may disappear through changes in the diplomatic grouping of Powers, as it has one so often in history, but the *absolute* psychological unity can perish never.

Chapter Twenty-Two

Li Dazhao: "Greater Asianism and New Asianism," 1919

Marc Andre Matten

Li Dazhao (Li Ta-Chao, 1889–1927) was born into a peasant family in Hubei (Hopei) province in China. Like many intellectuals of his generation, in his youth he went in 1913 to Japan, where he studied at the Faculty of Politics and Economics at Waseda University in Tokyo (Andō 1990; on Li's life, see Li 1994; Shimada 1990). During his stay in Japan, Li contributed various articles to *Jiayin zazahi* (The Tiger Magazine), founded by Zhang Shizhao (Chang Shih-chao, 1881–1973). When Yuan Shikai (Yüan Shih-k'ai, 1859–1916) promulgated a new constitution in 1914, Li criticized it harshly on the grounds that it concentrated the powers of government in Yuan's hands. His opposition grew after Yuan accepted the Twenty-One Demands issued by Japan in 1915. Li called on Chinese students throughout Japan to oppose these demands (see Meisner 1967).

After his return to Beijing in 1916, Li worked as the editor of the *Chenbao* (Morning Post) but in 1918 accepted the invitation of Cai Yuanpei (Ts'ai Yuan-p'ei, 1868–1940) to work as a librarian at Peking University. In 1920, he became professor of history, economics, and political science there. One of his students was Mao Zedong (1893–1976). His writings in the journal *Xin Qingnian* (New Youth, dubbing itself *La Jeunesse*, 1915–1925), which praised the Bolshevik Revolution in Russia as a victory for the common people, helped introduce Marxism to China. In 1926, Li participated in anti-imperialist student demonstrations in Beijing, for which he was arrested and executed in April 1927.

Together with Chen Duxiu (Ch'en Tu-hsiu, 1879–1942), one of the founders of the Communist Party of China in 1921, Li was one of the most important proponents of the May Fourth Movement in China (1915–1925). The movement originated in 1915 as a reaction against the Twenty-One Demands and reached its height in 1919 when, as a result of the Paris Peace Conference, the

German colonial possession on Shandong (Shantung) peninsula was not returned to China but transferred to Japan. The movement encouraged a reevaluation of Chinese traditional culture and created widespread nationalist consciousness among the Chinese population. It stressed Western ideas of science and democracy, which were deemed necessary for the progress of the nation.

In contrast to the strong nationalistic attitudes of many participants in the movement, Li's writings in 1919–1920 are characterized by his firm belief in internationalism—the result of his view of the Bolshevik Revolution as the beginning of a worldwide revolutionary transformation. He hoped for international solidarity and unity despite the fact that the prospects for a world revolution diminished after 1920.

Li was to a great extent inspired by Trotsky's 1915 book *The War and the International*, which argued that World War I signaled the downfall of the nation-state, that the proletariat was no longer interested in patriotism, and that its task was to create a republican United States of Europe as the foundation for a future United States of the World (cf. Li's essay "Bolshevism de shengli" [The Victory of Bolshevism], published in late 1918). If a United States of Europe could become a reality, Li wondered, why should it be impossible to form a United States of Asia? Li was here not simply arguing for a union of Asian states but also developing a vision of a socialist federation of Asian nations. In his article "Lianzhizhuyi yu shijie zuzhi" (Federalism and World Unity, published 1 February 1919 in *Xinchao*), he presented further arguments for a world federalist system, comprising three separate continental federations: one in Europe, one in America, and one in Asia. The removal of national boundaries, in his view, would create international harmony and made war impossible. Li's vision of Asianism was also shaped by Kodera Kenkichi's *Dai Ajiashugiron* (Greater Asianism, 1916, Chinese translation, 1918; see I:26) as well as by Wakamiya Unosuke (1879–1938)'s contribution in the Japanese journal *Chūō Kōron* (The Central Review), titled "Dai Ajia shugi to wa nan zo ya" (What Is Asianism?, April 1917).

Li's call for federation, however, did not imply an immediate dismissal of the notion of national self-determination. In the case of Asia, it was rather considered to be a necessary first step for the oppressed nations of the region (and not an end in itself). Further, the constant danger of imperialist aggression since the First Opium War (1839–1842) made it difficult for China to simply cast away the nation-state as a means and guarantee of liberation. The Japanese vision of ensuring liberty by forming an Asian community opposed to European imperialism was regarded critically by Chinese intellectuals after 1915. Calling for the creation of an Asian federation or union was thus a tricky issue, one that Li tried to solve by differentiating between New Asianism (*Xin Yaxiyazhuyi*) and Greater Asianism (*Da Yaxiyazhuyi*).

For Li, Greater Asianism was synonymous with the annexation of China and the realization of a Greater Japanism, which—though claiming to fend off the Americans and Europeans—achieved nothing more than subjugating China and the rest of Asia to Japan, a critique Li had already leveled in 1917 in his article "Da Yaxiyazhuyi" (Greater Asianism) published in *The Tiger Magazine* (this was a direct reply to Wakamiya Unosuke's article quoted previously).

In this respect, even an Asian version of the Monroe Doctrine did not promise a solution, a principle that already in 1903 had been critically assessed by Chinese nationalists in a journal called *Zhejiangchao* (The Tides of Zhejiang). They argued that America had used this doctrine for legitimizing its annexation of Hawaii, Cuba, and the Philippines by claiming that, in so doing, it would drive away European imperialists and help these countries regain their national self-determination. In fact, however, the Monroe Doctrine merely disguised America's own imperialist ambitions. As a consequence, Li rejected any pan-movement, which he considered aimed at nothing more than autocracy (see his article "Pan…ism zhi shibai yu democracy zhi shengli" [The Failure of Pan-isms and the Victory of Democracy], 15 July 1918, *Taipingyang*, 1: 10).

Li thus concluded that Japanese Asianism was not about returning Asia back into the hands of the Asian people but about turning Asia into the Asia of the Japanese. Greater Asianism was not a peaceful doctrine but an aggressive one; it was not a doctrine of national self-determination but an imperialist doctrine that would inevitably destroy the world. Instead of following Japanese thinkers such as Tokutomi Sohō (1863–1957) and Ukita Kazutami (1860–1946; Li's teacher at Waseda), who argued for an alliance between China and Japan while preserving the status quo, Li insisted that Asia should follow the doctrine of New Asianism and establish an Asian Union that had national liberation as its foundation and would later evolve into a World Union, the true source of happiness for mankind (cf. Andō 1990).

However, Li's vision of a new Asian order did not remain undisputed. In the same year, a certain Gao Chengyuan (also known as Gao Yuan) raised doubts about Li's analysis in an article published in the Beijing monthly *Fazheng Xuebao* (Journal of Law and Politics), questioning the necessity of first establishing continental alliances instead of enabling all nations to directly form a single alliance.

In late 1919, Li replied to this critique in an article titled "Zai lun Xin Yaxiyazhuyi" (Discussing the New Asianism Once Again) in *Guomin Zazhi* (Citizen Magazine), explaining in detail why the Asian peoples needed to unite in their fight against capitalism and imperialism. He asserted that he never excluded the possibility of establishing a World Alliance (although, he noted, such an alliance would be difficult to realize for practical reasons), and stated clearly that the most immediate threat to the freedom of the people of Asia came not from Westerners but from other Asians: "I advocate New Asianism in order to oppose Japanese Greater Asianism. . . . If within Asia the tyranny of Asians against Asians is not removed, there is no hope of ending the tyranny of those from other continents. . . . We only hope that all Asians will rise together to destroy Greater Asianism" (Meisner 1967: 187).

Li's differentiation between a Greater and New Asianism partly resembles Sun Yat-sen's later discussion of Kingly Way or rule through benevolence (Chinese: *wangdao*; Japanese: *ōdō*) and the Despotic Way, or rule through force (Chinese: *badao*; Japanese: *hadō*) (see also II:5). Considering that Sun and Li had been in contact with each other since 1919 and that Sun's writings on Asianism took on a more critical air precisely in April 1919 (see his article "Wu ren zhi da Yazhouzhuyi" [My Asianism]), it is almost certain that Li exerted some influence on Sun and thus left a lasting imprint on the development of Asianism in China (cf. Guan Wei 2003).

Source (translation from the Chinese original by Marc Andre Matten)
Da Yaxiyazhuyi yu xin Yaxiyazhuyi (Greater Asianism and New Asianism), *Guomin Zazhi*, 1 February 1919, reprinted in *Chenbao* (6 March and 21 March 1919) and in People's Press (ed.), *Li Dazhao Wenji* (Collected Writings of Li Dazhao), vol. 1, no. 2 (1984), Beijing, 609–11.

"GREATER ASIANISM AND NEW ASIANISM"

Recently some people in Japan have proposed a Greater Asianism. But when we Asians hear such terms, we are very concerned. It is people like Takebe Tongo, Ōtani Kōzui, Tokutomi Sohō and Kodera Kenkichi [see I:26 and I:28] who advocate such an ideology. We have to understand their proposals clearly before we can judge and criticize them.

First, one should know that the term "Greater Asianism" conceals the doctrine of China's annexation. The fate of China fully depends on the balance of power among the strong nations—only then it can continue to exist. There is no need to hide this fact. If Japan wants to conquer China by itself, then it must first drive away the other forces that constitute this balance. The Japanese have been pondering the question for a long time and finally come up with this phrase. On the surface, it seems to be no more than a familiar term for people who share the same language and race, but in reality it implies their intention to devour and swallow [China] all on their own.

Second, one should be aware that "Greater Asianism" is just another name for Greater Japanism (*Da Ribenzhuyi*). The Japanese want to use the language of the Asian Monroe Doctrine in order to fend off the Americans and Europeans and prevent them from spreading their influence in the Orient. All the Asian nations listen to orders from Japan; the problems of Asia are all being solved by the Japanese; Japan is the leading power in Asia, and Asia has become a stage for the Japanese. So Asia is not the Asia of the Europeans or Americans, and neither is it the Asia of the Asians—it is simply the Asia of the Japanese. From this perspective, "Greater Asianism" is not a peaceful doctrine, but an aggressive one; it is not a doctrine of national self-determination, but an imperialist doctrine that devours small and weak countries. It implies not Asian democracy, but Japanese militarism; it is not an order that promotes world order, rather it is the seed that destroys it.

It is because we consider we are of the same race and use the same language that we must say a few words to persuade the enlightened men of our neighboring countries. The fact that the last war in Europe shook the whole world and that large numbers of people were killed over many years, was this not the result of this "Greater-ism"? If one person propagates Greater Slavism, another propagates Greater Germanism; if one propagates Greater Asianism, another will propagate Greater Europeanism. Human greed is enormous and no nationality is as good as your own. . . . If we promote such an ideology, the outcome will be intolerable. The result will inevitably be one war after another, all fighting for the right to use the word "great." In the end this "Greater-ism" will die out—either as a result of the defeat of two great powers in conflict, or the mutual help offered by minor powers. In this context, Germany provides an excellent lesson. . . .

If one considers this ism to be a reaction to prejudice against yellow people shown by the Europeans and Americans, why should we not have another look at the outcome of the recent Peace Conference [in Paris]? If the Europeans and the Americans prove unreasonable and want to sacrifice our oriental nations, then it is not too late for us to reunify and resist them. If there is still no real solution to the issue of excluding Asians and if equal treatment is to be withheld, then this is really a common problem for the Asian people and must be solved by uniting the power of our Asian people. To fight for such a general principle, we will balk at nothing, even if it means war. If you fail to take this into account, blindly proposing a "Greater Asianism" is actually a very dangerous thing. It would present a danger not only to Japan, but would also harm every nation in Asia and endanger world peace. The responsibility for preventing such a danger falls not just on the East Asian nations (with the exception of Japan), but is an issue for all mankind. . . .

Looking at the world situation, the Americas will surely become an American Union, Europe will become a European Union and we Asians should also form such an organization, which will all be the foundation of a World Union. The Asian peoples should together advocate a New Asianism that will supersede the "Greater Asianism" advocated by some Japanese. This New Asianism would differ also from that advocated by Ukita Kazutami. He proposed a federation between China and Japan as its foundation while preserving the existing state forms. We, however, insist on national liberation (*minzu jiefang*) as the foundation and [call for] a radical transformation. Every Asian nation that has been annexed by another power must be liberated; it should carry out national self-determination, and then form a great federation, which will be established together with a European and American federations. Together they shall achieve a world federation that will promote the happiness of mankind.

Chapter Twenty-Three

Kurban Ali and the
Tatar Community in Japan, 1922

Selçuk Esenbel

Muhammed Gabdulhay Kurbangaliyef (1889–1972), or Kurban Ali for short, was born in the Russian city of Chelyabinsk in Orenburg province, the homeland of the Turkish Bashkir people. Kurban Ali was descended from a wealthy family of landowners and merchants who from the eighteenth century were prominent as *molla* or *imam*, Muslim leaders of their community. When his father was exiled after the tsarist government withdrew his appointment in 1912, Kurban Ali succeeded him as *imam*. The family took part in the civil war that ensued after the Bolshevik Revolution of November 1917. As local landlords, both father and son represented the conservative monarchist view hostile to communism. Elected as the *kadi* (Muslim judge) of his region in the early stages of the revolution, Kurban Ali formed a militia and soon joined forces with the antirevolutionary "White" Russians. However, as the Bolsheviks proved victorious, he was soon forced to escape to Manchuria, where from late 1917 he collaborated with the anti-Bolshevik forces of Admiral Kolchak and Ataman Semenov, a Cossack commander supported by the Japanese military.

In November 1920, Kurban Ali sought asylum in Tokyo, together with some other Bashkir militia members. After 1924 he settled in Tokyo permanently and began organizing Tatar Muslim refugees from Russia into Nihon Kaikyōto (Japan Muslim Community), an association of Muslims in Japan. Already introduced to important political figures in the pan-Asianist network during his first visit to Japan in 1920, Kurban Ali joined other Asian exiles fighting the colonial regimes in Asia from their base in Japan. Like India's Rash Behari Bose and Mouvli Barakatullah, Kurban Ali enjoyed the protection of the Kokuryūkai (see I:10). Through contacts to influential people like Shimano Saburō (1892–1982) from the South Manchurian Railways (SMR), Tōyama Mitsuru (see I:3), and Sugiyama Shigemaru (1864–1935), he got to know important political figures, such as Inukai Tsuyoshi (1855–1932),

Hirota Kōki (1878–1948) and Baron Hiranuma Kiichirō (see II:21), as well as pan-Asian activists, such as Kita Ikki (see I:27) and Mitsukawa Kametarō (1888–1936). Kurban Ali also got to know General Tanaka Giichi (1864–1929) and Matsuoka Yōsuke, the vice president of SMR. He apparently persuaded Matsuoka to pursue an active Islam policy (*kaikyō seisaku*) as part of his shift toward an Asianist foreign policy. Matsuoka was moving away from the Western orientation of previous Japanese governments whose dominant foreign policy stance had been conciliatory diplomacy within the framework of the Western treaty system in Asia (Shimano 1984: 450–60).

Funded by secret funds from the Ministry of Foreign Affairs, Kurban Ali propagated a combination of Pan-Asianism and Islam that he claimed was based on the common ethnoracial roots of the Japanese and the Ural Altaic peoples of Russia (e.g., in Kurbangaliev 1924). This was the so-called Altaic Brothers argument for realizing an Asian awakening under Japanese leadership, an initiative that would enable the Japanese to make an entry into the Islamic world via a strong alliance with Russia's Turkic minorities who were suffering under communist oppression (Esenbel 2002: 180–214; Nishihara 1980: 23). But more important than his writings was Kurban Ali's role as a practical community organizer. Men such as Abdürreşid İbrahim (see I:19), the leader of the pan-Muslim movement in Russia in the last decades of Romanov rule; Ayaz Ishaki, the talented nationalist writer; and Carullah, the most brilliant theologian of his generation, were all Russian Muslim intellectuals of Tatar origin who had already become major figures of the Tatar Muslim diaspora; all eventually ended up in Japan in the 1930s when the Japanese government adopted an active foreign policy toward Islam, and all were more prominent as intellectuals than Ali. Nevertheless, next to İbrahim, who had already formed contacts in Japan in the aftermath of Japan's 1905 victory in the Russo-Japanese War, Kurban Ali must be regarded as the second most important Central Asian figure who cooperated with Japanese pan-Asianist political and military groups in the period between the Russian Revolution and the end of World War II. He was particularly successful in setting up institutions that would ensure the survival of the Tatar community in Japan, which numbered 1,000 people in the early 1920s. In addition, almost 10,000 Tatar Muslims sought asylum in the Japanese-controlled territories of northeastern China, together with some 100,000 White Russians. Kurban Ali founded a Muslim school in Tokyo in 1927, the Tokyo Mohammedan School (Tōkyō Kaikyō Gakkō or Mekteb-I Islamiye) for Tatar children, which subsequently acquired a high reputation for its curriculum combining modern learning with courses in the Islamic faith that provided moral education. He also set up the Matbaa-I Islamiye or the Tokyo Mohammedan Press (Tōkyō Kaikyō Insatsusho). The press published numerous books and pamphlets in

Turkish, the Turko-Tatar language, and Arabic as a kind of Japanese public relations exercise directed at the Tatar diaspora as well as Muslims in other parts of the world. Journals such as *Yani Yapon Muhbiri* (News from New Japan) and school textbooks also fulfilled the needs of the Tatar diaspora community in the Far East (Esenbel 2004: 1154–59, 1170).

Kurban Ali played a significant role in intelligence activities, especially in Manchuria. By the late 1930s, the Japanese army and navy had been training Japanese Muslim agents and developing Islamic studies so as to support Japanese military policies toward the Dutch East Indies. The new interest shown by big firms such as Mitsubishi and Idemitsu in economic involvement in the Middle East, an interest tied to oil imports to support Japan's accelerating industrialization and the massive increase in Japanese exports to markets in the Near and Middle East, reduced the primary role of the Tatars as conduits between Japan and the Islamic world. Nevertheless, Kurban Ali again showed his organizational skills in his successful campaign for the construction of the Tokyo Mosque. He obtained official and business support, with the Mitsubishi Bank alone donating 150,000 yen toward the project, and ensured the involvement of the Tatar and Muslim communities in the campaign.

In 1933, Kurban Ali was involved in an intrigue in which Japanese ultranationalists led by Lieutenant General Baron Kikuchi Takeo (1875–1955) and Vice Admiral Viscount Ogasawara Naganari (1867–1958) brought Prince Abdul Kerim, an exiled member of the deposed Ottoman dynasty, to Japan in an abortive attempt to have him enthroned as sultan of the Islamic Turkestan Republic. The republic was declared by Uighur Turkestani separatists during the 1931–1936 Uighur rebellion in Xinjiang (also Hsin-chiang or Sinkiang) against Chinese rule.

In 1938, Kurban Ali's career in Japan underwent a rapid decline as he fell out of favor with the Japanese authorities. He was partly responsible for this himself because of his hostility to other Tatar émigré figures like Ayaz Ishaki and İbrahim, whom he regarded as rivals to his leadership of the Muslim diaspora. He frequently denounced his rivals to the Japanese authorities and sometimes even resorted to strong-arm tactics—such as his attempt to murder Ayaz Ishaki and his supporters in an ambush in cahoots with Japanese ultranationalist gangs and "White" Russian toughs. On 12 May 1938, the Tokyo Mosque, which was to become the major symbol of Japan's new official policy of friendship toward the world of Islam, was opened at an internationally attended convocation ceremony that coincided with the commemoration of Muhammad's birthday. Instead of Kurban Ali, İbrahim had recently been appointed as the official *imam* of the mosque and thus officiated at the ceremony. Kurban Ali had been arrested a week before to prevent him from attending. On 13 May 1938 he was deported to Dairen, Manchuria. However, in recognition of his contribution to the Islamic cause, as much as to keep up appearances, the Greater Japan Islamic League (Dai Nippon Kaikyō Kyōkai) continued to pay Kurban Ali a regular salary—ostensibly to make his move to Dairen appear as his own decision.

For the rest of the war, Kurban Ali worked for the Japanese in Manchuria and Central Asia against the Soviets. After the Japanese defeat in 1945, the Soviets arrested him, and, although he played down his role in anti-Soviet activities, he was sentenced to a lengthy term of imprisonment in a Siberian camp. However, toward the end of his life he was allowed to return to his hometown of Chelyabinsk. Kurban Ali was never able to see his wife and children, who remained behind in Tokyo.

The following translation is the text of two letters—originally written in Russian, the language of the Tatar exiles in Japan—soon after Kurban Ali had sought asylum in Japanese Manchuria. The first letter was addressed to the Japanese Minister of Education, and a copy was submitted with a second, brief letter urging the Japanese Foreign Minister to act on its recommendations. Both letters were written on 12 September 1922 and illuminate Ali's argument for an Altaic–Japanese collaboration that, he thought, would contribute to the rise of Asia. The letter written to the Japanese Minister of Education sets out the major points of the "Altaic brothers' argument," which would become a main component of the rhetoric of the Turkish version of Pan-Asianism used, with variations, to represent Japanese relations with the Turks of Turkey and the Turkish minorities in Russia. Kurban Ali envisages "a new Asia" in the process of formation by means of a special alliance between Japan and the newly emerging Turkic peoples of Russia and Siberia, with the revolutionary new Turkey as a supporting factor. His arguments are ethnoracial in character, a significant element in Japanese Pan-Asianism's interest in Turkic affairs and Central Asian peoples. His primary argument is that the Turkish peoples, who include the Tatars, Bashkir, Kirgiz, Azeri, and Ottoman Turks, are staunch friends of Japan in the Islamic world and are willing to promote friendship between Japan and the world's 200 million Muslims. This argument privileged the Tatar diaspora in Japan as Japanese Muslims who were accepted by the Japanese Empire as a friendly people who would help execute Japan's Islam policy in northern Asia against Russia and China. The argument also had a strong ethnoracial tone in its assertion that the Japanese are linguistically an Altaic people, originally from North Asia—a thesis propounded also by well-known academics such as Shiratori Kurakichi (1865–1942; Tanaka 1993: 88–98).

In these letters, Kurban Ali also appealed to the Japanese authorities to establish Turkic-language instruction in Japanese government schools as a first pioneering step to seal the racial and cultural bonds of the Japanese and Altaic peoples. The letter to the Minister of Education specifically names the Tokyo School of Foreign Languages (the present Tokyo University of Foreign Languages), the main Japanese institution offering courses in Asian languages, as the home of the proposed new language program. Kurban Ali provides a detailed list of major Russian dictionaries, grammars, and works on Turkic languages that he recommends should be procured for this purpose.

Kurban Ali also influenced Japanese approaches toward Turkic and Islamic studies by his emphasis on the study of Turkish in the historical Arabic script that would, in his own words, "make it easy for Japanese scholars to get to grips with Arabic and Persian as well." Interestingly enough, in 1928, the Turkish Republic replaced Arabic script with the Latin alphabet as part of its westernization program, while in the Soviet Union, Tatar, the language of Kurban Ali and the diaspora community, also replaced Arabic script— initially with the Latin alphabet and then, under Stalin, with the Cyrillic alphabet. This meant that Japanese students of Turkic languages in Japan were learning the prerevolutionary writing systems, which were no longer used in their home countries. The use of Arabic script in the Turkish-language publications of the Tokyo Mohammedan Press also reveals the restorationist character of Japanese links with the diaspora of the Turkish world that was out of step with the contemporary political and cultural character of both the Republic of Turkey and the Soviet Union. In fact, by aiding the Japanese plot to enthrone Prince Abdul Kerim, Ali antagonized the Turkish embassy in Tokyo, which ostracized him. This also caused temporary frictions in relations between Japan and the Turkish Republic.

The Japanese translation of Ali's letter also strikingly reveals the Japanese orientation of Kurban Ali as the émigré diaspora experience compelled him (and many others like him) to shift their identities away from their homelands, test different arguments, and undergo numerous shifts of allegiance according to the political exigencies of the day. The Russian original of the letter uses the term *Turci* (Turkic) in phrases such as "Turkic peoples" and "Turkic languages" in all references to anything concerning Turks, Turkish, and so on, thus revealing a firm orientation to the Turkic peoples of Russia. However, the Japanese translator is confused in many places and uses the term *Tyurkoman*—meaning Turcoman, the Turkic nomads of Central Asia—for the Russian term *Turci* but then sometimes corrects it to *Toruko*, actually the Japanese word for Turkey, specifically the present-day Ottoman/Republican Turks but referring also to the archaic *Tuerchi*, or ancient Turks of the Inner Asian steppe—nomads of the T'ang dynasty.

While at the beginning of the letter, *Torukojin* in Japanese obviously refers only to the Turkic peoples of Russia, by the end of the letter the same term is used to denote a single Turkish people uniting Central Asia and Turkey— thereby replacing the Russian tradition of distinguishing the Turkic peoples of Russia from the Ottoman or Republican Turks with a strong pan-Turkist orientation. On the other hand, Kurban Ali signed both letters as the representative of the Bashkir people of the Far East—referring to his specific ethnic identity but also to his role as the representative of the Council of the Mohammedans of the Far East, presumably an organization that he had set up during his brief period of collaboration with the Kolchak–Semenov forces. In official Japanese government records, the Tatars are frequently referred to simply as Muslim Russian émigrés. But as émigrés, they are instructed to form an official community for themselves Nihon Kaikyōto or Kaikyōzoku (Japanese–Muslim congregation) to be founded some time later. During the war, however, the members of the Tatar diaspora received Turkish citizenship from the republic, which solved their stateless status in Japan.

In conclusion, Kurban Ali was much criticized both for his self-assumed and dictatorial leadership of the Tatar community in Japan and for his relative unfamiliarity with Islamic theology. His friendship with the White Russians, plus his conservative traditionalist outlook, clashed with the modernist and nationalist views of such intellectually engaged figures as Ayaz Ishaki, who accused him of being pro-Russian. Nevertheless, Kurban Ali acted in a manner befitting a traditional landlord and communal leader who took responsibility for the survival of his people. He played a notable role in convincing Japanese pan-Asianists in the 1920s and early 1930s of the advantages of adopting a policy of cooperation with the Altaic peoples.

Source (translation from the Japanese by Selçuk Esenbel)
Letter of Kurban Ali to the Minister of Education of Japan; Gaimushō Gaikō Shiryōkan (Foreign Ministry Historical Archive), Tōkyō, Gaimushō Kiroku (Diplomatic Records) MT. 1.1.2.1.2, 03676-03694 for the Japanese translation, 03695-03700 for the original Russian letter addressed to the Minister of Education of Japan and included as an appendix to a letter addressed to the Minister of Foreign Affairs of Japan. (The text here is based on the Japanese translation, with any significant departures from the Russian original indicated in square brackets. Comments by the translator are also included in square brackets.)

Irak Sark'da Musluman Milletleri Murahhas ve Mumesssileri Surasi
Connciel [Council] of Moslem Representatives in the Far East

Your Excellency,

We hope for the safety of the whole of Asia and submit the following letter to your Excellency requesting your kind guidance, considering that it is of the utmost importance to work toward the close friendship of the Turkish peoples and Japan in both the cultural and economic spheres in order to realize the equality of the races based on a humanitarian ethic of international justice. At the present time, the territories occupied by the Turkish [Turkic in Russian] peoples cover more than half of Asia and the most important parts of South-east Europe and North-east Africa, and in addition, beginning from the Arctic Ocean, they include the Yakutsk territory near the Juen-Lun Plains all the way to the Turcoman tribes of Persia. Furthermore, the area stretching from the Kolyma and the banks of the Yellow River to Central Russia is inhabited by the Kasymov Tatars and the Macedonian Ottomans. In addition, it is possible to encounter Turkish peoples [Turkic in Russian] throughout all Siberia. All of these peoples hope to protect their independent existence and, in order to promote the economies of their respective regions, they desire to establish sincere and friendly relations with the great family of Ural-Altaic peoples as well as the powerful Asian peoples, of which only Japan has the capability of acting as a civilizing vanguard.

Following the end of the World War, the relations of all peoples are being reshaped. Without any doubt, every country in the world will have to be remodeled on this new foundation. As part of this change the Turcoman peoples, who appeared on the stage of world history 2000 years before Christ and left their imprint on the culture and civilization of the world, and who furthermore have today proved the strength of a national movement and armed struggle in Turkey, are now playing a pioneering role in shaping their destiny by establishing within Russia the seven [*sic*] autonomous republics of Turkestan, Kirgiz, Bashkurd, Tatar, Azerbaijan, and Crimea. The land of the Rising Sun, Japan, should provide humanitarian aid to them based on the ethics of humanitarianism and international justice.

The economic crisis in Europe comes hand in hand with a spiritual decline, and, in turn, has made the situation conducive to the rise of the Turkish [*Turki* in Russian, *Turkman* in Japanese corrected to *Toruko*, meaning "Turkish"] peoples upon the foundation of a completely new democracy. This movement is being strengthened by its foundation on the unyielding solidarity between the Turkish peoples [again *Turkman* in Japanese is corrected to *Toruko*] and the 200 million Muslims of the world.

If the peoples of Asia were to form mutually friendly relations, this in turn would help correct the historical errors that have produced Asia's present circumstances, which have been created by domestic infighting among Asian peoples and which are ruining Asia. To this end, it is necessary to study closely each other's culture and economy. The first important condition of achieving this goal is to learn the Turkish [*Turki* in Russian] languages. I appeal to your Excellency to address the issue of Turkish [*Turkman* in Japanese, corrected to *Toruko, Turki* in Russian] language instruction in government schools as a challenging first step, in view of the fact that the Turkish [*Turki* in Russian] peoples desire the formation of close relations between all Muslim peoples and Japan and to conclude friendship between our races.

Therefore, as a solution to this problem, I offer the following ideas. First, I suggest the establishment of a Turkish language division within the Tokyo School of Foreign Languages which serves Japan by educating a sizable number of Orientalist scholars. If this problem is to be solved successfully, I will not fail to offer any assistance I can regarding the employment of the best-qualified instructors and the selection of textbooks. Turkish language materials are all written in the Arabic script. Since all Muslim peoples use the Arabic script exclusively, if the Japanese were to study these works, it will also assist them in learning Arabic and Persian in the future. I am submitting two documents for reference in the appendix—the first on Turkic dialects, the second on Russian studies of the Turkish language.

12 September 1922

Bashkir People's Representative
M. G. Kurbangari
Respectfully

Seal in the Arabic Script
Kurban Ali

Chapter Twenty-Four

Rash Behari Bose: The Indian Independence Movement and Japan

Eri Hotta

Bose is undoubtedly a celebrated name in the narrative of Indian independence and Japan's Pan-Asianism. This owes much to Subhas Chandra Bose (1897–1945), a prominent anticolonial activist in preindependence India. As the leader of the Indian National Army, Bose played a major, if often uneasy, part in Japanese-led pan-Asianist programs during World War II (see Hauner 1981; Sareen 2004). But there was another Bose, Rash Behari Bose (1886–1945), who occupies an even more complicated—and arguably more interesting—place in Japan's pan-Asianist discourse (cf. Nakajima 2005; Hotta 2006). Though much less memorialized today, the life and thought of the latter Bose, who spent more than three decades in Japan, merit serious attention.

Rash Behari Bose was born in 1886 in northeastern Bengal to a family from the military Kshatria caste. As a student in Calcutta, he developed revolutionary ambitions, having been inspired by the literature of the 1857 Sepoy Rebellion. After dropping out of school, he began to engage in anti-British revolutionary activities while working as a forestry officer. In late 1912, Bose was implicated in a failed plot to assassinate Lord Hardinge (1858–1944), the viceroy and the governor-general of India. An investigation by British intelligence eventually revealed Bose as the mastermind behind the plot. This resulted in an extensive manhunt with a death warrant. Thus began Bose's life on the run. By May 1915, his options in India had run out, and he boarded a Japanese ship bound for Tokyo, feigning a family relationship with the great Bengali poet Rabindranath Tagore (1861–1941).

Over the next thirty years, Bose's career as a dissident Indian fighting for Indian independence would blossom in Japan. H. P. Ghose observed that "Rash Behari Bose was, so to say, not an individual but an institution from which emanated inspiration and instruction" (in Ohsawa 1954: vi) This may be an overstatement. Yet the degree to which Bose's proindependence, anticolonial cause was absorbed into the orthodoxy of Japan's pan-Asianist discourse cannot be dismissed so easily. His public roles included the editorships of journals such as *The New Asia* and *The Asian Review*, and he himself produced, in Japanese, a considerable number of books on India (Ohsawa 1954: 33). He was also a great clubman with excellent networking skills. He established cultural associations and study groups such as the Indian Society, the Indo-Japanese Friends Society, and a hostel for Asian students staying in Tokyo called "Villa Asians," in addition to organizing a series of international conferences on a pan-Asianist theme (cf. Hotta 2006).

Bose's family life too flourished in Japan. In late 1915, when the British first closed in on Bose and successfully put pressure on Tokyo to issue an extradition order, his Japanese supporters entrusted him to a Japanese couple. They were Mr. and Mrs. Sōma, who operated one of the first and hugely successful Western-style brasseries called *Nakamuraya*, still in business today. They were respected patrons of art and devout Christians who held regular literary and artistic discussion meetings. Defying all potential risks, the Sōma household provided Bose with a hideout. The Japanese government eventually reversed its extradition order, and in July 1918, Bose married the Sōmas' eldest daughter, Toshiko, with whom he had a son and daughter. But marital bliss did not slow down his revolutionary activities. It is thought that around this time he was actively supplying arms to India with the help of Japanese supporters, such as the pan-Asianist Ōkawa Shūmei (see II:4).

Bose's impressive Japanese success—and his life itself—owed much to the moral as well as financial support he received from Japan's prominent and influential pan-Asianists. His most powerful backer, aside from his in-laws, was Tōyama Mitsuru (1855–1944), a charismatic leader of the ultranationalist organization Genyōsha (see I:3) with a proven record of pan-Asianist sympathies. Inukai Tsuyoshi (1855–1932), a parliamentarian who would become Japan's prime minister, too, was among those who were charmed by the young Indian revolutionary.

As time went by, Bose's desire for India's independence grew more and more entangled with the rise of the ultranationalistic version of Pan-Asianism advocated by Tōyama and his followers. In the late 1920s and into the 1930s, the collapse of the world economy, impoverishment of Japan's countryside due to economic and natural disasters, and the increasing instability of Japan's international position had manifold effects. One of the most disastrous of these was the rise of Japanese chauvinism, which in turn gave credence to the ultranationalistic version of Pan-Asianism. The idea that Japan, as the chosen Asian nation, would spearhead the renaissance of Asia was at the heart of this brand of Pan-Asianism.

Bose too subscribed to the notion that Japan was to save Asia, including his India. Already in 1922, he was trumpeting Japan's unique leadership role in Asia's rebirth as the world's foremost civilization. In a piece that compared Pan-Asianism and Pan-Islamism (with a suggestion that the two were one and the same thing), he declared, "The Japanese defeat of Russia in 1904–1905 marked the beginning of Asia's renaissance. . . . But unlike the white men, Asia would never abuse its power and leadership" (Bose 1922: 129). Such an idea did not sit well with many other Asian nationalists outside of Japan, to be sure. But Bose's wholehearted embrace of the most radicalized and narcissistic form of Pan-Asianism found a welcome audience in Japan. Bose's pet thesis, which he reiterated in his writings and speeches, was the glory of Indian civilization, the strong tie between India and Japan, and, ultimately, the importance of establishing one Asia under Japan's leadership.

Through his public activities, Bose affirmed and gave authenticity to the ultranationalistic form of Pan-Asianism. Like Japan's other influential rightist thinkers/agitators, including Kita Ikki and Ōkawa Shūmei, Bose saw Japan's Pan-Asianism as providing a more egalitarian alternative to the existing international order dominated by the European and American powers. In such thinking, Japan became the ideal type for all other Asian nations to look up to. And so the argument ran that the Japanese way should prevail in Asia, even with force, if necessary.

Especially after the Manchurian Incident of 1931, when a Japanese army invaded the northeastern provinces of China, "Pan-Asianism" became the all-encompassing and morally unobjectionable umbrella to justify Japan's turn to militarism (cf. Hotta 2007). Bose was in the midst of that remarkable ascendancy of Pan-Asianism in Japan's foreign policy. That his position depended on support from Japan's radicalized and chauvinistic group of pan-Asianists determined the course of Bose's later career as a "collaborator" with Japan's wartime regime. Throughout the war, Bose sat on the boards of many cultural and political organizations of a pan-Asianist persuasion, continued to give lectures, wrote pamphlets, and maximized his rare and well-connected position, primarily to educate and enlighten the Japanese audience on India's cause of independence. The high point of Bose's wartime career came with his appointment as president of the Indian Independence League. He was also the first head, succeeded by Subhas Chandra Bose, of the Indian National Army organized in Singapore under Japanese auspices.

For Rash Behari Bose and others who agitated in support of Japan's war effort after Pearl Harbor, the war that Japan fought against the Allies was a clash between East and West. And moreover, he regarded it as a righteous war to liberate Asia led by Japan against the Anglo-American powers conspiring against the non-West. Bose himself said as much in an address he delivered at the Second Indian Independence League conference that he convened in Bangkok in June 1942:

> . . . the Greater East Asia War was declared on the 8th December, 1941. . . . I refuse to believe that there was a true Indian patriot who was not extremely delighted and gratified in his heart of hearts when the great news of the declaration of War by Japan against the Anglo-American races reached his or her ears. I refuse to believe there is any true Indian patriot, whatever be his or her career or conviction, who might not have rejoiced, as from day to day, the mighty Imperial forces of Japan on land and sea and in air went on administering crushing blows against their imperialism in Asia, and the British Imperialist bases in these parts began to totter one after the other like houses of cards. (Rash Behari Bose: "Address of Rash Behari Bose at the Bangkok Conference on 16 June 1942 Expressing Faith in Japan for the Liberation of India and Asking the People to Cooperate in the Struggle," National Archives of India, New Delhi, Indian Independence League Papers, F., no. 453) . . . Those of us, who were destined to live and work in Japan, had particular reasons to be overjoyed at these most welcome happenings.

But Japan's war was also a miscarried enterprise, we now know, that did not live up to its pan-Asianist objectives. And Bose's identification of Indian independence with Japan's wartime imperialism is unsettling for that reason. Had he decided to part ways with the Japanese once Japan's aggressive expansionist program in China and Southeast Asia became apparent, his reputation as an independence fighter might have survived intact (Hauner 1981: 103). That was exactly what other prominent Indian exiles in Japan, such as Ananda Mohan Sahay (1898–1991) and Raja Mahendra Pratap (see II:9), opted to do. But Bose was far more involved in what was by then the mainstream of Japanese society to do otherwise. It seems that the more success he had in Japan as the figurehead of Indian independence and the pan-Asianist cause, the more isolated he became from the reality of the independence movement at home.

Bose did not live to see Japan's defeat, as he died of tuberculosis in Tokyo in January 1945 at the age of sixty. By the end of his life, he stood not only physically but also ideologically apart from the mainstream of Indian nationalism, leading Indian observers to declare that Bose had become a mere Japanese puppet. His problem was by no means a unique one but perhaps a rather common one in any nationalist movement in exile. But this apparent point has too often been overlooked by the biographers of Bose in Japan, who have tended to overestimate his influence in India and overromanticize his activities. In contrast, Subhas Chandra Bose, despite his controversial associations with the Axis powers, occupies a legendary status in India's independence history, especially in Bengal. Perhaps the difference between the two is that having lived so far away for so long, Rash Behari Bose's credibility as an Indian patriot became more and more vulnerable to attack by his compatriots. The patriotism of Subhas Chandra Bose, on the other hand, is harder to challenge because even his reckless adventurism and flirtations with the fascist regimes (cf. Hauner 1981; Sareen 2004) were directly aimed at ousting British rule in India.

To dismiss Rash Behari Bose's Indian nationalism as well as his Pan-Asianism simply as disingenuous tools of Japan's more self-interested imperialist program would be all too easy, however. His view that the liberation of India and other Asian nations would arise from Japan's wartime program, in retrospect, was hopelessly misguided. But this does not explain why Bose should have been so attracted to Japan's Pan-Asianism and, in turn, Japan's pan-Asianists to Bose's independence struggle and over a substantial stretch of time too. The most remarkable aspect of the remarkable life of Rash Behari Bose then was the symbiotic relationship that he had with Japan's pan-Asianists. Ultranationalistic Japanese pan-Asianists found a powerful spokesman in the person of Bose. There he was, a real Indian independence fighter, giving his blessings to Japan's leadership in Asia with all the eloquence he could muster. This, to some Japanese, must have been proof that Japan was doing the right thing. Up until then, India, celebrated by Tagore and his art-historian friend Okakura Tenshin (see I:7 and I:8), had been an abstract, remote, and almost metaphysical idea in Japan. Direct contact of some politicized Japanese with Indian exiles such as Bose finally made India more real. And the Japanese were eager to embrace him and his cause. What Bose's Japanese friends did not realize was that it would have taken hundreds and thousands more Rash Behari Boses for Japan to lead India, let alone the rest of Asia.

Source (English in the original)
Rash Behari Bose: "Address of Rash Behari Bose at the Bangkok Conference (16 June 1942) Expressing Faith in Japan for the Liberation of India and Asking the People to Cooperate in the Struggle," National Archives of India, New Delhi, Indian Independence League Papers, F., no. 453.

Your excellencies, Friends and Compatriots!

Allow me to express my sincere thanks for the great honour you have done me by calling upon me to occupy this chair and guide the deliberations of this historic conference.

. . .

In our grim final struggle against British Imperialism, we shall have to offer great sacrifices. Many of us will have to lay down our lives before the world can see India free. It can be well said that these four comrades have given us the lead, of which our compatriots in Thailand and Malaya can be well proud of.

During and since 1857, when we first revolted against British Imperialism in India, hundreds of thousands of our most respected and beloved compatriots have laid down their lives in their efforts to free our Motherland. We cannot forget the fact that they have nourished the seeds of Swaraj with their blood and it is the result of their supreme sacrifices that we are to-day so near our goal and can hope with confidence to achieve independence in the near future. World knows only a part of the long list of those Indian victims of British Imperialism. Let us pay respects to the memory of those numberless known and unknown comrades. Placed as we are to-day, we can do very little beyond that. But the time is fast approaching when in every city and town in India, we shall find a worthy monument erected in their memory and we, Indians, will pay homage to them and look upon them with pride. . . .

I do not want to take your time by going into the details regarding India's struggle for freedom since 1857. Suffice it to say that although the failure of our revolt of 1857 was a great blow to the nation and although a general depression had overwhelmed the country, our efforts to overthrow British rule never ceased. Under the circumstances prevailing in those days, the activities had to be carried on underground and within a limited scope; and whenever there was an opportunity, a revolt was attempted. After minor preparatory stages our first effort on a large scale was made when the war of 1914–1918 started. Our workers were active everywhere. The Indian army was prepared to join the revolt. A part of the Indian army had actually revolted rather prematurely. We thought we were going to succeed. Unfortunately we did not meet with success on that occasion. Thousands of our compatriots had to pay the highest price of patriotism. Thousands were sent to the Andamans and Mandalay and hundreds of them still remain rotting in prisons and concentration camps. . . .

When in 1939 the war in Europe started, Britain once again began to indulge in jugglery of words on order to secure Indian co-operation and help. But to the great delight of us all, to this very day the nationalist leaders in India have refused to be misled and have continued to resist all British efforts to drag India into war. Our respect goes to Mahatma Gandhi [1869–1948] for the most admirable way, he has led the nation clear of all dangers of being entangled in this war.

With this background in India, the Greater East Asia War was declared on the 8th December, 1941. No matter in which part of the world he or she might be living, whatever might be his or her attitude towards Japan, I refuse to believe that there was a true Indian patriot who was not extremely delighted and gratified in his heart of hearts when the great news of the declaration of War by Japan against the Anglo-American races reached his or her ears. I refuse to believe there is any true Indian patriot, whatever be his or her career or conviction, who might not have rejoiced, as from day to day, the mighty Imperial forces of Japan on land and sea and in the air went on administering crushing blows against their imperialism in Asia, and the British Imperialist bases in these parts began to totter one after the other like houses of cards. For is there a man whose eyes cannot withhold joyous tears when he sees before his eyes the power of the greatest enemy of humanity and peace, the greatest aggressor of centuries being destroyed? Those of us, who were destined to live and work in Japan, had particular reasons to be overjoyed at these most welcome happenings.

We have been working in Japan for decades so that we can see Japan in a position to stand by the oppressed Asiatics and to liberate Asia. We were anxiously awaiting the day when Japan would fully realize the great significance of creating a free and united Asia and would feel convinced that it was in the interest of Japan herself, as also for the rest of Asia if not for the world as whole, that the octopus grip of the Anglo-Saxon Imperialism in the east must be destroyed root and branch. We all were fully convinced that Japan alone was in the position to take the honour. Thus when on the morning of the most auspicious day, the day of the Enlightenment of Lord Buddha, we heard the most auspicious news of Japan's declaration of war against our common enemy, we felt that our mission in Japan was fulfilled. We felt convinced that India's freedom was assured. Being in Japan for decades, I knew well that Japan was not in the habit of talking and debating unnecessary and meaningless things. I knew well that she was not in the habit of taking any serious step unless she had fully gauged her strength and was convinced of her success. I therefore did not share the views of those who thought that due to her continued military activities in China, she was too exhausted to challenge the mighty Anglo-Saxon, or the so called ABCD combined forces. I was one of those who had not the slightest doubt that the war in China was a prelude to the real war against Powers who were actually responsible for the continued fratricidal conflict between China and Japan. Happenings on the international chess board during the past more than ten years have been suggesting that such a worldwide conflict was inevitable. It was also apparent that the question of Indian freedom could be successfully solved only when Japan rose in arms against British Imperialism.

Now that Japan and Thailand have taken up arms against our common foe, the joint efforts of our worthy allies ensure the doom of the British Empire and our complete victory is assured.

These effective efforts on different fronts to destroy our common enemy, bring us a reminder regarding our own duties and responsibilities in this common effort for our common cause. We must ask ourselves what we have done and what we are going to do to contribute to this great cause. Only praising Japan, Germany and Italy will not entitle us to the position for which we are craving. We must contribute our might and must make the greatest sacrifice we can make. Then alone can we command the respect and consideration of our worthy allies and then alone we can claim a place worthy of a great nation like ours in a future international assembly.

Realising this very important fact, and our duty towards our motherland at this most important juncture, we in Tokyo promptly met on the 8th of December, 1941 at the Rainbow Grill and decided upon a programme of action. My Compatriots formed a committee and asked me to lead the movement and I gladly agreed to abide by their decision. We at first undertook to consolidate Indian opinion in East Asia in favour of a definite fight from without. Meetings were held in different centres of Japan and resolutions were passed emphasizing the solidarity of our compatriots, the great need of declaring Independence of India by destroying British Imperialism, and expressing confidence in our work.

On the 26th December, 1941, for the first time in the history of Indians in Japan, a Conference of nearly fifty representatives of the Indian residents in Kobe, Osaka, Yokohama and Tokyo—all the four cities, where Indians reside—was held at the Railway Hotel at Tokyo to consider the problems. A resolution was passed calling upon the Indians to realize the gravity of the situation and the danger ahead of India. The resolution reads as follows:

Whereas the continued defeat of the British and their allies in Europe and Africa has sealed the fate of the British Imperialism in Europe.

Whereas the most decisive destruction of British sea and land forces by Japan in the East has given a death-blow to the power and prestige of British Imperialism in Asia.

Whereas the war is fast approaching the shores and borders of India, the British stronghold, Axis powers may be obliged to invade India in order to destroy the main source of British fighting strength.

Whereas such an invasion will bring unimaginable and extremely unusual hardships, miseries and sufferings to millions of innocent and helpless Indians in cities, towns and villages, and

Whereas the only way to avoid this most unhappy situation is, to declare complete independence of India from British rule and to cut off all possible connections with British Imperialism in every possible way immediately;

The Indian Nationals residing in Japan assembled in this Conference, most seriously and earnestly appeal to the Indian National Congress and the people of India to immediately declare Independence and to capture all power from the British in India and to take immediate effective steps to stop each and every source of Indian aid to British Imperialist War and to declare on behalf of the people that India has no desire whatsoever to be involved in this conflict and has never been willing to help Britain. Our representatives were sent to Shanghai and on 26th of January this year, a huge gathering of the Indian residents of Shanghai was held in Young Men's Association hall when similar resolutions as passed in Tokyo were very enthusiastically passed and our movement was given unanimous support.

In the meantime we established contact with the military and civil high commands in Japan and began to impress upon them the necessity of helping India in her struggle for freedom for the very achievement of the great object for which Japan had declared war against British and America. We made it clear to them that so long as British Imperialism in India continued, Japan could not expect a final victory in this war. At last: we succeeded in prevailing upon them and General Tojo, the Prime Minister of Japan, openly declared before the Imperial Diet that his Government was prepared to help the Indians in our efforts to free our country from the long bondage. In his declaration before the Imperial Diet on the fall of Singapore he said:

"It is a golden opportunity for India, having, as it does, several thousand years of history and splendid cultural tradition, to rid herself of the ruthless despotism of Britain and participate in the construction of the Greater East Asia Co-Prosperity Sphere. Japan expects that India will restore its proper status of India for the Indians and will not stint herself in extending assistance to the Patriotic efforts of the Indians. Should India fail to awaken to her mission forgetting her history and tradition, and continue as before to be beguiled by the British cajolery and manipulation and act at their beck and call I cannot but fear that an opportunity for the renaissance of the Indian people would be forever lost."

The declaration offered us great encouragement and we felt convinced, that India could safely hope to be free before the East Asia War comes to an end. Counting upon the promises of General Tojo, we established our headquarters at Sanno Hotel and started our activities and preparations in right earnest. We decided that a Conference of the representatives of Indian organizations from various parts of East Asia should be held for exchanging views regarding our future move. With the help of the military authorities things were conveniently arranged and the representatives of our compatriots residing in Malaya, Hongkong and Shanghai along with us of Tokyo, sat in conference for three days and arrived at certain decisions and framed the preliminary constitution for the working and progress of our movement. Those friends from abroad, who participated in Tokyo Conference, had occasion to come in contact with responsible members of the Japanese Army in Tokyo and to know more and more about the standing of our movement. Discussions at the Tokyo Conference were varied and we did our best to lay down a solid

foundation upon which we could base our plan of action in future, We were deprived of the valuable help and advices of our friends in Thailand due to the unfortunate accident. Burma and Andamans were still in the hands of our enemies. We, therefore, were unable to come to a decision that could be claimed to be representative of the views of our compatriots in Asia as a whole. We, therefore, decided to hold a larger and most representative Conference at a later date when the decisions taken at Tokyo were to be ratified. This Assembly in which we are participating to-day is the result of that decision.
. . .

We should feel thankful to the Governments of Japan, Germany, Thailand and Italy for their most friendly attitude they have been showing towards our cause. We must be particularly thankful to Japan for the most encouraging and hopeful definite promise of help in our sacred cause. Let us not forget the words of Pandit Jawaharlal Nehru when he said:

Success often comes to those who dare and act, it seldom goes to cowards.

Part IV

THE BREAKDOWN OF THE IMPERIALIST ORDER: WORLD WAR I AND PAN-ASIANISM, 1914–1920

This part deals with the first peak of pan-Asian agitation in Japan during and immediately after World War I. Two related factors contributed to this activism. First, as the Western powers were fighting for their survival in Europe and paying much less attention to East Asia, Japanese pan-Asianists felt less restraint about expressing their ambitions openly. Second, as Japan had by this time become the leading power in the region, an increasing number of commentators, politicians, and even diplomats had begun to regard Pan-Asianism as a viable foreign policy option. Japan, these advocates argued, should now lead a united Asia in a war against the colonialist and racialist West. But this upsurge in pan-Asian discourse was not limited to Japan; Pan-Asianism was also the subject of lively debate in China during this period.

Although the Japanese Foreign Ministry continued to publicly deny that Japan was pursuing pan-Asian goals, Pan-Asianism had now entered mainstream political discourse. It was now even promulgated in English-language publications, directed primarily at a Western audience—a sign of Japan's growing self-confidence in the international arena.

It was in this atmosphere that terms such as "Pan-Asianism," "All-Asianism," "Greater Asianism," or simply "Asianism" appeared for the first time in Japanese newspapers and journals. The definitions of these terms, however, remained in flux—as indicated by the fact that some advocates were sufficiently flexible in their aims as to include Germany in plans for a pan-Asian league (I:25).

As this part shows, during this period pan-Asian ideas were propagated not only by Japanese but also by Chinese and Indian intellectuals and politicians. The Chinese revolutionary leader Sun Yat-sen, who had received Japanese support before and after the overthrow of the Qing (Ch'ing) dynasty in 1911–1912, also needed Japanese assistance during this period and—for this reason among others—continued to use pan-Asian arguments to appeal to Japan. Likewise, during World War I, the Indian independence fighter T. Das (I:31) sought Japanese (and German) support for India's independence struggle against Britain. While Germany supported Indian independence activities during World War I, the 1902 Anglo–Japanese alliance prevented Japan from openly assisting or encouraging the Indian independence movement.

The outpouring of publications on Asianism during this period, however, was also a by-product of the collapse of the old "diplomacy of imperialism," which occurred as a result of changes that took place during World War I. More and more voices demanded the establishment of a "new international order"—an order that would guarantee peace. The League of Nations, founded in 1919, was part of this scheme. However, the League was criticized in Asia as a tool to preserve the Anglo-American status quo and thus perpetuate Western colonial rule over Asia. It was in this political climate that Pan-Asianism emerged as an alternative to the universalistic claims of the League. It was seen as providing ideological foundations for the establishment of an "Asian League," a bloc that would ensure peace on a regional scale and that, it was argued, would create a more equitable environment than that established under the auspices of the League of Nations.

Chapter Twenty-Five

Germany, Sun Yat-sen, and Pan-Asianism, 1917–1923

Sven Saaler

The definition of "Asia" in the ideology of Pan-Asianism was always in flux and never free of contradictions. The inclusion of *Germany* in pan-Asian thinking is one of the most notable examples of stretching the "Asia" of Pan-Asianism to its limits. During World War I, when Germany was at war with England, France, Russia, and later the United States—the powers held responsible for the evils of colonialism by the pan-Asian movement—the idea emerged in Japan and China that Germany could (and should) be included in a pan-Asian alliance against the colonial "Western" powers, above all the Anglo-Saxon nations. The same idea, although more from a communist, ideology-driven rather than a "pan-Asian" perspective, also gained some prominence in Russia after the Bolshevik Revolution (Nicolaevsky 1949).

In 1916 and 1917, *The Far Eastern Review*, which had been published in Shanghai since 1904, ran a number of articles revealing the involvement of Chinese revolutionary leader Sun Yat-sen (see II:5) in schemes to include Germany in an anti-Western and anti-imperialist pan-Asian alliance. Sun strongly opposed the idea of China joining the "Great War" on the side of the entente powers against Germany. For him, notwithstanding its prewar participation in the imperialist partition of China, Germany was as much a victim of Anglo-Saxon imperialism as China and other Asian nations. Thus, Germany should be thought of as a potential ally, Sun argued. Sun was in close contact with Japanese politicians on this issue and had proposed a Sino–Japanese–German alliance to Japanese Prime Minister Katsura Tarō in 1913 (Tajima 2007: 3). He continuously advocated this scheme throughout World War I and long afterward.

After the revolution in Russia in 1917, Sun enlarged his vision of an anti-imperialist "continental bloc" and advocated a Sino–Japanese–German–Russian alliance to include not only the former imperialist power of Germany but also revolutionary Russia, which had explicitly renounced "the diplomacy of imperialism" with its emphasis on secret treaty policies. Similar ideas of a large anti-imperialist bloc including European powers were also voiced in other parts of Asia—for example, in India, where Taraknath Das (see I:31) argued for a rapprochement of Asian nations with Germany and Mahendra Pratap (see II:9) "began to feel decisive sympathy for the Germans who were fighting this dirty British empire" (Pratap 1947: 36). And in revolutionary Russia itself, although the Communist International in 1920 had dismissed Pan-Asianism as a product of Japanese imperialism, in later years Stalin stated that collaboration with Pan-Asianism might be possible "as a means of liberating Asia from 'Western imperialists'" (Nicolaevsky 1949: 286).

To be sure, in the context of World War I, an alliance between Germany and a pan-Asian league was not completely unrealistic, as ironic as this might sound considering the fact that German Emperor Wilhelm II was among the most vociferous proponents of the "Yellow Peril" before 1914. Indeed, even *after* the end of World War I, he still clung to his belief that a pan-Asian league would pose a threat to Europe one day, as can be seen in his memoirs published in the *New York Times* (Hohenzollern 1922: 104). However, during World War I, Germany was fighting a two-front war in Europe and had a strong interest in stimulating anti-British movements in Asia that would weaken the British Empire's integrity and force Britain to send troops to remote corners of its empire, thus bringing relief to the German Western Front. When Indian independence activists visited Germany during World War I, some of them were granted an audience with Emperor Wilhelm II (Pratap 1947: 41f, 58). In 1915, Germany even dispatched a mission to Afghanistan to assist the Provisional Government of India established there (Pratap 1947; see also II:9).

As a result of Germany's defeat in World War I, all these efforts petered out without any tangible results. However, pan-Asianists continued to consider the possibility of solidarity with "oppressed *European* nations" or with states that were considered victim or enemies of Anglo-American imperialism, such as, again, Germany after the Versailles Treaty but also with revolutionary Russia (after 1922 the Soviet Union). In 1923, it was again Sun Yat-sen who, in a letter to Inukai Tsuyoshi, expressed the wish to strengthen solidarity with oppressed European peoples. In this letter, which is reproduced here, Sun again refers to the possibility of a Chinese–Japanese–German alliance and places an even stronger emphasis on his hopes for the Soviet Union as the future savior of the oppressed peoples of Asia.

An "Asian" Russia had been a common trope in discourse on "Europe and Asia" since the eighteenth century, but the concept now became loaded with explosive potential for the postwar restructuring of international relations, particularly since the newly established government of Sun Yat-sen (the third government he had established in Canton within ten years) had announced that it would cooperate closely with the Soviet Union, following the signing of an agreement with Adolph Joffe (1883–1927), the Soviet Union's representative in China, on 26 January 1924. Soon after, Sun sent his confidant Den Jia-yan to Germany. In February 1924, Den here met with Hubert Knipping (1868–1955), director of the East Asia Department of the German Foreign Office and consul general in Shanghai until 1916, and came to an agreement involving cooperation with Germany in the industrial development of Southern China (Tajima 2007: 22). When considering the possibility of a Sino–German–Soviet alliance, we must not forget that, as a consequence of its isolation in Europe after World War I, Germany also had begun covert military cooperation with Soviet Russia after signing the Treaty of Rapallo in 1922. A rapprochement with China therefore was another way for Germany out of international isolation.

By stressing that China and other Asian countries might seek an alliance with the Soviet Union, Sun, in his letter, also warned Japan of the danger of its future isolation in Asia. For Sun, Japan had two choices: to join the Asian peoples' rapprochement with the Soviet Union and become, together with the Soviets, the savior of the oppressed peoples of Asia or to risk isolation in Asia—a warning that Sun repeated in a celebrated speech on "Greater Asianism" given in Kōbe in November 1924 (see II:5).

Source 1 (English in the original)
"Asia against the White Man," *Far Eastern Review*, April 1917, 409–12.

ASIA AGAINST THE WHITE MAN

Design to Free India from British Rule
Exposure of the Reasons Prompting Sun Yat-Sen and Co. to oppose a Break with Germany

In the preceding article we have intimated that the explanation of what would appear to be extraordinary opposition on the part of Dr. Sun Yat-sen, ex-President of the Chinese Republic; Mr. Tang Shao-yi, ex-Premier of the Chinese Republic [T'ang Shao-I, 1862–1938]; and Mr. Wen Tsung-yao [Wen Zongyao, 1867–1947], one of the most energetic leaders in the establishment of the Republic, to the forward step the Peking Government has taken to align China with the Powers fighting for the maintenance of the principles of International Law—upon the preservation of which China's future, more than that of any other country, depends—is due to their association with a Pan-Asian movement.

It is remarkable that foreigners have so far failed to realize that such a movement is vigorously afoot; that it has many adherents, chiefly in Japan, and that their plan is a far-reaching one, particularly with regard to the overthrow of British rule in India, and the ousting of the influence of the white men from the entire region covered by the term Asia—which embraces Japan, China, Siam, India, the Malayan Archipelago, and the islands of the Pacific—if not from Australia.

The movement has its genesis in Japan, whose ambitions for world dominion is not to be scoffed at. And in this connexion, and in view of the significant utterances of Dr. Sun Yat-sen and Mr. Tang Shao-yi—the new converts to the movement, who, as potential leaders of political parties in China, are now openly heading a campaign in China—we draw special attention to articles on the subject in previous issues of the Review, specially the July, 1916, number.

The startling telegrams which Dr. Sun Yat-sen has dispatched to the British Premier and to the Chinese Parliament, backed by the telegram to the Chinese Parliament jointly signed by Messrs. Tang Shao-yi and Wen Tsung-yao, in strong opposition to China breaking off diplomatic relations with Germany, will probably do more to focus the attention of the European and American nations on the sinister programme that these men have in view, than anything else could have done. . . .

That opposition [to breaking off diplomatic relations with Germany] is not, as may be supposed at first glance, due to any desire on the part of Sun Yat-sen and Co. to keep China out of the world purely because they believe that it is better in world interests that she remains neutral. It is solely and wholly because the co-operation of China with other foreign powers will do more to obstruct and perhaps entirely frustrate their plans for Asiatic union than anything else could have done. The most casual consideration, in the light of the following statements of Sun Yat-sen and Tang Shao-yi, will indicate to the most disinterested mind that China, when she throws her lot in with the Entente nations or America against Germany, will prevent a union with Japan in the movement to oust the white man from Asia. To effect such a purpose it is essential that China should be entirely free from foreign influences so that she might, under the hegemony of Japan, be at liberty to develop what plans are necessary to ensure ultimate success for the movement. . . .

It is only recently that the Japanese who foster the Pan-Asian movement have succeeded in recruiting active agents of some standing in the public mind to carry on propaganda work in China, and that they have enrolled men like the three above-mentioned shows that they must have been able to offer substantial inducements and practically guarantee success. . . .

Other nations may ignore the trend of events but it is significant that the Germans have not done so. German agents have done their best to bend to their purpose the projects of the three men mentioned, and to use the power it was believed they wielded to make it easy to launch an attack upon India through China. . . .

One of the first public utterances which disclosed the propaganda in which these men were engaged was made in the Japanese paper *Asahi*, when Dr. Sun Yat-sen . . . stated that Japan was really taking Chinese interests into primary consideration, the demands [a reference to the "21 Demands" of 1915] being but a first step in a great plan to bring about the union of Japanese and Chinese interests so that from Japan to Egypt there should be built up a great Asiatic confederation for the purpose of ousting the white man. . . .

The *Asahi* statement (translated by the "Herald of Asia") . . . is as follows:

Japan's acceptance of the Western doctrine of the "Open Door and Equal Opportunity" in China is the most potent cause of Sino-Japanese misunderstanding and friction, according to Dr. Sun Yat-sen, who recently discussed the subject with an *Asahi* representative. This noted revolutionist believes that all the trouble between the two countries is due to artificial causes, pointing out that the natural relations such as the ethical code common to both Japan and China, have all tended to draw the two peoples closer together, rather than to separate them as artificial causes have certainly done. Japan's avowal of the "principle" of the "open door and equal opportunity" is merely the foremost of these artificial causes.

The question as to what induced Japan to adopt this "principle," Dr. Sun answers by reminding us of the great disparity of international status between the two nations. While Japan has attained a position of equality with the Western Powers, China is now a helpless prey to their exploitation. The doctrine of equal opportunity owes its origin to the anxiety of every one of those Powers not to be left out when any one of them acquires "rights" or interests in China, and it is only natural that Japan, a rising nation situated nearer to China than any Occidental Power, should exercise every caution not to be forestalled by any other Power in the acquisition of rights and interests in China, since her own safety both as a nation, and as guardian to all the Orient, would be seriously affected if she allowed European Powers to exploit China as they pleased, whether politically or economically. Hence her assertion of the open door and equal opportunity before the Powers of Europe, and her claims of preferential rights in China.

But this position, assumed by Japan for her own interests, is at variance with the desires of the Chinese people, and is the primary cause of their distrust of Japan, and of their dissatisfaction with her attitude towards them.

Chinese of the new school of thought look to Japan for assistance in effecting political reforms and advancing the civilisation and power of their country, because they regard the Meiji Restoration and the political reformation of China as land-marks in the awakening of the yellow peoples as a race, and believe the Chinese political reformation to be in reality one of the fruits of the Meiji Restoration. At the same time they realize that their own political reformation is many times more difficult to accomplish than the Meiji Restoration, because international relations are far more complex to-day than they were fifty years ago, and the influence of Occidental Powers has penetrated China many times more deeply than it had penetrated Japan half-a-century ago. The removal of this foreign yoke is absolutely necessary to China's independence, which in turn is indispensable if a thorough political reformation is to be effected, but Japan has so far done little, if anything, to help China out of this foreign yoke. On the contrary, she has been content to avail herself of the European slogan for equal opportunities in China.

In the light of historical relations China and Japan are sisters. Unfortunately the elder sister, China, has been so enfeebled, physically and mentally, that she has to sit with folded arms while her property is taken away bit by bit by robbers operating in open daylight. What a contrast she is to her intelligent and vigorous younger sister, who can claim a share in the robbers' spoils and say to China, "Since you are giving away portions of your property to alien robbers, surely you can afford to give me a portion also"! So callous an attitude cannot but bitterly disappoint the Chinese people, and Dr. Sun's advice to us (Japanese) is, therefore, "Help China regain her national strength. Instead of exploiting her under cover of equal opportunity, help her, in the light of your experience since the Meiji Restoration, to set her house in order and free her from foreign influence." Then, and only then, will the Chinese be truly grateful to Japan for her moral support, and Dr. Sun thinks that the improvement of China's status among nations will mean an improvement in the position of the yellow peoples as a race, and conduce not a little to the raising of Japan's influence in the world. . . .

MR. TANG SHAO-YI WANTS A FREE INDIA

Mr. Tang Shao-yi's first public contribution to the propaganda appeared as an introduction to a book entitled "Is Japan a Menace to Asia," [see I:31] which is "dedicated to the Cause of Asian Independence." This book is designed to convince readers, especially Chinese, that Japan should be the leader of Asia and that she is "the pride of Asia." It claims that Japan's achievements "speak for Asia, and they demonstrate that China and India, under better environment, can at least do like Japan in all fields of human activity."

The author, who happens to be an obscure but active native of India claiming American citizenship, defends Japan's policy of aggression towards China as being justified by a wish to "preserve Asian supremacy in the Far East." The author is avowedly against what he terms "whitemanism," and works for a union of the Asiatics to destroy the dominance of Europeans, with particular reference to the British in India, or anywhere else in the Near or Far East for that matter. Mr. Tang writes as follows:

The future of Asia depends upon the ability of the Asiatic people to assert their rights politically. Political weakness of Asia has been the cause of many troubles and wars during the last century and a half. Asia as a whole, except Japan, affords for the strong Powers unbounded natural resources, cheap labor, markets, defencelessness and inefficient governments which give every incentive for aggression. . . . Political backwardness is not inherent among the Asiatic people, though it is the current opinion among the western students. China in the past had her bright periods of history, her glorious days of Imperialism. In the field of culture and civilization, China contributed her full share when she was politically strong. India of Asoka and Akbar was far ahead of any of the European countries of those ages. It is by contact with the Orient that Europe in the past has learnt many useful things for her present civilization. . . . To us it is quite clear that the Great Powers work unitedly to extract certain concessions from China. . . . The concert of the Great European Powers have had one motive before them—exploitation of Asia and Africa to their advantage.

This aggression of Europe in Asia can be stopped for the good of Asia and Europe by a solid Asiatic unity not merely from a cultural standpoint but from a political standpoint. [emphasis in original]

. . .

Because Japan is politically strong she is able to develop her country politically and culturally. China is struggling to be free and she should accept co-operation from any quarter that is truly friendly. Japan is China's disciple of the past and all far-sighted Japanese believe that "Japan without China and India, is, in the long run, without legs." . . .

The awakening of Asia is the most outstanding feature of the present age. The future of Asia is bright and glorious if the new spirit of Asia be rightly directed in cooperation with all the Asian people. *We hope, though we may not live to see it fully accomplished, that Japan and China and India will work united, standing for Asian independence against all outside aggressions.* [emphasis in original]

The following is from *The Labour Leader*, London, of January 11, 1917.
. . . We are indebted to the Indian *Modern World* for drawing attention to the pronouncement, which appears in the *Japan Magazine*:

The sun is full of caprice; it has its likes and dislikes, declares Mr. Unosuke Wakamiya in the *Chuo Koron*, and so it will finally decide the white man's fate as to occupation and exploitation of the tropics. On the yellow, the white, and the black races the sun has different effects; the king of day decides where races shall and shall not live. If one race trespasses on another, the sun will eventually come to the rescue. It is no use for races to defy the lord of light.

The sun favours the yellow man most; it places him in the largest and richest part of the world, and very probably he is the original representative of mankind, the first man. The three races mentioned occupy different portions of the globe. Of late, however, trespassing has begun. The white man has started to defy the sun; but he has neither the right nor the power to domineer over the yellow man; he can never succeed in planting himself permanently in Asia, which is the rightful home of the yellow man. He is likewise excluded from the home of the black man, by the same insistent sun.

The white man is now at the zenith of his power and glory and has assumed the dictatorship of mankind. But he has failed in his attempted conquest of the tropics, the climate of which proves fatal to him and his offspring. His adventure has turned out morally and physically disastrous to him. He cannot endure the races of the East nor the sun that created them. Yet, strange to say, though nature bans the white man from the tropics, she has made him dependent on tropical products. His tea, coffee, cocoa, dyes, and fruits; his cotton and tobacco; his rubber and numerous other necessaries of civilisation, all come from the tropics. But the sun decides that he shall obtain them through the yellow man, and not come to take them himself. He must be satisfied to purchase what he needs from Asia, and not try to take the country as well. It is, indeed, wonderful to what pains nature has gone to exclude the white man from Asia. The natives of tropical countries have a normal temperature lower than that of the European at home, so that a white man arriving in the tropics inevitably suffers from a rise of bodily temperature and becomes liable to tropical diseases of all kinds.

Thus the native can easily live where the white man will die. . . . The Japanese is a yellow man; he has the warm blood of the south; his temperature is normally below that of the European; and the cry of "Southward Ho!" is most natural to him. Japan, and not Europe or America, is to be supreme in Asia.

Source 2 (translation from the Japanese original by Sven Saaler)
Inukai Tsuyoshi ate shokan (Letter from Sun Yat-sen to Inukai Tsuyoshi, 16 November 1923), reprinted in Kojima Shinji et al. (eds.), *Chūgokujin*

no Nihonjinkan 100nenshi (Hundred Years' History of Chinese Views of the Japanese). Jiyū Kokuminsha, 1974, 153–58.

My dear friend, Bokudō,

Mr. Yamada has come and told me that you have joined the cabinet, that you are showing your political talents and that we will receive your support for our aims, which have not been fulfilled. The problems of East Asia will therefore be resolved soon, he says. I was extremely delighted [about this news]. . . .

Our [revolutionary] actions without doubt were obstructed by the Western powers [in the past]. Until now, Japanese policy towards China has been similar to that of the [Western] powers, and therefore Japan has lost much of its credibility among the peoples of Asia and in China. This is not to your advantage. When you enter the cabinet, I am sure you will end the policy of following the [Western] powers and choose a different way. . . .

The end of the European War has created a new situation in the world. What is this new situation? It is the awakening of all oppressed peoples and their rising up against rule by force. These [oppressed] peoples are most numerous in Asia, and therefore Asian nations will soon experience this worldwide trend and rise up against European rule. At present, Turkey stands at the forefront, but Persia and Afghanistan are following, and India and Malaya will soon follow. But there is one more [country], which is even larger and more important and more heavily involved with the struggle against the [Western] powers. These are the 400 million people of China. It is certain that the one who can enslave these 400 million will become the ruler of the world. Thus, the Western powers and others have tried to annex [it]. But, because they were obstructed, the idea of a partitioning [of China] was raised. Because Japan, as a matter of fact, is situated on the Eastern fringe of East Asia, she took part in these partition plans. At that time, everybody in Asia, including the 300 million (*sic*) Chinese, looked up to Japan as the savior (*kyūseishu*) of Asia. Contrary to these expectations, Japan, lacking far-sighted ambitions and any profound plan, imitated the European methods of aggression and eventually annexed Korea, losing the hearts of the people of all of Asia. This was truly sad. . . .

It is not too late [for Japan] to win back the hearts of the Asian people [by granting autonomy to Korea]. If she fails to do so, the hearts of the Asian people will surely be directed towards the Soviets. This will certainly be a misfortune for Japan.

Soviet Russia is the savior of the oppressed European peoples and an enemy of the [imperialist] European powers. As a result, the European governments dispatched troops to Siberia, but the peoples of the European countries attacked their own governments in turn. Eventually, as a result of internal strife, England, France, the United States and the others were forced to recall their conquering armies from Soviet Russia.

The oppressed Asian peoples are at present in an even worse situation than the European peoples. Thus they are fervently crying out for liberation. But in Asia, there is no country willing to help the weak and respect justice (*gi*). As a result, we must put our hopes on Soviet Russia. . . .

Many people say that the [coming] second world war [*nidome no sekai senso*] will surely be a war between the yellow and white [races]. However, I do not think it will be like this. Rather, it will be a contest between justice and oppression. Ridding themselves of oppression is the objective not only of the downtrodden Asian peoples, but also of the numerous oppressed peoples of Europe. Therefore, oppressed peoples everywhere must unite and defeat tyranny.

If this happens, in Europe, only Soviet Russia and Germany are qualified to become the core of the [resistance of the] oppressed, while England and France are the leaders of the oppressors. In Asia, India and China form the core of the oppressed, while the leaders of the oppressors are the same nations, England and France. The United States is part of this league of oppressors, although [sometimes] it is neutral—but it is surely not a friend of oppressed peoples. Only Japan is still an unknown quantity. Are they friend or enemy of the oppressed? I think this will depend on whether or not your ideals can be realized by the Yamamoto [Gonbei] cabinet. If you succeed in realizing your objectives, then Japan will become the friend of the oppressed. If this happens, we will have to prepare for a new world war. I want to suggest a few things to you about how to prepare for this war.

First, the Japanese government now has to help the Chinese revolution to achieve success—it must make possible the internal unification [of China] and break the yoke of the Western powers. . . .

Second, Japan must immediately recognize the Soviet government of Russia.

. . .

After the European War, not only did the international situation change fundamentally, but also the hearts of the people and the nature of ideology (*shiso*) changed completely. We have to acknowledge this. Japanese foreign policy, too, needs to be adjusted; Japan has to secure its position in the world. Otherwise, it will end up like Germany. Against whom are the fortifications of Honolulu and the defenses of Singapore directed? It has come to the point that Japan will have to ally itself with the Soviets—otherwise, it will be attacked from two sides by land and sea. Since the British and American navies are several times larger than that of Japan, it is important to realize that the Soviet armies are at present the most powerful military force in the world. An isolated Japan surrounded by strong neighbors will not have a hopeful future. Thus, a pro-Soviet foreign policy is the only way for Japan to survive. . . .

At the beginning of the European War, Japan chose the wrong direction and lost its chance of global leadership. It cannot make such a mistake again. My dear friend should think this over and make his plans swiftly!

Sun Yat-sen
November 16th, Year 12 of the Republic, Canton

Pan-Asianism during and after World War I: Kodera Kenkichi (1916), Sawayanagi Masatarō (1919), and Sugita Teiichi (1920)

Sven Saaler

This chapter traces changes in pan-Asian discourse in the late 1910s and early 1920s by focusing on some Japanese pan-Asian writings from around the time of World War I. These changes were the consequence of a transformation in international relations during that period. With the outbreak of World War I, the European powers could no longer pay much attention to East Asian affairs, in effect leaving Japan as the only great power in the region. Japan soon tightened its grip on China, culminating in the infamous "21 Demands" of 1915 that turned China into a quasi-protectorate of Japan. At the same time, growing friction between Japan and the West, fueled by the issue of racial discrimination, raised the prospect of a military conflict between the West on the one hand and the "colored races" on the other, with Japan leading Asia or even an anti-Western coalition of all the colored races. At least, this was the perception of pan-Asian writers and agitators during the final years of the war.

The writings of Kodera Kenkichi (1877–1949), Sawayanagi Masatarō (1865–1927), and Sugita Teiichi (1851–1929) illustrate these tendencies well. All three were influential figures in pan-Asian discourse in the 1910s and the early 1920s. Kodera (cf. Saaler 2007) was born in Sanda, Hyōgo prefecture, into a wealthy family. After a year in Tokyo at the private academy of Sugiura Shigetake (1855–1924), an ultranationalist scholar, educator, and priest associated with Tendai Buddhism, Kodera went abroad in 1897 and spent almost a decade overseas. He first studied at Columbian University (the present George Washington University), where he received a doctorate in civil law, and then went on to study at Johns Hopkins, Heidelberg, Vienna, and Geneva universities. In 1908, a year after his return to Japan, Kodera was elected to the Lower House of the Imperial Diet. At thirty-one years of age, he was the youngest-ever member of the Lower House. During his first term, he was affiliated with the Yushinkai, a small group of constitutionalists (*kensei yōgoha*). In 1910 he joined the Rikken Kokumintō, from which he defected to the newly founded Rikken Dōshikai (Association of Friends of the Constitution). In the following years, under the presidency of Katō Takaaki (1860–1925), Kodera rose quickly in the hierarchy of the party (renamed the Kenseikai or Association for Constitutional Politics) and was appointed a member of its board of directors (*sōmu*). However, he was forced to leave the Minseitō, the successor of the Kenseikai, after internal struggles in 1928, and in 1930 he retired from politics after failing to be reelected as an independent candidate.

Sawayanagi Masatarō was born in Nagano prefecture but went to Tokyo as an elementary school student. In 1888, he graduated from Tokyo Imperial University and entered the Ministry of Education (Monbushō), where he worked for the reform and unification of the elementary school system. After a two-year term as vice minister of education, in 1911 he was appointed the first president of Tōhoku Imperial University in Sendai. In 1913 he moved to become president of Kyōto Imperial University, and in 1916 he was named chairman of the Imperial Conference for Education. In that capacity Sawayanagi represented Japan at conferences abroad, such as the first World Conference on Education in San Francisco in 1923 (cf. Sawayanagi 1927; Sawayanagi 1937: I:11). At the same time, he was also engaged in the expansion of private education, holding influential posts at Seijō Gakuen and Taishō universities. In 1919, Sawayanagi was also named president of the Association for the Promotion of Popular Education (*Kokumin kyōiku shōreikai*), which had been founded on the initiative of Tokutomi Sohō (Sawayanagi 1937: 153; see I:28 on Tokutomi).

Parallel with these activities as an educator, during and after World War I Sawayanagi also began to express his views on international affairs in weekly and monthly journals, advocating a "cultural Asianism" and insisting on the unity of the "Asian race." Although Sawayanagi is known, above all, as an educator, his contribution to pan-Asian discourse cannot be underestimated. It is not entirely clear why he began promoting Pan-Asianism in 1917 by writing an article in Ōkuma Shigenobu's magazine *Shin Nippon* (New Japan) or even why the issue caught his attention. We can only suspect that Sawayanagi saw a chance to gain popularity by jumping on the pan-Asianist bandwagon; moreover, after his retirement as president of Kyoto Imperial University, he had plenty of time to study noneducational subjects. Furthermore, his lifelong connections with the Buddhist Jōdo Shinshū sect in Kyoto might well have influenced Sawayanagi, who was a close acquaintance of Kiyoyanagi Mitsuyuki, a Jōdo Shinshū priest. Sawayanagi himself had worked several years as an adviser (*komon*) to a middle school run by the Ōtani sect in

Kyoto (Nitta 1971: 46). The activities of Western Honganji head priest Ōtani Kōzui (1876–1948), who had led an expedition to investigate Buddhism in Central Asia in 1902 and financed three other expeditions in the following years, must have impressed Sawayanagi, just as they did many of his contemporaries. While these expeditions had primarily academic objectives, they also served the purpose of military reconnaissance since Ōtani was receiving funds from the Japanese army—not surprising at a time when war with Russia was considered imminent. Following his expedition Ōtani continued to propagate pan-Asian views, for example, in Tokutomi Sohō's *Kokumin Shinbun*. Since, as we have seen, Sawayanagi also had close links with Tokutomi, it can be safely assumed that Sawayanagi read some of Ōtani's writings on Pan-Asianism. In any case, the blending of educational policies with pan-Asian thought, as seen in Sawayanagi's writings, marked the beginnings of the acceptance of Pan-Asianism by mainstream politicians and bureaucrats as well as broader segments of society—and not only by the political opposition and "romantic" adventurers.

Sugita Teiichi, born in Echizen (the present Fukui prefecture), was already an established politician when Sawayanagi was still at school. He had participated in the antioligarchy Freedom and People's Rights Movement (*Jiyū minken undō*) of the 1870s and was elected to the Lower House of the Imperial Diet in the first elections to the newly established Diet in 1890 on the Jiyūtō (Liberal Party) ticket. Sugita had been writing on the necessity for Asian solidarity since the 1880s, when he published *Kōasaku* (A Policy for Raising Asia, 1884) (cf. Hashikawa 1980: 332f). However, it was the international situation in the aftermath of World War I that turned him into a fervent advocate of Pan-Asianism. By this time he had become an influential and well-known politician, being a former member (1890–1911) and president of the Lower House of the Diet (1906–1908) and a member of the House of Peers (since 1911). In 1916, in the journal *Nihon oyobi Nihonjin* (Japan and the Japanese), he called for the realization of the principles of "Greater Asianism" (*Dai Ajiashugi*) by creating an East Asian League (*Tōa renmei*) (Sugita 1916: 36f). His writings on Pan-Asianism after 1918 show that he was particularly troubled by the continuing racial discrimination against Japanese immigrants to the United States, Australia, New Zealand, and Canada. The rejection of a Japanese proposal to abolish racial discrimination at the Paris Peace Conference in 1919 (cf. Shimazu 1998) added fuel to Japanese suspicions of continuing Western racism and discrimination. Sugita felt that Japan, acknowledged internationally since the Russo-Japanese War of 1904–1905 as a "first-rate power" (*ittōkoku*), was being humiliated by not being treated equally. The League for the Equality of Races (Jinshu Sabetsu Teppai Kiseikai, literally the Association for the Abolition of Racial

Discrimination) founded in 1919 (see I:10), which was strongly supported by Sugita (cf. Mizushima 1978: 128) and, as we will see here, was an expression of Japanese sensitivity to Western discrimination and offered a strong critique of Western visions of a future world order.

The starting point of the new wave of pan-Asian writings in the late 1910s and early 1920s was the publication of Kodera Kenkichi's voluminous work *A Treatise on Greater Asianism* (1916). This was the first comprehensive treatment and definition of "Asianism"—its meaning, content, and objectives. Before Kodera's book appeared, the term "Asianism" (or "Pan-Asianism," "Asianism," "All-Asianism," and so on) had not been used in journals; indeed, Kodera's was the first book to use the term "Asianism" in the title. Even the Kokuryūkai (the Amur Society; see I:10), which is generally regarded as a pioneering pan-Asian organization, started using the term "Asianism" only after the appearance of Kodera's book. The earliest instance of the use of the term by the Kokuryūkai can be traced to an article in *Ajia Jiron* (Asian Review) in 1917 (cf. Saaler 2007; see also I:10). After Kodera's book was published, however, there was a flood of articles on "Asianism" (*Ajiashugi*), "Pan-Asianism" (*Han-Ajiashugi*), and "All-Asianism" (*Zen-Ajiashugi*). Major journals carried articles on the subject. For example, *Shin Nippon* (New Japan) published Sawayanagi Masatarō's "Bunkateki Han-Ajiashugi o teishō su" (Advocating a Cultural Pan-Asianism) in March 1917 (Sawayanagi 1917), *Tōhō Jiron* (The Eastern Review) published Kita Reikichi's "Gokai saretaru Ajiashugi" (Misunderstood Asianism; Kita 1917a), and *Taiyō* (The Sun) published Uchida Rōan's "Gakujutsuteki Han-Ajiashugi" (Academic Pan-Asianism; Uchida 1917), Ukita Kazutami's "Shin Ajiashugi" (The New Asianism; Ukita 1918), and Horiuchi Bunjirō's "Dai Ajiashugi to waga kokumin no shimei" (Greater Asianism and the Mission of Our People; Horiuchi 1918). By 1919, when Sawayanagi's book *Ajiashugi* (Sawayanagi 1919a) went on sale, the term "Asianism" had entered the common vocabulary of the Japanese.

What principles do these writings stand for and why did pan-Asian discourse reach such a pitch of intensity after 1916? As the excerpts from Kodera's "Treatise on Greater Asianism" show, Japanese distrust of the West and resentment at Western discriminatory racial practices greatly increased in intensity during World War I. They were further reinforced following the rejection of the antiracial discrimination clause, which Japan, during the Paris Peace Conference of 1919, wanted included in the Charter of the League of Nations (cf. Shimazu 1998). The rejection of the Japanese proposal—despite a clear majority in support of it among the participating states at the conference—caused a powerful anti-Western (particularly anti-U.S.) backlash in Japan, with demonstrations held by political associations such as the

Kokuryūkai. One demonstrator even committed suicide on the doorstep of the American embassy in Tokyo in protest against U.S. policy.

In his article "Asianism" in *The Japan Magazine* (Sawayanagi 1919b; quoted here), Sawayanagi explicitly cites the opposition of Australian Prime Minister William M. "Billy" Hughes (1862–1952) to the nondiscrimination clause (Australia was one of the ringleaders of the opposition to the Japanese proposal) as one source of his Asianist views. As his article shows, Sawayanagi did not restrict the propagation of Asianism within Japan and in Japanese—he was also one of the first Japanese writers actively to propagate Asianism as a Japanese policy option in relation to the West. While Okakura Tenshin (see I:8) had earlier written on the necessity of a "pan-Asian" alliance, his writings addressed the people of India, not a Western audience (nor a Japanese one). As Suematsu Kenchō's speech of 1905 shows (see I:12), prior to World War I the Japanese government put much effort into dispelling Western fears of Japan as a potential leader of a pan-Asian league. Now the tide had turned, and in *The Japan Magazine*—a journal addressed to foreigners—Sawayanagi openly challenged Western readers with his proclamation of "a federation of all the races of Asia"—the realization of Asianism as a preparation for "a war between East and West." As an educationalist, Sawayanagi is generally considered an advocate of liberal Western educational practices, a promoter of educational humanism (i.e., of child-centered methods that nourished children's "individuality"), and an admirer of Pestalozzi. However, in the field of international relations, he was harshly critical of the West and, above all, of Western racism. This is hardly surprising. The question of racial discrimination against Japanese in the United States, as seen in its anti-immigration laws, had received much attention in Japan as early as 1907, and this racial exclusionism of the Western countries (including the British dominions) was one of the reasons for the growth of pan-Asian discourse following the Russo-Japanese War (cf. Saaler 2008a).

Sugita presents the case against racial discrimination even more clearly. He was one of the leaders and a guest speaker at the founding rally of the League for the Equality of Races mentioned previously. This rally was held in Tsukiji, Tokyo, in 1919 and was attended by representatives of many political organizations, including several pan-Asian societies. For example, Ōkawa Shūmei (see II:4) attended as a representative of the newly founded All Asian Society (Zen Ajiakai). Members of the Kokuryūkai and the Genyōsha were also present, and the Kokuryūkai's organ *Ajia Jiron* covered the rally in great detail. The League for the Equality of Races advocated the inclusion of the previously mentioned nondiscrimination clause in the charter of the League of Nations and opposed the idea of Japan joining the League of Nations if the nondiscrimination clause were rejected. Sugita's speech was originally given in Japanese but was later translated into English, distributed to foreigners, and also included in a book by Paul Richard (on Richard, see I:29) published in India. Sugita's opposition to a League of Nations *without* a racial equality clause was one reason why he argued for the necessity of Asian solidarity. In the journal *Toyō Bunka* (Oriental Culture) in 1924, Sugita renewed his plea for "Uniting Greater Asia" (*Dai Ajia Gasshōron*) and an "East Asian League" (*Tōa renmei*), emphasizing that he had "already advocated this idea 40 years ago." Clearly, Japanese public opinion on foreign policy was becoming increasingly concerned with a "clash of races" and the possibility of a future war with the West and was moving toward spearheading a pan-Asian alliance.

Source 1 (translation from the Japanese original by Sven Saaler)
Kodera Kenkichi (1916), *Dai Ajiashugiron* (Treatise on Greater Asianism). Hōbunkan, 1, 3–5; 9, 13, 226f, 270, 275–81.

FOREWORD

Isn't it strange? In Europe, which controls Asia at will and has completely subdued it, these days we are hearing voices that warn of a Yellow Peril (*kōkaron*). However, among the colored races, which are subjugated and intimidated by the White race, hardly a peep concerning the White Peril (*hakka*) can be heard. Yet while there can be no doubt that the Yellow Peril is simply a bad dream, the White Peril is a present reality . . .

The idea of racial unity is the main tendency in world politics. Pan-Americanism, Greater Britainism, the unification of the English-speaking nations, Pan-Slavism, Pan-Germanism and Pan-Romanism are all representative of this tendency. Blood is thicker than water. A powerful Pan-Mongolism is set to develop and this Pan-Mongolism will be an ideology of the union of the yellow race. Japanese-Chinese cooperation, the opening up of [China's] wealth of natural resources and the harnessing of the Chinese people will lead to a reconstruction and revival of China in a very short time. . . . The harmonization of Eastern and Western culture and the deepening of Yellow and White thought will be the common task of China, the origin of ancient culture; and if Japan, the pioneer of a new civilization, can profit from China economically, and China from Japanese leadership in political matters, they will reach their objectives and this will be the first step toward the creation of a Greater Asianism. The objectives of this Greater Asianism must be the enlightenment of Asia and the promotion of her happiness through a newly created, unified, harmonized and developed new civilization.

Greater Asianism is no narrow-minded racist mindset. No, racial prejudice is the mindset of the Westerners and is found particularly among the White race. Their offensive and insulting idea of a Yellow Peril is evidence of this. The discriminatory treatment [of Asians] in the New World puts this notion into practice. Thus, when we condemn the White Peril in order to preach Greater Asianism it is a completely different matter from Europeans disseminating propaganda about the Yellow Peril in order to promote a league of the Whites. The former [Greater Asianism] is defensive, passive, peaceful, while the latter is offensive, aggressive and all-conquering.

INTRODUCTION

[Japan] must save East Asia from the threat of the White race—this is our highest mission (*saikō shimei*). To achieve this, we must become the leader (*meishu*) of the Yellow race and guide [other nations], preserve the territorial integrity of China, and strengthen its people and culture. Following the politics of "same culture–same race" (*dōbun dōshu*) and that of an [intimate] relationship like the one between the lips and the teeth, we have to promote mutual trust and cooperation, resist [negative] developments in the world, and create a new, glorious Asian civilization (*idai naru Ajiateki shin bunmei o kensetsu*). . . . [We must] revive the whole of the Yellow race under this new ideology (*shugi*), attain political freedom and sovereignty, and unite the Yellow race all over the world. . . . The [kind of] Asianism I am preaching can be summarized in the slogan: "Asia is the Asia of the Asians." . . .

THE CHINA POLICY OF THE [WESTERN] POWERS AND JAPAN

While China and India are the cradle of Asian civilization, Japan is the place where Asian civilization is being preserved. Indian civilization has had a particularly strong impact on Japanese religion and the fine arts, while Chinese civilization has been a leading influence on Japan in all other areas, such as politics, law, literature, arts and society, and has had a profound impact on Japan, but Indian civilization has also been introduced into Japan by way of China. This complex web of interaction makes up the history of Japan and China over the last few millennia. These two nations of the same color and the same stock use the same letters, they share proverbs, moral concepts and many aspects of daily living, and are similar in so many other ways that we hardly need to enumerate them. Moreover, there is little need to mention their geographical proximity and the resulting intimate relationship that is as close as the lips and teeth. One can say that the Japanese state and the Chinese state are the twin sons of one and the same nation. In accordance with this special relationship, Japan has a special duty to promote peace in the Far East and to protect China—but it also has the right to claim a special position. . . . . .

THE MEANING OF GREATER ASIANISM

The future history of Greater Asianism will be divided into four stages. In the first stage, the Yellow race—the strongest country of Mongol ethnicity (*Mōko minzoku*), Japan, and the largest country, China—must be united (*tōitsu*) under the banner of Greater Asianism. In the second stage, independent nations of the same ethnicity must be included. In the third stage, those of the same [Mongol] ethnicity that are under the rule of a different race (*ijinshu*) will have to be integrated. In the fourth stage, Greater Asianism must be extended gradually to all the nations of Asia. . . .

The task of the unification of Japan and China under the banner of Greater Asianism is no longer at the stage of discussion, but is soon to be brought to the stage of implementation. . . . The unification of the two countries is a natural process based on the following foundations. . . . First, China can receive military protection from Japan, and Japan can rely on China for a profitable economic relationship. . . . Second, [China and Japan] are connected to each other by virtue of their belonging to the same race. . . . Third, while [China and Japan] do not share a common language, they do share the same script. As a consequence, fourth, they share a common history of literature and ideas. . . . Fifth, concerning the political system and, sixth, concerning the legal system and customs as well as the judiciary—while there have been important changes in Japan [in recent years], . . . the origins of the Japanese legal system and the canons, as well as the ancient administrative systems . . . up to the Tokugawa period, were direct translations from Chinese ordinances. . . . Seventh, while peoples of Mongol ethnicities in general are not as devoted to religion as Westerners, . . . in this respect Japanese and Chinese again share much in common, since Japanese Buddhism was imported through China and furthermore, Confucianism, which dictates the morals of the Chinese, has also come to form the basis of the morals of the Japanese.

Source 2 (English in the original)
Sawayanagi Masatarō (1919b), "Asianism." *The Japan Magazine*, August, 141–44.

Asianism, as the word suggests, is not quite the same as cosmopolitanism: it is not so broad; neither is it so narrow as nationalism. The European Peace Conference [Paris Peace Conference, 1919] discusses such big problems as the elimination of race prejudice, and the League of Nations, but Asianism is not so ambitious as to include this. It involves principles that refer to the races of Asia only. It does not, however, conflict in any way with cosmopolitanism or any of the principles of humanity; it is only a process searching for certain high ideals.

Nationalism is concerned mainly with the things that pertain to certain countries, and cosmopolitanism deals with what pertains to all countries, but between these two comes racialism; and true nationalism can be understood only as we understand racialism. There are various opinions as to the meaning and significance of race. The Japanese race, for instance, includes the Yamato, the Korean, the Ainu and the Formosan races, yet not all of these belong to the Yamato race. . . . Thus race may be used sometimes in a broader or narrower sense. In the same way it is quite consistent to speak of all Asiatics as a race. In the same way we speak of the European race or the African race. Though the Europeans are spoken of as a race there are many contradictions among them and they often make war on one another; yet they are sufficiently alike in blood, manners and customs and language to be called a race.

While the definition of race is thus left rather vague, that of nationality is rather clear; and many nations that can assert its independence and establish stable government is entitled to become a nation, however small. In the same way, the Japanese race is marked off by its possessions and territories and its frontiers are clearly defined. . . . As civilization advances cosmopolitanism takes greater hold upon the mind of man. The League of Nations is but one more example of this, and offers one of the biggest problems with which the human mind has had to deal. The same idea has been practised in a lesser way among various races and nationalities for a hundred years or more. We see it in international leagues, in the universal postal union, the Red Cross Society and the Churches to some extent. While races and nations are talking of the possibilities of the future, whether of peace or war, my mind runs toward racialism as the solution of the difficulty.

While thought may jump from one extreme to another, human activity can never afford to do so. Nations cannot change from extreme nationalism to extreme cosmopolitanism at a bound: they must pass first through a period of racialism. Asia has to go through its time of Asianism and Europe through its period of Europeanism, and perhaps America will finish with its Americanism too. All are trying to understand and to be understood. Misunderstanding is bad for trade and for the spirit too. That it does not cost us much thought is no sign of a condition to be proud of or satisfied with. There is even misunderstanding between the races of Asia, and this should give us profound concern and regret. Japan is of kindred race with China and India, and they are further united by religious and social bonds. Is it not very strange that we are trying to curry favour with western nations that have little in common with us? Not that we should be hostile to western nations but that we should be still more anxious to understand and know our neighbours of Asia. . . . While disapproving of the discrimination practised among western nations we must hasten to correct our own errors in this respect. No nation today is perfectly consistent in regard to equality of treatment among races. So long as there is undue distinction of classes there will be undue discrimination of races.

The spirit of democracy seems to be spreading over the entire world; but even in England and America, where the doctrine had birth and where it is most admired, is there any tendency to avoid extreme nationalism? This is clear from the proceedings of the [Paris] Peace Conference. The delegates of each nation are busy enforcing and maintaining their interests. It is obvious that great patriotism is not the monopoly of the Japanese. Among us democracy is also raising its voice and threatening to weaken our patriotism. But if my idea of racialism or Asianism were accepted and acted upon this untoward tendency would be corrected. . . . Our goal must be Asianism as the most important step on our way toward cosmopolitanism. Japan is the most advanced of all the countries of Asia, and she is conscious of her responsibility toward the rest of Asia. The peace of the Orient rests with Japan. She cannot be content to remain just as she is. Unless she is ready to pursue development still further in every branch of national activity she will not be able to realize her ideal of Asianism. . . . Western nations are naturally afraid of orientals. The opposition of Premier Hughes of Australia shows this. When the Kaiser invented the "yellow peril" bogey he unconsciously confessed western fear of Asia. This fear is a nightmare at the heart of western nations. If something is not done it may some day lead to a war between the East and the West; and the oriental people must be prepared for any such emergency. A federation of all the races of Asia will be the best way to do this: in other words, we must realize Asianism. . . .

Source 3 (English in the original)
Sugita Teiichi (1920), "Address on the occasion of the founding of the League for the Equality of Races, 1919." Paul Richard, *The Dawn over Asia*. Madras: Ganesh & Co. Publishers, 90–92.

At its first meeting, the League [for the Equality of Races] thus formed under the Presidency of M. Teiichi Sugita, Member and former president of the House of Peers [*sic*], addressed to the Peace Conference the following message:

Tokio, February 11th 1919.

The Allied Nations now assembled at the Peace Conference are endeavouring to establish a League of Nations and found the permanent peace of the world.

We Japanese, whole-heartedly approve of this effort, and anxiously await its realisation.

But seeing that the racial discriminatory treatment in international intercourse, which still exists, is against all principles of liberty and equality, and forms a constant root of conflict between peoples;

That so long as this remains unchanged, all peace conferences and agreements will be as a house built on the sand, and that no true peace can be hoped for;

We, representatives of thirty-seven large Japanese associations call upon the nations of the world to found a permanent peace on justice and humanity; and, to this end,

Declare:

The Japanese Nation expects of the Peace Conference the final abolition of all racial discrimination and disqualification.

. . .

The Japanese Nation is entirely opposed to any League of the Nations founded upon the maintenance of Racial Discriminatory Treatment.

. . .

THE JAPANESE NATION REFUSES TO JOIN A LEAGUE OF NATIONS FOUNDED UPON THE MAINTENANCE OF RACIAL DISCRIMINATORY TREATMENT.

Source 4 (translation from the Japanese original by Sven Saaler)
Sugita Teiichi (1924), "Dai Ajia Gasshōron" (An Argument for Uniting Greater Asia). *Tōyō Bunka* 8, 7–13.

It is said that history always repeats itself. Several thousand years ago, during the era of the warring states [in China; the author refers to the period from the fifth century to 221 BC], it was argued that six kingdoms should form an alliance (*gasshō*) through a network of the [ruling] houses in order to prevent the capture of the city of Liang [the later Kaifeng] by the despotic [state] Qin [Ch'in, 778–207 BC]. In the same way, when we look at the situation in the world today, our Great Asia (*waga Dai Ajia*) must by all means unite now against the excessive tyranny of the white people (*hakujin*), and begin to resist. It is absolutely necessary that we awake and confront the white man on a level playing field. Expressed in contemporary language, the unity (*gasshō*) of Great Asia is today sometimes called the East Asian League (*Tōa renmei*).

I argued fervently for this idea 40 years ago [a reference to Sugita's own pamphlet entitled *Kōasaku*] and although I did not succeed, I spared no effort to work for the realization [of such a league] and took every opportunity to devote my activities to this cause.

As I recall, in 1884, it was the two countries of Britain and Russia which were exhibiting the strongest ambitions towards our Great Asia. . . . India had perished, Burma had collapsed, the foundations of Siam and Annam were shaken, the lands of our divine country (*shinshū*, Japan), which were supposed to be spared, were being trampled on by barbarians from far away, and the descendants of the Lord of Zhou [also Chou, an ancient Chinese Kingdom, 1045–256 BC], Confucius [551–479 BC], Qiuming [a court writer and disciple of Confucius], and Sima Qian [Ssǔma Ch'ien, ca. 145–86 BC, founding father of Chinese history], were quick to obey the ways of the foreigners. This was a time of dawning, when the patriots were beginning to rise up. I was in prison at that time and could not repress my feelings. I wrote "A Policy for Raising Asia" (*Kōasaku*) and "A Policy for an Oriental League" (*Tōyō Rengōsaku*), appealing to the men of virtue (*shishi jinjin*) in this world. . . . At that time, there was no other way of saving the world (*tenka*) than the speedy formation of an alliance (*dōmei*) of Japan, Qing (Ch'ing) China and Korea.

In September 1884, as autumn advanced, the wind soon became colder. In our immediate western neighbor [China], the old Empire that is as close to us as the lips to the teeth, just as in our country people were advocating freedom and civil rights, awakening from their sleep and uniting with us in a desire to prevent the further advance of the West[ern powers] toward the East. The patriots Nakae Chōmin, Kurihara Katsuichi, Suehiro Tetchō, Sō Zōsei, Haseba Noritaka, Ueki Emori, Kobayashi Baio and others plotted with these [Chinese] patriots and in Shanghai founded the Oriental Academy (*Tōyō Gakkan*), determined to devote their efforts to raising up patriots in both countries. As a matter of fact, this was the pioneer of the academies run by Japanese in China. Unfortunately, however, due to financial problems, it had to be discontinued; but shortly after Arao Sei (see I:4) took up the good work and founded the Research Institute for Japan-Chinese Trade with the intention, again, of raising up patriots (*shishi*). And these patriots fulfilled our expectations—the strenuous efforts of the young patriots for the national cause during the Japanese-Chinese War [1894–1895] are well known in the whole world (*tenka*) and I need not speak of them further. The present Tōa Dōbun Shoin (see I:9) is the successor [this institute].

When I went to Shanghai, I had several surprises. But the most astonishing thing I saw happened one evening when I wanted to enter a city park, and noticed a sign at the entrance: "No Chinese Allowed." . . . The peoples (*sho-minzoku*) of Great Asia (*Dai Ajia*) need to wake up, the countries of Great

Asia must form a union (*renmei*)! Today, the Americans are those with the strongest racial consciousness and the strongest sense of the omnipotence of materialism. While they are proud of their modern civilization, only a century has passed since the founding of their nation and their national character (*kokuminsei*) is that of *nouveaux riches* (*narikin*); they reveal a kind of colonial spirit that has nothing refined about it at all. Moreover, they proudly make [contradictory] announcements to the whole world, such as "Racial equality only has currency among the white race." On the other side, the history of the brutal, cruel and inhuman treatment meted out to their black slaves is thick with blood, and for people easily moved to tears, it is outrageous. . . . While they often use economic arguments as pretexts for initiating anti-Japanese actions, these arguments are only shallow excuses and their real intention is racial exclusion. Therefore, we must once again advocate Oriental Freedom. When Sun Yat-sen stayed at my cottage last year, I told him my opinions and asked him about his. He agreed to my plan [for advocating Oriental Freedom]. If we continue only to imitate the West (*Ōbei*) and to bow before the Westerners, Oriental Freedom can never be expected to have the slightest impact—not ever. And there is even less chance of the time coming when we will be able to eliminate anti-Japanese and anti-Chinese [discrimination] from the Eastern hemisphere. This is the time when we must realize a Japanese-Chinese Federation. Both within Japan and China, undertakings involving China and undertakings involving Japan, [respectively] are being initiated, but this is not the time to use phrases like *tai-shi* and *tai-nichi*. Both peoples have their own form of patriotism and thus, if concepts like *tai-shi* [China policy] and *tai-nichi* [Japan policy] continue to be invoked, our efforts will end up being directed toward our own country and attention will be diverted from the wider international situation. . . .

Although I have not mentioned his name, there is a Frenchman [Paul Richard; see I:29] who came to our country when peace was restored, whom I met one evening. He said: "The League of Nations as advocated by Westerners is only a product of their egoism. There is absolutely no need to listen to this. Above all, you must unite Asia. To that end, your country [Japan] must become the core." This was more than just simple flattery. What was the destiny of the League of Nations being advocated by the Americans? The Americans have always demanded that Asians open their doors and guarantee equal opportunities, but have they not failed to do the same regarding their own country and have they not betrayed our Greater Asia many times? So, what open door are we talking about? What equality of opportunity? . . . One candidate for the presidency [of the United States] from the Democratic Party lists the expulsion of Asians as a policy objective in his manifesto. What an inconsistency, what a contradiction! And now the anti-Japanese spirit has spread to Australia and is at its zenith in Canada. When the Kaiser loudly warned of the Yellow Peril, England went ahead and concluded an alliance with our country—but now the clouds of anti-Japanism hang low over its territories. . . . In the West, it was France where the ideas of Freedom and Equality developed from an early time and [consequently] the concept of racism is weak there. Also, the Russians are simple people and generally have a weak grasp of abstract concepts. . . . Japan, once bound to China, must proceed and reestablish diplomatic relations with Russia. We cannot agree with the present political ideology of Russia; however, we do not need to fear it. We have to assess every ideology from the perspective of the 3000 years of the history of our country. If our people (*kokumin*) are prepared, nothing untoward will happen. We must also support the development of a virile (*gōken*) literature. The urgent need for the development of Chinese studies (*kangaku*) is obvious.

Gentlemen, although I see that there is no progress on the formation of [a federation in] Asia at present, we will not stumble and therefore there is no need to lament. [As a classical Chinese poem says]: "Even if a country is destroyed, mountains and rivers remain." The rise and fall [of nations], the establishment and destruction of governments are inevitable [historical] events. However, what kind of person was Confucius? What kind of person was Sakyamuni [Gautama Buddha]? What kind of person was Mohammad? What kind of person was Christ? Who was Temujin [Genghis Khan], who overran the whole of Europe [*sic*] on horseback and made the mountains and rivers of Europe tremble? They were Asians! While even Asia has now grown old, are not their bodies still connected to us by blood? The fathers of European civilization were all products of our Greater Asia. Worshipping one's ancestors is part of Oriental tradition. . . .

What must happen to restore Greater Asia? Recently, we have seen that some people are doing good work for Asians, such as that fine Turkish fellow Kemal Pasha [Mustafa Kemal Atatürk, 1881–1938, founder of the Republic of Turkey and its first president in 1923]. Not intimidated by the large forces of the Allied armies and with only five million souls at his disposal, whom he personally guided and encouraged, he put an end to fears and performed an immeasurable service for the colored race (*yūshoku jinshu*). At this point, I feel deeply that we must further nurture our strength. This being said, Asians must become fearless when confronting Europe; we, the so-called Orientals, are always gentle and amenable vis-à-vis Europeans and Americans—but why is this so? It is for one reason only: the Oriental countries have always pursued a foreign policy of subordination towards the Euro-American countries. They have no independent foreign policy. This is most particularly true in the case of our Great Japanese Empire. I cannot help but regret this deeply. For the present, Japan must do everything it can to ally itself with

China and Russia, restore diplomatic relations [with Soviet Russia], increase its national strength and be fully equipped for national defense. Although the Anglo-Japanese Alliance [1902] was originally concluded against the common foe Russia, the situation in the contemporary world has changed from those days. America is constantly trying to pressure Japan to retreat from the [Asian] continent. But should Japan abandon the continent, the outlook for Japan will be nothing other than self-destruction. America, which preaches that our country is invading [the Asian continent], hides its own brutality and aggression behind sugared words, and gives wings to its own greed. While France has reduced the size of its reserve fleet, just look at the conduct of the British in Singapore and the behavior of America in Hawaii!

We are hurting: the great achievements of our former Emperor [Meiji] are about to fall out of favor, the great leaders of the Restoration are all leaving this world and the people's minds are empty. We, at the Oriental Culture Academy, must seriously consider these points, and my wish is that we will become the leaders of our generation and continue this great fight.

Chapter Twenty-Seven

Kita Ikki: "An Unofficial History of the Chinese Revolution," 1915, and "The Outline of a Plan for the Reconstruction of Japan," 1919

Christopher W. A. Szpilman

Kita Ikki (1883–1937), most historians agree, advocated the liberation of Asia from the yoke of Western imperialism and the formation of Asian states based on authentic (if undefined) Asian principles. He kept company with prominent pan-Asianists such as Miyazaki Tōten (1871–1922), Uchida Ryōhei (1874–1937), Ōkawa Shūmei (1883–1957) and Mitsukawa Kametarō (1888–1936; see II:2 and II:4). He took part in the Chinese Revolution of 1911–1912, which he hoped would replace the corrupt Qing (Ch'ing) regime with an Asian republic capable of resisting the encroachments of the West. For these reasons, Kita is recognized as a pan-Asianist. Yet, although Pan-Asianism forms an integral part of his image, Kita never tackled Pan-Asianism head-on: it is difficult to find a passage in his works that states his pan-Asian views. That was perhaps because he had concluded by 1919 that a sweeping totalitarian reform of Japan was a sine qua non for the liberation of Asia. Thus, his writing focused on this urgent task to the neglect of almost everything else.

The difficulty of writing about Kita's Pan-Asianism is compounded by the fact that for Kita and many other Japanese pan-Asianists, their pan-Asian visions often shaded into a more ambitious, if completely unrealistic, idea of the unification of the whole world under the leadership of the Japanese Empire. Such views often were colored by their religious persuasion. Thus Kita, under the spell of the Lotus Sutra, talked of a worldwide Buddhist federation (Kita 1959: 220), while some other pan-Asianists, influenced by fundamentalist Shintō doctrines, dreamed of the emperorization of the world (*sekai kōka*; Szpilman 2007: 98–99).

Kita Ikki (Terujirō; he adopted the name Ikki in 1915) was born in 1883 into a family of impoverished notables on the island of Sado, Niigata Prefecture. As a young man he moved to Tokyo, where he worked on a book titled

Kokutairon oyobi Junseishakaishugi (The Theory of National Polity and Pure Socialism), which, when privately published in 1906, caused a minor sensation before it was banned by the authorities.

At that time Kita, it would appear, was not preoccupied with Pan-Asianism, for his work pays no attention to it. Subsequently, however, Kita developed an interest in Asia. Seeking the company of like-minded men, he befriended Chinese students in the Chinese Revolutionary League (Tongmenghui or T'ung-meng-hui; Japanese: Chūgoku Dōmeikai) and their Japanese sympathizers at the Kakumei Hyōronsha (Revolutionary Review Society). Among the former was the future revolutionary leader Song Jiao-ren (Japanese: Sō Kyōjin, 1882–1913); the latter included Miyazaki Tōten (Torazō; see I:11). Through Miyazaki, Kita got to know Uchida Ryōhei, the leader of the Kokuryūkai (see I:10), who employed Kita as an editor for the society's publications.

When the Chinese Xinhai Revolution erupted in late 1911, Kita went to China as an observer for the Kokuryūkai. What he experienced in China inspired him in 1915 to write *Shina Kakumei Gaishi* (An Unofficial History of the Chinese Revolution), which circulated in stencil before finally appearing in print in 1921. Kita remained in Shanghai (except for a brief interlude in Tokyo) until the end of 1919. It was there that Kita wrote his celebrated *Kokka Kaizō Hōan Genri Daikō* (Outline of a Plan for the Reconstruction of Japan), in which he argued for a sweeping reform of the Japanese state on totalitarian lines. The unstated premise of the outline was that only such sweeping reforms would pave the way for the liberation of Asia.

In January 1920, Kita returned to Tokyo on invitation by Mitsukawa Kametarō and Ōkawa Shūmei (see II:4), who a few months earlier had formed the pan-Asianist association Yūzonsha (see II:2). Kita, they had hoped, would provide intellectual direction for the new organization. To some extent, they were not disappointed. Kita's *Kokka Kaizō Hōan Genri Daikō* exerted strong influence on Ōkawa and Mitsukawa, on other members of the Yūzonsha, and on Japan's radical right wing in general. And it was perhaps due to Kita's influence that the Yūzonsha assigned primacy to domestic reform over the realization of pan-Asian ideals. But Kita in general kept aloof from the activities of the organization. This was partly because he was too much of an individualist but chiefly because his primary passion was now religion, not politics. Since 1915 he had been in the thrall of Nichiren Buddhism or, more accurately, of the Lotus Sutra, and the religious practices in which he immersed himself took up more and more of his time. A personality clash between Kita and Ōkawa, who quickly realized they could not get on with each other, did not help. Soon the two quarreled openly, and by 1923 the Yūzonsha had disintegrated. After this fiasco Kita never joined another political organization.

He continued to dabble in political intrigues as a free agent, writing scurrilous political pamphlets—none of them pan-Asian in content—for financial gain. These pamphlets almost certainly reflected the views of those who commissioned them, but Kita probably believed most of what he wrote.

In the 1920s Kita formed a friendship with Nishida Mitsugi (1901–1937), an army lieutenant on the reserve list and a fellow worshipper of the Lotus Sutra. Nishida had extensive contacts among junior active duty army officers, and it was through Nishida that Kita is said to have exercised his charisma on the young officers. Some were impressed, but many others remained suspicious. It is nevertheless true that in the early 1930s some young army officers paid frequent visits to Kita's residence. When informed of their plans to stage a military coup, Kita tried to dissuade them but to no avail. The young officers rebelled in what is known as the February 26 Incident of 1936. They achieved nothing apart from the murder of a number of important political figures and surrendered after three days. Even before the coup was over, Kita was arrested. He was charged with leading the rebellion, and, after a court-martial, sentenced to death. He was executed, together with Nishida, in August 1937.

The problem with placing Kita as a pan-Asianist is that, in contrast to his erstwhile comrades Ōkawa, who wrote *Fukkō Ajia no Shomondai* (Various Questions concerning Revived Asia) in 1922, and Mitsukawa, who published *Ubawaretaru Ajia* (Stolen Asia) in 1921, he produced no work specifically dedicated to Pan-Asianism. His first book, *Kokutairon oyobi Junseishakai-shugi*, is a socialist tract with strong nationalist undertones. *Shina Kakumei Gaishi*, his second work, was a highly subjective account of the Chinese Revolution. As such, it was not strictly speaking a study of Pan-Asianism, either. His third and final work, *Kokka Kaizōan Genri Daikō* (1919), was a totalitarian tract whose theme was reform of Japan, not the propagation of Pan-Asianism. With its glorification of dictatorship and control economy, *Kokka Kaizōan Genri Daikō* gave rise to Kita's reputation as a Japanese fascist. It is doubtful whether Kita was a fascist, but he certainly was a nationalist. Yet though he never makes it explicit, it must not be overlooked that Kita's nationalism came in tandem with strong pan-Asian convictions. Kita's underlying assumptions were pan-Asian, and it seems certain that pan-Asian ideals (fused inseparably with dreams of a Greater Japan) were after 1907 always at the heart of Kita's concerns. They motivated him and inspired him to write; they impelled him to go to China and to participate in the Chinese Revolution. They lay at the core of his plans for a reorganization of Japan, for, in Kita's view, the realization of Japan's divine mission to liberate Asia was premised on the implementation of drastic domestic reforms. Only such reforms, he insisted, would make Japan strong enough to accomplish the mission. This insistence on complete and thoroughgoing reform of the Japanese state and society is the lesson Kita drew from World War I.

But even in *Shina Kakumei Gaishi*, which had been written in 1915–1916—that is, before the lessons of World War I, such as planned economy and total mobilization of society, fully sank in—Kita made a tacit assumption that domestic reform within Japan must precede Asian liberation. For, though he focused on the Chinese Revolution, he dedicated much space to criticizing Japan's foreign policy, which was shaped ultimately by domestic considerations. Reform these, Kita implied, and Japan's China policy would change for the better.

In the final analysis, Kita's Pan-Asianism was cultural. Though he did not oppose technological westernization, he rejected a cultural, ethical, political westernization of China and Japan. He was a proponent of "authentic" East Asian values that must be protected and from which neither Japan nor China should deviate, though unfortunately he failed to explain what these common Asian values were.

Kita, like many other Japanese pan-Asianists and conservatives, believed that Western ideas, before they could be accepted in Asia, must first be assimilated. According to Kita, Japan played and would continue to play an important role in this process of assimilation. Specifically, Japan would "fuse Eastern and Western civilizations" and then "enlighten modern peoples with low-level civilizations by means of Japanized and globalized Asian thought." This "renaissance," Kita predicted, would take place only "after a great war" that, he believed, was bound to break out sometime in the near future.

In his writings, Kita frequently resorted to analogies that were instantly comprehensible and no doubt highly stimulating to the Japanese reader but may be puzzling to the twenty-first-century Western reader. As this is also the case in the texts translated here, some explanation is in order. Kita, for example, refers to Japan as the Greece of Asia. Russia accordingly is cast in the role of "Persia," and the Battle off Tsushima (1905) becomes the Battle of Salamis, a turning point in ancient history when the naval forces of Greece destroyed the Persian fleet.

Alternatively, he refers to Japan as the Britain of East Asia. Parallels here are obvious: an island nation, a naval power, and colonization of neighboring nations (Ireland and Korea). In another striking mixture of metaphors Kita wrote that "the question of Indian independence will become the Sarajevo of the Second World War." When India took up arms against its colonial master, Japan would have to come to its assistance by offering naval support just as France had done when the American colonies rebelled against Britain. Without Japan's help, Indian efforts to gain independence were bound to fail as they had during World War I, when Japan behaved like Britain's "faithful servant" (Kita 1919: 274).

This method of explaining contemporary events in light of historical antecedents, stimulating though it can be, is, of course, grossly misleading. For, while undeniably there are some parallels between various historical situations, there are also many decisive differences, and this precludes drawing any valid inferences. Be it as it may, the limits of Kita's Pan-Asianism are apparent here, for Kita seems more indignant over Japan's alleged subservience to Britain than concerned with Asian liberation as such. So, it would be fair to say that in Kita's thought, Pan-Asianism was always subordinate to Japanese empire building. Japan after all was, as Kita noted, an "ambitious state" that was striving to become the "Germany of the East" (*Tōyō no Doitsu*; Kita 1919: 275). For those reasons Kita considered it "Japan's positive right" to occupy "Far Eastern Siberia" (this move, he claimed somewhat self-servingly, would protect China from Russian encroachments), and he entertained grandiose dreams of territorial expansion that also included Australia, whose annexation he hoped would solve Japan's population problem. Regardless of whether the motives were pan-Asian or imperialist, Kita was convinced that Japan's territorial expansion, "this great and unprecedented historic mission, would only be accomplished as the result of a cataclysmic war soon to erupt" (Kita 1919: 275–79).

As the passages translated here indicate, Kita represents a transition, albeit a tenuous one, between the idealistic Pan-Asianism of men like Miyazaki Tōten and the later Pan-Asianism that culminated in the Greater Asia Co-Prosperity Sphere that served as window dressing for Japan's aggression.

Source 1 (translation from the Japanese original by Christopher W. A. Szpilman)
Kita Ikki (1921 [1915]), *Shina Kakumei Gaishi* (An Unofficial History of the Chinese Revolution), Daitōtaku. Reprinted in Kita Ikki (1959), *Kita Ikki Chosakushū* (Collected Works by Kita Ikki), vol. 2. Misuzu Shobō, 115–16.

When explaining the causes of the collapse of the Tokugawa shogunate, Katsu Kaishū once said that it was not the Satsuma and Chōshū domains that had toppled the shogunate; the shogunate had collapsed of its own accord from within due to financial bankruptcy. His words can also be applied to describe the last days of Qing rule [in China] and the last days of the French monarchy.

The national revolution [in China] occurred because the finances of the Qing dynasty had collapsed.

It is not the case, as China experts think, that the finances collapsed because of the revolutionary turmoil. Their thinking is worthless as it confuses cause with effect just as if one were to claim that a flood, which occurs due to torrential rains, causes torrential rains to fall. Bankruptcy is not a matter to take place in the future. It is an accomplished fact in the present. Nor does it represent the kind of peripheral confusion that can be fixed by stopgap measures such as injection of foreign loans and foreign supervision. The only desirable thing is to smash the entire rotten structure and establish a new system nurtured by the revolutionary spirit, in other words, the only means is a revolution of the financial structure itself. Readers! How the French Revolution of the East [Chinese Revolution] proceeds from now on toward this destruction and construction, moreover how the Britain of the East [Japan] acts, will determine the fate of both Japan and China.

If we make one wrong step, I, like you, my readers, will have no option but to face the judgment of history.

In her relations with China in revolutionary chaos, Japan is a country that can forget her old grudges unlike Britain and France that cannot. Japan is not engaged in a contest over colonies as was the case when France prevented Britain from occupying North America and when Britain prevented France from occupying Egypt. So I really am struck speechless when I hear that Japan has on its own initiative joined the loan consortium of the Great Powers, whose purpose is to partition and destroy China. Will you also tell me that the preservation of the territorial integrity of China is too heavy a burden for Japan to bear? Will you tell me that the numerous difficult choices that Japan has to make in order to become Asia's Messiah (*Ajia no kyūshu*) are no longer being pursued; that Japan wants to take the easy option of becoming a running dog of the whites? Geographically speaking, Japan is the Britain of the East. Moreover as regards Japan's historical significance as the transmitter of Eastern and Western civilizations, Japan is the Greece of Asia. This Greece has already thwarted the aggression of powerful Russian Persia at the battle of Salamis that took place in the Sea of Japan. Ah, it is crystal-clear that the rising sun that shines over the Eastern Seas announces to us our divine mission. I can however categorically state that, regardless of the extent of revolutionary awareness in China, and taking into consideration the fact that Japan stands at a crossroads of its own diplomatic revolution, there is no point talking of the general situation in East Asia unless we realize that a great and unprecedented historic mission lies ahead.

Source 2 (translation from the Japanese original by Christopher W. A. Szpilman)

Kita Ikki (1919), *Kokka Kaizōan Genri Daikō* (Outline of a Plan for the Reconstruction of Japan), Yūzonsha. Reprinted in Kita Ikki (1959) *Kita Ikki Chosakushū*, vol. 2. Misuzu Shobō, 220 and 280–81.

The 700 million of our brothers in China and India have in fact no other means of achieving independence than with our guidance and protection. The population of our Japan, which has doubled over the last fifty years, will reach at least 250 million in a hundred years' time. This population increase will necessitate [the acquisition of] a large territory to support it. One hundred years in the existence of a state is equivalent to one hundred days in a man's life. How can those who worry about this inevitable prospect and deplore the miserable predicament of the neighboring nations be satisfied with the effeminate pacifism of socialists, whose views have been translated word for word from Western languages? I am not denying social evolution through class struggle. But how can one claim to be scientific while ignoring struggles between nations and between states that have been raging ever since the beginning of human history? All authorities on the Western kind of revolution without exception base their theories on this shallow and superficial philosophy and when in the end they cannot grasp the gospel of the sword, as soon as the Greece of lofty Asian civilization [Japan] completes state reconstruction based on its own spirit and raises the righteous flag of an Asian League, it will assume the leadership of a true world league that must come, and in this way, extending its limits eastward and westward, spread the heavenly way under which all men in the world are brothers as Buddha's children. The views of those who oppose military preparations by the [Japanese] state are in the final analysis childish.

. . .

The only question that the entire world confronts right now is which state, which nation is to become the Tokugawa Shōgun or the Holy Emperor [who rules the world]. The Japanese people . . . must internationally revive the supreme right to rule and await the advent of the highest state that would rule over other states. The Japanese people must face the imminent historically unprecedented national adversity by reforms of the political and economic structure of the state based on this Outline of Principles for National Reconstruction. Japan, the Greece of Asian civilization, has already destroyed mighty Russia, the Persia [of Europe], at the battle of "Salamis." The awakening of 700 million Chinese and Indians began precisely at that moment. Peace without war is not the way of heaven.

Chapter Twenty-Eight

Tokutomi Sohō and the "Asiatic Monroe Doctrine," 1917

Alistair Swale

Journalist, critic and historian Tokutomi Iichirō (better known under his pen name Sohō, 1863–1957) was born in Kumamoto to a farmer-samurai family (on Tokutomi's life, see Pierson 1980; Swale 2003). After studying at the Kumamoto School of Western Studies, he entered Dōshisha Academy for English studies in Kyoto but dropped out before graduation. Having become famous as the author of *Shōrai no Nihon* (The Future Japan, 1886), he moved to Tokyo and founded a political organization called the Minyūsha (Society of the People's Friends). Subsequently, he founded and edited the daily *Kokumin no Tomo* (The Nation's Friend, 1888–1898) and, after 1890, *Kokumin Shinbun* (The Nation Newspaper) and acquired a reputation as an outspoken advocate of popular rights (Ariyama 1992).

Tokutomi was so shocked by the Triple Intervention of 1895 that, as he confessed in his autobiography, he "became a different person intellectually" and turned into an apologist for state power. He now drew increasingly closer to the ruling elites and began actively to participate in politics. In 1911 he was appointed a member of the House of Peers. Tokutomi's ties to the government provided him with access to information and ensured a largely positive reception for his newspaper as an outlet for patriotic content especially after the Russo-Japanese War of 1904–1905 (Wada 1990: 229–46). As the Hibiya Riots that occurred after that war show, the peace treaty that Japan signed with Russia in 1905 was unpopular, and Tokutomi, who was identified with the government, saw his newspapers attacked by protesters. In reaction, Tokutomi sought to regain his popularity by finding a new cause—the threat posed by China and finding a solution to various issues concerning the Korean peninsula. To this end, he became involved in the expansionist Tōyō Kyōkai (Association of the East) in 1907. Following the formation of the second Katsura Cabinet in 1908 he redoubled his efforts in support of the government. He participated in the exhibition of "Meiji heroes" presented at Ueno Park in 1910, and following the annexation of Korea he launched the *Seoul Daily*.

Over the next thirty years Tokutomi continued as a leading figure of Japanese journalism, producing numerous best-sellers, such as *Taishō no Seinen to Teikoku no Shōrai* (The Youth of the Taishō Era and the Future of the Empire), as well as solid works of historical research, including the authorized multivolumed biographies of influential politicians such as Prince Katsura Tarō (1847–1913; *Kōshaku Katsura Tarō Den*, 1917) and Prince Yamagata Aritomo (1838–1922; *Kōshaku Yamagata Aritomo Den*, 1933).

During World War II, Tokutomi played a central role in the process of "spiritual mobilization" of public opinion for the war effort. In 1942, he became chairman of the Nihon Bungaku Hōkokukai (Patriotic Association for Japanese Literature; see Sakuramoto 1995) and the Dai Nihon Genron Hōkokukai (Great Japan Patriotic Writers Association). After the war, he was arrested as a class A war criminal and purged from public office, but he continued to write and in 1952 completed a monumental 100-volume *Kinsei Nihon Kokuminshi* (A History of the Japanese People in Early Modern Japan; Wada 1990: 7–13), the first volume of which had appeared in 1924.

The texts reproduced here, published in 1913 and 1917, are an expression of a growing self-confidence of Japan in the international arena. Tokutomi, by the time of World War I, had become an advocate of some form of East Asian regionalism premised on Japanese leadership in East Asia and a proponent of strong Japanese policy toward the Western powers. The texts call for the realization of an "Asiatic Monroe Doctrine," which held that non-Asian powers must not interfere in Asian affairs and that the East Asian region must be eventually unified under Japanese leadership (Nakamura 1991). They also express Tokutomi's views on Japan's "options" for imperial expansion onto the continent and out into the Pacific, along with a critical summary of the foreign policies of the nations that such expansion would affect (Wada 1990: 96–104).

"An Opinion on Current Issues" (1913) is particularly instructive in that it is a reflection of Tokutomi's thinking at a stage when he had become part of the political elite and held official posts. Two preoccupations emerge distinctly: one with the transformation of Japan into a great power and the other concerning the refining of a distinctive analysis of international relations based on a global balance of power and race. Drawing to some extent on the social Darwinist logic of connecting psychological traits of "national character" to natural environment, he argued for the modification of the Japanese people's insular outlook; the corollary of attempting this was in fact the development of a continental base not only in the sense of expanding the realm but also in order to obtain a physical environment capable of transforming the Japanese character. Such an expansion would naturally upset the balance of power in the region by challenging the European powers whose interests were ever expanding on the continent. This necessitated a new diplomatic line that would exclude Western interests but enable Japan to maintain an independent initiative: this is what provided the impetus behind developing an Asian Monroe Doctrine (Umetsu 2006: 16–31; Ariyama 1992: 62–67). Tokutomi was increasingly regional in his conception of the dynamics of international relations. However, his conclusions were pulling him away from his initial ideas of liberal internationalism. Tokutomi's view of Japan's relations with the Greater Asian region stemmed from social Darwinist musings about the relative vigour of the Western Great Powers and the series of plausible options available to the Far East's only state capable of standing up to them—Japan. "An Opinion on Current Issues" is replete with references to a balancing of the relative status of "white" and "yellow" races, and indeed it is clear that Tokutomi found it difficult to discuss relative international power without reference to the issue of race.

The evocation of the Asian Monroe Doctrine, a doctrine that Tokutomi had propounded since the mid-1910s (Yonehara 2003), was a highly adroit gambit to articulate a Japanocentric view of Asian affairs while maintaining the semblance of a parallel with a contemporary diplomatic line of thought. Tokutomi's version of the doctrine, as illustrated in the following excerpts, was not animated by a positive view of how Monroeism had played out hitherto. Indeed, in his "Opinion," Tokutomi highlighted the manner in which the original *American* Monroe Doctrine had become a cover for a particularly capricious brand of self-serving diplomacy. Nonetheless, he remained confident that Japan could construct an Asian Monroe Doctrine without hypocrisy.

Tokutomi subscribed to the notion that Japan must earn the respect of fellow Asians if it were to have any chance of fulfilling its manifest duty to defend the East from Western encroachment. However, this was countered by his pessimistic view of the capacity of any other major Eastern national entity, particularly China, to thwart Western ambitions. Tokutomi was inclined to view China as about to collapse, and the power vacuum would be filled by the Western powers or the Japanese. Tokutomi strongly believed that it was "best" for Japan to be prepared to fill that void. This, as "Japan's Mighty Mission" demonstrates, in Tokutomi's view, could be achieved only by establishing an Asiatic Monroe Doctrine. The timing was perfect since, after the outbreak of World War I, the Western powers were entangled in European affairs, producing a power vacuum in East Asia. However, sooner or later the Western powers were bound to return, making a clash between the West and Japan inevitable. In this way, Tokutomi's insistence on Japan as the leader of

Asia contributed to the deterioration of relations between the Western powers and Japan, becoming eventually a self-fulfilling prophecy.

After a period of abeyance in the 1920s, Tokutomi's Asiatic Monroe Doctrine acquired a new lease of life in the early 1930s when it was used to legitimize both the Japanese annexation of Manchuria and the foundation of the puppet state of Manchukuo (Takaki 1932; *New York Times*, 20 July 1933). The 1934 statement by the Foreign Ministry's Amau Eiji (1887–1968), which insisted that Western powers refrain from meddling in China, was generally interpreted by Western (as well as Chinese) observers as an expression of this resurgence of the Asiatic Monroe Doctrine (e.g., Hugh Byas's article in the *New York Times*, 26 August 1934; Wang 1934). Although the Amau statement was subsequently revised, this version of the doctrine soon became a quasi-official foreign policy of Japan (cf. Kamikawa 1939). This fact reflected an increasing popularity of pan-Asian sentiments in the Japan of the 1930s.

Source 1 (English in the original)
Tokutomi Iichirō, "Japan's Mighty Mission," in Taraknath Das, *Is Japan a Menace to Asia?* Shanghai: no publisher, 1917, 153–59.

The Japan Chronicle of January 19, 1917, published the following article as a translation of a portion of Mr. Tokutomi's recent work "The Rising Generation in the Taisho Era and the Future of the Japanese Empire," which is one of the most popular publications issued in Japan of recent years. The distinguished author is an ardent advocate of the policy known as "Asiatic Monroe Doctrine."

Japan's Mighty Mission
By
Hon. Mr. Iichiro Tokutomi
The Chief Editor and Proprietor of the Kokumin Shinbun, Crown Member of the House of Peers of Japan, etc.

. . .

What . . . is the mission of the Japanese Empire? In my opinion, it is of more urgent importance for Japan to try to restore the equilibrium between the White and Yellow races than to indulge in the chimerical theory of accomplishing the unification of the world, as is preached by some irresponsible Japanese. . . .

By the Asiatic Monroe Doctrine we mean the principle that Asiatic affairs should be dealt with by the Asiatics. As, however, there is no Asiatic nation except the Japanese capable of under taking these duties, the Asiatic Monroe Doctrine is virtually the principle of the Japanese dealing with Asiatic affairs.

There must be no misunderstanding as to the meaning of this doctrine. We do not hold so narrow-minded a view as to wish to attempt to drive the Whites out of Asia. What we want is simply that we become independent of the Whites, or Yellows free of the rampancy of the Whites. . . .

The not essential point that the Japanese people should bear in mind in carrying out the Asiatic Monroe Doctrine is that they must first win the respect and affection of the Eastern races and the deference of the Whites. The Asian Monroe doctrine is the principle of Eastern autonomy, that is, of Orientals dealing with Eastern questions. . . .

We are ready to leave the Europeans to attend to European affairs, and the Americans to American questions, but we demand that they should leave Orientals to attend to their own questions, just as we, Eastern peoples, do not interfere with their affairs. However earnestly they may preach the principle of universal brotherhood, the theory of the Whites, who regard not their property but other people's property as their own, is scarcely tenable before the impartial judgement of the Almighty. . . .

The mighty object of the [Meiji] Restoration was to place Japan on a par with the Great Powers. In other words, it consisted in safeguarding the independence of this country. The question of today is not the independence of the Japanese Empire but her expansion. This leads to the birth of the Eastern autonomy theory. Now that the national rights of this country are recovered, it is incumbent upon the Yamato race to try to recover for the weaker nations of the East their rights, which have been trampled underfoot by other powers.

If once Japan attains these objects, we must refrain from abusing our influence to bring pressure to bear on the Whites, but we must exert ourselves to break down the racial and religious prejudices to which the Whites are wedded, and show the world that the civilizations of the East and the West are reconcilable, that the White and the Yellow races are by no means natural enemies to each other, and that if they join hands on an equal plane, the ideal of universal brotherhood is not necessarily impossible to realise. . . .

Source 2 (translation from the Japanese original by Alistair Swale) Tokutomi Sohō, "Jimu Ikkagen" (An Opinion on Current Issues), reproduced in Tokutomi Sohō (1974), *Meiji Bungaku Zenshū* (Complete Collection of Meiji Literature) vol. 34, Chikuma Shobō, 301–14.

In the current tide of world trends I believe that there is no other case as exceptional in its significance as [the emergence of] the United States. And if George Washington himself were alive to see events as they now stand he would certainly feel that he had fallen from outer space onto a completely different planet. It was Washington who argued forcefully in print that America ought to be a nation remaining the total master of its own fate, presenting a threat to no other nation and in turn being threatened by no other nation. But what do we see today? We see that America, though already one of the great powers of the world, exercises that power almost as if it were in constant danger of being interfered with. While denying the right of others to "interfere" as a matter of course, it takes it upon itself to strut around in the world and undertake to solve all manner of problems.

I would like to attempt here an exposition of the so-called "Monroe Doctrine," although I acknowledge that definitions of the term have become more diverse and expanded over time. As the "Holy Alliance" [coalition initiated in 1815 by Russia, Austria, and Prussia that eventually included most European powers], more specifically Spain, attempted to restore its claim over territories in the New World, the then United States President [James] Monroe [1817–1825], stated that he regarded such a move as a pretext for interfering with the affairs of North America. It was at this point that he declared that the United States could not condone the colonizing activities of the European powers. In essence it was simply an embellishment of the sentiments earlier expressed by Washington.

However, by the time of President [Ulysses S.] Grant [1869–1877], the doctrine's meaning developed somewhat and came to signify something that was completely non-negotiable between the United States and Europe. Under [Grover] Cleveland [1885–1889 and 1893–1897] the implications of this [doctrine] were pursued more forcefully so that a clean break was declared with the powers of Europe and it was asserted that the sole right of adjudication in diplomatic affairs in the Americas lay solely with the United States. It almost precipitated a war with Britain. As it turned out, this war never happened as the British government backed down, but the result was that through this notion of the Monroe Doctrine, United States hegemony became almost complete throughout the Americas. And we do not know for sure what new "interpretations" of the doctrine might emerge from now on. . . .

The foreign policy of the United States today is the distillation of an utterly simplistic conception of the Monroe Doctrine. Problems are treated as being of concern to the United States even in matters that are in no way connected directly to it, with no external meddling permitted. It is as if the [Americans'] aim is not just to have control over their own country but to take the entire North American continent (Canada being in some ways separate) and exclude all other influences. Even in the case of Mexico they act as if it were their own.

It seems that, while outwardly projecting an image of promoting an open door policy, America is determined to follow the implications of the doctrine regardless of whether there is a special connection to that country or not. There is not much more that needs to be said about this, and it should suffice to raise the example of [U.S. Secretary of State Philander C.] Knox's memorandum on the "neutrality" of the Manchurian Railway [1909]. The world is now fully aware of what this means in terms of what I have described as America's misconceived foreign policy of no self-restraint. Even so, it must have come as something of a tremendous shock. But at least we can take some solace out of the fact that America's power, though substantial, does not exactly extend to the interior of Manchuria. It is the classic case of the rider whose whip is too long to use even on his own horse!

35: ADVANCE TO THE NORTH, ADVANCE TO THE SOUTH

How will China develop from now on? And what are we supposed to do about China? These are weighty questions that are far too difficult to deal with in just a few sentences. In any event, given that China is a neighboring country and a font of civilization that has had an enormous impact on the shape of our own nation, we are particularly obliged to maintain a view on China's position in relation to ourselves. It is this that I regard as being one of the primary reasons that we should continue to attach importance to the Manchurian Railway.

One of the primary justifications offered during the Triple Intervention which sought the retrocession of the Liaodung (Liaotung) Peninsula to China [1895] was that it [the Japanese annexation of this territory] would present an immediate threat to Peking and thereby undermine the independence of China. What of course happened is that no sooner had we returned that territory to China but the Russians came in and attempted to take control of the area for themselves. There is a great deal that we ought to learn from the facts of this matter. As it applied to Peking then so does it apply to our position in Manchuria now. Indeed not only Manchuria but even in relation to Mongolia as well. . . .

It is precisely with a view to securing the integrity of Chinese territory that we need to undertake the administration of Manchuria and Mongolia. And if it comes to the situation that the powers proceed to carve up that territory by force we need to be in Manchuria and Mongolia to ensure that we are amongst the lions to get our share. . . .

All going well, we will be able to promote the transplanting of our people and our economic development through Manchuria and Mongolia. If things do go amiss in China, we will most likely find that Chinese society will collapse much like a building with a high roof weighed down with tiles; that will give us an avenue to expand to the south. We should not be thinking of further ways in which to empower ourselves at present as we already have control over China by virtue of the current treaty port arrangement at Fujian [Fukien or Fu-chien], much as control over the thigh gives one control over the entire body. Success in this regard is little more than a repetition of the exploits of Koxinga [1624–1662, de facto ruler of Taiwan between 1661 and 1662] at the end of the Ming [1368–1644] and the beginning of the Qing [Ch'ing, 1644–1911] period.

This is a summary of the arguments in favor of moving into Manchuria and Mongolia: first, offensive defense; second, the formation of a continental empire for the Yamato people; third, moving into China; and fourth, there is the prospect that the vast skies and plains of the continent will cultivate a greater courage and nobility of character in our people. The biting winds and severe cold will nurture an indomitable spirit. It will constitute a great training ground for the people of a great nation, and we should recognize it as appropriate for us.

Chapter Twenty-Nine

Paul Richard: *To Japan,* 1917, and *The Dawn over Asia,* 1920

Christopher W. A. Szpilman

Dr. Paul Richard (1874–1967), a philosopher and an author of aphoristic books, lived in Japan for only four years. Though he neither spoke nor read Japanese, he exerted an indelible influence on Japanese Pan-Asianism.

Richard was born in the south of France in 1873. Raised strictly by his Protestant minister father, Richard at first pursued a military career. For some time he served in Tunisia as a cavalryman but decided it was not to his liking. After he was discharged, he decided to be a priest. He enrolled as a seminarian at the University of Toulouse but found the study of the "long and turgid history of Christianity" boring. Nevertheless, he completed his studies and duly became a Protestant minister. But bizarrely for a pastor, he saw no need for the ritual of baptism. Unable to reconcile his eccentric views with priesthood, he abandoned the latter to study law at the University of Lille. He qualified as a lawyer, but again his heart was not in his profession. After submitting a doctoral dissertation to the University of Paris in 1907, he dabbled in journalism, writing columns for newspapers and publishing his first book, *L'ether vivant et le realisme supra-nerveux* (Living Ether and Supra-Nervous Realism). The book's title suggests a very unlawyerlike preoccupation with paranormal phenomena.

This tendency toward mysticism was no new thing. Already as a young soldier Richard had experienced visions that triggered an interest in "esoteric, mystical, and occult subjects." These interests deepened considerably when, after divorcing his first wife, he married Mirra Elfassa Morriset (1878–1973), who was active in theosophist circles. India occupied a central place in theosophy. In 1910, Richard traveled to India, a mecca for theosophists, where, in Pondicherry, a French colonial enclave, he got to know Cambridge-educated Aurobindo Ghose (1872–1950), a proindependence activist turned mystic and religious leader. Richard and his wife, who had followed Richard to India in

1914, were deported in 1915 on the insistence of the British authorities, who were alarmed by Aurobindo's and the Richards' proindependence stance. Subsequently, the Richards traveled (via France) to Japan, where they arrived at the end of April 1916.

They remained in Japan for four years, leaving once again for Pondicherry in 1920. During their stay in Japan, Richard's marriage had come under strain, and shortly after their arrival in India, Mirra left him for Aurobindo. She went on to achieve international fame as The Mother, the leader of the religion that Aurobindo had started, with some 10 million followers. By contrast, without Mirra her former husband faded into obscurity. At first he sought solace by meditating in the seclusion of the Himalayas, but after several months he left India for France. In 1929 he traveled to the United States, where he eked out a living as a part-time French teacher. He died in 1967.

Richard appealed to Japanese with pan-Asian leanings for a number of reasons. First, there was his deportation from India in 1915 and his friendship with Aurobindo Ghose and other Indian proindependence activists. His aphoristic style was sufficiently ambiguous to please most readers, and he had a doctorate in the days when doctorates were still a rarity. But these things by themselves were insufficient to account for his popularity—Richard was admired above all for his ideas. Richard's condemnation of modern Western civilization, which he dismissed as materialistic and corrupt beyond repair, and his critique of Western hypocrisy, as exemplified by Western policies of racial discrimination, were music to the ears of his Japanese audience—as were, after 1918, his uncompromising rejection of the "Anglo-Saxon world order," his dismissal of the League of Nations, and his suspicions of Western-initiated disarmament and his condemnation of Western, Anglo-Saxon racism. Although Japanese audiences were exposed on a daily basis to such views expressed by other Japanese, they sounded much more convincing when communicated by a Western philosopher with a prestigious academic degree.

Richard's despair over the decline of Western civilization was linked to his theosophical convictions that only the East could save mankind. This led him, paradoxically for a European, to develop his own pan-Asian doctrine in which Japan played a central role. Only Japan, led by its "tenno," could liberate Asia from the yoke of Western imperialism. Only Japan, under the glorious leadership of its emperor, had the potential to save the world from the evils of soulless modernity and selfish materialism. But to accomplish these goals, Japan must first of all put its own house in order. In other words, the liberation of Asia and the world must commence with internal reform. Though Richard did not specify what he meant by these reforms, his was to be a spiritual reform with emphasis on the purification of the Japanese spirit.

Nevertheless, nothing in his views, couched as they were in sufficiently vague terms, appeared to contradict the ideas of even the most radical pan-Asianists. While in Japan, Richard propounded his views in lectures and in a number of highly popular pamphlets and articles that were translated into Japanese. The results were such that, virtually unknown in the West, Richard became a celebrity in Japan. In 1919–1920 it would probably have been difficult to find well-educated Japanese who did not recognize his name. Japan's men of letters lionized him. The playwright Akita Ujaku (1883–1962), for instance, spent many evenings with Richard. The famous Indian poet and pan-Asianist Rabindranath Tagore (1861–1941), who visited Japan in 1917, wrote a preface to Richard's *To The Nations*. The fact that the book was presented to the crown prince, the future Shōwa emperor, indicates the degree of Richard's popularity in Japan.

Lodged at first in Myōgadani and then in a luxurious villa in Sendagaya (later occupied by Kita Ikki), Richard came into contact with numerous Japanese pan-Asianists. He befriended Kawashima Naniwa (1865–1949), the notorious China hand who had been involved in an abortive attempt to set up a Japanese-controlled puppet state in Mongolia. He formed friendships with Tōyama Mitsuru, who was regarded in some quarters as a gangster or terrorist but, as Richard understood it, really wanted to achieve "Asian unity and freedom, and a renaissance of spiritual values" (Richard 1987: 89) and with Uchida Ryōhei, for whom he worked as editor of the English-language journal *The Asian Review* (see I:10). Richard even drafted a Kokuryūkai-sponsored declaration of racial equality that was sent to Woodrow Wilson (1856–1924) at the Paris Peace Conference.

Richard's extensive contacts also included pan-Asianists of a younger generation. Indeed, Richard's message, which included an insistence on Japan's unique role, its divine mission, and the necessity of domestic reform (which in his case meant restoring the purity of the spirit), closely resembled the ideas of some of these younger, more radical pan-Asianists. Ōkawa Shūmei (see II:4), Kanokogi Kazunobu (see II:14), and a number of other pan-Asianists were well acquainted with Richard's ideas, and his influence shows in their work. Ōkawa, who translated Richard's works into Japanese, even moved in with the Richards to be closer to the sage.

At times it is difficult to tell whether Japanese pan-Asianists borrowed from Richard or whether it was a case of intellectual convergence. Ōkawa, for one, openly acknowledged Richard's influence, but, in reaction to the same political and social changes, both Richard and Japanese pan-Asianists may have reached the same conclusions independently. For example, Richard's insistence on the unity of all religions, which he argued in *The Eternal Wisdom*, is reminiscent of the views of Tanaka Ippei (see II:6). In any event, pan-Asianists, old and young, condemned what they saw as Western materialism, Western prejudice against the East, and Western hypocrisy; extolled Eastern spirituality; and generally believed that Japan had a mission to save Asia; this was essentially also the message that Richard was putting across.

The first of the two fragments reprinted here was written in 1917, the second in 1919. The bloodbath of World War I, the outcome of which was still uncertain in 1917, was decided by 1919, and this accounts for certain differences between the two fragments—for instance, references to the League of Nations and the Paris Peace Conference. Like the Japanese pan-Asianists, amply represented in this volume, Richard rejected the League of Nations and, like them, regarded Wilson as a hypocrite (in the same vein, see Sugita Teiichi, quoted in I:26). But his essential anti-Westernism had already been shaped prior to the outbreak of World War I. The war, which he regarded as "a European colonial contest for the domination of Asia," did not affect his views.

His intense anti-Westernism did not, however, blind him completely to the defects of Japan's Asian policy. On a number of occasions he criticized Japan's colonial policy (Richard 1987: 122). He called on Japan to grant immediate independence to Korea and renounce any Japanese claims on Chinese territory. Such appeals, however, seem to have fallen on deaf ears; what his audience chose to remember was the praise for Japan.

Source 1 (English in the original)
Paul Richard, *To Japan*. Privately published; text in four languages, French (Au Japon), Chinese (translated by Matsudaira Yasukuni), Japanese (by Ōkawa Shūmei) and English (by Mirra Richard), 1917.

. . . Liberate and unify Asia; for Asia is thy domain. Asia is thy field of action and, if needed, thy field of war; thou knowest it well.

In this war, they wished thee to expend thyself elsewhere. Thou has understood that thou wert to await here thine hour. And thou hast not taken part in the bloody schism of Europe save in the measure demanded by the work in Asia. Thou hast acquired there that which will facilitate this work. Others have as their share the half of Europe. And they are striving to gain it. Thine own share is the whole of Asia, with her eight hundred million inhabitants, the half of Humanity. Thou hast but to set her free. Ally of those who say: "We fight for the liberty of Europe," say to them now: "I will complete your task and fight for the liberty of Asia." Thus thou wilt test the sincerity of their hearts. Thus, but only thus, thou wilt secure their respect for thee. For they only respect those they fear. They will respect thee if thou compellest respect for Asia. But only in becoming free will she be respected. Europe will not even have mercy on her, as long as she can consider her as a dependency, as long as she knows not that she herself is but a part of Asia. That which Nature has designed in outlining this continent, let thine own works inscribe it on the thought of the Occident. . . .

What wouldst thou be if thou didst not place thyself at the head of a free federation of Asia, necessary too for the next and splendid equilibrium of the world? Of whom wouldst thou be the servant if Asia remained enslaved, if thou didst not acquire, in liberating her, the power to unify her. But to liberate her, liberate thine own self from all the contrary suggestion, from all subjection. And to unify her, unify thyself to her. Her peoples must know that thou hast not denied them, that thou are not of those who speculate on their weakness and exploit it, that thou art the friend and not the enemy in disguise, the guide and not one of the false shepherds, the hero they are awaiting and not one more tyrant in lurking. Win their confidence, for with it full power will be given thee. See before thee; see and measure the power which Asia will give to him who has proved worthy of her trust. . . .

Only keep thy word. Give to this nation [China] that which thou hast reconquered for her; give her freely that which others had compelled her to yield by force. Thus thou wilt confound those who disarm thee against themselves in teaching thee to imitate them, and those who arm themselves against thee for fear that thou shouldst imitate the others. Thou wilt show the example to all. All must bow before thee if only thou wouldst make this sign.

Give to this nation that which she no longer asks or expects of thee. It is not too much; only a town. She will give thee a continent in exchange. . . .

"To the Sons of Japan"
Children of the Dawn and of the Oceans
Children of the Land of Flowers and Flame
The Land of Strength and Beauty

Harken to the chant of glory
Which all the waves of the vast seas
Chant to your islands of the Rising Sun.

They are seven the glories of your country
That is why seven also are its tasks.
Hear then the seven glories and the seven duties.
I
Sole people of Asia who hast remained free
Thou it is who must be the liberator of Asia.
II
Sole people of the world who hast never been enslaved
Thy role is to stand against all slaveries of the world.

III

Sole people who hast never been vanquished
Thy mission it is to vanquish all the enemies of human happiness.

IV

Sole people also who hast united in thyself the new science and the ancient wisdom,
the thought of Europe and that of Asia
It is thou who wilt reconcile these two worlds,
these two halves of the world to come.

V

Sole people whose religions have remained free from the shedding of blood
Thou it is who wilt reconcile all the gods in the harmony of a truth more divine.

VI

Sole people who hast known since thy birth
One line of Emperors, one immortal Emperor,
Thou wert born to teach the people of the earth, all children of Heaven, to form but
one Empire of which Heaven itself shall be the immortal Emperor.

VII

People most united of all peoples
Thou wert born to serve the future unity of all,
And, because thou art a warrior, to hasten the Peace of humanity.

Such are the seven glories and the seven labours of your Land of Flowers and
Flame
Children of the Dawn and of the Oceans.

Source 2 (English in the original)
Paul Richard (1920), *The Dawn over Asia*, translated from the French by
Aurobindo Ghose, Madras: Ganesh & Co, Publishers.

"THE CANTICLE TO ASIA."

But when she saw the Angel of the Nations she was greatly troubled and
searched in her mind what manner of salutation this might be.

And the Angel said unto her: "Fear not, Asia, for thou hast found favour
with the future.

And behold, thou shalt conceive, and bring forth a New Spirit, and shalt
call his name the Saviour of the Nations." . . .

Do you not see that Europe has need now to be saved—saved from her
hatreds and from her chaos by a creation of love; from her darkness by a light
of the soul; from her death by a resurrection? For the Europe that was is no
more. She is buried under her own crime. And the Europe that should be is

not yet. She waits: she waits for Asia. Is it not always from Asia that have come, and will yet come, the great renewals of the Spirit, the springtides of light and love and life? Is it not from Asia that have always come, and will yet come once again, the Saviours of the peoples? It is therefore that I, son of Europe, come and say to you: Awaken Asia!

Awaken her in two ways. For your work must be double: at once material and spiritual. Awaken Asia by organising her, by uniting her. And to that end, be not masters, but allies of her peoples. Cease you also to cherish against them prejudices of race. Treat them as brothers, not as slaves. Those are who slaves liberate that they may become your brothers. Form with them all one single family. Organise the League of Nations of Asia—the United States of Asia.

But that you may be able to do this, do more: for bodies are one only when the soul is one. Make one the Soul of Asia by awakening in her, in yourselves, her consciousness of Unity, of the One Soul in every being, of the One Being in all things. That is the sacred treasure of Asia, the only one that Europe could not take from her. It is her discovery and her heritage—her very truth. It is that which has made her true power, her enduring greatness. For the science of external things—the science of Europe—has the promise of the power that passes, leaving behind it only ruins, the science of internal things, the spiritual knowledge—which was always that of Asia—has a promise of the enduring life, the promise of a harmony that passes not away.

And therefore, while the empires of the West crumble—for which of them has ever been able to last? India, China, Japan, remain through the centuries. They remain on condition of renewing incessantly in themselves this profound and secret source, this only source of the true life; of renewing themselves at that source, in that consciousness of unity. It is on this that is founded the world that is to come.

Behold now all the peoples are in labour that it may be born. And each of them attempts to create it in its own image. Some, the conquerors of to-day, wish to build it upon force, on the inequalities of force. For they have inherited the very spirit that they claim to conquer. They are not its conquerors but its conquered. And therefore, when they assemble to speak of peace, all the gods of war assemble along with them. For under the name of peace they aim at establishing a dictatorship of Powers.

And see how others reply to this dictatorship from above by a dictatorship from below. To the reign of the rich, they oppose the reign of the little: they institute the kingdom of the Poor. They attempt to take the Kingdom of Heaven, the Kingdom of Equality, by violence. Why should you think yourselves obliged to imitate either? Rather give an example to all. Teach all by finding it in yourselves, the sole possible foundation of fraternity and human harmony: the foundation of love, of the divine unity of beings, races, worlds.

On this basis, at this height build! Build the civilisation of to-morrow—that of Asia. Build the true equality—that which does not exclude nobility. Build the true justice—that which does not exclude beauty; the true democracy—that which does not exclude divine symbols; the true "Tennoism"—that in which Earth and Heaven meet together. Build the empire of Unity; thus, thus alone will you destroy the reign of racial discrimination. . . .

Begin first with Asia. That is your proper role. Assemble the Congress of the free nations of Asia. For the time is coming when the nations, all the nations of Asia, must be free. None will be truly free so long as others remain slaves. None will be truly respected so long as all are not respected. If then you wish to be respected yourselves, secure respect first for the others. And that all maybe one day be free, liberate yourself by delivering those whom you have subjected. For to maintain the bonds of another is to be oneself bound. That is the true remedy: to save yourselves by saving Asia. And saving, by Asia, the world—for in her is the heart of the world. Yes, that is the true remedy: to build a new civilisation, that of Asia—for in her is the hope of the world. Thus, but thus only, shall the sorrow and humiliation of to-day vanish in the glory that calls you. . . .

Let us then cherish a dream. Let us imagine the finest programme that Japan can realise for herself, and offer as an example, as a gift to the world. The programme of a new civilisation, that of Asia. When one speaks of a civilisation of Asia, the people of Europe shrug their shoulders. They cannot imagine that there can ever be a more perfect, a more excellent civilisation than the one which has made of modern man a demon, and of his old world a hell. And yet another must needs replace it. For they may dance as much as they please—theirs is about to disappear! What then can Japan do to replace it? What can she do within at home; and without—for Asia, for Humanity? Three questions to which the reply must be—three splendid works.

Within, it must be discovered and shown to all how an ideal people is made, a people in which are harmonised and completed the two principles that are everywhere separated, everywhere corrupted; the two powers that are consecrated by each other: the people and its sovereign, who are in opposition only when they cease, the one or the other, to be divine. For if the true sovereign is the great symbol of Heaven, the people also is an expression of the great sovereign Soul. The former represents the unity, the other the multiplicity of the One. And the true democracy is only another name of the true "Tennoism."

Realise the true "Tennoism" by this faith of a whole people that permits Heaven to appear in the person of a sovereign. Realise also the true democracy by taking good care that between the people and its "Tenno," between these two halves of the one, nothing profane intervenes and darkens the earth, by veiling from it Heaven. You have driven away the Shogun and the rays from on high have illumined you. But the Shogun has returned under another form, another name. He calls himself now "Legion," he is named the "Narikin" [nouveaux riches]! Do you not hear Europe cry to you: "The end of the reign of wealth is bankruptcy and famine." And Russia also cries to you: "Always, always, the narikin precedes and prepares the Bolshevik."

Chapter Thirty

Kita Reikichi: "Misunderstood Asianism" and "The Great Mission of Our Country," 1917

Christopher W. A. Szpilman

Kita Reikichi, the younger brother of Kita Ikki (see I:27), was born on Sado Island, Niigata Prefecture, in 1885. He graduated in philosophy from Waseda University in 1908. Between 1914 and 1918 he lectured at his alma mater while writing articles in popular journals in which he took to task proponents of Taishō democracy, such as Yoshino Sakuzō, for what he believed were their logical inconsistencies and lack of realism. At the end of 1918 he left Japan to study abroad, first at Harvard and then, between 1920 and 1923, at the universities of Berlin and Heidelberg.

Back in Japan, he was appointed editor in chief of the daily *Nihon Shinbun*, founded by the pan-Asianist conservative lawyer-politician Ogawa Heikichi (1869–1942) to fight the alleged liberal bias of the Japanese press. While holding this position, Kita in 1926 launched the philosophical journal *Gakuen* (Academy), which, after he had founded the Sokoku Dōshikai (Association of Patriotic Comrades) in 1928, he replaced with the monthly *Sokoku* (Fatherland, with the Latin subtitle *Sciencia et Patria*). This journal propagated Kita's antiparty and hard-line foreign policy views to a wider readership than its specialist predecessor.

Parallel with his publishing ventures, Kita pursued a distinguished career in education. In the 1920s he taught philosophy at Daitō Bunka Gakuin (Greater East Culture Academy), and in the 1930s he taught at Taishō University while concurrently serving as president of the Teikoku Ongaku Gakkō (Imperial Music School) and Tama Bijutsu Senmon Gakkō (Tama Fine Arts College).

By the 1930s Kita had also developed political ambitions. Though he failed to get elected to the Diet on his first attempt in 1932, he was successful in 1936. Subsequently, except for a brief period in the early stages of the postwar occupation of Japan when he was purged by the American authorities, he served in the Diet continuously until his retirement from politics in 1956.

Though Kita was never a member of any cabinet, he played an important role in Japanese politics in the 1950s: in close collaboration with Hatoyama Ichirō (1883–1959), he was a founding member of the Jiyūtō (Liberal Party) and one of the architects of the conservative party coalition known as the Jiyū Minshutō (Liberal Democratic Party) formed in 1955. He died in 1961.

After his death, Kita Reikichi was quickly forgotten, outshone by the powerful and eccentric personality of his brother. In the prewar years, however, he had been better known than Ikki. Reikichi was a prolific writer, academic, and politician, whereas Ikki was a shadowy figure, largely unknown to the general public, as most of his writings were banned by the authorities as extremist.

Paradoxically, Ikki, who never explicitly claimed to be a fascist, is considered the father of Japanese fascism, whereas the thought and behavior of Reikichi, who in the 1930s openly declared himself "the leading fascist of Japan" (*Harvard Crimson*, 1 October 1932), have been consigned to historical oblivion—partly because, after Japan's defeat, he proclaimed himself to be a democrat and pacifist. This was indeed a radical change, since in 1917 he had denounced pacifism as a "poison" fatal to Japan's national strength, a view that he continued to adhere to unwaveringly until 1945.

In 1917, the heyday of "Taishō democracy," Kita Reikichi attacked not just pacifism but progressive ideas of every kind—such as liberalism, democracy, and individualism—that had become fashionable in Taishō Japan. In 1917, however, he felt also compelled to address the phenomenon of Pan-Asianism, which was being reasserted in Japan under the impact of World War I (see I:26). The European war had produced a power vacuum in China that Japan was only too ready to fill with the 1915 Twenty-One Demands. Japan's new aggressive policy toward China coincided with vociferous demands in the press for Japan to embark on a mission to liberate Asia from Western oppression. Such expressions of Asian solidarity were not new. Though they had been heard in the Meiji period, they now intensified to such an extent that new terms (*Dai-Ajiashugi* and *Ajiashugi*) were coined to describe the phenomenon (see the introductory chapter).

In three lengthy articles Kita critically discussed the pan-Asian ideas of Paul Richard (1874–1967; see I:29), Sawayanagi Masatarō (1865–1927), Sugita Teiichi (1851–1929; see I:26), and Ōtani Kōzui (1876–1948) and outlined his own version of Pan-Asianism.

Like those pan-Asianists whom he critiqued, Kita was influenced by the bloodbath of World War I, then in its third year and seemingly with no end in sight. Like them, he too was convinced that the world was in the throes of an "unprecedented crisis" (Kita 1918: 7), that Western civilization was on the verge of collapse, and that Western domination over Asia had been irreparably weakened. Like many Japanese right-wing intellectuals, Kita anticipated the end of the war with a mixture of hope and anxiety. He was hopeful because the decline of Western power in East Asia following the outbreak of war opened the prospect of Japanese territorial expansion at the expense of China and Russia and anxious because he feared that, once the war was concluded in Europe, the victors might then turn on Japan. Anticipating the ideas behind "Japan's quest for autonomy" (Crowley 1966), which were used to justify Japanese expansionism in the 1930s, Kita argued that only territorial expansion could ensure Japan's national survival by rendering her self-sufficient and impregnable to aggression. From this perspective, he characterized Japanese expansionism not as "aggression" but as a legitimate and "autonomous" (*jiritsu*) act of "self-defense" (*jiei*).

It is hardly surprising, given this kind of expansionist outlook, that throughout the 1920s Kita was unremittingly hostile to the Versailles–Washington treaty system and the League of Nations, rejected Shidehara's conciliatory foreign policy, and condemned as antistate the "poisons" of "effeminate" humanism and pacifism, which he claimed were pushing Japan to the brink of national extinction (Kita 1918: 8). With equal consistency, he fulminated against the 1930 London Naval Limitations Treaty as a "great infringement of the prerogative of Imperial command" (*tōsuiken no daikanpan*) and, in the 1930s, impressed by Hitler's successes, promoted national socialist ideas. But it would be unfair to describe Kita's views during World War I as fascism *avant la lettre*. At that time, he was a traditional imperialist with respect to foreign policy, and it was from this imperialist position that Kita approached the concept of Pan-Asianism.

Kita classified Pan-Asianism into four distinct categories: antibarbarian (*jōiteki*) Asianism, self-defensive Asianism, cultural (*bunkateki*) Asianism, and Asianism as "Japanism" (*Nihonshugi toshite no Ajiashugi*). Rejecting the first three categories as sentimental or impractical, he declared himself in favor of Asianism as Japanism. Kita argued that Asianism made sense only if it represented the Japanese national interest, in the same way that the Monroe Doctrine served to protect and promote America's national interest. In other words, if Pan-Asianism would assist Japanese expansionism, then he was all for utilizing it, but he rejected the sentimentalism of Asian solidarity. In the world of Realpolitik, he insisted, Japan should not entangle itself in alliances for sentimental reasons but should keep its options open and, if necessary, ally itself with a Western power. The Pan-Asianism he espoused was merely window dressing for Japan's naked aggression.

With his training in philosophy, Kita was always ready to pounce on any contradictions in the articles he criticized, but he himself was not immune from logical inconsistencies. For example, he was not troubled by the contradiction between his advocacy of naked aggression in China and his approval of Paul Richard's suggestion that Japan return Quingdao (Tsingtao) to China as a first step to the realization of Sino–Japanese friendship. And while he purported to reject culturalist Pan-Asianism, he espoused a form of the *wakon yōsai* ("Japanese spirit, Western knowledge") view of civilization that had gained currency in Japan as early as the mid-nineteenth century. Though Asian civilization was technologically inferior to Western civilization, it was morally and spiritually superior. Japan's "greatest mission," he believed, was to fuse these two cultural streams into a superior civilization, with "Japan's national character" acting as a catalyst (Kita 1918: 10–11, 183).

Although Kita's writings on Pan-Asianism formed just a small fraction of his copious journalistic output, his views anticipated the subservience of Japanese Pan-Asianism to the aggressive foreign policy that prevailed in the 1930s and 1940s and, as such, occupy an important place in the history of Japanese Pan-Asianism.

Source 1 (translation from the Japanese original by Christopher W. A. Szpilman)
Kita Reikichi (1917a), "Gokai Saretaru Ajiashugi" (Misunderstood Asianism). *Tōhō Jiron* 2:7, 8–10 (reprinted in Kita 1941: 40–43).

[The true sense of Asianism] is definitely not that it is expecting a great racial war between the yellow and white races and is striving to smash the "white clique"; or that it is aiming to prevent the aggression of the Whites by cooperating with weak Asian countries which have been oppressed by them; or that it must engage in a cultural war against all the Whites for the development of some diffuse concept of Eastern civilization. Rather, just like the Monroe Doctrine, its goal is to eliminate Western oppression in Asia and to establish Japan's commanding position in Asia in order to secure Japan's political survival and ensure the development of Japanese culture. The Monroe Doctrine, too, is not a creed of aggression which aims to topple the power of the European states and establish a single state combining North and South America—nor, needless to say, is it a cultural hegemonism striving to establish a unique culture peculiar to North and South America. It stands precisely for the elimination of interference by Western states in South and North America, and is based on the desire that old, doddering outsiders should not meddle in matters that affect the security and peace of the United States. There is no need to state that the Monroe Doctrine is neither a creed of aggression nor of culturalism. That it is not intended for the self-defense of South and North America is proven by various facts.

If it was purely an ideology of self-defense (*jieishugi*) for South and North America, with the increase in American power the necessity for self-defense would be reduced and therefore the Monroe Doctrine would have to be abandoned—whereas, on the contrary, it is being asserted with growing strength. Also, the United States is not obliged by any legal duty to protect weak South American states in case of aggression by European powers and, moreover, such facts as the American refusal to send a representative to the Panama Conference should not be overlooked. Thus the Monroe Doctrine is clearly a disguised form of Americanism (*gassshūkokushugi*). . . .

So, if the so-called Asianism with its slogan of "Asia for the Asians" has any significance, it must essentially be a Greater Japanism. To put it differently, because Japan's freedom and development are the only fundamental principles at issue, the only way to attain these principles is to get rid of white rule over Asia. Therefore, while there may be instances when we will ally ourselves with some peoples in Asia to attack a certain Western state, because an alliance of yellow peoples against all Whites would be an act of lunacy, it may also be necessary to ally ourselves with a Western country in order to attack another Western country—in accordance with the principle of "using a barbarian to conquer another barbarian." In short, the only significance of "Asia for the Asians" lies in the elimination of unjust white oppression in the interests of Japan's self-defense and need for expansion; I cannot accept as a national duty either the idea of provoking racial resentment and becoming the butt of white hatred, or sharing the fate of weak states out of some misguided sense of righteousness. Only I cannot help wondering to what extent we should respect Britain's vested interests for the sake of our future expansion. In my view, for the sake of Japan's future it will be necessary to challenge British commercial advantages in South China, to challenge Australia's exclusion policy to solve our population problem, and furthermore to challenge India's tariff regime in order to ensure freedom for Japanese trade. As a result of all this, the notion of "Asia for the Asians" will be realized to a certain extent—but this liberation of Asia will be mainly determined by the actual power of Japan and by [internal] divisions among the Whites, and cannot be expected to be realized through an anti-barbarian Asianism which pointlessly provokes racial resentment. In particular, given the fact that the United States is a country which contains all the European races (*jinshu*), the kind of Asianism advocated by Abbot Ōtani, which has as its goal competition with the United States, is extremely dangerous for the future of Japan because it incites antagonism between the yellow and white races. For this reason, I maintain that if one is to advocate Asianism, it is essential to have a closely worked-out plan and under no circumstances adopt an attitude based on shocking people with eccentric views.

Source 2 (translation from the Japanese original by Christopher W. A. Szpilman)
Kita Reikichi (1917b), "Waga Kuni no Daishimei" (The Great Mission of Our Country). *Tōhō Jiron* 2:12, 19–21 (reprinted in Kita 1918: 167–71).

What is especially noteworthy in [Paul Richard]'s argument is his demonstration of the significance of Asianism as Japan's highest mission.

For him, so-called Asianism is synonymous with the liberation of all Asia. It is the restoration of freedom. Japan is a state that has been preparing for several thousands of years to achieve this loftiest of goals. As long as this "Asianism" entails the liberation of Asia, it is only natural for [Richard] to warn Japan not to embrace petty ambitions that would give rise to resentment by the Asian peoples. There are some Japanese advocates of Asianism who endorse aggression in Asia. Is this not a gross contradiction? The liberation of all Asia and the invasion of one part of Asia—from the perspective of those who are on the receiving end of aggression, it is oppression and enslavement. This is the gross contradiction which Japanese Asianists lapse into. [Richard], suspicious on this point, advises Japan to return Tsingtao. The view which Richard takes is truly logical and I agree with his argument. Seen from the premise that Japan regards the liberation of all Asia as an article of faith, aggression would necessarily involve Japan abandoning a weak Asia and opting for the powerful West [reference to Fukuzawa Yukichi's 1884 "Argument for Leaving Asia," *Datsuaron*]. For how can a country that prostrates itself before the strong and humiliates the weak become the leader of a movement to liberate all Asia? Especially [when one considers] that, following the war, every country is bound to adopt an autarkic economic policy. Japan is a small country, short of natural resources, so a policy of self-sufficiency is out of the question. It will only be possible to realize such a policy by means of a union with China. For this reason, Sino-Japanese friendship is absolutely necessary both for the liberation of Asia and for Japan's independence. So [Richard's] argument, though it seems to be indirect, is extremely pointed.

In particular, he makes the crucially important point that Japan must boldly oppose Western demands that cannot be reconciled with the liberation of Asia. We are close to a scandalous situation when Japan acts as Britain's guard dog and messenger boy, terrorizing China and India. The warm sympathy which Richard feels for India and the Indians can scarcely fail to bring Japan's merciless attitude toward India [i.e., the official policy of cooperation with Britain and hostility to Indian aspirations for independence] into sharp contrast.

Richard also recognizes the glory of Japan's past. But he warns that, when all is said and done, this glorious past has been no more than a preparation for future tasks. Richard is not urging us to be proud of what we have been given, but rather to be proud of what we give. These words give the lie to Japan's shallow national pride. Whenever we open our mouths, we Japanese boast of our 2500 years of history and talk glibly of the synthesis of Eastern and Western civilizations. But we have made almost no attempt to study how Eastern and Western civilizations might be synthesized or how the resulting culture might be usefully propagated throughout the world. In a word, our venerable history and the fusion of Eastern and Western civilizations belong to the past. Finding ways of utilizing ancient history, of drawing on the fusion of Eastern and Western civilizations to develop Asia and, furthermore, of making a positive contribution to the whole world is a matter for the future. But Japan continues to indulge in reflection on the past without entertaining any radiant hopes for the future. That is why Mr Richard refers to Japan's past and present as a period of preparation and issues a challenge to the Japanese people. Japan must become what he calls "a nation of the future."

In conclusion, he cites the ability of the Japanese people "to reconcile opposites" as a characteristic that qualifies Japan to become a nation of the future. This point appeals to our ego in no small way. In Japan, all religions have been harmonized and there is no conflict between Shinto, Confucianism, Buddhism and Christianity. Moreover, the Japanese are a people who combine beauty and strength, a yearning for ideals with a clever practical streak, the feeling of an artist with the courage of a warrior. There can be no doubt that the state that is characterized by internal harmony and unity will be the state that brings both harmony and unity to the world. That is why Richard expects Japan to be a "nation of the future," the state at the center of world unification. Needless to say, I cannot help but note that Richard over-idealizes the Japanese in his vision. However, if one assumes that Richard is referring not to the Japanese as they actually are but rather as they should be, and if the Japanese as they should be represent the essence of Japaneseness, then it is not too difficult to reach some understanding of what the highest ambition of Japan and the Japanese ought to be.

In short, although I find nothing new in Richard's thinking, when I see in his writing—filled with the strength and beauty that comes from the hope and love he feels for the Japanese—a bright light illuminating some object hitherto hidden from sight, I thank him and cannot help but rejoice. But in order to realize the most noble mission which Richard demands and hopes from Japan, we must have sufficient determination. That is, if we wish to liberate oppressed countries, we must first of all become a free people ourselves. If we want to become the leader of Asia, we must first of all obtain autonomy from Western pressure. In the final analysis, the highest privileges come together with the highest duties. While granting Japan the highest privilege, Mr Richard imposes on us the highest duty.

Chapter Thirty-One

Taraknath Das: Pan-Asian Solidarity as a "Realist" Grand Strategy, 1917–1918

Cemil Aydin

Taraknath Das (1884–1958), an Indian intellectual, formulated one of the most articulate versions of "realist" Pan-Asianism as a form of regional solidarity against the British Empire that would benefit both the Japanese Empire and rising Indian nationalism. Das left Bengal in 1905 to study at the University of California and the University of Washington while remaining heavily involved as an organizer and publicist in popularizing the cause of Indian nationalism. Having become a naturalized U.S. citizen at the beginning of World War I, Das, on behalf of the revolutionary Ghadar Party, visited Germany, Turkey, China, and Japan during World War I to further the cause of Indian nationalism and disseminate anti-British propaganda. His most fruitful work in Japan was carried out in cooperation with Japanese pan-Asianists like Ōkawa Shūmei (see II:4), raising the awareness of the Japanese public about the Indian national struggle (Mukherjee 1997). As a result of his political activities during the war, in 1918 he was tried in America as part of the Hindu German Conspiracy Case (Brown 1948; Dignan 1971; Jensen 1979) and served eighteen months in prison. Das was a talented scholar who later in his life completed a PhD and taught Indian history at Columbia University while pursuing a prolific writing career. Nevertheless, Das's intellectual contribution to the formulation of a realist version of pan-Asian solidarity between the Japanese Empire and the rising nationalist movements in India and China is often overlooked. Yet, during World War I and its immediate aftermath, he made a name for himself as one of the most eloquent commentators on European racism and imperialism in Asia, advocating the need for Japan to abandon its alliance with Britain and support nationalism in India.

Das's most influential books on Pan-Asianism were written during his trip to China and Japan in September 1916 to engage in propaganda work against Britain and to solicit arms shipments from China to India. In 1916, there

already existed a network of Japanese pan-Asianists and Indian nationalists, and during his stay in Japan, Das utilized this network to meet not only
with Rash Behari Bose (I:24) and Sun Yat-sen (II:5) but also with leading
Japanese political figures, such as Inukai Tsuyoshi (1857–1932) and Ōkuma
Shigenobu (1837–1922), both supporters of Pan-Asianism. He also established a pan-Asiatic association with Ōkawa Shūmei, who served as the main
contact person between Das and pan-Asianist groups in Japan.

In 1917, Das published a book in Shanghai titled *Is Japan a Menace to
Asia?*, in which he argued that the interests of Britain and France conflicted
with Japanese interests in the region. He claimed that both these "white" great
powers were provoking anti-Japanese sentiments in the Far East in an effort
to limit Japanese influence (Das 1917b). Das urged Japan to act against British interests in the region by allying itself with Asian nationalist movements.
According to his argument, the Western powers had imposed an international
isolation on Japan, and Asian solidarity was the only way to overcome it. Das
also proposed that the Chinese should cooperate with Japan for the benefit of
both nations. The book contained an introduction by Tang Shao-yi, former
prime minister of the Republic of China and an appendix by Tokutomi Sohō,
an influential Japanese journalist known for his nationalist and pan-Asianist
views (see I:25 and I:28). The book was discussed extensively at the time
and received much attention in Japanese pan-Asianist circles. A Japanese-
language summary of the book was published by the leading nationalist
journal, *Nihon oyobi Nihonjin* (Japan and the Japanese) (Das 1917a). However, Shanghai's English-language *The Far Eastern Review*, denounced Das,
together with Sun Yat-sen, as promoters of Japanese colonial rule in Asia
under the cloak of Pan-Asianism and the Asian Monroe Doctrine (see I:28
for this article). The British authorities banned the book and tried to prevent
its distribution in countries friendly to Britain.

During 1917, Das gave several lectures in Japan and published a second
book that restated the main pan-Asian arguments against the Anglo-Japanese
Treaty. The book *Isolation of Japan in World Politics* was first published in
Ōkawa's Japanese translation by his All Asia Association under the pseudonym "An Asian Statesman" (Zen Ajiakai 1917); the English version followed
a year later (Asiatic Association of Japan 1918). The book focused on the
inevitable conflict of interest between the "yellow race" and the "white race"
in Asia, arguing that a long-term alliance between Japan and Britain was therefore impossible. Das added that, since Japan would never be treated as equal
by the Western powers, it should seek to create a new regional order in Asia
to overcome its isolation. An influential educator and former member of the
Japanese Diet, Oshikawa Masayoshi (1850–1928), wrote an introduction to
the book, criticizing the pro-British policies of the Terauchi Masatake cabinet

(1916–1918). The book contained appendices by the prominent philosopher-journalist Miyake Setsurei (1860–1945) and Senga Tsurutarō (1857–1929), a professor of philosophy at Kyoto Imperial University. Influential political figures such as Gotō Shinpei (in 1917 home minister and in 1918 foreign minister in the Terauchi Masatake cabinet) and Ōkuma Shigenobu, a former prime minister, praised the book. Restrictions on the distribution of the Japanese edition, enforced by the police at the request of the British embassy, had the opposite effect of serving as a successful promotional tool. To sum up, Das's campaign for Japanese support for Indian nationalism emphasized the long-term benefits that dissolving the Anglo–Japanese alliance would have for preparing the ground for Japanese leadership in Asia. This argument was based on the premise of Japan's international isolation as the only nonwhite great power. Das's activities, often in cooperation with Ōkawa Shūmei, contributed to a redefinition of Japanese Pan-Asianism by extending its scope from East Asia to India. His ideas on Japan's isolation—the result of racism—by the European great power "club" were well received by Japanese public opinion. The Japanese proposal at the Paris Peace Conference for including a clause on racial nondiscrimination in the charter of the yet-to-be-founded League of Nations reflected Japanese anxieties over unequal treatment by the great powers on racial grounds. But Taraknath Das changed his views about Japan's potential leadership in Asia as he became increasingly disillusioned with Japanese policies on nationalist movements in Asia during the interwar period. During the 1930s, Das expressed skepticism about the pan-Asian rhetoric of Japanese leaders and intellectuals. In an article he wrote in 1933 for *New Asia*, published by Rash Behari Bose, Das noted that Japan had done nothing to improve Indo–Japanese relations for about two decades, reinforcing his doubts over Japan's attempt to "return to Asia" after such a long period of indifference to nationalist movements (*The New Asia*, 7–8, November–December 1933, 3). During World War II, in an attempt to give official Pan-Asianism a historical lineage and international credibility, books by Das originally published during World War I were reprinted in Japan after more than twenty years (e.g., Das 1944). However, by the time the war broke out, Das himself was clearly opposed to Japanese policies in Asia.

   The following selections from Das's books reveal a very scholarly approach to his claims for Asian solidarity, based on the rationale of Realpolitik. In both of the books quoted, Das is often critical of earlier Japanese policies on China and argues that it is in the economic and political interests of the Japanese Empire to pursue friendly policies toward China. He also underlines the fundamental impossibility of Japan's cooperation with the Western powers due to racial discrimination and imperial rivalries. Another important aspect of Das's vision of Asian solidarity is his reliance on Western works of political science and international relations, illustrating how the notion of Asian solidarity was widely accepted by many observers of world events during World War I. Das refers frequently to books and articles in Western languages in order to demonstrate that pan-Asian solidarity is the best option for Japan, India, and China against a global Western imperial hegemony. His writings are a good example of the widespread appeal of the notion of Asian solidarity during World War I, demonstrating how Indian nationalists were attracted to the idea of Asian solidarity in their struggle against the British Empire, and how the arguments of Indian nationalists found strong echoes in pan-Asianist circles in Tokyo.

Source 1 (English in the original)
Das, Taraknath, *Is Japan a Menace to Asia?* Shanghai: no publisher, 1917, 119–20.

It is almost certain that after the conclusion of the European War a new readjustment between Powers is bound to come. In this matter of readjustment, the Far Eastern Problem and the question of the mastery of the Pacific will play an important part. England will try to win the good will of Germany so as to crush Japan. Germany may not agree to play second-fiddle to Great Britain, since the former has nothing to gain by so doing. Japan and Russia may stand aloof from Great Britain, though outwardly not opposed to her. Or these superior white nations may make a combination to crush "up-start" Japan, the disputer of their mastery in Asia. So, it seems, the outlook for peace is not bright, and I am afraid Asia will be the battle-ground of the next gigantic war for which the diplomats of the First Class Powers are now preparing. There is, it seems, no remedy against it, because China is not yet strong in the same way as Japan is to-day. A strong China with her 400 millions alone could have dictated a pacific policy to the world. Then, again, the peace in Asia will never be secure so long as Great Britain holds India as her exclusive property and excludes the people of India from the birth-right of independent government. Independent India will give equal opportunity to all nations of the world, but India under the British yoke will be a source of constant jealousy among the European Powers and all others interested in contesting British supremacy in Asia. . . .

Broadly speaking there are three great problems in the Far East: (1) Inevitable commercial and territorial expansion of Japan in Asia, specially towards the South, which will threaten the absurd European supremacy in Asia; (2) Evolution of a strong China, through friendly Japanese co-operation, as a champion of peace and protector of rights of other Asiatic people who are now under European domination; (3) [The] rise of Independent India to contribute her share to the cause of human progress as she did in the days of her ancient glory.

Source 2 (English in the original)
Asiatic Association of Japan (An Asian Statesman, pseudonym of Taraknath Das) (1918): *Isolation of Japan in World Politics.* Tokyo: Asiatic Association of Japan, 62–65.

The conclusion we have to make is that Japanese statesmen have committed grave blunders which have resulted in the loss of Japan's prestige in China. Japanese diplomacy has proved to be impotent in matters of winning the good will of China. Japan is about to be used by other Powers to make Russia and Japan enemies. Japan must not make the same blunders that Germany committed in the past, and she must take special care, for the sake of the future of the nation, that she may not have too many enemies to please some combinations.

Japan has a grave responsibility of championing the cause of Asian independence, and this can only be done through the strength of Japan in the field of economics, commerce, military, and naval matters, and especially in diplomacy. Failure in diplomacy may spell disaster for Japan in the long run and Japanese diplomacy must not be guided by a mere short-sighted policy of immediate gain, but by the policy which would be beneficial to the prosperity of Asia at large. In that case Japan can not very well be an adjunct of any European combination in matters of Eastern diplomacy, and Japan must have the courage and strength in chalking out her own policy, and she must have the diplomacy of using the European nations to the fulfillment of the end of Asian Independence and Japanese gain, instead of being used by the other nations for their gain, as has been done in the present European War. This is a stupendous task for the Japanese statesmen, but let us hope that they will be able to accomplish it through the unalloyed support of the Japanese nation and other Oriental countries. . . .

Let no Japanese forget that a strong Japan has a mission toward Asia. Let all Asia gather around Japan to strengthen her for the final issue of Asian Independence. Japan without Asian aid is in isolation. The Japanese statesmen should work with a long-sighted policy for the future generations of the people of the Rising Sun, and the first step toward this goal is to win the confidence of the Chinese nation.

Chapter Thirty-Two

Konoe Fumimaro:
"A Call to Reject the Anglo-American Centered Peace," 1918

Eri Hotta

Konoe Fumimaro (sometimes also called Ayamaro, 1891–1945) was born to one of the most ancient and aristocratic families descended from the Fujiwara clan. A three-time prime minister between 1937 and 1941, he was to preside over the intensification of Japan's de facto war with China. As Japan's premier, he issued a series of pan-Asianist proclamations, most famous of which was the "New East Asian Order" of November 1938 (see II:17). Formulated with the support of his brain trust, the Shōwa Research Association, his statement gave a pan-Asianist dimension to Japan's unplanned military engagement, effectively supporting and legitimating Japan's expansion in China and Asia. While clearly drawn to many aspects of fascism, Konoe was also a serious student of philosophy, trained in neo-Kantian idealism as well as Marxian economics. In politics, he had contacts with men of various political sympathies and was adept at navigating his career in the most tumultuous years of modern Japanese politics. In the end, however, his own convictions and ideas were rarely made explicit. This has led the historian Marius Jansen to conclude that "[m]odern Japanese history has not known a more enigmatic man" (Jansen 2000: 618; on Konoe's life, see Oka 1983).

The piece selected here, "Eibei Hon'i Heiwashugi o Hai Su" (A Call to Reject the Anglo-American Centered Peace), provides some clues to the Konoe enigma. It highlights the continuity of certain pan-Asianist beliefs held by Konoe. In fact, a sort of Pan-Asianism that highlighted Asia's plight and called for Japan's leadership in correcting it was a glue cementing the varying and often contradictory views that Konoe embraced. The article also sheds light on the broader question of how Japanese nationalism could coexist, however uneasily, with Pan-Asianism.

Indeed, Konoe's association with Pan-Asianism was in some sense predetermined before his birth. He was born as the first son of the pioneering pan-Asianist Prince Konoe Atsumaro (1863–1905; see I:6). The senior Konoe was the first president of the East Asian Common Culture Association (Tōa Dōbunkai; see I:9), formed in 1898, and advocated a Sino–Japanese alliance in a controversial 1898 article (Konoe 1898a; see I:6).

Atsumaro died when his son was only twelve years old, so it would be hard to see his Pan-Asianism as a causal influence on his son's political views. Indeed, as a student, the younger Konoe was much drawn to socialism and Marxian economics, leading him to pursue a course of studies at Tokyo and later at Kyoto Imperial universities. Besides, his Pan-Asianism developed under quite different historical circumstances and was also far more chauvinistic in character. Nonetheless, the polemical style of his writing reflected in the selected article and the binary view of the world infused with the language of social Darwinism and the racialist conception of international relations are not entirely unlike his father's and are noteworthy.

In 1916, at age twenty-five, he became a member of the House of Peers. The article "Eibei Hon'i Heiwashugi o Hai Su" was written on the eve of his departure for the Paris Peace Conference, to which he accompanied Japan's plenipotentiary Saionji Kinmochi. It was published in the December 1918 issue of the journal *Nihon oyobi Nihonjin* (Japan and the Japanese). It provided a general indictment of the state of the international system as well as a specific critique of the proposal for the League of Nations. Contrary to the polemical title of the piece and the sympathy he professed for the fellow "have-not" power Germany, however, Konoe was not entirely opposed to Woodrow Wilson's conception of establishing an intergovernmental league. He was nonetheless suspicious of the moral, egalitarian, and universalistic claims attached to it. Konoe asserted that the postwar peace settlements were dictated by the desire of Britain and the United States to maintain their international positions and to freeze the international political map to their advantage. In his mind, Japan's intellectual opinion was tipped in favor of the Anglo-American powers because too many of his compatriots were too easily impressed with their flowery language of peace and humanity. Telling his naive Japanese readers to wake up to reality, he identified, in a similar manner to his father's, his mission at the Paris Peace Conference as one of articulating Japan's support for the elimination of [Anglo-American] economic imperialism and equal treatment of the yellow race. His suspicion of the settlements as a Carthaginian peace and the Anglo-American attempt to check other rising powers—and especially a colored one—was to be further confirmed by the futile Japanese attempt at including clauses guaranteeing racial equality and religious freedom in the covenant of the League of Nations.

Konoe's indictment of such an Anglo-American peace was rather contradictory, however. On the one hand, he stated that Germany's resort to force was understandable and that her act of war constituted a legitimate means to correct an uneven distribution of power, wealth, and prestige in the society of nation-states. After all, would Japan not want to be a great power itself? But by becoming a "have" power itself, Japan would presumably end up oppressing other "have-not" powers, including those fellow yellow nations Konoe claimed that Japan would support and liberate. Konoe did not fully face up to this contradiction, much less resolve it in his writings. Thus, his argument can be crudely summarized as follows: We reject your exclusive club because you don't want us as a member, even though we really deserve to be one. If you change your mind, we would reconsider accepting your offer of membership (and we would probably end up excluding other nonmembers because it feels good to be privileged, though we might be nicer to them than you have been to us). If you don't take us seriously, you will regret it, because we might resort to forceful means just like the Germans.

Konoe's ambivalent position of desiring Japan to stand at a par with the great powers but not wanting it to appear overeager was also pronounced in a booklet he penned shortly after his return home from the Paris Peace Conference via the United States. In it, his obsession again focused on the question of how Japan should go about achieving great power status without feeling humiliated. His answer was for Japan to come up with a clear foreign policy framework. It revealed how his travels confirmed his view of the Anglo-American powers as the only true arbiters of the rules of international political game. In describing the rising anti-Japanese sentiments in the United States, Konoe says,

> That the white people—and the Anglo-Saxon race in particular—generally abhor colored peoples is an apparent fact, so blatantly observable in the US treatment of its black population. I for one felt a sort of racial oppression more in London than in Paris, and furthermore, that sense was heightened upon my arrival in New York. (Konoe 1981: 138)

He then goes on to discuss the success of Chinese propaganda in the United States and Japan's relative failure in promoting its national cause. Rather than regarding China as a fellow Asian power in Japan's fight against the discriminatory treatment by the Anglo-American powers, he sees China only as a competitor. Fearing that China might outdo Japan in the race for recognition by the Anglo-Americans, the very powers whose dominance he criticized only a few months ago, he dismisses the "glibness of Chinese propaganda, the one that paints a simplistic picture of Japan as a self-interested military expansionist" (Konoe 1981: 140).

Taken together, Konoe's firm belief from this period onward seems to have been that Japan should not let Britain and the United States coax it into doing whatever they tell it to do. His prescription for Japan's foreign policy then was to be confident enough to be able to assert its position and to have the dominant powers engage in listening to Japan's ambivalent position. His favorite themes of Japan having suffered from predatory Western economic imperialism, from being a late comer, and from lacking in natural resources were by no means original. But he was consistent and vocal in his protest without appearing reactionary. This might explain his immense popularity throughout his political life and beyond despite the instrumental roles he and his cabinet played in propelling Japan into a destructive war.

Put differently, Konoe promoted the idea of a "Japan that can say 'No'" well before the populist politician Ishihara Shintarō (see II:17 for Ishihara's views) popularized that phrase seven decades later (Ishihara 1991). Being able to say "No" means that Japan has its own unwavering foreign policy philosophy. For this reason, however much Konoe points to the "oppression of colored peoples," he sounds more like the xenophobic nationalists and fearmongering populist leaders of "have-not" revisionist powers, such as Italy and Germany.

Indeed, one of the most important facets of Konoe was his penchant for fascist ideas. In the late 1930s, Japan under his leadership became entangled deeper and deeper in the China quagmire. While claiming to want to end the conflict, Konoe's cabinet not only supported Japan's army in China but also dispatched reinforcements of almost a million men to the continent, quietly passing the General Mobilization Law (1938), and effectively converting Japan's semiwar economy into a fully fledged war economy. In his second term as premier, in October 1940, he pushed for the formation of the Imperial Rule Assistance Association (*Taisei Yokusankai*), ending Japan's party politics.

And so, the question that often fails to be asked, no doubt in large part because of general sympathy generated by his suicide on the eve of his arrest as a class A war criminal, as well as by his own and his surviving family's insistence on his personal preferences for peace, is concerning the nature of Konoe's role in the elevation of Japanese-centered Pan-Asianism to Japan's policy discourse. His fixed and hostile view of the outside world as being dominated by the Anglo-American powers, which he wished to reject, while desperately craving their recognition at the same time, comes across clearly in the article reproduced here. In the end, Konoe sought the answer to Japan's problems in fascistic—though not entirely fascist—ideology, mixed with the anti–status quo and dangerously romantic vision of Asia under Japanese leadership. The problem was that Asia did not invite such leadership, and Japan was not at all ready to exercise it. The resultant foreign policy was to push Japan onto an even more destructive as well as self-destructive showdown with Konoe's eternal object of envy and hatred: Britain and the United States.

Source (translation from the Japanese original by Eri Hotta)
Konoe Fumimaro, "Eibei Hon'i Heiwashugi o Hai Su" (A Call to Reject
the Anglo-American Centered Peace). *Nihon oyobi Nihonjin* no. 746 (12
December 1918), 23–26.

There is no denying that the postwar world is witnessing an ever flourishing rise of democratic humanitarianism. As our country too exists in the
world society of states, it is only natural that Japan too would not escape
being affected by such a philosophy. All in all, such a philosophy, be it democracy or humanitarianism, comes down to a feeling of equality amongst all
men. From a domestic perspective, that means having people enjoying democratic rights. The same thing, from an international perspective, means that
each state asserts its own right to survival on the basis of equality. Equality
does not imply that we sweep away all the differences between individuals,
or between nations. An individual should live up to his individual promise,
while a nation should cherish its distinctive national character. Equality really means that we endeavor to eliminate whatever social obstacles come in
the way of equal opportunities for individuals or nations to live up to their
unique potential. Such obstacles, for example, arise from having a political
preponderance [of a few states over the rest] or possession of special economic rights [by a few states]. . . .

In any event, it is my utmost wish that our country will be led positively by
this trend towards democracy and humanitarianism, so that the country can
develop. But what I find regrettable is that my fellow countrymen tend to be
overawed by British and American pronouncements. Without evaluating or
discounting anything they say, Japanese adopt and extol the Anglo-American
version of democracy and humanitarianism at face value. I am of course not
denouncing all Anglo-American politicians as lacking in sincerity. Like Wilson, or Lloyd George, there are those who earnestly and passionately promote
humanitarian principles. Nonetheless, there are people in this world who,
without being self-aware, commit acts of falsehood. Pure motives could more
often than not end up producing impure consequences. . . .

The Japanese press in recent years has been captivated by the flowery
language of Anglo-American politicians, and accepted their version of democratic humanitarianism, unable to detect their egoism—be that egoism of a
self-conscious or a non-self-conscious kind—lurking behind it. Forgetting
that they are Japanese, the press has praised the Anglo-American-centered
League of Nations unconditionally and uncritically. What is more, the press
seems to think that to do so automatically puts it on the side of justice and
humanity. I find this tendency rather pathetic. I cannot help but think in a

Japanese-centered way. Japanese-centeredness does not equate to egoism that thinks only of the Japanese people and neglects other nations. Such egoism is indeed an enemy of humanity, a bygone philosophy that does not agree well with the new postwar world. When I say we should think in a Japanese-centered way, I mean that the Japanese should confirm their legitimate right to survival. And when our right is unjustly suppressed, we must be prepared to fight for it. That is what humanitarianism dictates. Those who are still obsessed with peace, even when one's own legitimate right to survival is violated, are enemies of humanity. Pacifism and humanitarianism are not necessarily the same. We must sometimes abandon peace for humanity. Advocates of Anglo-Americanism treat pacifism and humanitarianism as the same thing. In our country too, there are those who follow their lead and mistakenly believe that peace equals humanity. . . .

The European War was a battle between existing great powers and great powers in the making. It was a battle between those who found it convenient to sustain the status quo and those who found it convenient to destroy it. Those who prefer the *status quo* cry out for peace, while those who prefer the collapse of the status quo call for war. . . . As the colonial histories of Britain or France show, the *status quo* powers have taken for themselves most of the less civilized countries and made them their colonies a long time ago, monopolizing all the profits. As a result, not only Germany but all other late comers find no room for expansion and development. Such a state of affairs contradicts the principles of equal opportunity for the human race and is a menace to the right of equal existence and survival of every nation. It was a legitimate demand on Germany's part to want the destruction of this state of affairs. But Germany's method lacked moderation, and she placed primacy on force and militarism, thereby inviting the criticism of the world. I, as a Japanese, empathize with Germany's difficult position in which it was compelled to act as it did. . . .

Nevertheless, Japan's opinion makers, drunk with high-sounding claims, are taken with the Anglo-American-centered pacifism and worship the League of Nations like a heaven-sent gospel. This in spite of the fact that Japan, being in an international position rather like Germany's, should be desiring the destruction of the *status quo*. I find such an attitude of the Japanese people fawning. From the standpoint of justice and humanity, it should be detested. But I am not at all opposed to the idea of the League of Nations *per se*. If this League could be organized around the principle of justice and humanity in their true meaning, it should be welcomed with open arms for the happiness of humanity and for all nation-states. . . .

But this League could be used as an instrument for the great powers to gobble up lesser powers economically. . . .

Britain and the United States were the greatest economic beneficiaries of this war. They instantaneously became the world's economic hegemons. Now, with the League's arms reduction plans . . . , they are bent on controlling the world. . . . Other nations, without the forceful means to express their aspirations, . . . would have to follow Britain and the United States like a herd of obedient sheep. . . .

[At the Paris Peace Conference] I will demand the following. First, for the benefit of not only Japan, but also other late comers who face a similar fate, and for the establishment of equal opportunities of existence and survival for all nations based on justice and humanity, I call for the elimination of economic imperialism. I demand that every nation decolonize its colonies, and open them up as markets for industrial products as well as suppliers of natural resources, which will be equally open to all nations without few powers monopolizing them. Second, as a Japanese, I demand the elimination of racial discrimination against the yellow race. From the United States to the British colonies [*sic*] of Australia and Canada, the doors are open to white immigrants. Japanese and other yellow races are regarded as inferior and are being persecuted. Such a situation, needless to say, has been a source of great discontent amongst us Japanese. The yellow man is kept from securing a job or renting a house or land. One even needs a white guarantor in order to stay just one night in some hotels. Such a situation is, from the perspective of humanitarianism, a grave problem. . . .

At the coming Peace Conference, I would demand that British and Americans deeply repent their past arrogant attitudes and eliminate, on the principle of justice and humanity, all rules and regulations discriminating against yellow people, and not just in terms of their discriminatory immigration policies. I think that the coming Peace Conference provides a great challenge for humanity, testing us whether we would be able to reform the world on the basis of justice and humanity. Should Japan be critical of the Anglo-American-centered pacifism, assert true justice and humanity, and try its utmost to bring them about in reality, her glory as a fighter for justice would be forever praised in human history.

Consolidated Bibliography

Unless otherwise stated, all Japanese titles are published in Tokyo and all Korean titles in Seoul.

Abdürreşid İbrahim (1910), *Alem-I Islam ve Japonya'da Intisari Islamiyet* (The Future of the Japanese from the Perspective of Religion). Istanbul: Ahmed Saki Bey Matbaasi.

Abe Hirozumi (1980), "Mori Kaku: Fuashizumu Taisei no Senku" (Mori Kaku: The Pioneer of the Fascist System), Andō Minoru et al., *Nihon Seiji no Jitsuryokusha* (Influential Figures in Japanese Politics), vol.2. Yūhikaku.

Aibara Shigeki (1998), "Konoe Atsumaro to Shina Hozenron" (Konoe Atsumaro and the Preservation of China's Territorial Integrity Principle). Okamoto Kōji (ed.), *Kindai Nihon no Ajiakan* (*Modern Japan's View of Asia*). Kyoto: Minerva Shobō, 51–77.

Aizawa Yasushi (1833), *Teki-ihen* (A Guide to Morals), reprinted in Aizawa Yasushi, *Shinron/Teki-ihen* (New Thesis/A Guide to Morals). Iwanami Shoten, 1931.

Akashi, Motojiro (1988), *Rakka Ryusui: Colonel Akashi's Report on His Secret Cooperation with the Russian Revolutionary Parties during the Russo-Japanese War.* Translated by Inaba Chiharu. Helsinki: SHS.

Akif, Mehmet (Ersoy) (2003), *Safahat* (Passages). Istanbul: Inkilap Kitabevi.

Ampiah, Kweku (2007), *The Political and Moral Imperatives of the Bandung Conference of 1955: The Reactions of the US, UK and Japan.* Folkestone: Global Oriental.

An Chung-gŭn (1910), "Tongyang Pyŏnghwaron" (A Discourse on Peace in East Asia), reprinted in Ch'oe Wŏn-sik and Paek Yŏng-sŏ (eds.), *Tongasia, Munje-wa Sikak* (East Asia, Problems and Points of View). Munhak-kwa Chisŏngsa, 1997, 205–15.

An Kyong-su (1900), "Nisshinkan Dōmeiron" (Argument for a Japanese-Chinese-Korean Alliance). *Nihon oyobi Nihonjin,* nos. 116–123 (8 parts).

Anderson, Benedict R. (1983), *Imagined Communities: Reflections on the Origin and Spread of Nationalism.* London: Verso.

Andō Hikotarō (1990), "Nihon Ryūgaku Jidai no Ri Daishō" (Li Dazhao during His Time as a Foreign Student in Japan). *Shakai Kagaku Tōkyū* 36:2, 347–72.

Ano, Masaharu (1997), "Yosuke Matsuoka: The Far-Western Roots of a World-Political Vision." *Oregon Historical Quarterly* 98:2, 164–204.

Aoe Shunjirō (1997), *Ishiwara Kanji* (Ishiwara Kanji). Chūō Kōronsha.

Aoe Shunichirō (1992), *Ishiwara Kanji* (Ishiwara Kanji). Chūō Kōronsha.

Arano Yasunori (2007), "Kinsei Nihon ni okeru 'Higashi Ajia' no 'Hakken'" (The 'Discovery' of 'East Asia' in Early Modern Japan). Kishi Toshihiko et al. (eds.), *"Higashi Ajia" no Jidaisei* (The Temporality of 'East Asia'). Keisuisha, 21–52.

Archer, Clive (2001), *International Organizations*. London and New York: Routledge.

Arendt, Hannah (1985), *The Origins of Totalitarianism*. San Diego: Harcourt.

Ariyama Teruo (1992), *Tokutomi Sohō to Kokumin Shinbun* (Tokutomi Sohō and the *Kokumin Shinbun*). Yoshikawa Kōbunkan.

Arrighi, Giovanni, Takeshi Hamashita, and Mark Selden (eds.) (2003), *The Resurgence of East Asia: 500, 150 and 50 Year Perspectives*. London and New York: Routledge.

Asiatic Association of Japan (Author Taraknath Das) (1918), *Isolation of Japan in World Politics*. Tokyo: Asiatic Association of Japan.

Association of Southeast Asian Nations (2009), "ASEAN Plus Three Cooperation." Official website of the Association of Southeast Asian Nations, Internet: http://www.aseansec.org/16580.htm (last accessed 1 June 2010).

Aydin, Cemil (2007a), "A Global Anti-Western Moment? The Russo-Japanese War, Decolonization and Asian Modernity." Sebastian Conrad and Dominic Sachsenmaier (eds.), *Conceptions of World Order, ca. 1880–1935. Global Moments and Movements*, 213–36. Basingstoke: Palgrave Macmillan.

―――― (2007b), *The Politics of Anti-Westernism in Asia: Visions of World Order in Pan-Islamic and Pan-Asian Thought*. New York: Columbia University Press.

Banerjee, Taransankar (1977), *Sardar K. M. Panikkar: A Profile of a Historian: A Study in Modern Indian Historiography*. Calcutta: Ratna Prakashan.

Bayly, Christopher, and Harper, Tim (2007), *Forgotten Wars: The End of Britain's Asian Empire*, London: Penguin Books.

Beasley, William G. (1987), "Japan and Pan-Asianism. Problems of Definition." Janet Hunter (ed.), *Aspects of Pan-Asianism*. London: Suntory Toyota International Centre for Economics and Related Disciplines, London School of Economics and Political Science (International Studies 1987/II), 1–16.

Berger, Gordon M. (1977), *Parties Out of Power in Japan, 1931–1941*. Princeton, NJ: Princeton University Press.

―――― (1979), "The Three-Dimensional Empire: Japanese Attitudes and the New Order in East Asia, 1937–1945." *The Japan Interpreter* 12:3–4, 355–83.

Bharucha, Rustom (2006), *Another Asia: Rabindranath Tagore and Okakura Tenshin*. New Delhi: Oxford University Press.

Bose, Rash Behari (Ras Bihari Bōsu) (1922), "Han Kaikyōshugi to Han Ajiashugi. Toruko Fukkō no Igi" (Pan-Islamism and Pan-Asianism—The Meaning of the Re-Emergence of Turkey). *Kaizō* 1922:11, 123–29.

Boyle, John Hunter (1972), *China and Japan at War, 1937–1945: The Politics of Collaboration*. Stanford, CA: Stanford University Press.

Brandt, Max von (1903), *Die Zukunft Ostasiens* (The Future of East Asia). Stuttgart: Strecker and Schröder (first edition 1895).

Brown, Giles (1948), "The Hindu Conspiracy, 1914–1917." *The Pacific Historical Review* 17:3, 299–310.

Brown, Roger H. (2007), "Visions of a Virtuous Manifest Destiny: Yasuoka Masahiro and Japan's Kingly Way." Sven Saaler and J. Victor Koschmann (eds.), *Pan-Asianism in Modern Japanese History: Regionalism, Colonialism and Borders*. New York: Routledge, 133–50.

——— (2009), "Shepherds of the People: Yasuoka Masahiro and the New Bureaucrats in Early Shōwa Japan." *Journal of Japanese Studies* 35:2, 285–319.

Caprio, Mark E. (2009), *Japanese Assimilation Policies in Colonial Korea, 1910–1945*. Seattle: University of Washington Press.

Chen Laixing and Yasui Sankichi (eds.) (1989), *Son Bun Kōen "Dai-Ajiashugi" Shiryōshū. Nihon to Chūgoku no Kiro* (Collected Sources Relating to Sun Yat-sen's Lecture "Pan-Asianism": The Crossroads of Japan and China). Kyoto: Hōritsu Bunkasha.

Cheung, Andrew (1995), "Slogans, Symbols, and Legitimacy: The Case of Wang Jingwei's Nanjing Regime." *Indiana East Asian Working Paper Series on Language and Politics in Modern China*, 6.

Chō Gun (Zhao Jun) (1997), *Dai-Ajiashugi to Chūgoku* (Greater Asianism and China), Aki Shobō.

Choi Hong-gyu (2004), *Sin Ch'ae-ho ŭi yŏksahak kwa minjok undong* (Historiography and the National Movement of Sin Ch'ae-ho). Inchi Publishing.

Cohen, Paul A. (1974), *Between Tradition and Modernity: Wang T'ao and Reform in Late Ch'ing China*. Cambridge, MA: Harvard University Press.

Coudenhove-Kalergi, Richard N. (1931), "Japans Monroe-Doktrin" (Japan's Monroe Doctrine) *Pan-Europa* 7:1, 256–63.

——— (1932), "Kyokutō Monrōshugi o Mitomeyo" (Let's Recognize the Far Eastern Monroe Doctrine). *Tairiku* no. 221, 19–22.

Crowley, James B. (1966), *Japan's Quest for Autonomy, 1930–1938*. Princeton: Princeton University Press.

——— (1971), "Intellectuals as Visionaries of the New Asian Order." James W. Morley (ed.), *Dilemmas of Growth in Prewar Japan*. Princeton, NJ: Princeton University Press, 319–73.

Da Yaxiyazhuyi yu xin Yaxiyazhuyi (Greater Asianism and New Asianism). *Guomin Zazhi*, 1 February 1919, reprinted in *Chenbao* (6 March and 21 March 1919) and in People's Press (ed.), *Li Dazhao Wenji* (Collected Writings of Li Dazhao), 1, no. 2 (1984), Beijing, 609–11.

Dai Ajia Kyōkai/Dai Tsuran Kyōkai (1922), *Dai Ajia* (Greater Asia). Dai Ajia Kyōkai.

Daniels, Roger (1977), *The Politics of Prejudice: The Anti-Japanese Movement in California and the Struggle for Japanese Exclusion*. Berkeley: University of California Press.

Das, Taraknath (1917a), "Ajia no Kyōisha wa Hatashite Nihon ka" (Is It Really Japan That Is a Menace to Asia?). *Nihon oyobi Nihonjin* 706 (1 June 1917), 68–75.

—— (1917b), *Is Japan a Menace to Asia?* Shanghai: no publisher.

—— (1936), *Foreign Policy in the Far East.* New York: Longmans, Green and Co.

—— (1944), *Indo Dokuritsuron* (On Indian Independence). Hakubunkan.

de Bary, William Theodore (ed.) (1960), *Sources of Indian Tradition.* New York: Columbia University Press.

de Bary, William Theodore, et al. (eds.) (1960), *Sources of Chinese Tradition.* New York: Columbia University Press.

Delpai Research (1995), "Tongasia Munmyŏng Chindan—Hanchungil Kongdong Yŏn'gu Kyŏlgwa Pigyo" (Diagnosis of Civilization in East Asia—Comparison of Research in China, Japan and South Korea). *Korea Forum* 21:14, 92–113.

Dennehy, Kristine (2007), "Overcoming Colonialism at Bandung, 1955." Sven Saaler and J. Victor Koschmann (eds.), *Pan-Asianism in Modern Japanese History: Regionalism, Colonialism and Borders.* New York: Routledge, 213–25.

Dignan, Don (1971), "The Hindu Conspiracy in Anglo-American Relations during World War I." *The Pacific Historical Review* 40:1, 57–76.

Dikötter, Frank (ed.) (1997), *The Construction of Racial Identities in China and Japan.* Honolulu: University of Hawai'i Press.

Doak, Kevin M. (1994), *Dreams of Difference: The Japan Romantic School and the Crisis of Modernity.* Berkeley: University of California Press.

Duara, Prasenjit (1998), "Transnationalism in the Era of Nation-States: China, 1900–1945." *Development and Change* 29:4, 647–70.

—— (1998) "Transnationalism in the Era of Nation-States: China, 1900-1945." *Development and Change,* 29:4.

—— (2001), "The Discourse of Civilization and Pan-Asianism." *Journal of World History* 12:1, 99–130.

—— (2003), *Sovereignty and Authenticity: Manchukuo and the East Asian Modern.* New York: Rowman & Littlefield.

Dufourmont, Eddy (2008), "Matsumura Kaiseki et l'Eglise du Japon (Nihon Kyōkai): Un Asiatisme Chrétien?" Christian Galan and Arnaud Brotons (eds.), *Japon Pluriel 7. Actes du Septième Colloque de la Société Française des Études Japonaises.* Paris: Picquier, 159–68.

Duus, Peter (1970), "Nagai Ryūtarō: The Tactical Dilemmas of Reform." Albert M. Craig et al. (eds.), *Personality in Japanese History.* Berkeley: University of California Press, 399–424.

—— (1971), "Nagai Ryūtarō and the 'White Peril,' 1905–1944," *Journal of Asian Studies* 31:1, 41–48.

—— (1995), *The Abacus and the Sword. The Japanese Penetration of Korea, 1895–1910.* Berkeley: University of California Press.

—— (2001), "The 'New Asianism.'" Arne Holzhausen (ed.), *Can Japan Globalize? Studies on Japan's Changing Political Economy and the Process of Globalization in Honour of Sung-Jo Park.* Heidelberg: Physica, 245–56.

Eizawa Kōji (1995), *"Daitō-A Kyōeiken" no Shisō* (The Ideology of the "Greater East Asia Co-Prosperity Sphere"). Kōdansha.

Esenbel, Selçuk (2002), "Japan and Islam Policy during the 1930s." Bert Edstrom (ed.), *Turning Points in Japanese History*. Manchester: Japan Library/Curzon Press, 180–214.

—— (2004), "Japan's Global Claim to Asia and the World of Islam: Transnational Nationalism and World Power, 1900–1945." *The American Historical Review* 109:4, 1140–70.

—— (2007), "The Legacy of the War and the World of Islam in Japanese Pan-Asianist Discourse: Wakabayashi Han's Kaikyō Sekai to Nihon. Rotem Kowner (ed.), *Rethinking the Russo-Japanese War 1904–05. Vol. 1. Centennial Perspectives*. Folkestone: Global Oriental, 263–80.

Esenbel, Selçuk, and Inaba Chiharu (eds.) (2003), *The Rising Sun and the Turkish Crescent: New Perspectives on the History of Japanese Turkish Relations*. Istanbul: Boğaziçi University Press.

Fairbank, John K., Edwin O. Reischauer, and Albert M. Craig (1989), *East Asia: Tradition and Transformation*. Boston: Houghton Mifflin Company.

Fallows, James (1989), "Containing Japan." *The Atlantic Monthly* (May 1989), 40–54.

Fletcher, William Miles III (1982), *The Search for a New Order: Intellectuals and Fascism in Prewar Japan*. Chapel Hill: University of North Carolina Press.

Forman, Michael (1998), *Nationalism and the International Labor Movement: The Idea of the Nation in Socialist and Anarchist Theory*. University Park: Pennsylvania State University Press.

Furukawa Takahisa (1998), *Kōki, Banpaku Orinpikku: Kōshitsu Burando to Keizai Hatten* (Imperial Calendar, the Expo and the Olympic Games: The Imperial Brand and Economic Development). Chūō Kōronsha.

Furuya Tetsuo (ed.) (1996), *Kindai Nihon no Ajia Ninshiki* (The Perception of Asia in Modern Japan). Ryokuin Shobō.

Gayle, Curtis Anderson (2003), *Marxist History and Postwar Japanese Nationalism*. London: RoutledgeCurzon.

Genyōsha Shashi Hensankai (ed.) (1917), *Genyōsha Shashi* (The Official History of the Genyōsha). Genyōsha Shashi Hensankai.

Ghose, Aurobindo (1972a), "Asiatic Democracy." *Bande Mataram*, 16 March 1908, 757–60.

—— (1972b), "India and the Mongolians." *Bande Mataram*, 1 April 1908, 812–17.

—— (1972c), "The Asiatic Role." *Bande Mataram*, 9 April 1908, 842–45.

—— (1972d), "Facts and Opinions." *Bande Mataram*, 31 July 1909, 230–31

—— (1972e), "Facts and Opinions." *Bande Mataram*, 9 October 1909, 247–58.

—— (1972a–1972e), Reprinted in Sri Aurobindo Birth Centenary Library (ed.) (1972), *Bande Mataram. Early Political Writings*, Vol. I. Pondicherry: Sri Aurobindo Ashram Trust.

Gluck, Carol (1993), "The Past in the Present." Andrew Gordon (ed.), *Postwar Japan as History*. Berkeley: University of California Press.

Go Toshi (ed.) (1944), *The Assembly of Greater East-Asiatic Nations*. The Nippon Times.

Goodman, Grant K. (1991), *Japanese Cultural Policies in Southeast Asia during World War Two*. New York: St. Martin's Press.

Consolidated Bibliography

Goto, Ken'ichi (1997), *"Returning to Asia": Japan-Indonesia Relations 1930s–1942*. Ryūkei Shosha.

Gotō Ken'ichi (2007), "1930-nendai 'Ajia Kaiki' Ron to Dai Ajia Kyōkai: Sono Konnichiteki 'Imi' o Kangaeru" (The 1930s "Return to Asia" Debate and the Greater Asia Association: Considering Its Modern "Meaning"). Nishikawa Jun and Hirano Ken'ichirō (eds.), *Higashi Ajia: Kyōdōtai no Kōchiku* (East Asia: The Formation of a Community), Vol. 3, *Kokusai Idō to Shakai Hen'yō* (International Movements and Social Changes). Iwanami Shoten, 73–104.

—— (2008), "Hajime ni, Kaisetsu ni Kaete: Shōwa Senzenki Nihon to Dai Ajia Kyōkai," (Introduction, in Place of a Commentary: Japan in the Prewar Shōwa Period and the Greater Asia Association). Gotō Ken'ichi and Matsuura Masataka (eds.), Dai Ajiashugi *Kaisetsu Sōmokuroku* (*Dai Ajiashugi*: Commentaries and a Complete Catalogue), Ryūkei Shosha, 1–20.

Guan Wei (2003), "Lun Li Dazhao de Xin Yaxiya Zhuyi Jian tan Sun Zhongshan Da Yazhouzhuyi Zhi Bianqian" (On the New Asianism of Li Dazhao and the Transformation of Sun Yat-sen's Great Asianism). *Beifang Luncong* 6, 51–55.

Gulick, Sidney Lewis (1905), *The White Peril in the Far East: an Interpretation of the Significance of the Russo-Japanese War*. New York: Fleming H. Revell.

Hamanaka, Shintaro (2009), *Asian Regionalism and Japan: The Politics of Membership in Regional Diplomatic, Financial and Trade Groups*. London: Routledge.

Hamashita, Takeshi (2008), *China, East Asia and the Global Economy*, edited by Linda Grove and Mark Selden. London: Routledge.

Han, Sang Jin (2003), "Theoretische Reflexionen über die Asiatischen Selbstbehauptungsdiskurse (Theoretical Reflections on Asian Discourse on Self-Assertion)." Iwo Amelung and Sven Saaler et al. (eds.), *Selbstbehauptungsdiskurse in China–Korea–Japan*. Munich: Iudicium, 325–52.

Hannaford, Ivan (1996), *Race: The History of an Idea in the West*. Washington, D.C., and Baltimore: The Woodrow Wilson Center Press and Johns Hopkins University Press.

Hanzawa Kōkan (1940), *Kōa Shokumin Kyōkasho* (Asia Development Textbook). Dai Nihon Tosho.

Hashikawa, Bunsō (1980), "Japanese Perspectives on Asia: From Dissociation to Coprosperity." Akira Iriye (ed.), *The Chinese and the Japanese. Essays in Political and Cultural Interactions*. Princeton, NJ: Princeton University Press, 328–55.

Hashim Makaruddin (ed.) (2000), *Politics, Democracy and the New Asia: Selected Speeches of Dr. Mahathir Mohamad, Prime Minister of Malaysia*. Selangor Darul Ehsan (Malaysia): Pelanduk.

Hatada Takashi (1969), *Nihonjin no Chōsen-kan* (Japanese Views of Korea). Keisō Shobō.

Hatano [Uho] (1912), *Asya Tehlikede* (Asia in Danger). Translated from Japanese by Mehmet Hilmi Nakawa and Abdürreşid İbrahim. İstanbul: Ahmed İhsan ve Şürekası.

Hatano Sumio (1996), *Taiheiyō Sensō to Ajia Gaikō* (The Pacific War and Asian Diplomacy). Tokyo Daigaku Shuppankai.

Hatsuse Ryūhei (1980), *Dentōteki Uyoku Uchida Ryōhei no Kenkyū* (A Study of Uchida Ryōhei, a Traditional Right Winger). Fukuoka: Kyushu Daigaku Shuppankai.

Hauner, Milan (1981), *India in Axis Strategy: Germany, Japan, and Indian Nationalists in the Second World War*. Stuttgart: Klett-Cotta.

Haushofer, Karl (1931), *Geopolitik der Pan-Ideen* (The Geopolitics of Pan-Ideas). Berlin: Zentral-Verlag.

Hay, Stephen N. (1970), *Asian Ideas of East and West. Tagore and his Critics in Japan, China, and India*. Cambridge, MA: Harvard University Press.

Hayashi Fusao (1974), *Dai Tōa Sensō Kōteiron* (Affirmation of the Greater East Asian War). Roman (reprinted as expanded edition Banchō Shobō 1975; reprinted Natsume Shobō, 2001).

Hazama Naoki (2001), "Shoki Ajiashugi ni tsuite no shiteki kōsatsu" (A Historical Inquiry into Early Pan-Asianism). *Tōa*, nos. 410–417 (2001–2002, 8 installments).

He, Jing (2006), *China in Okakura Kakuzō with Special Reference to His First Chinese Trip in 1893*. PhD diss., University of California, Los Angeles.

Heisig, James W., and John C. Maraldo (1995), *Rude Awakenings: Zen, the Kyoto School, and the Question of Nationalism*. Honolulu: University of Hawai'i Press.

Hinohara Shōzō (1884), "Nihon wa Tōyōkoku taru bekarazu" (Japan Must Not Be an Oriental Country). *Jiji Shinpō*, 11, 13, and 14 November 1884.

Hirai, Kazuomi (2005), "Sengo Shakai Undō no naka no Beheiren Undō no chiikiteki Enkai o Chūshin ni" (Citizen's Federation for Peace in Vietnam [Beheiren] and the Social Movements in Postwar Japan). *Hōsei Kenkyū/Journal of Law and Politics* 71:4, 355–87.

Hiraishi Naoaki (1994), "Kindai Nihon no 'Ajiashugi'" (The "Asianism" of Modern Japan). Mizoguchi, Yūzō et al. (eds.), *Sekaizō no Keisei* (Ajia kara kangaeru 5). Tokyo Daigaku Shuppankai.

Hirano Kuniomi (1863), *Seiban Sosaku* (Fundamental Measures for Expelling the Barbarians), reprinted in Hirano Kuniomi Kenshōkai (ed.), *Hirano Kuniomi Denki oyobi Ikō* (Biography and Posthumous Writings of Hirano Kuniomi). Shōzansha, 1980, 54.

Hirano Yoshitarō (1945), *Ajiashugi no Rekishiteki Kiso* (The Historical Foundations of Asianism). Kawade Shobō.

Hiranuma Kiichirō Kaikoroku Hensan Iinkai (ed.) (1955), *Hiranuma Kiichirō Kaikoroku* (The Memoirs of Hiranuma Kiichirō). Gaiyō Shobō.

Hohenzollern, William [Wilhelm von] (1922), "Memoirs of the Ex-Kaiser." *New York Times*, September/October 1922 (10 installments).

Holland, William L. (1955), *Selected Documents of the Bandung Conference: Texts of Selected Speeches and Final Communique of the Asian-African Conference, Bandung, Indonesia, April 18–24, 1955*. New York: Institute of Pacific Relations.

Horiuchi Bunjirō (1918), "Dai Ajiashugi to waga kokumin no shimei" (Great Asianism and the Mission of Our People). *Taiyō* 24:9.

Hosoi Hajime (1932), *Nihon no Ketsui* (Japan's Resolve). Nihon Yūben Taikai Kōdansha.

Hoston, Germaine (1984), "Marxism and Japanese Expansionism: Takahashi Kame-kichi and the Theory of 'Petty Imperialism.'" *Journal of Japanese Studies* 10:1, 1–30.

Hotta, Eri (2006), "Rash Behari Bose and His Japanese Supporters." *Interventions* 8:1, 116–32.

—— (2007), *Pan-Asianism and Japan's War 1931–1945*. New York: Palgrave Macmillan.

Hughes, Thomas L. (2002), "The German Mission to Afghanistan, 1915–16." *German Studies Review* 25:3, 447–76.

Huntington, Samuel P. (1996), *The Clash of Civilizations and the Remaking of World Order*. New York: Simon & Schuster.

Hwang, Dongyoun (1998), "Some Reflections on War-Time Collaboration in China: Wang Jingwei and His Group in Hanoi." *Working Papers in Asian/Pacific Studies* 98-02.

Ichikawa Fusae, "Mite Kita Shin Shina" (The New China I Saw). *Fujō Shinbun*, no. 2080 (21 April 1940), 2, and no. 2081 (28 April 1940), 8.

Iida, Yumiko (1997), "Fleeing the West, Making Asia Home. Transpositions of Otherness in Japanese Pan-Asianism, 1905–1930." *Alternatives* 22, 409–32.

Inabe Kōjirō (2002), *Ikki to Reikichi: Kita Kyōdai no Sokoku* (Ikki and Reikichi: The Fatherland of the Brothers Kita). Niigata: Niigata Nippō Jigyōsha.

Inoue Hide, "Joshi Kyōiku no Dōkō" (Trends in Women's Education). *Kōa Kyōiku* 3:3 (1944), 18–24.

Inoue Hisakazu (2006), *Ajiashugi o Toinaosu* (Reconsidering Asianism). Chikuma Shobō.

Inoue Kiyoshi (1966), *Nihon no "Kindaika" to Gunkokushugi* (Japan's "Modernization" and Militarism). Shin Nihon Shinsho.

Inoue Masaji (1910), *Kyojin Arao Sei. Tsuketari Jūni Resshiden* (The Giant Arao Sei. Including The Lives of Twelve Patriots). Sakura Shobō.

—— (1944), *Kōa Gojūnen no Saka o Yojite* (Fifty Years in the Uphill Struggle to Raise Asia). Self-published.

Ishidō Kiyotomo (1985), "Tenkō ni tsuite" (Concerning Apostasy). *Undōshi Kenkyū* 16: 72–92.

Ishihara, Shintaro (1991), *The Japan That Can Say "No."* Translated by Frank Baldwin. New York: Simon & Schuster.

Ishiwara Kanji (1993), *Saishū Sensōron Sensōshi Taikan* (Treatise on the Final War and an Outline of War History). Chūō Kōronsha.

Itō Takashi (1978), *Taishōki "Kakushin"-ha no Seiritsu* (The Formation of the "Radical Faction" in the Taishō Era). Hanawa Shobō.

—— (1983), *Konoe Shintaisei: Taisei Yokusankai e no Michi* (The Konoe New Order: The Road to the Imperial Rule Assistance Association). Chūō Kōronsha.

—— (comp.) (2006), *Gendaishi o Kataru: Matsumoto Gaku* (Talking of Modern History: Matsumoto Gaku). Naiseishi Kenkyūkai Danwa Sokkiroku. Gendaishi Shiryō Shuppan.

—— (1989), "'Dai Ajiashugi' to 'Sanmin shugi.' Ō Seiei [Wang Jingwei] Kairai Seikenka no Shomondai ni tsuite" ("Greater Asianism" and "The Three People's

Principles." On Some Problems under Wang Jingwei's Puppet Government). *Yokohama Shiritsu Daigaku Ronsō* 40:1, 225–47.

Itō Teruo (ed.) (1990), *Ajia to Kindai Nihon: Han Shinryaku no Shisō to Undō* (Asia and Modern Japan: Anti-Invasionist Thought and Action). Shakai Hyōronsha.

Iwakura Tomomi (1875), "Tomomi Saido Kokusei o Hitsurokushi Goran ni Kyōzurukoto" (Tomomi Writes and Submits Another Proposal on the State Policy). Tada Kōmon (ed.), *Iwakura Kō Jikki* (Diary of Prince Iwakura), Vol. 2, (Kunaishō/Ministry of Imperial Household), 1906, 1270.

Jansen, Marius B. (1954), *The Japanese and Sun Yat-sen*. Cambridge, MA: Harvard University Press.

—— (1980), "Konoe Atsumaro." Akira Iriye (ed.), *The Chinese and the Japanese: Essays in Political and Cultural Interactions*. Princeton, NJ: Princeton University Press, 107–23.

—— (2000), *The Making of Modern Japan*. Cambridge, MA: Harvard University Press.

Jensen, Joan (1979), "The 'Hindu Conspiracy': A Reassessment." *The Pacific Historical Review* 48:1, 65–83.

Johnson, Chalmers (1964), *An Instance of Treason: Ozaki Hotsumi and the Sorge Spy Ring*. Stanford, CA: Stanford University Press.

—— (1993), "The State and Japanese Grand Strategy." Richard Rosecrance and Arthur A. Stein (eds.), *The Domestic Bases of Grand Strategy*. Ithaca, NY: Cornell University Press.

Kada, Tetsuji (1939), "The Theory of an East Asiatic Unity." *Contemporary Japan* July 1939 (VIII:5), 574–81.

Kajima Kenkyūjo (ed.) (1971), *Nihon Gaikōshi, 24-kan: Daitōa Sensō, Senji Gaikō* (History of Japanese Foreign Relations, Vol. 24: The Greater East Asian War, War Time Diplomacy). Kajima Kenkyūjo Shuppankai.

Kamachi, Noriko (1981), *Reform in China: Huang Tsun-hsien and the Japanese Model*. Cambridge, MA: Council on East Asian Studies, Harvard University.

Kamikawa, Hikomatsu (1939), "The American and Japanese Monroe Doctrines." *Contemporary Japan* 8:6, 740–50.

Kan Sō-ichi (Han Sang-il) (1984), *Nikkan Kindaishi no Kūkan: Meiji Nashonarizumu no Rinen to Genjitsu* (The Space of the Modern History of Japan and Korea: The Ideals and Reality of Meiji Nationalism). Nihon Keizai Hyōronsha.

Kaneko, Toshiya (2002), *Cultural Light, Political Shadow: Okakura Tenshin (1862–1913) and the Japanese Crisis of National Identity*. PhD diss., University of Pennsylvania.

Kang Sang-jung (2001), *Tōhoku Ajia Kyōdō no Ie o Mezashite* (Towards a Common House in Northeast Asia). Heibonsha.

Kanlidere, Ahmet (1997), *Reform within Islam: the Tajdid and Jadid Movement among the Kazan Tatars, 1809-1917*. Beyoğlu, Istanbul: Eren.

Kanokogi Kazunobu (1937), *Sumera Ajia* (Imperial Asia). Dōbun Shoin.

Karl, Rebecca (2002), *Staging the World: Chinese Nationalism at the Turn of the Twentieth Century*. Durham, NC: Duke University Press.

Katsube Mitake, Matsumoto Sannosuke, Ōguchi Yūjirō (eds.) (1972), *Katsu Kaishū Zenshū* (Collected Writings of Katsu Kaishū), Vol. 18. Keisō Shobō, 50.

Katzenstein, Peter, and Takashi Shiraishi (eds.) (1997), *Network Power: Japan and Asia*. Ithaca, NY: Cornell University Press.

—— (eds.) (2006), *Beyond Japan: The Dynamics of East Asian Regionalism*. Ithaca, NY: Cornell University Press.

Katzenstein, Peter, et al. (2000), *Asian Regionalism*. Cornell East Asia Series. Ithaca, NY: East Asia Program, Cornell University.

Kawahara Hiroshi (1979), *Shōwa Shisōshi Kenkyū* (The Study of Shōwa Intellectual History). Waseda Daigaku Shuppankai.

Kawai Yoshihiro (2006), *Yasuoka Masahiro no Kenkyū: Minponshugi no Keisei to sono Tenkai* (A Study of Yasuoka Masahiro: The Formation and Development of "People-as-the Base" Thought). Meisō Shuppansha.

Kawakami, K. K. [Kiyoshi Karl] (1919), *Japan and World Peace*. New York: Macmillan.

—— (1921), *What Japan Thinks*. New York: Macmillan.

Keene, Donald (1964), "Japanese Writers and the Greater East Asia War." *Journal of Asian Studies* 23:2, 209–25.

Kim Bongjin (2007), "Kindai Chōsen to Higashia Ajia Ninshiki" (Modern Korea and Asian Consciousness). Kishi Toshihiko et al. (eds.), *"Higashi Ajia" no Jidaisei* (The Temporality of "East Asia"). Keisuisha, 53–90.

Kim Dae-Jung (1994), "Is Culture Destiny? The Myth of Asia's Anti-Democratic Values." *Foreign Affairs*, November–December, 189–94.

Kim, John Namjun (2007), "The Temporality of Empire: The Imperial Cosmopolitanism of Miki Kiyoshi and Tanabe Hajime." Sven Saaler and J. Victor Koschmann (eds.), *Pan-Asianism in Modern Japanese History: Regionalism, Colonialism and Borders*. New York: Routledge, 151–67.

Kingston, Jeffrey (2004), *Japan's Quiet Transformation: Social Change and Civil Society in the Twenty-First Century*. London: RoutledgeCurzon.

Kita Ikki (1921 [1915]), *Shina Kakumei Gaishi* (An Unofficial History of the Chinese Revolution), Daitōtaku, reprinted in Kita Ikki (1959), *Kita Ikki Chosakushū* (Collected Works by Kita Ikki), Vol. 2. Misuzu Shobō, 1–213.

—— (1919), *Kokka Kaizōan Genri Daikō* (Outline of a Plan for the Reconstruction of Japan), Yūzonsha, reprinted in Kita Ikki (1959), *Kita Ikki Chosakushū*, Vol. 2. Misuzu Shobō, 215–81.

—— (1959), *Kita Ikki Chosakushū* (Collected Works of Kita Ikki), Vol. 2. Misuzu Shobō.

Kita Ikki, Ōkawa Shūmei, and Mitsukawa Kametarō (2008), *Ajiashugishatachi no Koe 3: Yūzonsha to Kōchisha, aruiwa Kokka Kaizō e no Kokoromi* (Pan-Asianist Voices, Vol. 3: The Yūzonsha and the Kōchisha, or An Attempt at State Reform). Shoshi Shinsui.

Kita Reikichi (1917a), "Gokai Saretaru Ajiashugi" (Misunderstood Asianism). *Tōhō Jiron* 2:7, 8–10.

—— (1917b), "Waga Kuni no Daishimei" (The Great Mission of Our Country). *Tōhō Jiron* 2:12, 19–21.

—— (1918), *Hikari wa Tōhō Yori* (The Light from the East). Dai Nihon Yūbenkai.

—— (1941), *Haigeki no Rekishi* (The History of Rejection). Dairi Shobō.

Kitaoka Shin'ichi (1988), *Gotō Shinpei. Gaikō to Vision* (Gotō Shinpei. Foreign Policy and Vision). Chūō Kōronsha.

Kiyofuji Kōshichirō (ed.) (1981), *Ten'yūkyō* (The Band of Heroes Assisted by Heaven). Kōryū Shorin (reprint).

Kobayashi Hideo (1995), *"Nihon Kabushikigaisha" o Tsukutta Otoko: Miyazaki Masayoshi no Shōgai* (The Man Who Created "Japan Inc.": The Life of Miyazaki Masayoshi). Shōgakukan.

—— (2005), *Mantetsu Chōsabu* (The Research Department of the Southern Manchurian Railway Co.). Heibonsha.

Kodera Kenkichi (1916), *Dai Ajiashugiron* (Treatise on Greater Asianism). Hōbunkan.

Koizumi, Junichiro, Prime Minister of Japan (2002), "Japan and ASEAN in East Asia: A Sincere and Open Partnership" (14 January). Prime Minister of Japan and His Cabinet website, http://www.kantei.go.jp/foreign/koizumispeech/2002/01/14speech _e.html (last accessed 30 March 2010).

Kojima Shinji et al. (eds.) (1974), *Chūgokujin no Nihonjinkan Hyakunenshi* (Hundred Years' History of Chinese Views of the Japanese). Jiyū Kokuminsha.

Kokuryūkai (1934), *Nikkan Gappō Kinentō Shashinchō* (Monument to the Union of Japan and Korea). Kokuryūkai Honbu.

—— (1966a), *Nikkan Gappō Hishi* (Secret History of the Union of Japan and Korea). Hara Shobō (first published 1930 by Kokuryūkai Shuppanbu, ed. by Kuzuu Yoshihisa).

—— (ed.) (1904), *Seiro Annai* (Guidebook to Conquering Russia). Futendō.

—— (ed.) (1966b), *Tōa Senkaku Shishi Kiden* (Biographies of Pioneer East Asian Patriots), 3 vols., Hara Shobō (first published 1933–36 by Kokuryūkai Shuppanbu, ed. by Kuzuu Yoshihisa).

Kokuryūkai Honbu (1924), Kokuryūkai Kakuchō Shuisho (Program for an Expansion of the Kokuryūkai), reprinted in Uchida Ryōhei Monjo Kenkyūkai (ed.), *Uchida Ryōhei Kankei Monjo*, Vol. 7, Fuyō Shobō, 20f.

—— (ed.) (1904), *Kokuryūkai Mankan Shinzu* (Kokuryūkai's New Map of Manchuria and Korea). Kōbunkan Yoshikawa Hanshichi.

Kokuryūkai Shuppanbu (ed.) (1918), *Ajia Taikan* (Overview of Asia). Kokuryūkai Shuppanbu.

Komagome Takeshi (1994), "'Manshūkoku' ni okeru Jukyō no Isō: Daidō, Ōdō, Kōdō" (Tenets of Confucianism in Manchukuo: The Great Way, the Kingly Way, the Imperial Way). *Shisō* 841, 57–82.

Kondō Kuniyasu (1979), "Kaisetsu" (Commentary). Nishi Junzō (ed.), *Genten Chūkoku Kindai Shisōshi*, Vol. 3 (A History of the Foundations of Modern Chinese Thought). Iwanami Shoten, 3–26.

—— (1981), *Chūgoku Kindai Shisōshi Kenkyū* (Studies in Modern Chinese Intellectual History). Keisō Shobō.

Konoe Atsumaro (1898a), "Dōjinshu Dōmei, Tsuketari Shina Mondai Kenkyū no Hitsuyō" (An Alliance of the Same Race and the Necessity of Studying the Chinese Question). *Taiyō*, 24:1 (1 January 1898), reprinted in Konoe Atsumaro Nikki

Kankōkai (ed.), *Konoe Atsumaro Nikki*, supplement. Kajima Kenkyūjo Shuppankai, 1969, 62–63.

—— (1898b), "Teikoku no Ichi to Gendai no Seijika" (The Position of Our Empire and the Politicians òf Today). *Tōa Jiron* 1 (December), 5–7.

Konoe Atsumaro Nikki Kankōkai (ed.) (1968–1969), *Konoe Atsumaro Nikki* (The Diaries of Konoe Atsumaro), 6 vols. Kajima Kenkyūjo Shuppankai.

Konoe Fumimaro (1918), "Eibei Hon'i Heiwashugi o Hai Su" (A Call to Reject the Anglo-American Centered Peace). *Nihon oyobi Nihonjin* 746 (12 December), 23–26.

—— (1981), *Sengo Ōbei Kenbunroku* (Travels in Post-War Europe and the United and States). Chūō Kōronsha (first edition Gaikō Jihōsha, 1920).

—— (1937), "Manchukuo, Precursor of Asiatic Renaissance and the Government by Wang-Tao (Kingly Way) Based on Theocracy." *Contemporary Manchuria* 1:2, 1–17.

Koo Jong-Suh (1995), "Pan-Asianism. Primacy of East Asia." *The Monthly Joongang*, April.

Koschmann, J. Victor (1997), "Asianism's Ambivalent Legacy," in Peter J. Katzenstein and Takashi Shiraishi (eds.), *Network Power: Japan and Asia*. Ithaca, NY: Cornell University Press, 83–110.

Kurbangaliev, M. (1924), "Ajia no Roshia ni okeru Uraru Arutai Minzoku" (The Ural-Altaic Peoples in Russian Asia). *Manmō* 10, 20–32.

Kuroki Morifumi (2002), "Ueki Emori no Taigai Shisō (1)" (On the Foreign Thought of Emori Ueki [1]). *Fukuoka Kokusai Daigaku Kiyō* 7, 15–27.

—— (2005), "Kōakai no Ajiashugi" (The Asianism of the Kōakai). *Hōsei Kenkyū* (Kyūshū Daigaku) 71:4, 247–87.

—— (2007), "The Asianism of the Kōa-kai and the Ajia Kyōkai: Reconsidering the Ambiguity of Asianism." Sven Saaler and J. Victor Koschmann (eds.), *Pan-Asianism in Modern Japanese History*. London: Routledge, 34–51.

Kuroki Morifumi and Masuzawa Akio (eds.) (1993), *Kōa-kai Hōkoku/Ajia Kyōkai Hōkoku* (Bulletin of the Kōakai, Bulletin of the Ajia Kyōkai). Reprint, 2 vols. Fuji Shuppan.

Kushner, Barak (2006), *The Thought War: Japanese Imperial Propaganda*. Honolulu: University of Hawai'i Press.

Laffan, Michael Francis (2003), *Islamic Nationhood and Colonial Indonesia: The Umma below the Winds*. London: RoutledgeCurzon.

Lee, Chong-sik (1985), *Japan and Korea: The Political Dimension*. Stanford, CA: Hoover Institution Press.

Lee, Peter et al. (eds.) (2000), *Sources of Korean Tradition*. New York: Columbia University Press.

Li Cai-hua and Suzuki Tadashi (2007), *Ajia to Nihon: Heiwa Shisō toshite no Ajiashugi* (Asia and Japan: Asianism as an Ideology of Peace). Nōbunkyō.

Li Narangoa (2007), "Universal Values and Pan-Asianism: The Vision of Ōmotokyō." Sven Saaler and J. Victor Koschmann (eds.), *Pan-Asianism in Modern Japanese History: Colonialism, Regionalism and Borders*. London: Routlege, 52–66.

Li Quanxing (ed.) (1994), *Li Dazhao Yanjiu Cidian* (Dictionary for Research on Li Dazhao). Beijing: Hongqi Chubanshe.

Mackie, Jamie (2005), *Bandung 1955: Non-Alignment and Afro-Asian Solidarity*. Singapore: Editions Didier Millet.

Maeno Ryōtaku (1777), *Kanreihigen* (Humble Opinion from Limited Observation), reprinted in Numata Shirō et al. (eds.), *Nihon Shisō Taikei, Vol. 64: Yōgaku* (Survey of Japanese Thought, Vol. 64: Western Science). Iwanami Shoten, 1973.

Mahathir Mohamad (2004), *Achieving True Globalisation*. Interview and composition by Kohei Hashimoto. Selangor Darul Ehsan (Malaysia): Pelanduk.

Mahathir Mohamad and Shintarō Ishihara (1995), *The Voice of Asia: Two Leaders Discuss the Coming Century*. Translated by Frank Baldwin. Kōdansha, 1995. Originally published as *"No" to ieru Ajia* (The Asia That Can Say "No"), Kōbunsha, 1994.

Mannheim, Karl (1953), *Essays on Sociology and Social Psychology*, edited by Paul Kecskemeti. London: Routledge and Kegan Paul.

Mantetsukai and Shimano Saburō Denki Kankōkai (eds.) (1984), *Shimano Saburō* (Shimano Saburō). Hara Shobō.

Mark, Ethan (2006), "'Asia's' Transwar Lineage: Nationalism, Marxism and 'Greater Asia' in an Indonesian Inflection." *Journal of Asian Studies* 65:3, 461–93.

Maruyama Masao (1964), "Nihon Fuashizumu no Shisō to Undō" (The Thought and Movement of Japanese Fascism), Maruyama Masao, *Gendai Seiji no Shisō to Undō* (The Thought and Movement of Modern Politics). Miraisha, 29–87.

—— (2002), "Fukuzawa Yukichi no 'Datsuaron' to sono Shūhen" (Fukuzawa Yukichi's *Datsuaron* and Its Context). *Maruyama Masao Techō* 20, 1–42.

Maswood, S. Javed (ed.) (2001), *Japan and East Asian Regionalism*. London: Routledge.

Matsui Iwane (1933), "Dai Ajiashugi" (Greater Asianism). *Kingu*, May Issue Supplement "Jikyoku Mondai: Hijōji Kokumin Taikai" (The Problems concerning the Current Situation: A People's Rally in Times of Emergency), 2–9.

Matsumoto Gaku (1933), "Nippon Bunka Renmei no Teishō: Daigo Intaa (Nihon Seishin Intaa) ni Tsuite" (A Call for a Japan Culture League: On the 5th International [The International of the Japanese Spirit]). *Kokui* 14, 3.

—— (1940), "Eastern Culture and Its Peculiar Features." *Cultural Nippon* 8:4, 1–15.

Matsumoto Ken'ichi (2000), *Takeuchi Yoshimi "Nihon no Ajiashugi: Seidoku* (Careful Reading of Takeuchi Yoshimi's "Japan's Asianism"). Iwanami Shoten.

Matsumura Masayoshi (1987), *Pōtsumasu e no Michi. Kōkaron to Yōroppa no Suematsu Kenchō* (The Road to Portsmouth. The Yellow Peril and Suematsu Kenchō during His Time in Europe). Hara Shobō.

Matsuoka Yōsuke (1941a), Address by the Foreign Minister of Japan before the 76th Session of the Imperial Diet, 21 January 1941. *Contemporary Japan*, February.

—— (1941b), *Kōa no Taigyō* (The Gigantic Task of Raising Asia). Naikaku Insatsukyoku/Daiichi Kōronsha.

Matsuura Masataka (2007a), "Han-Ajiashugi ni okeru 'Indo Yōin'" (The Indian Factor in Pan-Asianism). Ishida Ken (ed.), *Bōchō Suru Teikoku, Kakusan Suru Teikoku* (The Growing Empire, the Disintegrating Empire). Tokyo Daigaku Shuppankai, 3–53.

—— (ed.) (2007b), *Shōwa-Ajiashugi no Jitsuzō* (The True Picture of Shōwa-Period Asianism). Kyoto: Minerva Shobō.

—— (2010), *Taiheiyō Sensō wa naze Okita no ka: Han-Ajiashugi no Seiji Keizaishi* (Why Did the Pacific War Come About? The Political and Economic History of Pan-Asianism). Nagoya: Nagoya Daigaku Shuppankai.

Matsuzawa Tatsuo (1939), "New Chosen." *Contemporary Japan*, June, 455–64.

Matsuzawa Tetsunari (1979), *Ajiashugi to Fashizumu* (Asianism and Fascism). Renga Shobō Shinsha.

Mazumdar R. C. (1927), "Introduction." *Ancient Indian Colonies in the Far East*, Vol. I. Champa: The Punjab Sanskrit Book Depot and Lahore, i–xxiv.

McCormack, Gavan (2000), "The Japanese Movement to 'Correct' History." Laura Hein and Mark Selden (eds.), *Censoring History: Citizenship and Memory in Japan, Germany, and the United States.* Armonk, NY: M. E. Sharpe.

McWilliams, Wayne C. (1975), "East Meets East: The Soejima Mission to China, 1873." *Monumenta Nipponica* 30:3, 237–75.

Meisner, Maurice (1967), *Li Ta-Chao and the Origins of Chinese Marxism.* Cambridge, MA: Harvard University Press.

Miki Kiyoshi (1938), "Tōa Shisō no Konkyo" (The Basis of East Asian Philosophy). *Kaizō*, December, 8–20.

Minichiello, Sharon (1984), *Retreat from Reform: Patterns of Political Behavior in Interwar Japan.* Honolulu: University of Hawai'i Press.

Mitani Hiroshi (1997), *Meiji Ishin to Nashonarizumu* (The Meiji Restoration and Nationalism). Yamakawa Shuppansha.

Mitsukawa Kametarō (1921), *Ubawaretaru Ajia* (Stolen Asia). Kōbundō Shoten (reprinted 2007 by Shoshi Shinsui).

—— (1935), *Sangoku Kanshō Igo* (After the Triple Intervention). Heibonsha (reprinted 1977 by Dentō to Gendaisha and 2004 by Ronsōsha).

Miwa Kimitada (1973), "Ajiashugi no Rekishiteki Kōsatsu" (Historical Examination of Asianism). Hirano Ken'ichirō (ed.), *Nihon Bunka no Hen'yō.* Kōdansha, 385–461.

—— (1990), "Japanese Policies and Concepts for a Regional Order in Asia, 1938–1940." James W. White, Michio Umegaki, and Thomas R. H. Havens (eds.), *The Ambivalence of Nationalism: Modern Japan between East and West.* Lanham, MD: University Press of America, 133–54.

—— (1999), *Kakusareta Perii no "Shirahata"* (Perry's Hidden "White Flag"). Sophia University Press.

Miyadai Shinji (2004), *Ajiashugi no Tenmatsu ni Manabe* (Learn from the Development of Asianism!). Jissensha.

Miyagawa Torao (1972), *Okakura Tenshin.* Tokyo University Press.

Miyagi Taizō (2001), *Bandon Kaigi to Nihon no Ajia Fukki* (The Bandung Conference and Japan's Return to Asia). Soshisha.

Miyai Kanejirō (1925), *Dai Ajia Renpō no Kensetsu* (The Construction of a Greater Asian Federation). Ajia Shinbunsha.

Miyamoto Moritarō (1984), *Shūkyōteki Ningen no Seiji Shisō: Abe Isoo to Kanokogi Kazunobu no Baai* (The Political Thought of Religious Men: The Case of Abe Isoo and Kanokogi Kazunobu). Bokutakusha.

Miyazaki Masayoshi (1938), *Tōa Renmei Ron* (On the East Asian League), Kaizōsha.

Miyazaki Ryūsuke and Onogawa Hidemi (eds.) (1971), *Miyazaki Tōten Zenshū* (Complete Works of Miyazaki Tōten), Vol. 2. Heibonsha.

Miyazaki Tōten (1902), *Sanjūsannen no Yume* (Thirty-Three Years' Dream). Kokkō Shobō.

—— (1915), "Rikkōho Sengen" (Election Manifesto), reproduced in *Miyazaki Tōten Zenshū* (Complete Works of Miyazaki Tōten), Vol. 2, Heibonsha, 1971, frontispiece.

—— (1919), "Tokyo yori" (From Tokyo, 1919), *Miyazaki Tōten Zenshū* (Complete Works of Miyazaki Tōten), Vol. 2, Heibonsha, 1971, 128.

—— (1982), *My Thirty-Three Years' Dream: The Autobiography of Miyazaki Tōten*. Translated, with an introduction by Etō Shinkichi and Marius B. Jansen. Princeton, NJ: Princeton University Press.

Miyazaki Tōten, Kayano Nagatomo, and Kita Ikki (2008), *Ajiashugisha no Koe 2: Kakumei Hyōronka aruiwa Chūgoku Kakumei e no Kan'yo to Satetsu* (Pan-Asianist Voices, Vol. 2: Critics of Revolution or Engagement and Failure in the Chinese Revolution). Shoshi Shinsui.

Mizoguchi Yūzō et al. (eds.) (1993–1994), *Ajia kara Kangaeru* (Asian Perspectives). 7 vols. Tokyo Daigaku Shuppankai.

Mizuno Naoki (1996), "1920-nendai Nihon: Chōsen, Chūgoku ni okeru Ajia Ninshiki no Ichidanmen: Ajia Minzoku Kaigi o Meguru Sangoku no Ronchō" (Japan in the 1920s: One Aspect of Asia Awareness in Korea and China. Debates Concerning the Conference of Asian Peoples in the Three Countries). Furuya Tetsuo (ed.), *Kindai Nihon to Ajia Ninshiki* (The Perception of Asia in Modern Japan). Ryokuin Shobō, 509–48.

Mizushima Naofumi (1978), *Sugita Junzan Ō Shōden* (Short Biography of the Venerable Sugita Junzan). Fukui: Yasuda Shoten/Himawari Shoten.

Mori Kaku (1941), "Hijōji no hijō shudan" (Extraordinary Means for Extraordinary Times). *Diamond*, July 1932, reprinted in Yamaura Kan'ichi, *Tōa Shintaisei no Senku: Mori Kaku*. Mori Kaku Denki Hensankai, 1941, 26–29.

Mori Rintarō (Ōgai) (1904), *Kōkaron Kōgai* (An Outline of the Yellow Peril). Shun'yōdō.

Morishima Michio (2000), *Collaborative Development in Northeast Asia*. Basingstoke: Palgrave Macmillan.

Mukherjee, Tapan (1997), *Taraknath Das: Life and Letters of a Revolutionary in Exile*. Calcutta: National Council of Education in Bengal.

Mulgan, Aurelia George (2009), "Hatoyama's East Asia Community and Regional Leadership Rivalries." Internet: East Asia Forum, http://www.eastasiaforum. org/2009/10/13/hatoyamas-east-asia-community/ (last accessed 1 June 2010).

Murayama Tomiichi (1995), "Statement by Prime Minister Tomiichi Murayama 'On the Occasion of the 50th Anniversary of the War's End' (15 August 1995)." Internet: *Ministry of Foreign Affairs*, http://www.mofa.go.jp/announce/press/pm/ murayama/9508.html (last accessed 1 March 2010).

Muro Kiyoshi (1999), *Tōjō Utsubeshi: Nakano Seigō Hyōden* (Tōjō Must Be Struck: A Critical Biography of Nakano Seigō). Asahi Shinbunsha.

Murobuse Kōshin (1926), *Ajiashugi* (Asianism). Hihyōsha.

Mutō Shūtarō (2003), "Hirano Yoshitarō no Dai Ajiashugiron" (Hirano Yoshitarō's Theory of Greater Asianism). *Ajia Kenkyū* 49:4, 44–59.

Nagai, Ryūtarō (1913), "The White Peril." *The Japan Magazine*, 39–42.

—— (1920), *Kaizō no Risō* (The Ideal of Renovation). Seikadō.

—— (1937), "Ajia saiken no seisen" (Holy War for the Reconstruction of Asia). *Nihon Bunka* 10 (November), 27–42.

—— (1944), *Nagai Ryūtarō shi Kōa Yūbenshū* (Speeches of Nagai Ryūtarō concerning the Raising of Asia). Ryūginsha.

Nagami Shichirō (1942), *Kōa Ichiro: Inoue Masaji* (Inoue Masaji: Path to a Prosperous Asia). Tōkō Shoin.

Naimushō Keihokyoku Hoanka (1926), *Zen Ajia Minzoku Kaigi Tenmatsu. Tsuketari Puratappu no Torai* (The Circumstances of the Conference of Asian Peoples. Addendum: The Arrival of Pratap). Gaimushō Gaikō Shiryōkan (Diplomatic Record Office of the Ministry of Foreign Affairs of Japan), Gaimushō Kiroku (Diplomatic Records), MT I.4.6.0.1-1, Minzoku Mondai Kankei Zakken (Miscellaneous Matters Relating to the Question of Asian Nationalities), Vol. 2: Ajia Minzoku Mondai (The Question of Asian Nationalities).

Najita, Tetsuo (1971), "Nakano Seigō and the Meiji Restoration in Twentieth-Century Japan." Morley, James (ed.), *Dilemmas of Growth in Prewar Japan*. Princeton, NJ: Princeton University Press.

Nakagawa Hidenao (2006), "Atarashii Ajiashugi" (A New Asianism). Abe Shinzō et al., *Nitchū Taiwa* (Japanese-Chinese Dialogue). Genron NPO.

Nakajima Takeshi (2005), *Nakamuraya no Bōsu: Indo Dokuritsu Undō to Kindai Nihon no Ajiashugi* (The Bose of the Nakamuraya: The Indian Independence Movement and the Asianism of Modern Japan). Hakusuisha.

—— (2009), *Bose of Nakamuraya: An Indian Revolutionary in Japan*. New Delhi: Promilla & Co. Publishers in association with Bibliophile South Asia.

Nakamura Naomi (1991), "Tokutomi Sohō no 'Ajiashugi'" (Tokutomi Sohō's "Asianism"). *Shakai Kagaku Kenkyū* 37:2, 415–37.

Nakamura Tetsu (2003), "Military Action Prompting Afghan Backlash." *International Herald Tribune/Asahi Shimbun*, 13 December (accessible online at http://www1a.biglobe.ne.jp/peshawar/eg/naka13dec03.html).

Nakano Seigō (1917), "Bōkoku no Sanga" (The Mountains and Rivers of a Fallen State), *Sekai Seisaku to Kyokutō Seisaku* (Global and Far Eastern Policy). Shiseidō Shoten.

—— (1942), "Kono Issen: Kokumin wa ika ni Tatakaubeki ka!" (This One War: How the People Should Fight!), Tōhōkai, Tokyo, January, 13–16.

Nakano Yasuo (1988), *Ajiashugisha Nakano Seigō* (The Pan-Asianist Nakano Seigō). Aki Shobō.

Nakashita Masaharu (1996), *Shinbun ni Miru Nitchū Kankeishi: Chūgoku no Nihonjin Keieishi* (Sino-Japanese Relations as Seen through Newspapers: China's Japanese-Run Newspapers). Kenbun Shuppan.

Nakatani Takeyo (1985), "Matsui Taishō to Dai Ajiashugi. Jo ni Kaete" (General Matsui and Greater Asianism. In Place of a Preface). Tanaka Masaaki (ed.), *Matsui*

Iwane Taishō no Jinchū Nisshi (General Matsui Iwane's War Diary). Fuyō Shobō, 4–6.

—— (1989), *Shōwa Dōranki no Kaisō: Nakatani Takeyo Kaikoroku* (Recollections of the Upheavals of the Shōwa Period: The Memoirs of Nakatani Takeyo). 2 vols., Tairyūsha.

Nicolaevsky, B. (1949), "Russia, Japan, and the Pan-Asiatic Movement to 1925." *The Far Eastern Quarterly* 8:3, 259–95.

Nihon Bunka Chūō Renmei (ed.) (1938), *Nihon Bunka Dantai Nenkan* (The Year Book of Japan's Cultural Bodies), Nihon Bunka Chūō Renmei.

Nish, Ian (2005), "Suematsu Kencho: International Envoy to Wartime Europe," *Discussion Paper no. IS/05/491.* The Suntory Centre. Suntory and Toyota International Centres for Economics and Related Disciplines.

Nishihara Yukio (1980), *Zenkiroku Harubin Tokumu Kikan: Kantō-gun Jōhōbu no Kiseki* (Complete Records of the Harbin Special Service Agency: Traces of the Kwantung Army's Intelligence Section). Mainichi Shinbunsha.

Nitta Kiyo (1971), *Sawayanagi Masatarō. Sono Shōgai to Gyōseki* (Sawayanagi Masatarō. His Life and Work). Seijō Gakuen Sawayanagi Kenkyūkai.

Norman, E. Herbert (1944), "The Genyosha: A Study in the Origins of Japanese Imperialism." *Pacific Affairs* 17:3, 261–84.

Northedge, F. S. (1986), *The League of Nations: Its Life and Times, 1920–1946.* Leicester: Leicester University Press.

Oates, Leslie Russell (1985), *Populist Nationalism in Prewar Japan: A Biography of Nakano Seigo.* Sydney: Allen and Unwin.

Obi Toshito (ed.) (1962a), "Dai 20-kai [Ozaki Hozumi] Jinmon Chōsho" (The 20th [Ozaki Hozumi] Interrogation Report). *Zoruge Jiken* (Sorge Incident), Vol. 2, Gendaishi Shiryō (Sources on Modern History), Vol. 2, Misuzu Shobō, 197–210.

—— (ed.) (1962b), "Ozaki Hotsumi no Shuki (1)" (Ozaki Hotsumi's Memorandum, part 1), *Zoruge Jiken* (Sorge Incident), Vol. 2, Gendaishi Shiryō (Sources on Modern History), Vol. 2. Misuzu Shobō, 1–25.

—— (ed.) (1962c), "Rishaado Zoruge no Shuki (1)" (Richard Sorge's Memorandum, part 1), *Zoruge Jiken* (Sorge Incident), Vol. 1, Gendaishi Shiryō (Sources on Modern History), Vol. 1. Misuzu Shobō, 139–70.

O'Connor, Peter (2004–2005), *Japanese Propaganda: Selected Readings.* Folkestone: Global Oriental and Tokyo: Edition Synapse.

Office of Strategic Services (1944), "Japanese Attempts at Infiltration among Muslims in Russia and Her Borderlands," *O.S.S./State Department Intelligence and Research Reports, I. Japan and Its Occupied Territories during World War II.* R&A Report no. 890.2.

Oguma Eiji (1995): *Tan'itsu Minzoku Shinwa no Kigen* (The Myth of the Homogenous Nation). Shin'yōsha.

—— (1998), *"Nihonjin" no Kyōkai* (The Boundaries of the "Japanese"). Shin'yōsha.

—— (2002), *A Genealogy of "Japanese" Self-Images.* Melbourne: Trans Pacific Press.

—— (2007), "The Postwar Intellectuals' View of 'Asia.'" Sven Saaler and J. Victor Koschmann (eds.), *Pan-Asianism in Modern Japanese History: Regionalism,*

Colonialism and Borders. New York: Routledge, 200–212 (revised version accessible online at http://www.japanfocus.org/-Oguma-Eiji/2350).

Ogura Kazuo (1982), *Nichi-Bei Keizai Masatsu: Omote no Jijō Ura no Jijō* (US-Japan Economic Tension: The Publicly Known Circumstances and the Behind-the-Scenes Circumstances). Nihon Keizai Shinbunsha.

—— (1983), *Trade Conflict: A View from Japan.* Japan Economic Institute.

—— (1993), "A Call for a New Concept of Asia." *Japan Echo* 20:3 (Autumn 1993) (abridged translation of "Ajia no Fukken no tame ni," *Chūō Kōron*, July 1993: 60–73).

—— (1999), "Creating a New Asia." *Japan Echo* 26:3 (March–April).

Ohsawa, J. G. (1954), *The Two Great Indians in Japan. Sri Rash Behari Bose and Netaji Subhas Chandra Bose.* Calcutta: Sri K. C. Das for Kusa Publications.

Oka, Yoshitake (1983), *Konoe Fumimaro.* University of Tokyo Press.

Okakura Kakuzo [Tenshin] (1920), *The Ideals of the East, with Special Reference to the Art of Japan.* London: J. Murray (originally published in 1903, accessible online at http://www.archive.org).

Okakura Kakuzō (1981), *Okakura Tenshin Zenshū* (Complete Works of Okakura Tenshin), Vol. 8, edited by Kumamoto Kenjirō et al. Heibonsha.

—— (1984), *Okakura Kakuzō Collected English Writings.* Heibonsha.

Okakura Tenshin (1940a), *The Awakening of the East*, with notes and an introduction by Akira Asano. Seibunkaku (originally published in 1905).

—— (1940b), *The Awakening of Japan*, edited with notes by Hiroshi Muraoka. Kenkyūsha (originally published in 1904, accessible online at http://www.archive.org).

Ōkawa Shūmei (1913), "Nihon Bunmei no Igi oyobi Kachi" (The Significance and Value of Japanese Civilization). *Tairiku* 3 (September), 22–32.

—— (1916), "Kokuminteki Risō Juritsu no Kyūmu" (The Urgent Task of Establishing a National Ideal). *Michi*, February, 35–40.

—— (1943), *Kaikyō Gairon* (A General Outline of Islam). Keiō Shobō.

—— (1961), *Anraku no Mon, Ōkawa Shūmei Zenshū* 1 (The Gate to Comfort, Complete Works of Ōkawa Shūmei). Iwasaki Shoten, 724–865.

—— (1993), *Fukkō Ajia no Shomondai* (Various Problems of Asia in Revival). Chūō Kōronsha (originally published in 1922 by Daitōkaku).

Ōmae Ken'ichi (1994), *Ajiajin to Nihonjin: Mahatiiru Marēshia Shushō to no Taiwa* (Asians and Japanese: A Dialogue with Mahathir, the Prime Minister of Malaysia). Shōgakukan.

Otabe Yūji (1981), "Nihon Fuashizumu Keisei to 'Shin Kanryō': Matsumoto Gaku to Nihon Bunka Renmei" (The Formation of Japanese Fascism and "the New Bureaucrats": Matsumoto Gaku and the Japan Culture League). Nihon Gendaishi Kenkyūkai (ed.), *Nihon Fuashizumu (1): Kokka to Shakai* (Japanese Fascism [1], State and Society). Ōtsuki Shoten, 79–117.

Ōtani Kōzui (1939), *Ōtani Kōzui Kōa Keikaku* (Ōtani Kōzui's Plan to Raise Asia). 3 vols., Yūkōsha.

Ōtsuka Takehiro (1995), *Ōkawa Shūmei* (Ōkawa Shūmei). Chūō Kōronsha.

Ōuchi Chōzō (1934), "Konoe Kazan-kō to Tōa Dōbun Shoin" (Prince Konoe Kazan and the Tōa Dōbun Shoin). *Shina* 25:2/3, 143–47.

Ōyama Ikuo (1916), "Dai Ajiashugi no Unmei Ikan" (What Is the Fate of Greater Asianism?). Ōyama Ikuo: *Ōyama Ikuo Chosakushū* (Collected Works by Ōyama Ikuo), Vol. 1. Iwanami Shoten, 1987, 134–52.

Pané, Sanoesi (1930), "De Boodschap van India" (The Embassy of India). *Timboel* 4:8–9, 112–13.

Panikkar, K. M. (1953), *Asia and Western Dominance: A Survey of the Vasco Da Gama Epoch of Asian History, 1498–1945.* London: George Allen & Unwin.

Peattie, Mark R. (1975), *Ishiwara Kanji and Japan's Confrontation with the West.* Princeton, NJ: Princeton University Press.

Peshawar-kai (2009), *About Us,* http://www1a.biglobe.ne.jp/peshawar/eg/annai.html (accessed 21 May 2009).

Pierson, John D. (1980), *Tokutomi Soho, 1863–1957: A Journalist for Modern Japan.* Princeton, NJ: Princeton University Press.

Pratap, Mahendra (1947), *My Life Story of Fifty-Five Years.* Dehradun: World Federation.

Reynolds, Douglas R. (1986), "Chinese Area Studies in Prewar China: Japan's Tōa Dōbun Shoin in Shanghai, 1900–1945." *Journal of Asian Studies*, 45:5, 945–70.

——— (1989), "Training Young China Hands: Tōa Dōbun Shoin and Its Precursors, 1886–1945." Peter Duus, Ramon H. Myers, and Mark R. Peattie (eds.), *The Japanese Informal Empire in China, 1895–1937.* Princeton, NJ: Princeton University Press, 210–71.

——— (1993), *China, 1898–1912: The Xinzheng Revolution and Japan.* Cambridge, MA: Harvard University Press.

Richard, Michel Paul (1987), *Without Passport: The Life and Work of Paul Richard.* New York: Peter Lang Publishing.

Richard, Paul (1917), *To Japan.* Privately published; text in four languages, French (Au Japon), Chinese (translated by Matsudaira Yasukuni), Japanese (by Ōkawa Shūmei), and English (by Mirra Richard).

——— (1920), *The Dawn over Asia,* translated from the French by Aurobindo Ghose. Madras: Ganesh & Co., Publishers.

Romulo, Carlos (1956), *The Meaning of Bandung.* Chapel Hill: University of North Carolina Press.

Rōyama, Masamichi (1934), "The Meaning of the Manchukuo Empire." *Contemporary Japan*, 3:1, 27–33.

——— (1938), "Tōa Kyōdōtai no Riron" (Theory of East Asian Cooperative Body). *Kaizō*, November, 6–26.

——— (1941), *Foreign Policy of Japan: 1914–1939.* Westport, CT: Greenwood Press Publishers.

Rozman, Gilbert (2004), *Northeast Asia's Stunted Regionalism.* Cambridge University Press.

Saaler, Sven (2002), *Pan-Asianism in Modern Japanese History: A Preliminary Approach.* Tōkyō: Deutsches Institut für Japanstudien (DIJ Working Paper 02/4).

—— (2005), *Politics, Memory and Public Opinion. The History Textbook Controversy and Japanese Society.* Munich: Iudicium.

—— (2007), "The Construction of Regionalism in Modern Japan: Kodera Kenkichi and His 'Treatise on Greater Asianism' (1916)." *Modern Asian Studies* 41: 1261–94.

—— (2008a), "The Russo-Japanese War and the Emergence of the Notion of the 'Clash of Races' in Japanese Foreign Policy." John Chapman and Inaba Chiharu (eds.), *Rethinking the Russo-Japanese War, Vol. 2.* Folkestone: Global Oriental and University of Hawai'i Press, 274–89.

—— (2008b), "Taishō-ki ni okeru Seiji Kessha. Kokuryūkai no Katsudō to Jinmyaku" (Political Societies in the Taisho Era: The Activities and the Social Network of the Kokuryūkai). Inoki Takenori (ed.), *Demokurashii to Chūkan Dantai— Senkanki Nihon no Shakai Shūdan to Nettwaku* (Democracy and Intermediary Organizations—Social Organizations and Networks in Interwar Japan). NTT Shuppan, 81–108.

Saaler, Sven, and J. Victor Koschmann (eds.) (2007), *Pan-Asianism in Modern Japanese History: Colonialism, Regionalism and Borders.* London: Routledge.

Said, Edward (1995), *Orientalism.* London: Penguin Books.

Sakai Tetsuya (2007), *Kindai Nihon no Kokusai Chitsujoron* (The International Order of Modern Japan). Iwanami Shoten.

Sakeda Masatoshi (1978), *Kindai Nihon ni okeru Taigaikō Undō no Kenkyū* (A Study of the Movement for Hardline Foreign Policy in Modern Japan). Tokyo Daigaku Shuppankai.

Sakurai Yoshiyuki (1964), *Meiji to Chōsen* (Meiji [Japan] and Korea). Sakurai Yoshiyuki Sensei Kanreki Kinenkai.

Sakuramoto Tomio (1995), *Nihon Bungaku Hōkokukai* (Patriotic Association for Japanese Literature). Aoki Shoten.

Sanbō Honbu (ed.) (1985), *Sugiyama Memo* (The Sugiyama Memorandum), Vol. 2. Hara Shobō.

Sareen, T. R. (2004), "Subhas Chandra Bose, Japan and British Imperialism." *European Journal of East Asian Studies* 3:1, 69–97.

Sarkar, Benoy (1916), *Chinese Religion through Hindu Eyes: A Study in the Tendencies of Asiatic Mentality* (originally published in Shanghai in 1916, reprinted by Oriental Publishers & Distributors, Delhi, 1975), 245–80.

—— (1922), *The Futurism of Young Asia and Other Essays on the Relations between the East and the West.* Berlin: J. Springer.

Satō Dōshin (1999), *Meiji Kokka to Kindai Bijutsu—Bi no Seijigaku* (The Meiji Nation State and Modern Fine Arts—Political Science of Aesthetics). Yoshikawa Kōbunkan.

Sawayanagi Masatarō (1917), "Bunkateki Han-Ajiashugi o Teishō su" (I Advocate Cultural Pan-Asianism). *Shin Nippon* 7/3.

—— (1919a), *Ajiashugi* (Asianism). Daitōkaku.

—— (1919b), "Asianism." *The Japan Magazine,* August, 141–44.

—— (1927), "The General Features of Pacific Relations as Viewed by Japan." *News Bulletin* (Institute of Pacific Relations), 1: 24–27.

Sawayanagi Reijirō (1937), *Waga Chichi Sawayanagi Masatarō* (My Father Sawayanagi Masatarō). Toyama Shobō.

Schmid, Andre (2002), *Korea between Empires 1895–1919.* New York: Columbia University Press.

Sheng Banghe (2000), "19 Shiji Yu 20 Shiji Zhi Jiaode Riben Da Yazhouzhuyi" (Japanese Asianism in the Transitional Period from the 19th to the 20th Century). *Lishi Yanjiu* 3: 125–35.

Shi Guangshang (2006), "Ajia Keizai no Mirai to Nitchū no Keizai Kyōryoku" (The Future of the Asian Economy and Sino-Japanese Economic Cooperation). Abe Shinzō et al., *Nitchū Taiwa* (Japanese-Chinese Dialogue). Genron NPO.

Shi Jiafang (2002), *"Tongwen Tongzhu" de Pianju. Ri wei Dongya Lianmeng Yundong de Xingwang* (The Fraud of "Same Culture, Same Race." The Rise and Fall of Japan's Fake East Asian League Movement). Beijing: Shehui Kexue Wenxian Chubanshe.

Shillony, Ben-Ami (1981), *Politics and Culture in Wartime Japan.* Oxford: Clarendon Press/Oxford University Press.

Shimada, Kenji (1990), *Pioneer of the Chinese Revolution: Zhang Binglin and Confucianism.* Translated by Joshua A. Fogel. Stanford, CA: Stanford University Press.

Shimano Saburō Denki Kankōkai (ed.) (1984), *Shimano Saburō: Mantetsu Soren Jōhō Katsudō no Shōgai* (Shimano Saburō: A Life in the Intelligence Service of the South Manchurian Railway against the Soviets). Hara Shobō.

Shimazu, Naoko (1998), *Japan, Race, and Equality: The Racial Equality Proposal of 1919.* London: Routledge.

Shin, Gi-Wook (2005), "Asianism in Korea's Politics of Identity." *Inter-Asia Cultural Studies* 6:4, 616–30.

——— (2006): *Ethnic Nationalism in Korea: Genealogy, Politics and Legacy.* Stanford, CA: Stanford University Press.

Shindō Eiichi and Hirakawa Hitoshi (eds.), (2006), *Higashi Ajia Kyōdotai o Sekkei Suru* (Construction of an East Asian Community). Nihon Keiyai Hyōronsha, 2006.

Shisō no Kagaku Kenkyūkai (ed.) (1959), *Kyōdō Kenkyū: Tenkō* (Cooperative Research: Conversion), Heibonsha, Vol. I.

Sima, Josef (1974), "On the Character of the So-Called Pan-Mongol Movement after 1911." *Archiv Orientalni* 42:4, 97–119.

Sin Il-ch'ol (1981), *Sin Ch'ae-ho ŭi Yŏksa Sasang Yŏn'gu* (A Study of the Historical Thought of Sin Ch'ae-ho). Korea University Press.

Sin Yong-ha (1984), *Sin Ch'ae-ho ŭi Sahoe Sasang Yŏn'gu* (A Study of the Social Thought of Sin Ch'ae-ho). Hangil Publishing.

Singh, Bhubhindar (2002), "ASEAN's Perceptions of Japan: Change and Continuity." *Asian Survey* 42:2, 276–96.

Smith, Warren W. (1959), *Confucianism in Modern Japan: A Study of Conservatism in Japanese Intellectual History.* The Hokuseido Press.

Snyder, Louis (1984), *Macro-Nationalisms. A History of the Pan-Movements.* Westport, CT: Greenwood Press.

Sŏ Chaep'il Kinyŏmhoe (ed.) (2003), *Sŏ Chaep'il Kwa kŭ Sidae* (Sŏ Chaep'il and His Times). Samhwa Press.

So Wai-Chor [Su Wei Chu/So I Sho] (2007), "Ō Seiei [Wang Jingwei] to Dai Aji-ashugi" (Wang Jingwei and Greater Asianism). Matsuura Masataka (ed.) (2007), *Shōwa Ajiashugi no Jitsuzō. Teikoku Nihon to Taiwan, "Nanyō," "Minami Shina"* (The True Picture of Shōwa Asianism. Imperial Japan and Taiwan, the Southern Islands, and Southern China). Kyoto: Minerva Shobō, 182–204.

Sokarno (1955), "Sokarno, President of the Republic of Indonesia at the Opening of the Asian-African Congress in Bandung, Indonesia, on 18 April 1955," The Ministry of Foreign Affairs, Republic of Indonesia (ed.), *Asia-Africa Speaks from Bandung.* Djakarta: Ministry of Foreign Affairs, 19–29.

Son Bun [Sun Yat-sen] (1974), "Dai-Ajiashugi." Kojima Shinji et al. (eds.), *Chūgokujin no Nihonjinkan Hyakunenshi* (Hundred Years' History of Chinese Views of the Japanese). Jiyū Kokuminsha, 158–63.

Stalker, Nancy K. (2006), "Suicide, Boycotts and Embracing Tagore: The Japanese Popular Response to the 1924 US Immigration Exclusion Law." *Japanese Studies* 26:2, 153–70.

—— (2008), *Prophet Motive: Deguchi Onisaburō, Oomoto, and the Rise of New Religions in Imperial Japan.* Honolulu: University of Hawai'i Press.

Steinhoff, Patricia G. (1991), *Tenkō Ideology and Societal Integration in Prewar Japan.* New York: Garland.

Storry, Richard (1957), *The Double Patriots: A Study of Japanese Nationalism.* London: Chatto and Windus.

Sudo, Sueo (2002), *The International Relations of Japan and South East Asia: Forging a New Regionalism.* London: Routledge.

Sugimori Hisahide (1963), *Tsuji Masanobu* (Tsuji Masanobu), Bungei Shunjū Shinsha.

Sugita Teiichi (1916), "Waga Gaikō to Tōyō Renmei" (Our Foreign Policy and the Oriental League). *Nihon oyobi Nihonjin* 674 (11 February), 25–30.

—— (1920), "Address on the Occasion of the Founding of the League for the Equality of Races, 1919." Paul Richard, *The Dawn over Asia.* Madras: Ganesh & Co. Publishers, 90–92.

—— (1924), "Dai Ajia Gasshōron" (An Argument for Uniting Greater Asia). *Tōyō Bunka* 8: 7–13.

Suh Sung (2005), "Japanese Neo-Nationalism and an Idea of East Asian Community." *Inter-Asia Cultural Studies* 6:1, 609–15.

Sun Ge (2000), "How Does Asia Mean?" *Inter-Asia Cultural Studies* 1:1, 13–47, and 1:2, 319–41.

—— (2003), "The Habit of Thinking." *EMPIRE. A Symposium on the Emerging World Order.* Internet: http://www.india-seminar.com/2003/529.htm (last accessed 1 May 2010).

Sun Yat-sen (1923), "Inukai Tsuyoshi ate Shokan" (Letter to Inukai Tsuyoshi). Kojima Shinji et al. (eds.), *Chūgokujin no Nihonjinkan 100 Nenshi* (Hundred Years' History of Chinese Views of the Japanese). Jiyū Kokuminsha, 1974, 153–58.

—— (1941), "Pan-Asianism." *China and Japan: Natural Friends—Unnatural Enemies,* Shanghai: China United Press, 141–51.

Suyematsu, Baron (Suematsu Kenchō) (1905), *The Risen Sun.* London: Archibald Constable & Co.

Swale, Alistair (2003), "Tokutomi Sohō and the Problem of the Nation-State in an Imperialist World." Dick Stegewerns (ed.), *Nationalism and Internationalism in Imperial Japan: Autonomy, Asian Brotherhood, or World Citizenship?* London: RoutledgeCurzon, 69–88.

Szpilman, Christopher W. A. (1998a), "Conservatism and Its Enemies in Prewar Japan: The Case of Hiranuma Kiichirō and the Kokuhonsha." *Hitotsubashi Journal of Social Studies* 30:2, 101–33.

—— (1998b), "The Dream of One Asia: Ōkawa Shūmei and Japanese Pan-Asianism." Harald Fuess (ed.), *The Japanese Empire in East Asia and Its Postwar Legacy*. Munich: Iudicium, 49–63.

—— (2002), "Kita Ikki and the Politics of Coercion." *Modern Asian Studies* 36:2, 467–90.

—— (2004), "Fascist and Quasi-Fascist Ideas in Japan, 1918–1941." Bruce E. Reynolds (ed.), *Japan in the Fascist Era*. New York: Palgrave Macmillan, 73–106.

—— (2007), "Between Pan-Asianism and Nationalism: Mitsukawa Kametarō and His Campaign to Reform Japan and Liberate Asia." Sven Saaler and J. Victor Koschmann (eds.), *Pan-Asianism in Modern Japanese History: Colonialism, Regionalism and Borders*. London: Routledge, 85–100.

Tajima Nobuo (2007), "Son Bun no 'Chū-Doku-So Sangoku Rengō' Kōsō to Nihon, 1917–1924" (Sun Yat-sen's Idea of a "Chinese-German-Soviet Alliance," 1917–1924). Hattori Ryūji et al. (eds.), *Senkanki no Higashi Ajia Kokusai Seiji*. Chūō Daigaku Shuppanbu, 3–52.

Takaki, Yasaka (1932), "World Peace Machinery and the Asia Monroe Doctrine." *Pacific Affairs* 5:11, 941–53.

Takamure Itsue (1940), "Shin Shina no Kensetsu to Nihon Fujin" (The Establishment of a New China and Japanese Women). *Josei Tenbō* 14:4 (April), 5.

Takegoshi [Takekoshi] Y[osaburō] (1919), "The Future of Japan." W. H. Morton-Cameron (comp.), *Present-Day Impressions of Japan: The History, People, Commerce, Industries and Resources of Japan and Japan's Colonial Empire, Kwantung, Chosen, Taiwan, Karafuto*, Vol. 1. London: The Globe Encyclopedia, 83–89.

Takeuchi Yoshimi (1942), "Tabi Nikki Shō" (Extracts from My Travel Diary), reprinted in *Takeuchi Yoshimi Zenshū* (Complete Works of Takeuchi Yoshimi), Vol. 14. Chikuma Shobō, 1980, 395–428.

—— (1944), *Rojin* (Lu Xun), reprinted in *Takeuchi Yoshimi Zenshū* (Complete Works of Takeuchi Yoshimi), Vol. I. Chikuma Shobō, 1980, 1–175.

—— (1948a), "Kindai to wa Nani ka (Nihon to Chūgoku no Baai)" (What Is Modernity? The Case of China and Japan), reprinted in *Takeuchi Yoshimi Zenshū* (Complete Works of Takeuchi Yoshimi), Vol. IV. Chikuma Shobō, 1980, 128–71.

—— (1948b), "What Is Modernity? The Case of China and Japan." Richard F. Calichman (ed.), *What Is Modernity? Writings of Takeuchi Yoshimi*. New York: Columbia University Press, 2005, 53–81.

—— (1958a), "Kindai no Chōkoku" (Overcoming Modernity), reprinted in *Takeuchi Yoshimi Zenshū* (Complete Works of Takeuchi Yoshimi), Vol. VIII. Chikuma Shobō, 1980, 3–67.

—— (1958b), "Overcoming Modernity." Richard F. Calichman (ed.), *What Is Modernity? Writings of Takeuchi Yoshimi*. New York: Columbia University Press, 2005, 103–47.

—— (1960a), "Asia as Method." Richard F. Calichman (ed.), *What Is Modernity? Writings of Takeuchi Yoshimi*. New York: Columbia University Press, 2005, 149–65.

—— (1960b), "Hōhō toshite no Ajia" (Asia as Method), reprinted in *Takeuchi Yoshimi Zenshū* (Complete Works of Takeuchi Yoshimi), Vol. V. Chikuma Shobō, 1980, 90–115.

—— (ed.) (1963a), *Ajiashugi* (Asianism). Chikuma Shobō (Gendai Nihon Shisō Taikei, Vol. 9).

—— (1963b), "Ajiashugi no tenbō" (The Prospect of Asianism), in Takeuchi Yoshimi (ed.), *Ajiashugi* (Asianism) (Gendai Nihon Shisō Taikei, Vol. 9), Chikuma Shobō.

—— (1963c), "Nihon no Ajiashugi" (Japan's Asianism), reprinted in *Takeuchi Yoshimi Zenshū* (Complete Works of Takeuchi Yoshimi), Vol. VIII. Chikuma Shobō, 1980, 94–156.

—— (1966), "Kaisetsu" (Commentary), reprinted in *Takeuchi Yoshimi Hyōronshū, Vol. III: Nihon to Ajia* (Collection of Takeuchi Yoshimi's Essays, Vol. III: Japan and Asia). Chikuma Shobō, 421–31.

—— (1969), "Ōkawa Shūmei: Profile of Asian Minded Man." *The Developing Economies* 7:3, 367–79.

Takeuchi Zensaku (1948), "Meiji Makki ni okeru Chūnichi Kakumei Undō no Kōryū" (The Exchanges between the Chinese and Japanese Revolutionary Movements in the Late Meiji Period). *Chūgoku Kenkyū* 1948:5, 74–95.

Takushoku Daigaku Sōritsu Hyakunenshi Hensanshitsu (ed.) (2002–2005), *Tanaka Ippei*. Takushoku Daigaku, 5 vols.

Tanaka Ippei (1924), *Isureamu to Dai-Ajiashugi* (Islam and Asianism). Self-published.

Tanaka Keiichi (ed.) (1996), *Shibata Shūzō Nikki* (Diaries of Shibata Shūzō). 2 vols. Heibonsha.

Tanaka Sōgorō (1930), *Tōyō Shakaitō Kō* (Thoughts on the Eastern Socialist Party). Ichigensha.

—— (1971), *Kita Ikki: Nihon no Fasshisuto no Shōchō* (Kita Ikki: The Symbol of Japanese Fascists), Expanded Edition, San'ichi Shobō.

Tanaka, Stefan (1993), *Japan's Orient—Reading Pasts into History*. Berkeley: University of California Press.

Tang Zhijun (ed.) (1977), *Zhang Taiyan Zheng Lun Xuan ji* (Collected Works on Zhang Taiyan's Political Writings). Beijing: Zhonghua Shuju, Vol. 1.

—— (1991), "Guanyu Yazhou Heqin hui" (On the Asiatic Humanitarian Brotherhood). Wuchang Xinhai Geming Yanjiu Zhongxin (ed.), *Xinhai Geming yu Jindai Zhongguo; 1980–1989 Nian Lunwen Xuan*. Wuhan: Hubei Renmin Chubanshe.

Tang, Leang-Li (ed.) (1941), *China and Japan: Natural Friends, Unnatural Enemies*. Shanghai: China United Press.

Tankha, Brij (ed.) (2009), *Okakura Tenshin and Pan-Asianism: Shadows of the Past*. Global Oriental.

Tano Daisuke (2009), "Yoka no Sūjiku. Sekai Kōsei Kaigi to Nichidoku Bunka Kōryū" (The Axis of Leisure. The World Welfare Congress and Japanese-German Cultural Exchange). *Geshihite* 2, 21–39.

Tarling, Nicholas (1992), "'Ah-Ah': Britain and the Bandung Conference of 1955." *Journal of Southeast Asian Studies* 23:1, 74–111.

Tarui Tōkichi (1893), *Daitō Gappōron* (Arguments on Behalf of the Union of the Great East), reprinted in *Fukkoku Daitō Gappōron* (Chōryō Shorin/Wakatsuki Shoten, 1975).

Thompson, Richard Austin (1978), *The Yellow Peril, 1890–1924*. New York: Arno Press.

Tikhonov, Vladimir (2002), "Korea's First Encounters with Pan-Asianism Ideology in the Early 1880s." *The Review of Korean Studies* 5:2, 195–232.

Tōa Renmei Kyōkai (ed.) (1940), *Tōa Renmei Kensetsu Yōkō* (Prospectus for Constructing the East Asian League). Ritsumeikan Shuppanbu.

Tōjō Hideki (1943), "Taishō o Haishi Tatematsurite—Kōa no Seigyō kono Issen (Revering the Imperial Edict: This One War [Is] the Holy Task of Raising Asia). *Seinen* 27:1 (1 January), 38–39.

Tokugawa Yoshichika (1973), *Saigo no Tonosama: Tokugawa Yoshichika Jiden* (The Last Lord: The Autobiography of Tokugawa Yoshichika). Kōdansha.

Tokutomi Iichirō (1917), "Japan's Mighty Mission," in Taraknath Das, *Is Japan a Menace to Asia?* Shanghai: no publisher, 153–59.

Tokutomi Sohō (1913), "Jimu Ikkagen" (An Opinion on Current Issues), reprinted in Tokutomi Sohō (1974), *Meiji Bungaku Zenshū* (Complete Collection of Meiji Literature), Vol. 34. Chikuma Shobō, 301–14.

Tomioka Kōichirō (2006), *Shin Daitōa Sensō Kōteiron* (A New Affirmation of the Greater East Asian War). Asuka Shinsha.

Torpey, John (ed.) (2003), *Politics and the Past: On Repairing Historical Injustices*. Lanham, MD: Rowman & Littlefield.

Tōyama Mitsuru, Inukai Tsuyoshi, Sugiyama Shigemaru, and Uchida Ryōhei (2008), *Ajiashugisha no Koe 1: Gen'yōsha to Kokuryūkai, aruiwa Kōdōteki Ajiashugi no Genten* (Pan-Asianist Voices, Vol. 1: The Gen'yōsha and the Kokuryūkai, or: The Origin of Activist Asianism). Shoshi Shinsui.

Tsuji Masanobu (1950), *Ajia no Kyōkan: Tatakai o Tsūjite Mita Chūgoku* (Empathy with Asia: The China I Saw through My Struggle). Atō Shobō.

Tsukui Tatsuo (1956), *Uyoku Kaigan: Chūkyō to Nikkyō* (The Opening of the Right Wing's Eyes: The Chinese Communist Party and the Japanese Communist Party). Takubunkan.

Tsunoda, Ryusaku et al. (eds.) (1958), *Sources of Japanese Tradition*. New York: Columbia University Press.

Uchida Rōan (Roansei) (1917), "Gakujutsuteki Han-Ajiashugi" (Academic Pan-Asianism). *Taiyō* 23:4, 65–75.

Uchida Ryōhei (1918), "Jo'" (Preface). Kokuryūkai Shuppanbu (ed.), *Ajia Taikan* (Overview of Asia). *Kokuryūkai Shuppanbu*, 1–4.

—— (1920), "The Asian Review and the Kokuryu-kai." *The Asian Review* 1:1, 3–5.

Uchida Ryōhei Monjo Kenkyūkai (ed.) (1992), *Kokuryūkai Kankei Shiryōshū* (Collection of Sources Relating to the Kokuryūkai), Vol. 1. Kashiwa Shobō.

Uhl, Christian (2009), "Displacing Japan: Takeuchi Yoshimi's Lu Xun in Light of Nishida's Philosophy—and Vice Versa." *Positions: East Asia Cultures Critique* 17:1, 207–38.

Ukita Kazutami (1918), "Shin Ajiashugi" (New Asianism). *Taiyō* 24:9, 2–17.

Umetsu Jun'ichi (2006), "Tokutomi Sohō to 'Chikara no Fukuin': *Shōrai no Nihon* kara *Jimu Ikkagen e*" (Tokutomi Sohō and "The Gospel of Power": From *The Future of Japan* to *An Opinion on Current Issues*). *Seigakuin Ronsō* 19:1, 16–31.

Utsunomiya Tarō Kankei Shiryō Kenkyūkai (ed.) (2007), *Nihon Rikugun to Ajia Seisaku. Rikugun Taishō Utsunomiya Tarō Nikki 3* (The Japanese Army and Asia Policy. The Diary of Army General Utsunomiya Tarō, 3). Iwanami Shoten.

Valliant, Robert B. (1974), "The Selling of Japan: Japanese Manipulation of Western Opinion, 1900–1905." *Monumenta Nipponica* 29:4, 415–38.

Wada Haruki (2003), *Tōhoku Ajia Kyōdō no Ie: Shinchiikishugi Sengen* (North Western Asian Common Homestead: The Declaration of a New Regionalism). Heibonsha.

—— (2008a), "The Comfort Women, the Asian Women's Fund and the Digital Museum." Internet: *JapanFocus*, http://japanfocus.org/-Wada-Haruki/2653 (last accessed 1 March 2010).

—— (2008b), "Okinawa to Hokutō Ajia" (Maritime Asia and the Future of a Northeast Asia Community). *Ryūkyū Shinpō,* 7–9 January.

Wada Mamoru (1990), *Kindai Nihon to Tokutomi Sohō* (Modern Japan and Tokutomi Sohō). Ochanomizu Shobō.

Wakabayashi, Bob Tadashi (1986), *Anti-Foreignism and Western Learning in Early-Modern Japan: The New Theses of 1825.* Cambridge, MA: Harvard University Press.

Wakabayashi Nakaba [Han] (1937), *Kaikyō Sekai to Nihon* (The World of Islam and Japan). Dainichisha.

Wang, C. C. (1934), "The Pan-Asiatic Doctrine of Japan." *Foreign Affairs* 13:1, 59–67.

Wang Jingwei (1940), "Minzuzhuyi yu Da Yazhouzhuyi" (Nationalism and Greater Asianism). *Da Yazhouzhuyi* (Greater Asianism), 1:4 (November), 1–5.

Wang Ping (2004), *Jindai Riben de Yaxiyazhuyi* (Modern Japanese Asianism). Beijing: Shangwu Yinshuguan.

Wang Yi (2006a), "Ajia no Shōrai oyobi Nitchū Ryōkoku no Yakuwari" (The Future of Asia and the Roles of Japan and China). Internet: http://jp.chineseembassy.org/jpn/sgxx/t282546.htm (last accessed 4 October 2009).

—— (2006b), "Sikao Ershiyi Shiji de Xin Yazhouzhuyi" (Considering Neo-Asianism in the Twenty-First Century). *Waijiao Pinglun* (Foreign Affairs Review) 89: 6–10.

Watanabe Kyōji (2006), *Hyōden Miyazaki Tōten* (Critical Biography of Miyazaki Tōten). Shoshi Shinsui (first edition by Yamato Shoten, 1976).

Weber, Torsten (2009), "'Unter dem Banner des Asianismus': Transnationale Dimensionen des japanischen Asianismus-Diskurses der Taishō-Zeit (1912–1926)" (Under the Banner of Asianism: The Transnational Dimensions of Japanese Discourse on Asianism in the Taishō Era [1912–1926]). *Comparativ. Zeitschrift für Globalgeschichte und Vergleichende Gesellschaftsforschung* 18:6, 34–52.

Wilson, George M. (1969), *Kita Ikki: Radical Nationalist in Japan*. Cambridge, MA: Harvard University Press.

Wilson, Sandra (2005), "The Discourse of National Greatness in Japan, 1890–1919." *Japanese Studies* 25:1, 35–51.

Wong, Yong-tsu (1989), *Search for Modern Nationalism: Zhang Binglin and Revolutionary China, 1869–1936*. Hong Kong: Oxford University Press.

Worringer, Renée (2006), "Pan-Asianism in the Late Ottoman Empire, 1905–1912." Camron Michael Amin, Benjamin C. Fortna, and Elizabeth B. Frierson (eds.), *The Modern Middle East: A Sourcebook for History*. Oxford: Oxford University Press, 331–38.

—— (ed.) (2007), *The Islamic Middle East and Japan: Perceptions, Aspirations, and the Birth of Intra-Asian Modernity*. Princeton, NJ: Markus Wiener Publishers.

Yamagata Bantō (1820), *Yumenoshiro* (A Castle of Dreams), reprinted in Tominaga Nakamoto and Mizuta Norihisa (eds.), *Nihon Shisō Taikei, Vol. 43: Yamagata Bantō* (Survey of Japanese Thought, Vol. 43: Yamagata Bantō), Iwanami Shoten, 1973, 223, 433.

Yamamoto Shigeki (2001), *Konoe Atsumaro: Sono Meiji Kokkakan to Ajiakan* (Konoe Atsumaro: His Views on the Meiji State and Asia). Kyoto: Minerva Shobō.

Yamamuro Shin'ichi (1993), *Kimera: Manshūkoku no Shōzō* (Chimera: A Portrait of Manzhouguo). Chūō Kōronsha (translated into English as *Manchuria Under Japanese Dominion* by Joshua Fogel, Philadelphia: University of Pennsylvania Press, 2005).

—— (2001), *Shisō Kadai toshite no Ajia* (Asia as an Intellectual Theme). Iwanami Shoten.

—— (2005), *Nichiro Sensō no Seiki* (The Century of the Russo-Japanese War). Iwanami Shoten.

Yamanokuchi Kōichi (1996), "Kokuryūkai: Uchida Ryōhei no Dōkōkai Katsudō (The Kokuryūkai: The Activities of Uchida Ryōhei in the Dōkōkai). *Nihon Hōsei Gakkai Hōsei Ronsō* 32: 155–65.

Yamaura Kan'ichi (1941), *Tōa Shintaisei no Senku: Mori Kaku* (Mori Kaku, the Pioneer of the East Asian New Order). Mori Kaku Denki Hensankai.

Yasko, Richard A. (1973), *Hiranuma Kiichirō and Conservative Politics in Pre-War Japan*. PhD diss., University of Chicago.

Yasuoka Masahiro (1922), *Fukkō Ajia no Shisōteki Konkyo* (The Ideological Basis for a Revived Asia). Yūzonsha Shōsatsu no. 2, November.

—— (1933), "Seiji Tetsugaku yori Mitaru Gendai Nihon: Sekai Topikku" (World Topics: Contemporary Japan from the Perspective of Political Philosophy). *Kōen* 234, Kigen 2, 593.

—— (1938), "Shina Jihen no Shisa suru Kongo no Kyōyō Mondai" (The Future of the Matter of Personal Cultivation as Indicated by the China Incident). *Kinkei Gakuhō* 12: 1–22.

—— (1943a), *Daitōa Kyōeiken no Shidōsha taru beki Nihonjin no Kyōiku* (Education for Japanese Capable of Being Leaders of the Greater East Asia Co-Prosperity Sphere). Keimeikai.

—— (1943b), *Naigai Jisei no Konpon Mondai* (Fundamental Issues of Current Domestic and Foreign Political Trends). Chōsa Hōkokusho no. 15. Nihon Gaikō Kyōkai.

Yeo Lay Hwee (2006), "Japan, ASEAN, and the Construction of an East Asian Community." *Contemporary Southeast Asia* 28:2, 259–75.

Yi, Chin-o (2000), Orientalisŭm-kwa Oksidentalisŭm-ŭl Nŏmŏsŏ (Beyond the Orientalism and Occidentalism). Onŭl-ŭi Munye Pip'yŏng, Internet: http://home.pusan.ac.kr/~jino/Jeosul/gt02.htm (last accessed 31 March 2010).

Yō Teruko (2007), "Kanokogi Kazunobu ni okeru Nihon Seishin to Nachizumu" (The Japanese Spirit and Nazism in Kanokogi Kazunobu). Mochida Yukio (ed.), *Kindai Nihon to Doitsu* (Modern Japan and Germany). Minerva Shobō.

Yokoi Shōnan (1860), *Kokuze Sanron* (Three Theses on State Policy), reprinted in Satō Shōsuke et al. (eds.), *Nihon Shisō Taikei, Vol. 55: Watanabe Kazan, Takano Chōei, Sakuma Shōzan, Yokoi Shōnan, Hashimoto Sanai* (Survey of Japanese Thought, Vol. 55: Watanabe Kazan, Takano Chōei, Sakuma Shōzan, Yokoi Shōnan, Hashimoto Sanai). Iwanami Shoten, 1971, 450–51.

Yonehara Ken (2003), *Tokutomi Sohō: Nihon Nashonarizumu no Kiro* (Tokutomi Sohō: Japanese Nationalism at a Crossroads). Chūō Kōronsha.

Yonetani Masafumi (2006), *Ajia/Nihon* (Asia/Japan). Iwanami Shoten.

Yoshimi Yoshiaki (1987), *Kusa no Ne no Fashizumu* (Grass-Roots Fascism). Tokyo Daigaku Shuppankai.

Young, Louise (1998), *Japan's Total Empire: Manchuria and the Culture of Wartime Imperialism*. Berkeley: University of California Press.

Zachmann, Urs Matthias (2007), "Blowing Up a Double Portrait in Black and White: The Concept of Asia in the Writings of Fukuzawa Yukichi and Okakura Tenshin." *Positions: East Asia Cultures Critique* 15:2, 345–68.

—— (2009), *China and Japan in the Late Meiji Period: China and the Japanese Discourse on National Identity, 1895–1904*. London: Routledge.

Zen Ajiakai (1917), *Kokusaikan ni okeru Nihon no Koritsu* (The Isolation of Japan in International Relations). Zen Ajiakai.

Zhai Xin (Teki Shin) (2001), *Tōa Dōbunkai to Chūgoku: Kindai Nihon ni okeru Tai-gai Rinen to sono Jissen* (The Tōa Dōbunkai and China: The Ideal and Practice of Foreign Relations in Modern Japan). Keiō Gijuku Daigaku Shuppankai.

Zhang Weixiong (1999), *Bunjin Gaikōkan no Meiji Nihon: Chūgoku Shodai Chūnichi Nihon Kōdan no Ibunka Taiken* (The Meiji Japan of the Literati-Diplomats: The First Chinese Diplomatic Mission to Japan and Its Experience of a Foreign Culture). Kashiwa Shobō.

Zhongnan Diqu Xinhai Geming Shi Yanjiuhui (ed.) (1980), *Xinhai Geming Shi Cong Kan* (Materials on the History of the Xinhai Revolution), Vol. 1. Beijing: Zhinghua Shuju.

Zhou Huaren, (1940), "Da Yazhouzhuyi yu Sanminzhuyi" (Greater Asianism and the Three People's Principles). *Da Yazhouzhuyi* (Greater Asianism), 1:2 (September), 11–15.

Zumoto Motosada (1927), "Japan and the Pan-Asiatic Movement." *News Bulletin* (Institute of Pacific Relations), 8–15.

Index

List of Contributors to Volume 1

Cemil Aydin is an associate professor of history and chair in Islamic studies at the History and Art History Department of George Mason University, where he is also the director of the Ali Vural Ak Center for Islamic Studies. He received his PhD from Harvard University in 2002. He is author of *Politics of Anti-Westernism in Asia: Visions of World Order in Pan-Islamic and Pan-Asian Thought* (2007).

Yuan P. Cai is a doctoral candidate at the University of Adelaide, Australia. His thesis examines the rise and fall of the pan-Asian movement in China, 1850–1950. He has taught history and international relations at the universities of Adelaide, Oxford, and the Australian National University and is currently an assistant editor at East Asia Forum in Canberra, Australia.

Peter Duus, Emeritus William H. Bonsal Professor of History, Stanford University, is the author of *Party Politics and Political Change in Modern Japan* (1968), *Feudalism in Japan* (1976, 1993), *The Abacus and the Sword: The Japanese Penetration of Korea, 1895–1910* (1995), *Modern Japan* (1976, 1989), and *The Japanese Discovery of America* (1997).

Selçuk Esenbel is professor of history at Bogazici University in Istanbul. She received her PhD from Columbia University. She is the author of *Even the Gods Rebel: The Peasants of Takaino and the 1871 Nakano Uprising in Japan* (1998) and coeditor of *The Rising Sun and the Turkish Crescent* (2003).

Jing He is an independent scholar of modern Japanese intellectual history. She received her PhD from the University of California, Los Angeles, in 2006. Her dissertation focused on Okakura Kakuzō's conception of national identity.

Eri Hotta, an independent scholar based in New York, received her doctorate in international relations from Oxford, where she taught for four years and where she was also a junior research fellow until 2005. She has since held several visiting research and teaching posts in the United States and Japan. Her book *Pan-Asianism and Japan's War 1931–1945* was published in 2007.

Joël Joos, associate professor of history of Japanese thought and culture at Kochi Women's University, wrote his PhD on Maruyama Masao (Catholic University of Leuven, 2001). His recent publications include "Memories of a Liberal, Liberalism of Memory: Tsuda Sōkichi and a Few Things He Forgot to Mention," in Sven Saaler and Wolfgang Schwentker (eds.), *The Power of Memory in Modern Japan* (2008).

Kim Bongjin is professor of international relations at Kita Kyushu Metropolitan University, Japan. He is the author of *Higashi Ajia "Kaimei" Chishikijin no Shii Kūkan: Chon Kwan-in, Fukuzawa Yukichi, Yu Kil-jun no Hikaku Kenkyū* (The Thinking-Space of East Asian "Enlightened" Intellectuals: A Comparative Study of Cheng Kuan-ying, Fukuzawa Yukichi, and Yu Kilchun; 2004).

Kyu Hyun Kim is associate professor of Japanese and Korean history at the University of California, Davis. A Harvard PhD in history and East Asian languages who specializes in modern Japanese history, he is the author of *The Age of Visions and Arguments: Parliamentarianism and the National Public Sphere in Early Meiji Japan* (2009).

Eun-jeung Lee, professor of Korean studies at the Free University of Berlin, was previously an Alexander von Humboldt Foundation fellow and a Japan Foundation fellow. Her publications include *Anti-Europa: Die Geschichte der Rezeption des Konfuzianismus in Europa* (Anti-Europe: The History of the Reception of Confucianism in Europe; 2003).

Matsuda Kōichirō is professor of Japanese political thought at Rikkyo University, Tokyo. His works include *Edo no Chishiki kara Meiji no Seiji e* (From Edo Knowledge to Meiji Politics; 2008) and *Japan and the Pacific, 1540–1920* (coeditor; 2006).

Marc Andre Matten is assistant professor of contemporary Chinese history at the University Erlangen-Nuremberg, Germany. He previously held teaching and research positions at the universities of Tokyo and Leiden (Netherlands) and at the Academia Sinica (Taiwan). He is the author of *The Borders of Being Chinese: The Creation of National Identity in Twentieth Century China* (in German; 2009).

Sven Saaler, associate professor of modern Japanese history at Sophia University in Tokyo, was formerly head of the Humanities Section of the German Institute for Japanese Studies and Associate Professor at the University of Tokyo. He is the author of *Politics, Memory and Public Opinion* (2005) and coeditor/coauthor of *Pan-Asianism in Modern Japanese History* (2007) and *The Power of Memory in Modern Japan* (2008).

Michael A. Schneider is professor of East Asian history and chair of the Asian Studies Program at Knox College, Illinois. He has also served as an exchange professor and visiting scholar at Waseda University. He has published a number of articles on Pan-Asianism and Japanese colonial policy in Korea.

Alistair Swale, chair of the School of Arts at the University of Waikato, New Zealand, received his PhD in Japanese intellectual history from Kyoto University. He is the author of *The Political Thought of Mori Arinori: A Study in Meiji Conservatism* (2000) and *The Meiji Restoration: Monarchism, Mass Media and Conservative Revolution* (2009).

Christopher W. A. Szpilman, professor of modern Japanese history at Kyushu Sangyo University, Fukuoka, received his PhD from Yale University. He is the coeditor of *Mitsukawa Kametarō's Diaries* (2011) and of a new revised edition of Kita Ikki's *National Polity and Pure Socialism* (in Japanese; 2007) and the author of a number of articles on Japan's prewar right wing and conservatism.

Brij Tankha is professor of modern Japanese history, Department of East Asian Studies, University of Delhi. His publications include *Shadows of the Past of Okakura Tenshin and Pan-Asianism* (editor; 2008) and *A Vision of Empire: Kita Ikki and the Making of Modern Japan* (2003).

Renée Worringer is assistant professor of Islamic and Middle East history at the University of Guelph in Ontario, Canada. She is the editor of and contributor to the collection *The Islamic Middle East and Japan: Perceptions, Aspirations, and the Birth of Intra-Asian Modernity* (2007).

Urs Matthias Zachmann is assistant professor at the Japan Center of the University of Munich. He is the author of *China and Japan in the Late Meiji Period: China Policy and the Japanese Discourse on National Identity, 1895–1904* (2009) and of a number of articles on late Tokugawa and Meiji diplomatic and intellectual history.